Japanese and
Continental
Philosophy

Japanese and Continental Philosophy

Conversations with the Kyoto School

EDITED BY

Bret W. Davis, Brian Schroeder,
and Jason M. Wirth

Indiana University Press

BLOOMINGTON & INDIANAPOLIS

This book is a publication of

Indiana University Press
601 North Morton Street
Bloomington, Indiana 47404-3797 USA

www.iupress.indiana.edu

Telephone orders	800-842-6796
Fax orders	812-855-7931
Orders by e-mail	iuporder@indiana.edu

Library of Congress Cataloging-in-Publication Data

Japanese and Continental philosophy : conversations with the Kyoto
School / edited by Bret W. Davis, Brian Schroeder, and Jason M. Wirth.
  p. cm. — (Studies in Continental thought)
Includes bibliographical references and index.
  ISBN 978-0-253-35544-7 (cloth : alk. paper) — ISBN 978-0-253-
22254-1 (pbk. : alk. paper) 1. Philosophy, Japanese. 2. Philosophy, Com-
parative. 3. Continental philosophy. 4. Nishida, Kitaro, 1870–1945. 5.
Nishitani, Keiji, 1900– 6. Tanabe, Hajime, 1885–1962. I. Davis, Bret W. II.
Schroeder, Brian. III. Wirth, Jason M., [date]
  B5241.J36 2011
  181'.12—dc22
                                                          2010020772

1 2 3 4 5 16 15 14 13 12 11

In memory of the generous spirit of two

extraordinary cross-cultural bridgebuilders:

Jan Van Bragt (1928–2007) and Horio Tsutomu (1940–2006)

Contents

Acknowledgments

We would like to thank, first of all, the contributors to this volume for their scholarship, collaboration, and patience. In particular we would like to express our gratitude to Professor Ueda Shizuteru for the inspiration of his life's work and way of life, as well as for his contribution to this project. We are grateful to John Sallis for including this work in his series Studies in Continental Thought, and especially to Dee Mortensen, Laura MacLeod, Marvin Keenan, and the staff at Indiana University Press. Bret Davis would like to thank the Center for Humanities at Loyola University Maryland and the Society for Nishida Philosophy for research grants in support of his work on this project.

Abbreviations of Works
by the Kyoto School

Ch.   Chinese
Fr.   French
Gn.   German
Gr.   Greek
Jp.   Japanese
Sk.   Sanskrit

HISAMATSU Shinichi

ZFA   *Zen and the Fine Arts,* trans. Tokiwa Gishin (Tokyo: Kodansha, 1971).

MIKI Kiyoshi

MKZ   *Miki Kiyoshi zenshū* [*The Complete Works of Miki Kiyoshi*] (Tokyo: Iwanami
       Shoten, 1966–1968).

NISHIDA Kitarō

NKZ   *Nishida Kitarō zenshū* [*The Complete Works of Nishida Kitarō*], 19 vols.
       (Tokyo: Iwanami Shoten, 1988).
AM   *Art and Morality*, trans. David A. Dilworth and Valdo H. Viglielmo
       (Honolulu: University of Hawai'i Press, 1973).
FP   *Fundamental Problems of Philosophy*, trans. David A. Dilworth (Tokyo:
       Sophia University Press, 1970).
IG   *An Inquiry into the Good,* trans. Masao Abe and Christopher Ives (New
       Haven, Conn.: Yale University Press, 1990).

IN   *Intelligibility and the Philosophy of Nothingness,* trans. Robert Schinzinger
      (Honolulu: East-West Center Press, 1958).
LW   *Last Writings: Nothingness and the Religious Worldview,* trans. David A.
      Dilworth (Honolulu: University of Hawai'i Press, 1987).

NISHITANI Keiji

NKC   *Nishitani Keiji chosakushū* [*The Collected Writings of Nishitani Keiji*], 26
      vols. (Tokyo: Sōbunsha, 1986–1995).
NK   *Nishida Kitarō,* trans. Yamamoto Seisaku and James W. Heisig (Berkeley:
      University of California Press, 1991).
RN   *Religion and Nothingness,* trans. with intro. Jan Van Bragt (Berkeley:
      University of California Press, 1982).
SN   *The Self-Overcoming of Nihilism,* trans. Graham Parkes with Setsuko Aihara
      (Albany: State University of New York Press, 1990).

TANABE Hajime

THZ   *Tanabe Hajime zenshū* [*The Complete Works of Tanabe Hajime*], 15 vols.
      (Tokyo: Chikuma Shōbō, 1964).
PM   *Philosophy as Metanoetics,* trans. Takeuchi Yoshinori (Berkeley: University
      of California Press, 1986).

UEDA Shizuteru

NKY   *Nishida Kitarō o yomu* [*Reading Nishida Kitarō*] (Tokyo: Iwanami Shoten,
      1991).
USS   *Ueda Shizuteru shū* [*The Ueda Shizuteru Collection*] (Tokyo: Iwanami
      Shoten, 2002–2004).

WATSUJI Testurō

WTR   *Watsuji Tetsurō's Rinrigaku: Ethics in Japan,* trans. Yamamoto Seisaku and
      Robert E. Carter (Albany: State University of New York Press, 1996).

Japanese and
Continental
Philosophy

Introduction:
Conversations
on an Ox Path

The principal aim of this volume is to promote dialogue between Western and Japanese philosophy, and more specifically between Continental philosophy and the Kyoto School. In the West, this dialogue is still at a nascent stage. In Japan, it began with great intensity upon the opening of this Far Eastern island nation to the West in the latter decades of the nineteenth century, and it continues unabated to this day. While (with a few exceptions) Western philosophers have concerned themselves mostly with their own tradition, Japanese philosophers have been avidly seeking to build dialogical bridges between their own conceptual and linguistic horizons and those of the West.

The Eurocentrism of the West has in fact spread to many sectors of Japanese society as well, academia included. When the Japanese begin to radically philosophize, however, rather than stopping at mere importation and reflection on Western schools of thought, they inevitably also embark on a hermeneutical retrieval of their own traditions of thought. No group of thinkers has done this more ardently and productively than the Kyoto School, which has justifiably become the most famous group of modern Japanese philosophers.[1] Its members are noteworthy not only for the rigor and originality of their individual thought, but also for their shared attempt to think in dialogue with the West while keeping firmly in touch with their own native traditions, particularly those of Mahāyāna Buddhism.

The Kyoto School is a name given to a group of twentieth- (and now twenty-first-) century philosophers who are united by the fact that they are all inspired by Nishida Kitarō[2] (1870–1945), who is widely considered to be Japan's first and still greatest modern philosopher, as well as by the fact that they all studied and/or taught at Kyoto University. Nishida's junior colleague, Tanabe Hajime (1885–1962), as well as many of his students, most notably Nishitani Keiji (1900–1990), are generally considered members of the School, as are more recent thinkers such as Nishitani's student Ueda Shizuteru (b. 1926). It is important to point out that the School is not constituted by any dogmatically accepted creed. Although it can be said to be held together by an evolving set of shared concerns and vocabulary, even such common terms as "absolute nothingness" are often the subject of contention (see for example the intense debate that took place between Nishida and Tanabe, as explicated by Sugimoto in chapter 3). What all the members of the School *can* be said to have in common, however, is a firm commitment to engaging in East-West dialogue on a rigorously philosophical level.

Over the last few decades, the importance of the Kyoto School has become increasingly recognized, and the School is now studied and researched in many North American and European universities. A number of translations, monographs, and edited volumes have appeared in response to a growing demand for primary and secondary sources on the Kyoto School. Thus far, however, the available literature has been for the most part limited to introduction and interpretation,[3] or has focused on the relevance of the Kyoto School to Buddhist-Jewish-Christian dialogue,[4] or has been concerned with critically assessing the politics and political thought of the School during World War II.[5]

Japanese and Continental Philosophy: Conversations with the Kyoto School is the first anthology to be fully committed to developing *philosophical exchanges* between the Kyoto School and modern and contemporary Western philosophers in the Continental tradition.[6] Such a volume is not only overdue, it is also, we think, a most appropriate response to the philosophical and dialogical overtures made by the Kyoto School itself.

It needs to be stressed that the members of the Kyoto School thought of themselves first and foremost as *philosophers,* rather than as religious, cultural, or political theorists. Moreover, the philosophies of the Kyoto School are themselves inherently dialogical, commuting between Eastern and Western philosophical and religious traditions. The original Kyoto School thinkers were conversant in particular with continental European schools of thought such as German idealism, Marxism, existentialism, hermeneutics, and phenomenology. Contemporary successors to the Kyoto School in Japan, including several contributors to the present volume, have continued this tradition by engaging in dialogue with recent schools and figures in Continental philosophy.

Most of the essays in this volume develop dialogues with the three central figures of the Kyoto School: Nishida, Tanabe, and Nishitani. Some essays treat other important members of the School, such as Ueda and Hisamatsu Shinichi (1889–1980), as well as significant Japanese philosophers whose connections to the School were more peripheral, most notably Miki Kiyoshi (1897–1945),

Watsuji Tetsurō (1889–1960), and Kuki Shūzō (1888–1941). Our Japanese contributors include Fujita Masakatsu, who heads the department of the History of Japanese Philosophy at Kyoto University, the current hub of Kyoto School studies in Japan, as well as Ōhashi Ryōsuke, a prolific philosopher who represents what might be considered the School's fourth generation. We are especially honored to have Ueda Shizuteru—the leading figure of the third generation of the School and undoubtedly one of the most significant contemporary Japanese philosophers—compose the lead essay especially for this volume.

Our European and North American contributors, for their part, attempt not just to introduce the Kyoto School to a Western readership, but more importantly to bring their philosophies into critical and innovative conversation with some of the most significant figures in recent Western philosophy. Although we have focused the Western side of this volume on Continental philosophy, we have intentionally not restricted its scope to the familiar and expected figures of Kant, Hegel, Nietzsche, and Heidegger, who in the past exerted the most influence on the Kyoto School philosophers, and with whom they most often engaged in critical dialogue. In the interest of continuing—rather than merely reflecting on—the dialogue between Japanese and Continental philosophy, we have also included essays that address the thought of such figures as Arendt, Derrida, Habermas, Irigaray, Levinas, Löwith, Marion, Merleau-Ponty, Plessner, Ricoeur, Scheler, Schelling, and Mark C. Taylor.

Our intention is to invite new voices into this dialogue with Japanese philosophy. In particular, it is our hope that students and scholars trained in Continental philosophy will use this book as an opportunity to expand the horizons of their thinking. This is not just a question of filling a multicultural quota. It is a question of genuinely philosophizing in today's globalizing world, where "philosophy" is understood not simply as a Western academic discipline, but rather as a rigorous loving quest for wisdom that refuses to stay confined within established borders of language, culture, tradition, and academic specialization. For modern Japanese as for all non-Western intellectuals, cross-cultural thinking is not an option; given the spread of Western capitalism, technology, and culture around the world, they cannot evade the exigency of living and thinking between their native traditions and those of the West. Only Westerners have the apparent luxury—which may in fact all too easily become an intellectual blindfold—of ignoring other traditions of thought. This volume invites Western philosophers to take the risk of learning from dialogical encounters with a significant group of philosophers outside their familiar cultural and academic purview.

This is not, however, an invitation to escapism. We should not allow the pendulum to swing from arrogant Eurocentrism into idealizing Orientalism. Just as Western philosophers today should not stubbornly or timidly stay within the borders of the Western tradition, neither should they forgo a thorough hermeneutical reflection on their own cultural and intellectual background or a critical engagement with other traditions of thought. Hence the theme of our volume: genuinely philosophical conversations between Continental and Japanese philosophies. It is true that many of our essays are notably sympathetic to—which does not mean uncritically accepting of—the thought of the Kyoto School. We think this is justified, however, not only because many of us find much of their thought to be philosophically compelling, but also because of the nascent stage of the philosophical reception of their thought. We are concerned more with giving new readers reasons for entering into serious engagement with their thought than with pushing them away by issuing what may be prematurely critical judgments of it.

We have made a point of including a broad spectrum of contributors from Europe, North America, and Japan, ranging from many of the most established scholars to a couple of rising stars in the field. While nearly all the contributors have a background in Continental philosophy, many have also been trained in Japanese and Buddhist thought. And while we recognize the importance of language ability for understanding the subtle—and at times crucial—nuances of philosophical texts, we nevertheless made it a point *not* to require that all of our contributors possess an ability to read Japanese. Certainly one should ideally read Nishitani in Japanese, just as one should ideally read Plato in Greek. But in neither case should this be an all or nothing affair. When asked about the scarcity of explicit references to Asian thought in Heidegger's texts, despite his known interest in it, Gadamer suggested that Heidegger may well have been hesitant to refer to a thought he could not read in the original language.[7] Even though this hermeneutical hesitancy (or scholarly pride) may have some role to play in academia, it should not get in the way of the philosophical urge to follow the scent of wisdom wherever it may lead. The study of Japanese philosophy will, of course, always need its linguistically trained experts. If linguistic ability is treated as an entry permit, however, then the discussion room will remain underpopulated, and the field of philosophy in general—not just the field of

Japanese philosophy—will suffer the missed opportunities of a multilateral cross-cultural dialogue.

The book is arranged in five main parts that present major themes with which the Kyoto School is engaged: (1) The Kyoto School and Dialogue; (2) Self and World; (3) God and Nothingness; (4) Ethics and Politics; and (5) Grammar, Art, and Imagination.

The Kyoto School and Dialogue

Part 1 opens with Ueda Shizuteru's "Contributions to Dialogue with the Kyoto School," in which he discusses both the difficulties and the world-historical significance of the birth of "Japanese philosophy" in the Kyoto School's attempt to think in the dialogical space between Western and Eastern traditions. Ueda explains how, in contrast to the Western ontology of being or substance, the Kyoto School thinkers drew their central thought of "absolute nothingness" or "emptiness" from East Asian thought, and from Mahāyāna Buddhism in particular. In critical dialogue with Western thought, they also went beyond the traditional thought of the East in attempts to develop *philosophies* based on nothingness/ emptiness rather than on being/substance. Ueda then addresses the vexing question of why Nishitani chose to reappropriate the traditional Mahāyāna term "emptiness" instead of adopting Nishida's locution of "absolute nothingness," a choice which Ueda argues must be understood in light of the historical advent and global spread of European nihilism. Ueda closes by reflecting on the contemporary challenge posed to philosophers by the worldwide menace of this self-dissimulating nihilism, a challenge which he suggests can be met by furthering a dialogue between Nietzsche, Heidegger, and deconstruction on the one hand, and the philosophies of Nishida and Nishitani on the other.

In "Dialogue and Appropriation: The Kyoto School as Cross-Cultural Philosophy," Bret W. Davis introduces the Kyoto School by way of reflecting on hermeneutical, ethical, and political issues central to their cross-cultural philosophy. In particular, Davis focuses on the tension between cultural appropriation and creative synthesis, on the one hand, and dialogue and respect for irreducible cultural differences, on the other. He begins by raising the question of whether and to what extent the cultural appropriation found in modern Japan can be compared with that found in ancient Greece. This leads to a discussion of Karl Löwith's criticism of modern Japanese intellectuals for purportedly failing to "critically appropriate" Western thought, a failure

Löwith sharply contrasts with the Greco-European tradition of "making what is other one's own." Davis develops two critical responses to Löwith, the first being that he neglected to take account of the Kyoto School's significant attempts to navigate through the pendulum swing in modern Japan between deferential Eurocentrism and reactionary Japanism. Second, from the Kyoto School Davis gleans both a critique of willful cultural appropriation and intimations of a philosophy of genuine cross-cultural dialogue, wherein cultural differences would neither be obliterated nor reified. The essay ends with a reflection on the tension between the pluralistic ideals and the political entanglements of the Kyoto School.

It is important to note that the Kyoto School was not only engaged in substantive conversation with the Western tradition, but that there were also critical debates occurring between its own members, debates which exercised a powerful, formative influence on subsequent philosophical reflection in Japan as a whole. Sugimoto Kōichi's essay, "Tanabe Hajime's Logic of Species and the Philosophy of Nishida Kitarō: A Critical Dialogue within the Kyoto School," examines the critical exchange between Nishida and Tanabe, an exchange which laid the groundwork for the formation of the Kyoto School as a group of original thinkers with an often shared, yet at times also contested philosophical orientation and vocabulary. Sugimoto organizes his essay into three main sections, in which he focuses on Tanabe's "logic of species" and Nishida's response to it. He begins by briefly describing the problems posed by Tanabe's logic of species, based on two important articles written by Tanabe, "The Logic of Social Existence" (1934–1935) and "The Logic of Species and the World Schema" (1935). In particular, Sugimoto discusses Tanabe's implicit and explicit critique of Nishida in these articles. In the second section, Nishida's objections to the logic of species as articulated in his *Philosophical Essays II* (1937) are examined. Sugimoto concludes by showing that, despite both Tanabe's frequent and unequivocal criticism of Nishida's philosophy and Nishida's no less critical objections to Tanabe's logic of species, there nevertheless exists a common basis that underlies their philosophies.

Self and World

Part 2 opens with "Philosophy as Auto-Bio-Graphy: The Example of the Kyoto School," by Ōhashi Ryōsuke. This essay develops the idea of philosophy as auto-bio-graphy in three theses, and does so by way of the example of the Kyoto School. Ōhashi maintains that one can understand several aspects of the Kyoto School's conception of philosophy in these terms. Ōhashi's first thesis is that philosophy is knowledge of *to autō,* that is, of the "self." In other words it is, to use Socrates' famous phrase, a matter of coming to "know oneself" (Gr. *gnōsi sauton*). The second thesis is interrelated to the first, namely, that philosophy always concerns the *biōs* of the *autōs,* the life in which the ego-less self of the actual I expresses itself and establishes itself as an I. And finally, Ōhashi argues, as the life of the self, philosophy requires *graphē,* that is, a writing of its determinative meaning. Philosophy as the *descriptive* writing of the life of the self is, in accord with its form, an auto-bio-graphy.

In Buddhist philosophy, any consideration of the self necessarily entails a thinking of what the self is not. The egoless self (Sk. *anātman;* Jp. *muga*) finds strong resonances in the thinking of Nietzsche, who offers what is perhaps the West's most influential and incisive treatment of the problem of nihilism. Nishitani Keiji has responded to the increasingly global problem of nihilism by developing a philosophy of Zen Buddhism. In "Nishitani after Nietzsche: From the Death of God to the Great Death of the Will," Bret W. Davis considers and develops a central aspect of Nishitani's project of "overcoming nihilism by way of passing through nihilism," namely, his dialogical encounter with Nietzsche's thought. By first elucidating the debate in the West over the relation between nihilism and the will, and then turning to Nishitani's development of the Buddhist critique of "craving" in terms of an "infinite drive," Davis assesses Nishitani's interpretation of Nietzsche's thought—both his sympathetic interpretation of the idea of *amor fati* and his critique of the will to power. Although Nishitani was influenced by and remained deeply appreciative of Nietzsche's attempt at a "self-overcoming of nihilism," in the end he argues that Mahāyāna Buddhism, and Zen in particular, offers a more profound way through and beyond what he calls the "field of nihility." Whereas Nietzsche primarily sought to affirm the ubiquity of the will to power after the death of God, Nishitani claims that Zen's "Great Death" takes one beyond all standpoints of will to a rebirth of non-egoistic freedom and compassion.

The deep relationship between Nietzsche and Nishitani is also at issue in David Jones's "Empty Soul, Empty World: Nietzsche and Nishitani," which investigates the idea of *śūnyatā,* or "emptiness," to present a new understanding of the Buddhist ideal of non-ego (or no-self) as seen in the work of Nishitani and his encounters with Nietzsche. For Nishitani, to arrive at the Good entails the deployment of the non-differentiating love of *agapē,* which is tantamount to "emptying oneself." This emptying of the soul first shows itself as a flowing-over beyond the field of the ego into the indifferent realm of the non-ego, and then extends beyond selfhood altogether. This extension has an ethical and ecological dimension since self-emptying is the perfect mode of being issuing from Buddhist compassion. The lack of selfishness is ultimately what is meant by non-ego, the realization of emptiness on the existential plane, and this constitutes the "Great Compassion" of Buddhism. On Jones's interpretation, this flowing-over the field of ego into the realm of the non-ego is also envisaged by Nietzsche's identification of the individual soul with the undifferentiated Dionysian flow of all things. For Nietzsche this is an act of love, and though it involves the erotic, it is without object except (re)union with the reality that we are. Such love resonates with the *agapē* of Nishitani's self-emptying. And according to Jones, Nietzsche unknowingly follows in the footsteps of the Buddha's teaching, as evinced in the *Diamond* and *Heart Sutras,* to reveal his own Great Compassion, in which visible forms of the experienced world are radically transformed by losing substantiality. This Great Compassion reverberates with deep ecology, the philosophical-religious worldview of which is envisioned and constituted on a deeper level by Nietzsche and Nishitani.

Generally considered to be the Kyoto School's principal representative today, Ueda Shizuteru has creatively developed the philosophies of Nishida and Nishitani, and he has done so in dialogue not only with medieval Western mystics (Eckhart) and modern philosophers (Descartes), but also with twentieth-century phenomenologists. In "Ueda Shizuteru's Phenomenology of Self and World: Critical Dialogues with Descartes, Heidegger, and Merleau-Ponty," Steffen Döll notes that much of Ueda's work has focused on the dual problem of the "self" and its "place." In his phenomenological analysis of the self, Ueda shows the self to exist in a twofold structure, for which he coins the term "twofold being-in-the-world." Insofar as this twofold structure of the self signifies that the self exists simultaneously in a concrete, contingent place, as well as in the "infinite openness of Nothingness," Ueda's phenomenology of the self is both a phenomenology of the life-world and paradoxically a phenomenology of "that which does not appear"—namely, the all-embracing place of emptiness or absolute nothingness. Döll traces Ueda's interpretation of Merleau-Ponty's conception of the self as well as his dialogue with Heidegger's thought on the question of nothingness. Both European thinkers have significantly influenced Ueda and his conception of self and world, even though at times only implicitly. Hermeneutically reconstructing this relationship, Döll argues, deepens our understanding of Ueda's development of the Kyoto School's philosophy as well as enriches our view of modern phenomenology.

God and Nothingness

The Kyoto School is often touted for being the first to develop a genuinely comparative religious philosophy, and part 3 focuses on this central aspect of their thought. In "Nothing Gives: Marion and Nishida on Gift-giving and God," John C. Maraldo points out that the Christian philosopher Jean-Luc Marion and the Buddhist philosopher Nishida, as vast as their differences may be, both have proposed alternatives to thinking of God in terms of being, and being in terms of ground. Maraldo contends that both Nishida and Marion offer a way out of onto-theology that is markedly different from Heidegger's. Maraldo begins his essay by sketching Marion's alternative of God revealed as gift and giving, rather than as a being. He then presents Nishida's alternative of the Absolute as a nothingness to which we nevertheless can relate. Nishida's name for that relation is "inverse correspondence," which is explained through an explication of Buddhist senses of giving and gift. Maraldo concludes by suggesting that "Marion's notion of God as giving needs a notion like Nishida's absolute nothing to make it work."

The interrogation into religious and theological dimensions and implications of the Kyoto School is continued in "Language Games, Selflessness, and the Death of God: A/Theology in Contemporary Zen Philosophy and Deconstruction," by Gereon Kopf. Contrary to most interpreters of Nishida, who find traces of mysticism, or at least absolutism, in his philosophy, Kopf draws our attention to certain affinities between Nishida's philosophy and Jacques Derrida's deconstructionist project. Some of Nishida's terminology is remarkably similar to Derrida's language of *differánce* and *khōra*, as well as to Mark C. Taylor's conception of the "divine milieu" as that which "neither is nor is not" and of the self as "both desubstantialized and deindividualized." In addition, two of Nishida's main critics, Tanabe and Takahashi Satomi, argue that Nishida's notion of the absolute, if developed correctly, renders an "absolute criticism" or a "self-corrective dialectics," respectively. Kopf contends that the concept of the "absolute" as it can be found in the work of the later Nishida functions not unlike Tanabe's "absolute criticism" and Takahashi's self-corrective dialectics, and implies a philosophy that, while not identical with Derrida's deconstruction or Taylor's "postmodern a/theology," combines insights from both Kyoto School and postmodern philosophy. Such thinking furnishes an a/theology that is not only strengthened by postmodern criticisms but that also provides a new methodological and terminological framework for interreligious dialogue and cross-cultural philosophy.

Kenotic theologian Thomas J. J. Altizer was a pioneer in recognizing the School's importance for conceiving a new theological vision in the West, and "Buddha and God: Nishida's Contributions to a New Apocalyptic Theology" presents his latest reflections on this topic. This essay is a response to Nishida and the Kyoto School which attempts to raise the possibility that Christianity can now be liberated theologically by incorporating a Buddhist understanding of absolute nothingness and absolute self-negation. While these categories have only a limited presence in historical Christianity, Altizer notes they have become prominent in late modernity, and most clearly so in uniquely modern realizations of apocalypse itself. The Kyoto School has made it possible, he claims, to grasp the full theological significance of apocalypse through its radical interpretation of *śūnyatā*. For Altizer, this is most clearly the case with the themes of crucifixion, resurrection, and apocalypse: If these themes can be understood as an absolute negation realizing an absolute nothingness, then that nothingness is tantamount to the apocalypse of the Godhead, which makes possible a total human freedom. According to Altizer, nothing is more challenging theologically than thinking such a conception of nothingness, and above all, understanding the actuality of such a nothingness. This is the point where Christianity faces its deepest challenge from Buddhism, and one that is decisively present in the Kyoto School.

Ethics and Politics

For many, the most controversial dimension of Kyoto School thinking concerns their ethics and politics, which provide the theme of part 4. Brian Schroeder's "Other-Power and Absolute Passivity in Tanabe and Levinas" engages the later thought of Tanabe and that of Emmanuel Levinas in order to assess their respective interpretations of alterity in light of their mutual attempts to establish a fundamental conception of ethics and religion. Central to both, Schroeder contends, is the possibility of the ethical transformation of the self in response to an imperative posed by the passive power of the other, a necessary condition for confronting the problem of evil—a pressing issue in the wake of recent world terrorism, and especially since terrorist activities have been repeatedly cast as a matter in which religion predominates. To bring about this self-transformation, the concept of "breaking through," employed by both Tanabe and Levinas, will be examined in order to acquire an adequate understanding of the dialectic between good and evil, power and passivity, response and reconciliation, mediation and proximity, self and other, humanity and divinity, and God and absolute nothingness. Standing on common ground regarding the priority of religion over philosophy, Tanabe and Levinas each formulate a religious philosophy as the heart of their thinking, and abandon ontological philosophy as the principal means to realize the meaning of the ethical. In both, there occurs a conversion from philosophy to religion wherein the notion of responsibility becomes central. Schroeder concludes by arguing that Tanabe's philosophy *as* metanoetics (a going-beyond knowledge together with a change of heart and mind) and Levinas's "metaphysical" ethics are complementary standpoints that can each help advance the other position by exposing certain philosophical difficulties inherent in it.

Bringing together Watsuji Testurō and the French feminist philosopher Luce Irigaray, Erin McCarthy explores the idea that the body is of central importance for ethical being-in-the-world, and further develops a concept of (ethical) selfhood that is not dualistic. McCarthy points out that while feminists, phenomenologists, and Asian philosophers have addressed the body and its place in ethics and selfhood/identity, they have yet to speak to one another. In "Beyond the Binary: Watsuji Testurō and Luce Irigaray on Body, Self, and Ethics," Watsuji and Irigaray each speak to the universality of the place of the body in ethical being-in-the-world and cultivate a notion of self that includes the body as that which provides a base for cross-cultural dialogue and understanding while at the same time creating a space for recognition of and respect for difference. Globalization and technocracy alike threaten to level off any difference under the guise of universality in its most dangerous sense. In establishing a dialogue between Irigaray and Watsuji, McCarthy assumes the challenge of making philosophy "radically plural." This dialogue takes each beyond their own philosophy as a step toward a vision of where we might go, how we might live a different kind of selfhood wherein we would accept, respect, and cultivate a fully embodied ethics that allows the genders to flourish together. McCarthy performs a double reading of both Irigaray and Watsuji—that is, a feminist reading of Watsuji and a Watsujian reading of Irigaray—and by thus exploring each through the other, begins to move toward a new vision of self, the body, and ethics.

The topic of a now famous symposium that took place in 1942, the question of "overcoming modernity" is an important issue for many in the Kyoto School. From a contemporary standpoint, Bernard Stevens reflects on this controversial issue in his essay "Overcoming Modernity: A Critical Response to the Kyoto School," attempting to clarify not only what is meant by the philosophical concept of modernity, but also what is signified by "postmodernism." For Stevens, it is of vital importance to recall the disastrous ideological consequences caused by the project of "overcoming modernity" during the Japanese imperial regime at the time of the Fifteen Year War (1931–1945). Stevens's aim, however, is not simply to reopen past controversies. Rather, his concern is twofold: to salvage the philosophical and humanistic message of the Kyoto School by extricating it from its political failings, and to address the recent emergence of neo-fascism around the world.

Since the early 1990s, prominent North American and British critics of the Kyoto School have decried the political writings of its members for having "defined the philosophic contours of Japanese fascism," usually by way of suggesting guilt-by-association with the ideas of Martin Heidegger. Graham Parkes overtly challenges this widely echoed characterization of the Kyoto School thinkers in "Heidegger and Japanese Fascism: An Unsubstantiated Connection." Parkes contends that on closer examination the scholarship turns out to be sadly short on facts and to depend on misquotations or mistranslations of passages that are couched in or interspersed with neo-Marxist jargon and quasi-deconstructionist rhetoric. In 1997, Parkes published an influential article in *Philosophy East and West* titled "The Putative Fascism of the Kyoto School" (subsequently shortened and revised for publication in Japanese translation), in which he argued that "politically correct" Japanology obscures critical issues surrounding the Kyoto School. The critics in question never responded to this piece, and have instead simply kept up a stream of innuendo. In order to confront this ever-widening perception that the Kyoto School thinkers were fascists inspired by Heidegger, Parkes argues that it is time for another refutation, and a further demonstration of the extent to which the politics of the contemporary academy continue to cloud our understanding of the political philosophy of the Kyoto School.

Grammar, Art, and Imagination

The final part of *Japanese and Continental Philosophy* commences with Rolf Elberfeld's "The Middle Voice of Emptiness: Nishida and Nishitani." Elberfeld initially notes that even though the middle voice belongs to the oldest grammatical forms of the Japanese language, in English- and German-speaking descriptions of the modern Japanese language this form is not mentioned, since the middle voice exists neither in German nor in English. He then argues that one comes to understand the grammatical forms and the philosophical potential of the middle voice by starting from an analysis of the ancient Japanese language; yet it also becomes clear that the middle voice remains alive in modern Japanese: Elberfeld's thesis is that the philosophies of Nishida and Nishitani can be read in a new perspective if one is aware of the history and the modern use of the middle voice in the Japanese language. Both thinkers use this form, yet presumably without knowing the grammatical background of it. The word *kangaerareru*, which constantly appears in the texts of Nishida, and the word *mieru*, which is used by Nishitani to explain the nonduality of an event of perception, are, grammatically speaking, forms of the middle voice. Starting with an understanding of the middle voice in old Japanese texts, such pivotal terms in Nishida's and Nishitani's texts—and indeed, their philosophical approach in general—can be seen in a new light. Specifically, this interpretive perspective of the middle voice allows us to clarify the central yet enigmatic metaphors of "place" (*basho, tokoro*) and "emptiness" in the philosophies of Nishida and Nishitani.

Aesthetics is conventionally considered to be an elective problem within philosophy. In "Truly Nothing: The Kyoto School and Art," Jason Wirth contests that claim, as well as the assumptions underlying it, and does so by providing some preliminary considerations of Kyoto School aesthetics. According to Wirth, the latter is not an application of allegedly Kyoto School principles to the question of art, nor is it an issue that speaks within the narrow philosophical parameters of a "School." Rather, Wirth argues, not only is this issue fundamental to the manner of philosophizing particular to the Kyoto School, it is also an important clue to the coming-to-the-fore of the site of philosophizing itself. This position is developed in the essay by concentrating on the thinking of Nishida, Nishitani, and Hisamatsu in dialogue with Western philosophers and writers such as Schelling, Kant, Heidegger, and more recently François Berthier, Hermann Broch, and Roger-Pol Droit.

The book concludes with Fujita Masakatsu's "*Logos* and *Pathos:* Miki Kiyoshi's Logic of the Imagination," which introduces Miki's major work *Logic of the Imagination,* and shows how Miki—in dialogue with Nishida, Kant, and a number of his contemporary German and French philosophers—seeks to provide a philosophical anthropology that can account for the unification of the two dimensions of human being, *logos* and *pathos.* Fujita considers Miki's argument that the human being cannot be understood simply in terms of consciousness, but must be grasped as an embodied existence, which means a being imbued with *pathos*. Specifically, Miki understands embodied human praxis to involve an intermingling of affectivity and intellect, and he thinks that it is precisely the power of imagination that opens up a place for this intermingling. Fujita concludes that Miki's work, while never fully completed, nevertheless makes an original and important contribution to the post-Kantian discourse on the enigmatic yet indispensable faculty of imagination.

Having introduced the contents of the essays in this volume, it is worthwhile to point out that what is often at stake in these conversations among and about Japanese and Continental philosophers is not only the content, but also the very methods and aims of philosophy. In the course of such cross-cultural encounters, philosophy indeed has the opportunity to become once again a question to itself. If one of the gifts that Western philosophy has been able to offer the Japanese is its methods of rational inquiry and critical dialogue, one of the gifts that the Japanese tradition has to offer the West is an existential-religious path that proceeds by way of holistic practice as well as conceptual thought. Can these mutual gifts be brought together into the formation of such a "way" of doing philosophy that would offer a genuine alternative to those caught today in the standoff between passionate yet dogmatic faith and sober yet listless reason? Can philosophy retain its rational rigor and yet become, once again, a holistically praxis-oriented way of life?[8]

While respecting the variety of their approaches and subject matter, we editors would like to suggest that the essays in this book could be thought of as a collection of "conversations on an ox path." With this phrase we are alluding specifically (though not restrictively), on the one hand, to Heidegger's "conversation on a country path" in which a scientist, a scholar, and a guide converse their way down a path toward "releasement" (Gn. *Gelassenheit*) as the authentic way of being human;[9] and, on the other hand, to the classic Zen text, *The Ten Ox-herding Pictures,* which illustrates and comments on a search for the elusive "Ox" that represents one's true self or "Buddha nature"— a provisional image which is itself cast aside (Jp. *hōge*) along the path toward existential liberation (*gedatsu*).[10] Like the characters in these texts, the conversations in the present volume do not have—or at least do not remain attached to—a pre-established idea of the goal toward which they are heading. Indeed, with respect to the diversity of the contributions here, it would be more appropriate to say that they are each on "an" ox path, rather than on "the" ox path. In any case, for the Kyoto School thinkers, as for many of us, philosophy should ultimately be a quest for liberating wisdom, not simply an academic exercise; and it is a quest that must be made neither simply in solitude nor simply in solidarity, but rather in dialogue—which entails, as Ueda suggests, the experience of being irreducibly "alone together" as singular yet interrelated individuals in conversation.[11] Conveying a renewed sense of practicing philosophy as a dialogical way of life is one of the aims we hope to accomplish with this gathering of conversations.

Notes

1. The Kyoto School is certainly not the only group of philosophers in modern Japan, nor even the most popular, but they are the most original, owing no doubt in large part to the fact that they draw deeply on Asian as well as on Western traditions of thought. For an overview of the history of modern Japanese philosophy, see Gino K. Piovesana, *Recent Japanese Philosophical Thought, 1862–1996: A Survey,* the revised edition of which includes a new survey by Naoshi Yamawaki, "The Philosophical Thought of Japan from 1963 to 1996" (Richmond, Surrey: Japan Library, Curzon Press, 1997); also see John Maraldo, "Contemporary Japanese Philosophy," in Brian Carr and Indira Mahalingam, eds., *Companion Encyclopedia of Asian Philosophy* (London and New York: Routledge, 1997). For an anthology of Japanese phenomenology, see Nitta Yoshihiro and Tatematsu Hirotaka, eds., *Japanese Phenomenology,* in *Analecta Husserliana* 8 (Boston: Reidel, 1979). For an anthology of contemporary Japanese postmodern and feminist thought, see Richard Calichman, ed., *Contemporary Japanese Thought* (New York: Columbia University Press, 2005).

2. Japanese names are written here in the Japanese order of family name first, followed by given name, except when Japanese authors have used the Western name order for their publications in Western languages.

3. For general introductions to the Kyoto School, see James W. Heisig, *Philosophers of Nothingness: An Essay on the Kyoto School* (Honolulu: University of Hawai'i Press, 2001); and Bret W. Davis, "The Kyoto School," in *The Stanford Encyclopedia of Philosophy* (Summer 2010 edition), ed. Edward N. Zalta, at http://plato.stanford.edu/archives/sum2010/entries/kyoto-school/. Both of these sources contain extensive bibliographies of primary and secondary literature on the Kyoto School.

4. See, for example, Hans Waldenfels, *Absolute Nothingness: Foundations for a Buddhist-Christian Dialogue,* trans. James W. Heisig (New York: Paulist Press, 1980). Noteworthy anthologies focusing on the philosophy of religion include Taitetsu Unno, ed., *The Religious Philosophy of Nishitani Keiji* (Berkeley, Calif.: Asian Humanities Press, 1989); and Taitetsu Unno and James W. Heisig, eds., *The Religious Philosophy of Tanabe Hajime* (Berkeley, Calif.: Asian Humanities Press, 1990).

5. The politics and the political philosophy of the Kyoto School is, to be sure, one important aspect of their thought that needs to be both critically and dialogically addressed. In addition to chapters 2, 4, 13, and 14 of the present volume, see most notably James W. Heisig and John C. Maraldo, eds., *Rude Awakenings: Zen, the Kyoto School,*

and the Question of Nationalism (Honolulu: University of Hawai'i Press, 1994); and Chris Goto-Jones, ed., *Re-politicising the Kyoto School as Philosophy* (London: Routledge, 2007).

6. There have been several important monographs in Western languages that embark on such a philosophical dialogue, including those by Kyoto School–oriented Japanese philosophers, such as the English works of Masao Abe (Jp. Abe Masao) and the German works of Ryosuke Ohashi (Jp. Ōhashi Ryōsuke), as well as works by Western scholars, several of whom contribute to this volume; see the bibliographies referred to in note 3, above. Robert Wilkinson's monograph, *Nishida and Western Philosophy* (Burlington, Vt.: Ashgate, 2009), appeared as the present volume was going to press.

7. Related from Gadamer's personal correspondence by Graham Parkes in his introduction to *Heidegger and Asian Thought* (Honolulu: University of Hawai'i Press, 1987), 5–7; also see Heidegger's own remarks in this regard in his letter to the 1969 conference held in Hawai'i on "Heidegger and Eastern Thought," in Eliot Deutsch, ed., *Philosophy East and West* 20, no. 3 (July 1970): 221. Heidegger's famous "A Dialogue on Language between a Japanese and an Inquirer" (in *On the Way to Language,* trans. Peter D. Hertz [New York: Harper & Row, 1971]) is an exception here, although one that is not without its own problems of monological distortion. For a collection of documents and essays regarding the relation between Heidegger and Japanese philosophy, especially the Kyoto School, see Harmut Buchner, ed., *Japan und Heidegger: Gedenkschrift der Stadt Messkirch zum 100. Geburtstag Martin Heideggers* (Sigmaringen: Jan Thorbecke, 1989).

8. For a compelling account of how Western philosophy has indeed been practiced, particularly by the ancients, as a "way of life," see Pierre Hadot, *Philosophy as a Way of Life: Spiritual Exercises from Socrates to Foucault,* ed. Arnold I. Davidson, trans. Michael Chase (Oxford: Blackwell, 1995).

9. Martin Heidegger, "Zur Erörterung der Gelassenheit: Aus einem Feldweggespräch über das Denken," in *Gelassenheit* (Pfullingen: Neske, 1959); "Conversation on a Country Path about Thinking," in *Discourse on Thinking,* trans. John M. Anderson and E. Hans Freund (New York: Harper & Row, 1966). The full original text of this "conversation" was included in *Feldweg-Gespräche (1944/45),* vol. 77 of Heidegger's *Gesamtausgabe* (Frankfurt am Main: Vittorio Klostermann, 1995), and is newly translated by Bret W. Davis in Heidegger's *Country Path Conversations* (Bloomington: Indiana University Press, 2010).

10. See Yamada Mumon, *Lectures on the Ten Oxherding Pictures,* trans. Victor Sōgen Hori (Honolulu: University of Hawai'i Press, 2004). Also see Ueda Shizuteru and Yanagida Seizan, *Jūgyūzu: Jiko no genshōgaku* [The ten ox pictures: A phenomenology of the self] (Tokyo: Chikuma, 1992); and for a Heidegger/Kyoto School–inspired German translation of this text, see Tsujimura Kōichi and Harmut Buchner, *Der Ochs und Sein Hirte* (Pfullingen: Neske, 1958).

11. See *Ueda Shizuteru shū* [Collected writings of Ueda Shizuteru] (Tokyo: Iwanami, 2002), 10: 269–98.

PART ONE

The Kyoto School
and Dialogue

1

Contributions to Dialogue with the Kyoto School

UEDA SHIZUTERU

"Japanese Philosophy" in the World

Since philosophers have often spoken of Greek philosophy, French philosophy, English philosophy, American philosophy, and so on, it would seem plausible to speak of "Japanese philosophy." Nevertheless, until about twenty or thirty years ago, philosophers in Japan generally did not take this to be a philosophically meaningful locution. It was from the beginning regarded as out of the question. If one did speak expressly of "Japanese philosophy," this tended to be understood as stressing the "Japanese" character of the philosophy in question, and this was deemed inappropriate to the scholarly nature of philosophy as an objective and universal discipline. The universality of philosophy was implicitly understood to mean the scholarly nature of Western philosophy. When one spoke of "philosophy" in Japanese academia, this was understood to obviously imply "Western philosophy," and if one studied philosophy at a Japanese university, one studied as a matter of course—and often exclusively—Western philosophers from Plato and Aristotle, through Descartes, Kant, and Hegel, to Husserl and Levinas. Of course, one might focus on a particular topic in order to clarify the relations between these different figures or to trace the history of a certain problematic; or one might go a step further and develop one's own philosophical path of thinking through one's study of these Western philosophers. But it remained the case that philosophy in modern Japan was an imported academic discipline of Western origin. The above state of affairs is historically explicable insofar as in premodern times there was, as Nakae Chōmin famously quipped, "no philosophy in Japan"—assuming, that is, that we strictly adhere to the Western concept of "philosophy."

While this state of affairs had its historical conditions, the situation is beginning to change as we enter into a new era in which we can say—as Nishida Kitarō foresaw in the midst of the world-historical developments of his time—"the world is today becoming real." In the wake of a shift away from the past identification of Western philosophy with philosophy as such, and in a movement toward opening up a discourse of "world philosophy," new and important contributions to philosophy can be expected to come from ideas that originate in non-Western traditions of culture and thought. One reason for this is that the European philosophical tradition, the tradition that Japanese philosophers have long held up as a model, has entered an era of radical self-questioning. In particular, certain dominant ways of thinking in modern European philosophy, certain foundational ideas that were previously held to be certain and even self-evident, have fallen into question. The ontological notion of substance, the logical principle of identity, subject/object dualism in epistemology, the strict division between reason and sensibility, and underlying everything the idea of "God" or the distinctively modern idea of the absolute "subject"—all of these at once dominant and fundamental ways of thinking, have fallen into question. We can look upon "deconstruction" as one palpable manifestation of this state of affairs.

The turn away from the previous identification of European philosophy with philosophy as such, and the development of world philosophy, will no doubt advance a philosophical thinking that is no longer restricted to the specific "love of wisdom" and "science of principles as the science of sciences" that originated in the West. Contact between different traditions promises to help shed light on shared fundamental structures of human existence, and it will encourage new ways of bringing to awareness the understandings of the world and the self found in our various manners of being-in-the-world. What is being heralded as "the end of philosophy" concerns the system of knowledge that places metaphysics in the position of first philosophy. "World philosophy" calls for a transformation of philosophy itself along with a transformation of the world. For Western philosophy as well, an "other beginning" of thinking is called for; and the possibility of discovering indications for such an other beginning in the insights of traditions outside of Europe is now being realized.[1]

Now, in order for Japanese philosophy to be capable of making a meaningful contribution to world philosophy, Japanese philosophers need to go beyond their specialized research in European philosophy in order to discover, by way of a dialogical confrontation, what Nishida called a "deeper basis" between traditions. Then, concrete efforts of thinking must be carried out in the newly shared world-horizon that opens up on this deeper basis. Two examples which met the above conditions, and which were articulated so as to be comprehensible to Westerners, are Suzuki Daisetsu's (Daisetz Suzuki) "Eastern Way of Seeing" and Izutsu Toshihiko's "Eastern Philosophy." It is the content of their works, and not just the fact that many of them were written in English, which made them significant initial formulations of what Japanese thinkers can contribute to world philosophy. While both concerned themselves with "Eastern" ideas, these ideas were reinterpreted within a world-horizon and were creatively transformed to address the world. Beyond these contributions, on a properly philosophical level stands the thought of Nishida Kitarō, who took up the theme of the "world." And after Nishida, in the wake of changes in the spiritual climate of the world, the philosophy of Nishitani Keiji assumes special significance.

Just as European philosophy as such should not be inflated into world philosophy, non-European traditions as they are cannot contribute directly to world philosophy. While European philosophy must be deconstructed and perhaps even pass through what Heidegger calls the end of philosophy to an other beginning from which it can undergo a transformative turn to world philosophy, the insights harbored in Eastern traditions need to be transformed into "philosophical principles" before they can contribute to world philosophy. Nishida's key ideas, such as "pure experience," "place," and "contradictory self-identity," can be viewed as traditional insights transformed into philosophical principles. Nishitani took Mahāyāna Buddhism's key term "emptiness" and refashioned it into a fundamental philosophical category.

The potential for Japanese philosophy to contribute to the development of world philosophy is based in at least the following two aspects of its historical foundations. First of all, the "place" of Japan—which is constituted in the understanding of self and world by means of the Japanese language—is not simply that of Japan alone, since the Japanese tradition harbors the influence of a number of traditions, including those of India, central Asia, China, and Korea. Shaped by these cross-fertilizations, the "place" of Japan developed as one great confluence of the rich sediments of these non-Western traditions, one that can undoubtedly serve as a significant reservoir of ideas for the formation of world philosophy.

Secondly, this "place" of Japan now contains within it the experience, accumulated over the course of a century and a half, of a monumental encounter, collision, and exchange with Western culture and its products. Traversing the two stages of the "opening of the country" (*kaikoku*) in the Meiji period and the country's defeat in World War II, and despite the fact that Japanese society on the whole—albeit with some exceptions—was characterized by a turning of its back on tradition (this too is a phenomenon of cross-cultural encounter), there were exceptional individuals who placed themselves in the gap between these radically different traditions and took up the challenge of rethinking the fundamental principles of the world from this vantage point. We inherit the fruits of the efforts of these great thinkers who subjected their very existence to their cross-cultural experiments. Examples include Natsume Sōseki in literature, Nishida Kitarō in philosophy, and Suzuki Daisetsu in religion. Such intercultural experience in the "place" of Japan may well come to be seen as one paradigm for the interculturality and multiculturalism that is becoming such a prevalent concern in the world today. Japanese philosophy unfolds in the world and for the world, and Japanese philosophers are called on to show the world what and how they think.

A positive contribution to world philosophy can be made by Japanese philosophers only if they engage in genuine self-criticism, that is to say, in self-criticism made real by taking into account criticism from the world. The present anthology, *Japanese and Continental Philosophy: Conversations with the Kyoto School,* which includes critical interpretations of and dialogues with the Kyoto School by European and North American scholars, is certainly a timely and significant venture. Confronted with Western philosophy, Nishida realized that the Eastern tradition was lacking in "logic," and so he took as his life's task the formulation of such a logic. Japanese philosophy became in this situation a *topos* of thought which lets Japan be reflected in the world and lets the world be reflected in Japan. What is needed today is a world brought together by the fruits of mutual critique and mutual supplementation between different traditions. In order to discuss more specifically the kind of contributions that can be made by Japanese philosophy, let us look more closely at the philosophy of the Kyoto School.

The Core of the Kyoto School:
Nishida's Nothingness and Nishitani's Emptiness

The core issue that animates both Eastern and Western philosophical thinking is that of "being," "nothingness," and "being and nothingness." It would be oversimplifying to categorically characterize the West in terms of a philosophy of being, and the East in terms of a philosophy of nothingness. Among

European philosophical thinkers who were deeply moved by an idea of nothingness, Meister Eckhart and Nietzsche immediately come to mind. And yet, even in these cases, when we compare them to Nishida and Nishitani and the intellectual tradition in their background that conceives of what is originary in terms of nothingness, it does after all seem that in European philosophy what is originary is ultimately grasped in terms of being. That is to say, in the West nothingness is understood as non-being, that is, as the negation of being, and in this sense is based on being. Even when negativity is actively or even ardently grasped, in the end it is grasped as a self-negation of being that serves to elevate being itself.[2] By contrast, in the intellectual tradition behind Nishida and Nishitani, nothingness (*mu*) is not only non-being (*hi-u*) as the negation of being (*u*), but also contains a sense that goes beyond this, and this "additional sense" is brought to life when the originariness of nothingness is existentially realized and thoughtfully cultivated. When nothingness is limited to non-being as the negation of being, it is restricted to the horizon of being. Nothingness does not then tear through the horizon of being (which includes non-being), but rather, on the basis of what might be called a transcendental ontological preeminence of being, it is from the start posited as what can be comprehended in terms of non-being.

In the Western tradition, the thinker who has most thoroughly inquired into the mutual interpenetration of being and nothingness is the later Heidegger. When he writes, "As the shrine of Nothing, death harbors within itself the essential presencing of being,"[3] he is almost pronouncing being-qua-nothingness and nothingness-qua-being. Yet it remains the case that Heidegger's ultimate concern is still with being. Being (*das Sein*) is spoken of in terms of nothingness to clearly distinguish it from beings (*das Seiende*), but nothingness is not the origin. Even when be-ing—verbally understood as the event of appropriation/expropriation (*Ereignis/Enteignis*)—approximately expresses the dynamic of "from nothingness/toward nothingness," it is an event of being, not of nothingness.

In short, there are two orientations of thinking being and nothingness. On the one hand, there is the orientation of seeing nothingness as more than the negation of being, and of realizing the ultimate origin of nothingness in a higher level of negativity, namely that of *neither* being *nor* nothingness. On the other hand, there is the orientation of seeing the negativity of nothingness over against being in terms of non-being, and of subsuming the negativity of non-being into being so as to elevate being to the level of absolute being. While these two directions cannot be further elucidated here, let us note that they correspond to different ways of thinking the being and nothingness of the subject—in other words, life and death. On the one hand, one can be oriented by the idea of life and death as an inseparable pair and by the ideal of true enlightened existence in the midst of the recurrence of life and death;[4] on the other hand, one can be oriented by the idea of a transcendence of death's negation of life that leads to a transformation into eternal life. What is at stake here is not a comparative question, a matter of judging which orientation is superior, but rather an existential question, a matter of how one is to live and die as a human being.

With these issues of being and nothingness in the background, and amid the encounter—the collision and exchange—of Eastern and Western traditions of culture and thought, Nishida Kitarō and Tanabe Hajime first developed philosophies based on the idea that the absolute must be thought in terms of nothingness. The fundamental category of their philosophies was therefore "absolute nothingness" (*zettai-mu*). While following the methodologies of Western philosophy, they took into consideration the East Asian notion of a primordial origin of "nothingness" (Ch. *wu;* Jp. *mu*) as well as Mahāyāna Buddhism's notion of "emptiness" (Sk. *śūnyatā;* Jp. *kū*). With absolute nothingness as their philosophical principle, they set out on a difficult road toward bridging the differences between East and West, with the aim of conceiving the world anew within a horizon that included these differences.

Despite their commonalities, there are also differences between Nishida's and Tanabe's conceptions of "absolute nothingness." While Nishida's conceived of it in terms of "place" (*basho*), Tanabe's conceived of it in terms of "praxis" (*jissen*). Nishida developed a philosophy of "the place of absolute nothingness" (including "contradictory self-identity" as the "logic of place"), while Tanabe developed a philosophy of "the working of absolute nothingness" (absolute nothingness-qua-love). It is beyond the scope of the present essay to enter much further into the vast topic of—and the profound questions regarding—absolute nothingness. Here I wish to merely draw attention to the potential for Western philosophy to garner from Nishida's philosophy indications for a radical turn in thought, a potential that arises in the contemporary world-situation. Nishida's philosophy of absolute nothingness developed the ideas of "place" rather than "substance," "contradictory self-identity" rather than the "principle of identity," a "movement from a place preceding the subject/object split to a unification of the mutual opposition of subject-and-object" rather than a "dualism of subject and object," and a thoughtful cultivation of the reason inherent in sensibility rather than the supposition of a strict division between reason and sensibility. Such are the indications that can be gleaned from Nishida for developing new principals of philosophical thought.

Succeeding Nishida in the lineage of the Kyoto School, Nishitani's "philosophy of emptiness" is perhaps exerting a more direct impact on Western philosophy, meeting with positive as well as critical reception in Europe and North America. As a key term in Mahāyāna Buddhism, "emptiness" has received a nearly exhaustive amount of attention and has been discussed in a variety of manners. I will not delve into these discussions here, but will focus rather on Nishitani's "standpoint of emptiness" and sketch the development of his notion of emptiness in relation to Nishida's notion of nothingness.

Despite his direct connection to Nishida, Nishitani worked out a novel standpoint of emptiness. Why did Nishitani speak of the standpoint of emptiness rather than absolute nothingness? It can be said that the reason for this was the significant role that the arrival of nihilism played in Nishitani's thought, a problem which had not been an issue for Nishida. Nishida's project was aimed at uniting the cultures of East and West in their differences, deepening the possibilities of human existence, and constructing a comprehensive and concrete system of thought which would include the sciences. Put simply, this was a matter of uniting the spirit of modern science with Mahāyāna Buddhism. In contrast, Nishitani, who began to philosophize thirty years after Nishida did, faced a different problem, a problem which was increasingly shaking the spiritual and intellectual ground of the world. Nishitani wrote: "The space for a primordial relation with the transcendent is closing, and because of this the world and human existence are becoming fundamentally meaningless and aimless. This condition is lurking at the base of the way of being of modern civilization and human being. Such a situation is what is called the arrival of nihilism" (NCK 11: 163). In that modern science destroyed the teleological worldview, according to Nishitani it too bears the mark of nihilism.

Exposing his thinking and his very existence to this problem of nihilism, Nishitani's fundamental task became that of "overcoming nihilism by way of passing through nihilism." The crux of his inquiry into and response to nihilism was reached in the central chapters of his *What is Religion?* (translated as *Religion and Nothingness*), "Nihility and Śūnyatā" and "The Standpoint of Śūnyatā" (NKC 10: 87–187; RN 77–167). In the opening remarks of his final lecture at Otani University in June 1987, Nishitani reflected on his decades-long path of thought and remarked: "If pressed to say what the central issue is, it is thinking in response to the basic problem of nihilism" (NKC 26: 287). Born in the year of Nietzsche's death, as if by a fateful coincidence of the intellectual and spiritual history of the world, Nishitani inherited Nietzsche's penetrating nihilism and found a way to live through and beyond it. "Overcoming nihilism by way of passing through it" thus characterized the urgent matter pervading both his life and thought.

The problem is the unrelenting sense of meaninglessness and nihility that comes from the impermanence and nihility of human existence. Nietzsche positively accepted this nihility by proclaiming that "God is dead," and that in the place left vacant by "God" as the ultimate ground of everything and basis of all meaning is found an abysmal nihility which threatens everything with an "eternal meaninglessness." To the extent to which nothingness is enfolded back into being as non-being, nothingness is approached as a bottomless nihility. This is the nihility which encroaches upon the modern spirit and its quest for endless freedom and total independence. It is a nihility which rises up to an ever higher level to nihilate any and all attempts to oppose it with some kind of substantial being. What Nietzsche revealed as "European nihilism"— as the culmination of two thousand years of Europe's intellectual and spiritual history (including its religion, metaphysics, science, etc.), a nihilism which he says will haunt Europe for two hundred years to come—this has now, as a consequence of the Europeanization of the world, become nihilism for the world.[5] Moreover, the Europeanization of non-European lands has brought about a severance from their native traditions, and this severance has made the nihilism in these lands all the more severe.

In the midst of this abysmal nihility unveiled by nihilism, the idea of "absolute nothingness" could not help but be impacted. In a thoroughgoing nihilism, the very notion of the "absolute" rings hollow. Even if one repeatedly stresses that the absolute must be thought in terms of nothingness, and even if one adds the warning that this nothingness is not to be understood as the simple contrary to being, "absolute nothingness" remains a fundamental term within the horizon of ontology, and ontology as such has been rendered ineffective. For Nishitani, the effects of nihilism were not limited to the "death of God" in Europe; even "absolute nothingness"—an idea conceived in the horizon of the world and with Eastern traditions in its background—had ceased to be effective in its present form. Although the idea of "absolute nothingness" originated out of Nishida's bold venture of thought, it had quickly become a ready-made concept for the next generation of thinkers, and, in a rapidly changing world that was covering over differences between East and West, it was left suspended within the nihility of this superficial "one world." This shallow global nihility is, as it were, a nihilation of the abysmal depth of the abyss of nihility that was revealed by Nietzsche. Nihilating the nihilism witnessed by Nietzsche, this endlessly nihilistic nihility of shallowness is the end-stage of nihilism. (In passing let me add that Nishitani saw in this end-stage of nihilism what can be spoken of as the "wickedness" [ma] that runs rampant in the present world-historical era.) The issue at stake in the world today is not the reality of "East and West," as it was for Nishida, but rather what makes meaningless the distinction of East and West, namely, the "superficial one world and its nihility." This is the true problem of the "world" today, a problem now shared by all those whose being is that of being-in-the-world. And this is where Nishitani's thought is situated.

Because of the collapse of the absolute, the loss of the horizon of ontology, and the endless nihilization of nihility, "absolute nothingness," which would accommodate within itself even absolute being, could no longer be the basic category of thought in a world horizon. What was direly needed was a simple basic category that could accommodate as an ambiguous possibility absolute nothingness on the one hand and nihility on the other, and, moreover, which could convey the dynamic of a qualitative obversion, conversion, and recovery from the reality of nihility (and the nihility of reality) to absolute nothingness. Nishitani found this basic category in "emptiness" (śūnyatā, kū), an idea that was, as he said, "demanded by the problem of nihilism." From the standpoint of thought and existence within the modern world, Nishitani developed a concrete and embodied understanding of this key term of Mahāyāna Buddhism. At the same time, Nishitani proceeded to develop a penetrating account of thought and existence within the modern world in light of this notion of emptiness. He dialectically demonstrated his philosophy of emptiness by way of carrying out an extensive dialogue and confrontation with the Western history of thought. This dialogue took into consideration nearly all the dimensions of the questions of "being and nothingness" and "life and death," including a dialogue and confrontation with Western ontology and its idea of substance, with Christian theology and its idea of a personal God, and with Western philosophy of human existence and its idea of the subject.

Although "emptiness" is a fundamental concept in the tradition of Mahāyāna Buddhism, given its unprecedented use in this modern context, Nishitani tells us that he "borrowed" it and used it "rather freely" from a "standpoint that attempts to stand at once within and outside of tradition" (NKC 10: 5; RN xlix, translation modified). Precisely for this reason, in a world that included traditions which did not know such an idea of emptiness, the term was able to take on new significance through the medium of

Nishitani's thought. When one simply hears the word "emptiness," even if one knows that its core meaning is that of Mahāyāna Buddhism's *śūnyatā,* one can freely put in play other possible connotations, such as: (1) futility, vacuity, and nihility; (2) the sky,[6] and in particular a vast blue sky. Nishitani speaks of the sky as the invisible infinite become visible, as the visible eternal, and of the open expanse (*kokū*)[7] as an image of the fundamentally invisible infinite. He suggests that "the blue sky is this open expanse as it appears in visible form to human sensibility," and that "the sight of the blue sky with the eyes of the body is directly transferred to the sight of the open expanse with the eyes of the mind/heart";[8] and finally (3) the wind, which is closely related to emptiness and the sky for Nishitani. (In 1980 he titled a collection of his essays *The Heart of the Wind* [NKC 20].) Nishitani was the first to use "emptiness" as a basic category of thought in such a way as to put all of these nuances into play, and to think through their interrelations.

The core issue is that of breaking free of nihility, and the positivity of the freedom that emerges from this break. And furthermore, the structure of the self-awareness that arises in this process is at issue. Nishitani writes: "As a valley unfathomably deep may be imagined set within an endless expanse of sky, so it is with nihility and emptiness. . . . Emptiness is an abyss for the abyss of nihility. Furthermore, the abyss of emptiness opens up more to the near side, more immediately here and now than what we call ego, or subjectivity." And yet, because it is more to the near side of us than we ourselves are, "we fail to realize that we stand more to the near side of ourselves in emptiness than we do in self-consciousness" (NKC 10: 110–11/RN 98). The question is whether, in the bottomless self-awakening that leaps into nothingness, the nihility that endlessly nihilizes our being-in-the-world is itself emptied and converted into the emptiness that lies open underfoot. The insight reached at the end of Nishitani's path of thought was that the transcendence out of the limitless nihilizing of nihility is only possible—if it is indeed possible—by way of this emptying and conversion into emptiness, in other words, by way of the realization that "nihility too resides within emptiness." The endless futility of the hollow vacuum and the bottomless brightness of the open expanse are two revolving sides of the 360-degree modulations of emptiness.

What was the "living God" for Nishida became the "dead God" for Nishitani. Both the word "God" and the word "absolute nothingness" were engulfed in a vacuum of nihility wherein they rang hollow. But what Nishitani called "emptiness" is an infinitely deep and open expanse that is able to empty and convert (or obvert) even this hollow vacuum of nihility, such that once again "God" lives and "absolute nothingness" takes on significance.

Now, what one becomes aware of in the realm of thought as the problem of nihilism is, more originally and immediately, the problem of life as such—that is to say, the problem of life and death. The idea of "overcoming nihilism by way of passing through nihilism" could be said only because it was lived. This is conveyed by the various impressions recorded by those who had the opportunity to meet Nishitani and get to know him personally.[9]

We have seen that for Nishitani "overcoming nihilism by way of passing through nihilism" was an event of nihility/emptiness. The concreteness of the affirmative aspect of the standpoint of emptiness—in the language of Mahāyāna Buddhism, this would be the "marvelous being" aspect of the key phrase "true emptiness, marvelous being"—became a central concern of Nishitani's after the 1961 publication of *What is Religion?* (*Religion and Nothingness*). A noteworthy example of this is his 1981 essay, "Emptiness and Sameness" (NKC 13: 111–60).[10]

The Modern World as a Problem

It is possible to view the basic tendency of the Western philosophies of Nietzsche, Heidegger, and deconstruction as heading "toward nothingness." By contrast, we can view the thought of Nishida and Nishitani, with the Eastern traditions in their background, as on the whole moving in a direction "from nothingness." While moving solely in the direction of "toward nothingness" may lead to a negative questioning that persists in problematizing everything, moving in the direction of "from nothingness" harbors the possibility of discovering creative responses. However, the power of these responses weakens if one moves solely in a direction "from nothingness"; one can even degenerate into a lukewarm complacency of inactivity. The reinvigoration of responses requires exposure to the severity of questioning that "toward nothingness" provokes.

In this sense, it has perhaps become possible for the directions of "toward nothingness" and "from nothingness" to converse by standing back-to-back, as it were, each contacting the other by means of the nothingness shared between them. The collision and rift between East and West has ultimately given rise to this possibility. Responding "from nothingness" was occasioned by the questioning "toward nothingness," and this questioning together with this responding can bring about a mutual enhancement of East and West. It might even be said that the vitality of this questioning and responding could give birth to new world-philosophical principles. These would be principles for a world that would include the rich content of the variety of different traditions, a world wherein each of these traditions could be revitalized. Yet this world remains but a possibility; and it may vanish without ever having become anything more than a possibility.

It must be said that the grim global reality of today is the formation of a mono-world which renders meaningless the differences between East and West, and which thus invalidates the historic undertaking of Nishida and Nishitani alike. A hypersystematization of the world is bringing with it a swift and powerful process of homogenization that is superficial and yet thoroughgoing. This in turn is engendering friction and even confrontation between ethnic groups and their cultures; the accelerating destruction of nature; human physiological irregularities and disorders as well as the deepening of internal psychological fissures; the spread of a feeling of vacuity; and an endless mad frenzy of vacuous activity. Despite efforts to bring about a world full of diversity that is yet unified by means of contact between different traditions, it does not appear that such efforts today are able to clear the way for a worldwide countercultural movement that would oppose the contemporary hypersystematization of the world and its concomitant homogenization. The uniform world system increasingly covers over a variety of areas and arenas, such that this variety itself is becoming meaningless. Just like asphalt in a metropolis, the cement of the uniform world system is gradually yet thickly covering the entire world, including so-called outer space, and the thickness of this covering corresponds to the hollowness of the vacuum that is being spread. It is as if, without regard for this historically vital moment of raising and responding to the question of nothingness, this nothingness—situated at the point of contact between the backs of questioning and responding—has itself been nihilated, and the cement of the uniform world system has been poured in to fill up this gap of nihility. And now, drowning out the voices of both questioners and responders, if not indeed clogging up their mouths and sweeping them away, this cement spreads out endlessly.

Situated between the possibilities of a mutual enhancement of East and West on the one hand and a uniform world system that is becoming a global reality on the other, what is philosophy able to do? This is the question that we who live in the world today are facing. Philosophy is almost powerless. And yet, precisely such dire straits can become an authentic opportunity for philosophy to recollect and retrieve its original radicality. For human beings, who think while living and live while thinking, the very act of living originally entailed the act of philosophizing. Philosophy ignited the quest for knowledge of life, and activated the knowledge that springs forth from life. As the classic sources tell us, philosophy is at once an elevated science of sciences and an immediate concern of the soul. Precisely in the midst of despair in the modern world, this unadulterated radical origin of philosophy as a practice of thinking while living and living while thinking can be revived. But this too is a possibility that might remain unrealized.

Nishida spoke of "digging down in between East and West." Today it is necessary to dig down beneath the bottom of the homogenized world. With a shared sense of dismay, and by means of mutual questioning, we are called upon to dig down deeper. This may be thought of as the task of the present anthology.

Translated from the Japanese by Bret W. Davis

NOTES

1. The fact that at the first annual meeting of the Society for Nishida Philosophy in 2003 there were present, alongside many Japanese philosophers specializing in European philosophy, quite a number of foreign scholars of Nishida's philosophy, provides some evidence of the state of philosophy in the world today. And perhaps we can view this as one sign of an impending new stage in the *world* history of philosophy.

2. This issue requires a thorough examination. In this regard see Ueda Shizuteru, "Mu to kū o megutte" [On nothingness and emptiness], *Nihon no tetsugaku* [Japanese philosophy] (2006) 5: 3–18.

3. Martin Heidegger, *Vorträge und Aufsätze*, 7th edition (Pfullingen: Neske, 1994), 171. Translator's note: The English passage can be found in *Poetry, Language, Thought*, trans. Alfred Hofstadter (New York: Harper & Row, 1971), 178–79, translation slightly modified.

4. Translator's note: Ueda is using Mahāyāna and specifically Zen Buddhist terminology here. In Chinese and Japanese, *saṃsāra* (the cycle of birth and death) is often referred to by a word that conjoins the characters for "birth/life" and "death." The Mahāyāna and especially Zen ideal is then expressed as that of becoming a "true person existing in the coming and going of life-and-death" (*shōjikyorai-shinjitsunintai*).

5. Translator's note: For Nietzsche's notebook writings on European nihilism, see Friedrich Nietzsche, *The Will to Power*, trans. Walter Kaufmann and R. J. Hollingdale (New York: Vintage, 1967), 7–82. Also see Shizuteru Ueda, "Das absolute Nichts im Zen, bei Eckhart und bei Nietzsche," in Ryōsuke Ohashi, ed., *Die Philosophie der Kyōto-Schule* (Munich: Alber, 1990).

6. Translator's note: In Chinese and Japanese "sky" is written with the same character as "emptiness" (Ch. *kung*; Jp. *kū*).

7. Translator's note: In Buddhism *kokū* metaphorically refers to an "empty space" that envelops all things without getting in their way.

8. Translator's note: See NKC 13: 111–12; Nishitani Keiji, "Emptiness and Sameness," in Michele Marra, *Modern Japanese Aesthetics: A Reader* (Honolulu: University of Hawai'i Press, 1999), 179–80.

9. See the leaflets inserted into Nishitani's Collected Works (NKC) and *Keisei Nishitani Keiji kaisō-hen* [Keisei Nishitani Keiji: Reminiscences] (Kyoto: Tōeisha, 1992).

10. Translator's note: For an English translation of this essay, see above note 8.

2

Dialogue and Appropriation:
The Kyoto School
as Cross-Cultural Philosophy

Bret W. Davis

This essay introduces the Kyoto School by way of reflecting on hermeneutical as well as ethical and political issues that are central to the cross-cultural philosophical endeavors of its members, especially Nishida Kitarō and Nishitani Keiji, the pivotal figures of the School's first two generations. The thematic focus will be on the tension between cultural appropriation and creative synthesis on the one hand, and dialogue and respect for irreducible cultural differences on the other.

To begin with, the question is raised of whether and to what extent the cultural appropriation found in modern Japan can be compared with that found in ancient Greece. Next, Karl Löwith's criticism of modern Japanese intellectuals for purportedly failing to "critically appropriate" Western thought, a failure he sharply contrasts with the Greco-European tradition of "making what is other one's own," is discussed. Two critical responses to Löwith are then developed: first, Löwith neglected to take account of the Kyoto School's significant attempts to navigate a passage through the pendulum swing within modern Japan between deferential Eurocentrism and reactionary Japanism. And second, from the Kyoto School can be gleaned both a critique of willful cultural appropriation and intimations of a philosophy of genuine cross-cultural dialogue, wherein cultural differences would neither be obliterated nor reified. The essay ends with some remarks on the tension between the pluralistic ideals and the political entanglements of the Kyoto School.

Cultural Appropriation: Greek and Japanese

Under political pressure and military threat but never outright colonization (and not until 1945, occupation) by Western powers, the Japanese have to a significant degree been able to modernize/Westernize on their own terms. They have selectively adopted things Western and adapted—or "translated"— them into things Japanese. Yet the Japanese today often find themselves stereotyped as imitators of the West, in whose imitations something essential is, if not tragically, at least comically "lost in translation." If we are tempted to laugh at their appropriations of things Western, we should be reminded that our pop-culture adaptations of Zen and the art of making California rolls and karate movies may appear just as strange from a Japanese perspective.

A more serious case of amnesia is found in the fact we often forget that our Western cultures themselves are hardly products of homogeneous inbreeding. Modern Western cultures are heirs not only to the ancient Greek cultural synthesis of Mediterranean, Near Eastern, and probably also South Asian cultures,[1] but also to the subsequent wedding of that synthesis with the Judeo-Christian tradition as well as with various regional indigenous European cultures—not to mention subsequent influences from African, Native and Latin American, Islamic, and Far Eastern cultures.

Indeed, all complex cultures could be thought of as multicultural in the sense that they are products of multiple cultural translations, through which new developments are always made by way of alteration and metamorphosis. To borrow an insight from Gadamer, "understanding is not merely reproductive but always a productive activity as well." And therefore "we understand in a *different* way, *if we understand at all.*"[2] Insofar as both Western and Eastern cultures developed in large part through efforts to understand and assimilate foreign cultural achievements, cultural origins are more or less always productively lost in translation.[3] Cultural purity is thus an ideological construct. Acknowledging this fact, however, need not lead to a blanket and uncritical affirmation of "hybridity."[4] There are, I think, still significant—if often fine and politically sensitive—lines to be drawn between eclectic syncretism and creative synthesis, between imitative colonialism and critical appropriation, and between missionary conversion and mutually transformative dialogue. In any case, the vitality of a culture would seem to depend not on its ability to preserve a purported purity, but rather on its ability to take in and accommodate the foreign without losing, in some sense, its own integrity and autonomy. The *manner* of cultural infusion would thus be crucial.

In this regard it is interesting, and perhaps provocative, to put the following two quotations next to one another; the first is from Nietzsche on the ancient Greeks, while the second is from Nishida Kitarō (1870–1945) on the modern Japanese.

It has been pointed out assiduously, to be sure, how much the Greeks were able to find and learn abroad in the Orient, and it is doubtless true that they picked up much there. . . . Nothing would be sillier than to claim an autochthonous development for the Greeks. On the contrary, they invariably absorbed other living cultures. The very reason they go so far is that they knew how to pick up the spear and throw it onward from the point where others had left it.[5]

[Japanese culture] is what might be called a culture without form; put [metaphorically] in terms of art, it is a musical culture. It is for this reason that up until now it has taken in various foreign cultures. If it had a firmly fixed culture, then it would have had to either make the foreign culture over into its own or be destroyed by it. But Japan has the special character of repeatedly taking in foreign cultures as they are and transforming itself. The reason for its excellence lies in the fact that Japanese culture progressively synthesizes various cultures. (NKZ 14: 416–17)

Reading these two passages together invites us to compare the cultural synthesis of ancient Greece with that of modern Japan. Both cultures deliberately open themselves to foreign influence, and yet in the process of appropriation everything entering Greece became Greek as does everything entering Japan become Japanese.

The Need for Critical Appropriation: Karl Löwith's Critique of Modern Japan

Is there any reason, then, that modern inheritors of the Greek cultural synthesis (and subsequent Western cultural syntheses) should disparage the cultural synthesis that has been taking place for the last century and a half in Japan? Some would say that there is indeed.

Karl Löwith—a student and critic of Heidegger who spent five years (1936–1941) in Japan after fleeing Nazi Germany—would strongly disagree with a comparison of the ancient Greeks and the modern Japanese, at least a comparison that puts one on par with the other. At the end of a 1941 essay on European nihilism,[6] which was translated into Japanese, Löwith wrote an "Afterword to the Japanese Reader." Writing at a time of reactionary self-assertion of Japanese culture and a "renunciation of Europe," Löwith offered his reflections as a "justification of European self-critique and a critique of Japanese self-love." He writes:

When in the latter half of the previous century Japan came into contact with us and took over our advances with admirable effort and feverish rapidity, our culture was already in decline, even though on the surface it was advancing and conquering the entire earth. But in contrast to the Russians of the nineteenth century, at that time the Japanese did not open themselves critically to us; instead they first of all took over, naively and without critique, everything in the face of which our best minds, from Baudelaire to Nietzsche, experienced dread because as Europeans they could see through themselves and Europe. Japan came to know us only after it was too late, after we ourselves lost faith in our civilization and the best we had to offer was a self-critique of which Japan took no notice.[7]

According to Löwith, because Japan never really questioned its fundamental "self-love," and was thus never really self-critical, its wholesale acceptance, and then later rejection of Western culture, also remained uncritically superficial. Mired in their unexamined self-adoration, the Japanese had purportedly failed to learn the most important lesson of Europe, namely that of self-critique. Later Löwith might have also agued that, both before and after the reactionary self-affirmation of the war years, Japanese self-love too easily turns over into self-hate, and thus imperialistic national assertion converts over into colonial subservience. In either case, what is missing is a Japanese ability to "think for themselves,"[8] to *critically* reflect on their own tradition and to *critically* appropriate the foreign. The ability for such self-criticism and critical appropriation, on the other hand, is for Löwith a key element of the Greek heritage of the West.

Before examining what Löwith understands as the Greco-European manner of "genuine appropriation" of the foreign, let us reflect further on his critique of the Japanese. Löwith could be accused of over-generalizing. Given the time period of his sojourn, one wonders whether he is passing judgment on all of post-Meiji Japan from the perspective of a certain reactionary Japanism that was most prevalent in the late 1930s and early 1940s. Certainly in the Meiji (1868–1912), Taishō (1912–1926), and Early Shōwa (1926–) periods we find a number of great Japanese intellectuals struggling mightily with the question of what to introduce from the West and how to appropriate it in relation to their own traditions. Even figures at relatively opposite ends of the spectrum, like Fukuzawa Yukichi and Kiyozawa Manshi, could hardly be simply accused of either colonial subservience or uncritical self-adoration.

Nevertheless, by way of hyperbole Löwith does manage to clearly articulate the dilemma of modern Japanese intellectuals. He writes that they "live as if on two levels [or stories, *Stockwerken*]: a lower, more fundamental one, on which they feel and think in a Japanese way; and a higher one, on which the

European sciences [*Wissenschaften*] from Plato to Heidegger are lined up."[9] In other words, Japanese intellectuals live in a "two-storey house without a ladder" mediating the two levels. Unwilling to question an attachment to their Japanese identity, they were also unable, argues Löwith, to *critically* appropriate Western thought by way of engaging it in dialogue with their own traditions.

Elaborating on Löwith's critique, we need stress that besides the schizophrenia of leaping back and forth between these "levels" or the homelessness of "falling between two stools,"[10] there were also more perilous pitfalls to be found in this two-storey dwelling of modern Japan—namely, there were those who attached themselves uncritically to one level and virulently rejected the other. This led to an intra-Japanese antagonism between opposing camps of Eurocentrism and Japanism.[11] Broadly speaking, we also find a historical (and sometimes individual) pendulum swing between these academic encampments, with a general swing West during the Meiji, Taishō, and postwar periods, and a counter-swing East, or rather to Japan, during the first two (ca. 1925–45) and partially again during the last two decades (ca. 1970–90) of the Shōwa period.[12]

One contemporary Japanese scholar reflects critically on the pitfalls of the early decades of Japan's encounter with the West as follows: What the early modern Japanese thinkers often lacked was "a reflection on the very nature of an encounter with a different tradition, a reflection on what it means to encounter an Other. Because of this lack, they found themselves caught in a squeeze between an inferiority-complex with regard to Western civilization on the one hand, and a reactionary self-love on the other. They found themselves forced into the bottle-neck of an either/or choice between the camp of Western Learning and that of Japanism."[13] How to live and think in the tension between their native traditions and those imported from the West—without falling into either of these pitfalls—remains to this day a great task for Japanese intellectuals.

Steering through a Pendulum Swing between Eurocentrism and Japanism

Yet were there not Japanese intellectuals who did more or less successfully attempt to steer a "middle way" through the pendulum swing between deferential Eurocentrism and reactionary Japanism? It is in this context that we can speak of the contributions of the Kyoto School to Japanese academia, and from there to the wider world of cross-cultural dialogue. As if in direct response to Löwith's critique, James Heisig has written that the aim of the Kyoto School philosophers was twofold: "an introduction of *Japanese* philosophy into world philosophy while at the same time using western philosophy for a second look at Japanese thought trapped in fascination with its own uniqueness."[14] In other words, the Kyoto School consistently attempted (sometimes more and sometimes less successfully) to steer a course between Japanism and Eurocentrism, and to bring both "levels," and indeed the multiple cultural "layers"[15] embedded in modern Japan, into critical and innovative dialogue with one another.

Conspicuously missing from Löwith's afterword is any mention of the Kyoto School, even though they were clearly the most important group of Japanese philosophers at the time he was writing.[16] Löwith went to Japan as a visiting professor, in order to "disseminate through writing and teaching" what he thought valuable in European philosophy and culture, and not primarily as a student of Japanese culture or even as a partner in dialogue.[17] Yet the Japanese were, for their part, willing to learn from him, and generations of Japanese thinkers have paid serious attention to his critique.[18]

In his own 1949 book on European nihilism, Nishitani Keiji wrote a concluding chapter, titled "The Meaning of Nihilism for Us," in which he acknowledges and responds to Löwith's critique. Nishitani writes:

> Löwith compares the undiscriminating nature of the Japanese with the free mastery of the ancient Greeks when they adopted neighboring cultures: they felt free among others as if they were at home, and at the same time retained their sense of self. There is no such unity of self and others in the case of Japan. Löwith says that modern Japan is itself a "living contradiction." What he says is true—but how are we then to resolve such a contradiction? (NKC 8: 179; SN 176)

Nishitani goes on to say that the answer to this question can only come by way of first clearly recognizing the cultural crisis and "spiritual void" in modern Japan: "The reason the void was generated in the spiritual foundation of the Japanese in the first place was that we rushed earnestly into Westernization and in the process forgot ourselves" (NKC 8: 181–82; SN 178). Moreover, along with Löwith (as well as Nietzsche, Heidegger, and the many other European intellectuals cited in Löwith's study), Nishitani sees the West itself as having fallen into a crisis of nihilism. According to Nishitani, for the Japanese there are two lessons—and two tasks—to be learned from European nihilism:

> [It] teaches us, first, to recognize clearly the crisis that stands in the way of Western civilization—and therefore in the way of our Westernization—and to take the analysis of the crisis by "the best minds in Europe," and their efforts to overcome the modern period, and make them our own concern. This may entail pursuing the present course of Westernization to term. Secondly, European nihilism teach-

es us to return to our forgotten selves and to reflect on the tradition of oriental culture. (NKC 8: 183; SN 179)

While his *Nihilism* book undertook the first task, that of understanding and appropriating European efforts to overcome nihilism, most of Nishitani's subsequent thought—namely his philosophizing on and from "the standpoint of Zen"—took up the second task of reappropriating an Asian tradition.

Nishitani is careful to distinguish his project from that of Japan's Romantic School[19] and other reactionary thinkers who sought to reject the infusion of Western culture and return to a purportedly pure culture of premodern Japan. Nishitani writes:

> There is no turning back to the way things were. What is past is dead and gone, only to be repudiated or subject to radical critique. The tradition must be rediscovered from the ultimate point where it is grasped in advance as "the end" (or *eschaton*) of our Westernization and of Western civilization itself. Our tradition must be appropriated from the direction in which we are heading, as a new possibility. (NKC 8: 183; SN 179)

Nishitani was thus self-consciously undertaking a dual task: that of critically and creatively appropriating Western thought and culture while at the same time critically and creatively reappropriating Asian and Japanese traditions. Ultimately, moreover, his aim was not just to foster an autonomous yet international Japanese culture, but to make a Japanese contribution to thinking through the increasingly global problem of nihilism.

The problem of "nihilism" per se was a central theme of Nishitani's thought in particular,[20] a topic with which other Kyoto School thinkers, such as Nishida, were less directly engaged. However, the dual endeavor of critically and creatively appropriating Western culture and philosophy while also critically and creatively reappropriating Asian thought, was shared by all members of the Kyoto School, as well as by a number of important thinkers closely related to them.[21] The philosophers associated with the Kyoto School were not only keenly aware of the issues pointed out in Löwith's critique; they had in fact set out to address them long before Löwith arrived in Japan to teach them the ways of Western appropriation.

Questioning Willful Appropriation: A Counter-Critique of Löwith, Hegel, and the Greeks

But it is not enough to merely point out how the Kyoto School managed to learn from or even preempt Löwith's lessons on critical cultural appropriation.

For even if they could—*should* the Japanese simply imitate the Greeks? *Should* the Japanese simply appropriate Western manners of appropriation? Löwith holds up the Greeks as a paradigm of authentic cross-cultural encounter. But is there not often something rather *willful* and, to put it bluntly, self-centered about Greco-European cultural appropriation?

In his 1949 text, "The Meaning of Nihilism for Us," Nishitani follows Nietzsche in calling for a recovery of what he calls a "primordial will" to forge a path into the future by way of critically retrieving what is noble in the culture and philosophy of one's ancestors. However, while the theme of "looking back in order to look ahead" remains a constant, a radical critique of the notion of "will" becomes a central theme in Nishitani's thought by the 1961 appearance of his magnum opus, *What is Religion?* (translated as *Religion and Nothingness*).[22]

There Nishitani claims that all "standpoints of will" are in the end bound to one type or another of "self-centeredness," be it that of an individual or collective egoism, or that of an ethnocentrism that is backed up by the will of a personal god (NKC 10: 222–23; RN 202–203). What he calls the field of *śūnyatā* (emptiness) is reachable only by means of "an absolute negativity toward 'the will' that underlies every type of self-centeredness." The Buddhist standpoint of non-ego (*muga,* on the field of *śūnyatā,* he writes, "implies an orientation directly opposite to that of will" (NKC 10: 276; RN 251; translation modified). And it is only from a standpoint of non-willing that a genuine "responsibility to every neighbor and every other"—which entails a non-dual (that is, "not one and not two") relation which neither alienates nor incorporates the other—becomes possible (NKC 10: 281; RN 255).

The non-willing and non-dualistic standpoint of *śūnyatā* is ultimately realized by way of an intuitive wisdom (*prajñā*) that transcends the limits of subjective reason; and the holistic practice of self-emptying that leads to this wisdom is something Nishitani thinks the West can learn from the East.[23] On the other hand, however, a dialogical suspension of egoistic will in submission to reason is something that he thinks the East can learn from the West. Commenting favorably on the legacy of Platonic dialogue, Nishitani writes: "Dialogue begins . . . from a letting go of the ego and a submission to reasonableness." Moreover, the philosophical spirit introduced by Plato's dialogues is said to be that of "inquiry aimed at the gradual discovery of something new, something not yet known to the participants" (NKC 9: 56; NK 43).[24] Dialogue involves, therefore, a suspension of egoistic will that opens one up to what one can learn from, and together with, one's interlocutor, as opposed to a willful appropriation of the other in a battle for the preservation and expansion of the domain of one's own ego. In his multifaceted critique of the will itself, we see how Nishitani brings both Eastern and Western sources into fruitful dialogue.

Nishida—for whom philosophical inquiry involved not just intellectual self-reflection but also an *askēsis* of self-negation[25]—characterized Japanese culture not only as "musical" (that is, affective, harmonious, and fluid), but also as harboring an ego-negating spirit of "going to the truth of things" by "bowing one's head before the truth." Only by "emptying oneself" can one "see things by becoming them," and this practice of self-emptying is said to be both the wellspring of artistic creativity and the Japanese correlate to, and thus point of reception for, the discipline of Western science and rational inquiry (NKZ 12: 343–46). Nishida thus sought to reappropriate sources in the Japanese tradition that would open it up to mutually enhancing dialogue, and not antagonistic competition, with the West.

Not only was Nishida critical of Western imperialism and exploitation, but he was also strongly opposed to Japan-centric ideologues who wanted to either reject Western culture altogether or more often—as expressed in the popular slogan *wakon-yōsai* (Japanese spirit, Western technique)—reduce its role to that of a technical handmaid to an uncritically reified sense of Japanese spirit. According to Nishida, Japan should neither retreat from the world into its own isolated cultural shell, nor should its goal be to unilaterally appropriate or "digest" (*shōka*, literally "erase and transform") Western culture by incorporating it into a purportedly unchanging culture or spirit of it own (NKZ 14: 399–400). For Nishida, tradition is not a static heritage, but rather a dynamic process wherein "the new is guided by the old and, at the same time, the new changes the old" (NKZ 14: 384).[26] Moreover, what was most valuable in the life of Japanese tradition was a spirit of self-emptying opening to others and to truth, not an attachment to one's own cultural artifacts and dogma or a will to appropriate the foreign and make it conform to one's designs. Rather than conservative retreat from or willful appropriation of other cultures, Japan should genuinely open itself to dialogue with them, in order to both learn and contribute. Only in this way could the world become truly worldly, in the sense that cultures would, in dialogue, be free to creatively transform themselves while maintaining their fluid integrity as living traditions (NKZ 14: 402).[27]

According to Nishitani, such cross-cultural dialogue would be made possible only by way of what he calls "a shift from today's 'egoistic' way of being a nation to a 'non-egoistic' way of being a nation" (NKC 4: 69).[28] For Nishida, too, an internal principle of self-negation is a condition for becoming open to other cultures and thus a participant in world history (NKZ 8: 45). Rolf Elberfeld has well articulated this important aspect of Nishida's thought when he writes: "If a particular historical world possesses no self-negation, then the will arises in it to become the entire world and it attempts to wipe out all other worlds." According to Nishida, insofar as a culture is open to dialogue with other cultures, "then it possesses in itself [a principle of] self-negation, which means that it does not understand itself as the one and only comprehensive world." Only by way of such self-negation is such a culture "free from itself in its intercourse with other worlds and cultures that are foreign to it."[29]

In light of this critique of willful cultural appropriation that we have gleaned from the Kyoto School, let us return to critically examine Löwith's account of the "genuine appropriation" (*echte Aneignung*) he finds in the West, and in the West alone. Löwith writes:

> The appropriation of something other and foreign would presuppose that one can *alienate* or distance oneself from oneself, and that one then, on the basis of the distance one has acquired from oneself, makes what is other one's own as something foreign. . . . In this way, the Greeks took a world whose roots were foreign and made it into their home. "Of course they received the substantial beginnings of their religion, education, and social cohesion more or less from Asia, Syria, and Egypt; but they wiped out, transformed, processed, and changed what was foreign in this origin; they made something different out of it, to such an extent that what they, like us, value, acknowledge, and love in it is precisely what is essentially their own."[30]

Self-alienation—a partial analogue to the Kyoto School's self-emptying or ego-negation—plays the role here of a means to the end of self-enhancing appropriation of what is foreign. If there is an unmistakably Hegelian ring to Löwith's account of cultural appropriation, this is no accident; indeed the second half of the above passage is quoted from Hegel, and is followed by Löwith's statement: "This means that [the Greeks] were, in the Hegelian sense, with themselves [*bei sich*] or free in the other." The Japanese, by way of contrast, are said to "not have any impulse to transform what is foreign into something of their own. They do not come from others back to themselves; they are not free, or—to put it as Hegel does—they are not with themselves in being-other."[31]

For Löwith, as for Nishida, a "failure to critique oneself rests on the inability to see oneself as another and to go out of oneself."[32] Yet whereas Nishida had emphasized self-negation and becoming "free from oneself" as an opening to dialogue with others and to the indigestible alterity of the other in the depths of the non-substantial self, for Hegel and Löwith such "self-alienation" is ultimately a step on the way to "transforming the foreign into something of one's own" so that one can come back to an expanded "freedom for oneself."

Undoubtedly there is much to learn from Löwith and Hegel with regard to self-enhancing cultural appropriation. However, it is highly questionable that we should turn to Hegel—in many ways the philosophical godfather of Eurocentrism—in order to learn how to enter into a genuine *dialogue* with other cultures. According to Hegel, "world history," as the historical process of Spirit's self-othering and self-recollecting, "goes from East to West; for as Europe is the absolute end of world-history, Asia is its beginning."[33] Since the Greeks had purportedly already "internalized" (*er-innert*) all that was of value in Eastern culture and "Oriental wisdom," these are now only a memory (*Er-innerung*) for the West; and thus for Hegel there could be no reason to return to engage in a *dialogue* with the East.

In a number of ways Hegel is here taking up and radicalizing the ancient Greek stance toward foreign cultures.[34] The ancient Greeks tended to see their appropriations as improvements on the originals, and it is perhaps for this reason that they rarely cite their Near Eastern and Indian sources. Although the ancient Greeks are generally considered the origin of Western culture, they did not in fact simply pride themselves on originality. Wilhelm Halbass writes: "It is precisely the openness for the possibility of alien sources, the readiness to learn and the awareness of such readiness which sustains the Greek claim of being different from the Orient."[35] There is a profound ambiguity here. On the one hand, the Greeks demonstrated a marked openness, or at least an inquisitiveness toward the foreign; on the other hand, they were motivated by a drive to appropriate the foreign, stripping it of its alterity and transforming its achievements into something of their own. And precisely this ability and will to appropriate the foreign is taken by the Greeks to be an essential trait that distinguishes them from the Orient.

This conceit of a supposedly unique ability to take an interest in and comprehend other cultures is clearly echoed two millennia later in Hegel's presumption that "Asian thought is comprehensible and interpretable within European thought, but not vice versa."[36] Hegel epitomizes the Western spirit of conquest and comprehension of alterity; and his grand narrative of the self-alienation and self-recovery of Spirit provides a most cunning justification for a Eurocentric teleological account of world history. Yet, as Gadamer recognizes, "Hegel's dialectic is a monologue."[37] It is not a cross-cultural dialogue that is genuinely open to the alterity of other traditions, an alterity which exceeds the Western philosopher's powers of self-recollection.

"The step from Hegel to Nishida [and the Kyoto School] is the step from a single 'world history' which derives from a principle of uniformity, to a history of 'worldly worlds' which is in itself structured polycentrically."[38] It is a step from a Eurocentric monologue to a pluralistic *polylogue,* where each participant not only alienates itself from its self-attachment so as to better receive the gifts of others, but also empties itself of its imperialistic drive in order to let others be, not just elsewhere, but also in the very heart of the interrelational self (NKZ 6: 381).[39]

PLURALISTIC DREAMS AND POLITICAL NIGHTMARES

As Edward Said has demonstrated, a monological Orientalism has characterized much of what modern Western intellectuals have had to say about the East.[40] Moreover, a teleological Eurocentrism pervades not only much of modern Western philosophy, but also more overtly political theories of "development" and "sociocultural evolution."[41] Such theories often tend to shift the geographical center from Europe to the United States, today's juggernaut of globalization. Francis Fukuyama even provides us with a grand-narrative legitimization of teleological Ameri-centrism.[42] He argues that all societies, even those who are dragging their feet or violently resisting, are destined to progress along the "caravan trail" toward us (i.e., the U.S.). The United States is thought to be the beacon of liberal democracy and free-market capitalism, the ultimate political and economic form of a nation in which all individuals are free at last to compete against one another for fame and fortune, instead of fighting over ideas. Indeed Fukuyama sees the last bulwark against the nihilism of what Nietzsche calls the "last man," in the *thumos* (ambition) of capitalistic competition. This is because, in the globalized American world-culture that Fukuyama envisions as his teleological "end of history," there are no more grand ideological battles to fight. On the other hand, Samuel Huntington has (in)famously argued that the global ideological wars are just getting started, and will usher in an inevitable life-or-death struggle between eight or nine fundamentally incompatible civilizations.[43] Must we acquiesce to either global Americanization or a clash of civilizations?

The Kyoto School attempted to develop an alternative global vision. Its members were among the first non-Western philosophers to thoroughly criticize the trend toward Euro/Ameri-centric cultural homogenization, and to do so without calling for a regressive parochialism and without resigning us to a clash of cultures.

Nishida both affirmed the synthetic character of cultures, Japan in particular,[44] and argued that this need not and should not imply an annihilation of cultural integrity and cultural differences. In a true "worldly world" or "world of worlds" (*sekai-teki sekai*),[45] each culture would be allowed to open itself up to other cultures *in its own way*. Nishida denies that the individuality of the world's cultures should (or even could) be reduced to a global oneness: "The loss of specificity entails the disappearance of culture itself. . . . A true world culture will be formed [only] by various cultures which, while maintaining their own respective standpoints, develop themselves through the mediation of the world" (NKZ 7: 452–53). A culture would develop, not dissipate itself, by opening up to dialogical engagement with others. In this way Nishida attempts to resolve the tension between maintaining a fluid sense of cultural identity and bringing about a cooperative exchange between cultures.

It needs to be pointed out that Nishida did not always think of cultural interaction in terms of peaceful harmony (Jp. *wa*); he accepts that it also entails mutual strife and struggle (Gr. *polemos*).[46] In places, Nishida speaks of the worldly world of "contradictory identity" not only in terms of "mutual supplementation" (NKZ 12: 392), but also in terms of a "mutual struggle" (see NKZ 8: 529; 12: 334).[47] Nishida accepts that historical ages have in the past always been established by a nation taking charge and unifying a world, and that the global world as a whole was first unified by Western imperialism. And yet, he goes on to write, we stand on the brink of a radically new world-historical era in which we must go beyond the simple paradigm of mutual competition between "nations in opposition." Above all, Nishida repeatedly emphasizes, "the imperialistic idea that puts one ethnic nation in the center surely belongs to the past." The new global paradigm must be pluralistic rather than imperialistic, and this implies moving beyond competitive antagonism to mutually transforming dialogue, to the collaborative construction of a "world of worlds," a unity-in-diversity to which each nation contributes on the basis of its own world-historical perspective (NKZ 10: 256, 337).

Hence, when Nishida claims that Japan has a special ability to assimilate foreign cultures, this does not mean that it fails to achieve or loses its own identity in the process. And it *should* also not mean that *only* Japan is capably of a synthesis of the world's cultures. If this were his assertion, then he would be subject to the criticism that "Nishida attacked . . . Eurocentrism by promoting an equivalent Japanism."[48] It is true that Nishida, along with the rest of the Kyoto School, did think that Japan was in a special position to help usher in a new age of both post-isolationism and post-imperialism. They thought that, precisely because of Japan's ability to assimilate the strengths of others cultures—and in particular to modernize/Westernize—without abandoning its own tradition, it could lead other Asian nations in a resistance to Western imperialism and to the establishment of a "Greater East Asian Co-Prosperity Sphere" (*daitōa kyōeiken*).

Unfortunately, the reality of Japan's political construction of the so-called Co-Prosperity Sphere had little to do with the ideality of the Kyoto School's visions, which were themselves not unproblematic. Whether, to what extent, and in what manner Nishida and the other Kyoto School philosophers did end up supporting and promoting Japan's disastrous imperialistic revolt against Western imperialism are questions that have fueled a controversy that has surrounded the Kyoto School for several generations. While clearly their political thought must be read critically, it is also clear by now that the Kyoto School can hardly be accused of simply proffering an ideological justification for Japanese militaristic imperialism.[49] Their political engagements are more aptly described in terms of what Ōhashi calls "oppositional cooperation" (*hantaisei-teki kyōryoku*).[50] In other words, they attempted to reform Japanese political thought from within by redefining its terms and introducing a rational and "world-historical" standpoint to what was quickly degenerating into an irrational Japan-centric fever.

It is beyond the scope of this essay to delve into this controversy. There has been a lot of work done, and there remains much still to be done on the political entanglements of the Kyoto School during the Pacific War.[51] In any case, here I have attempted to take up the Kyoto School philosophers at their cross-cultural best, rather than to try to catch them at their political worst. I hope at least to have shown that they offer us an invaluable set of dialogue partners in the *de facto* post-isolationist and *de jure* post-imperialist meeting of Eastern and Western cultures.

Nishida and the other members of the Kyoto School were "philosophers *of* interculturality" in both senses of the genitive in this phrase: They thought *from out of* their experience of the meeting of Eastern and Western cultures in modern Japan; and they thought *about* what a cross-cultural encounter does and should entail.[52] What I have suggested that we can glean from their experience and thought is this: Cross-cultural encounter should be motivated not only by a will to self-enhancing appropriation of the foreign, and not ultimately by a teleological drive toward synthetic (monological) unity, but rather first and foremost by a non-willful openness to dialogue without end.

NOTES

1. On the cultural and philosophical interactions between ancient Greece, Persia, Egypt, and India, see Thomas McEvilley, *The Shape of Ancient Thought: Comparative Studies in Greek and Indian Philosophies* (New York: Allworth Press, 2002).

2. Hans-Georg Gadamer, *Truth and Method,* 2nd rev. edition, trans. Joel Weinsheimer and Donald Marshall (New York: Crossroad Publishing, 1989), 297. Gadamer, however, restricts his philosophical hermeneutics to the Western tradition. For a critique of Gadamer in this regard, see my "Taiho to kaikō: Seiyōtetsugaku kara shisakuteki-taiwa e" [Step back and encounter: from Western philosophy toward a dialogue of thought], *Nihontetsugakushi kenkyū* [Studies in Japanese philosophy] 1 (2003): 36–66.

3. On the insurmountable limits and productive possibilities of translation between linguistic and cultural "frameworks," see Fujita Masakatsu, "Ibunkakan no taiwa (honyaku) no kanōsei o megutte" [On the possibility of dialogue (translation) between different cultures], in Fujita Masakatsu and Bret Davis, eds., *Sekai no naka no Nihon no tetsugaku* [Japanese philosophy in the world] (Kyoto: Shōwadō, 2005). Ōhashi Ryōsuke interprets "Japanese modernity" as a "trans-lation" (Gn. *Über-setzung*) of European modernity, wherein the "Buddhist and Shinto mindset that underlies Japanese culture provides the peculiarly malleable basis on which the foreign European world and its products, science and technology, were taken over, cultivated and modified" (*Japan im interkulturellen Dialog* [Munich: Iudicium, 1999], 129, 201; my translation). Rolf Elberfeld writes that Nishida "finds . . . a new and different beginning in philosophy by means of the '*trans*-lation' of Western philosophy into the Japanese cultural world" (*Kitarō Nishida (1870–1945): Moderne japanische Philosophie und die Frage nach der Interkulturalität* [Amsterdam: Rodopi, 1999], 53; my translation). Also see in this regard John Maraldo, "Tradition, Textuality, and the Trans-lation of Philosophy: The Case of Japan," in Charles Wei-hsun Fu and Steven Heine, eds., *Japan in Traditional and Postmodern Perspectives* (Albany: State University of New York Press, 1995).

4. On the debated use of this term in postcolonial theory, see Ania Loomba, *Colonialism/Postcolonialism* (London and New York: Routledge, 1998), 173–83.

5. Friedrich Nietzsche, *Philosophy in the Tragic Age of the Greeks,* trans. Marianne Cowan (Washington, D.C.: Regnery, 1962), 29–30.

6. Karl Löwith, "Der europäische Nihilismus," in Karl Löwith, *Sämtliche Schriften* (Stuttgart: J. B. Metzler, 1983–1986), 2: 532–40; an English translation is available in Karl Löwith, *Martin Heidegger and European Nihilism,* ed. Richard Wolin, trans. Gary Steiner (New York: Columbia University Press, 1995), 228–34. Incidentally, the Japanese translation of Löwith's text, *Yōroppa no nihirizumu* (Tokyo: Chikuma Shobō), appeared in 1948, but the original German was not published until its inclusion in volume 2 of Löwith's *Sämtliche Schriften.*

7. Löwith, *Sämtliche Schriften,* 2: 533–34; *Martin Heidegger and European Nihilism,* 229.

8. See Fujita Masakatsu, "'Kindai no chōkoku' o megutte" [On the idea of "overcoming modernity"], in *Nihonjin no jikoninshiki* [The self-perception of the Japanese], ed. Aoki Mamoru et al. (Tokyo: Iwanami, 1999), 32–33.

9. Löwith, *Sämtliche Schriften*, 2: 537; *Martin Heidegger and European Nihilism*, 232. Elsewhere Löwith further develops his critique of "modern Japan," which he says is "a contradiction in terms, which, however, exists"; see *Sämtliche Schriften*, 2: 543–47, 556–59, 588ff. He contrasts the superficiality of modern Japan's assimilation of Western culture with ancient Japan's assimilation of Chinese culture: "The Chinese culture is indeed integrated, the Western civilization is only adjusted and adopted" (ibid., 545; see also 557, 593).

10. See Löwith, *Sämtliche Schriften*, 2: 547, 558.

11. In his sweeping polemic against *nihonjinron* (theories of Japanese uniqueness), *The Myth of Japanese Uniqueness* (New York: St. Martin's Press, 1986), Peter Dale misleadingly lumps Nishida and other thinkers related to the Kyoto School together with a range of reactionary Japanists. Bernard Faure, while warning against falling into "sociopolitical reductionism," and while expressly not attempting to address "the strengths of the philosophical ideas" of Nishida and the Kyoto School, nevertheless characterizes the effects of the Kyoto School as "reverse Orientalism" ("The Kyoto School and Reverse Orientalism," in *Japan in Traditional and Postmodern Perspectives*). During the war, however, the "world-historical philosophy" of the Kyoto School was censured by the ideologues of "Imperial Way Philosophy" for being too worldly and failing to be Japancentric (see Ōhashi Ryōsuke, *Kyōtogakuha to Nihon-kaigun* [The Kyoto School and the Japanese navy] [Kyoto: PHP Shinsho, 2001], 71–72). John Maraldo reviews the debate regarding the Kyoto School's relation to Japanism, and insightfully concludes that the apparent standoff between nationalism and internationalism may be a false one, as we "come to recognize world philosophers as people who speak to others out of a particular tradition, rather than those who would pretend a view from nowhere" ("Ōbei no shiten kara mita Kyoto-gakuha no yurai to yukue" [The whence and whither of the Kyoto School from a Western perspective], in *Sekai no naka no Nihon no tetsugaku,* 51).

12. Cf. Dale, *The Myth of Japanese Uniqueness,* 213.

13. Kioka Nobuo, "Kaikō no ronri: Kuki Shūzō" [The logic of encounter: Kuki Shūzō], in Tsunetoshi Sōzaburō, ed., *Nihon no tetsugaku o manabu hito no tame ni* [For those studying Japanese philosophy] (Kyoto: Sekaishisōsha, 1998), 142.

14. James W. Heisig, *Philosophers of Nothingness: An Essay on the Kyoto School* (Honolulu: University of Hawai'i Press, 2001), 270.

15. Watsuji characterizes Japanese culture in terms of layers (*jūsō*) (see Watsuji Tetsurō, *Shinpen Nihonseishinshi kenkyū* [New edition of studies in the spiritual history of Japan], ed. Fujita Masakatsu [Kyoto: Tōeisha, 2002], 239–46). According to Watsuji, it is precisely the contemporaneous coexistence of such cultural layers, rather than the exclusive replacement of one with the other, that characterizes Japanese culture.

16. In a later text from 1943, Löwith does refer to Nishida as the sole original thinker in Japan, "who is comparable to any of the living philosophers of the West in depth of thought and subtlety." "But even this man's work," he goes on to say, "is no more than an adaptation of Western methodology, the use of it for a logical clarification of the fundamental Japanese intuitions about the world" (*Sämtliche Schriften*, 2: 560). In 1960, after having apparently read a few more German translations, Löwith acknowledges that "Nishida is one of the few Japanese philosophers who, thanks to

their education in Zen Buddhism, have their own productive viewpoint on European thinking, and do not only reproduce it in a disengaged manner" (ibid., 582).

17. Löwith, *Martin Heidegger and European Nihilism*, 234. However, Löwith did come to think that "some years in the Far East are almost indispensable for a critical, i.e., discriminating understanding of ourselves" (*Sämtliche Schriften*, 2: 541), and he apparently did at times appropriate Japanese culture, Zen in particular, into his thought (see the editor's introduction to *Martin Heidegger and European Nihilism*, 3). Moreover, upon emigrating to America from Japan, he wrote in English two critical reflections on Japanese culture, "Japan's Westernization and Moral Foundation" (1942–1943) and the revealingly titled "The Japanese Mind: A Picture of the Mentality that We Must Understand if We are to Conquer" (1943). Years later, Löwith also published a comparative essay, "Bemerkungen zum Unterschied von Orient und Okzident" [Remarks on the difference between Orient and Occident] (1960). In addition to the "Afterword to the Japanese Reader" in his book on European nihilism, my references to the second volume of Löwith's *Sämtliche Schriften* have been to these three essays.

18. For two noteworthy, more recent responses to Löwith's critique, see Ōhashi, *Nihon-tekina mono, Yōroppa-tekina mono* [Things Japanese and things European], 152ff.; and Ōkōchi Ryōgi, *Ibunka rikai no genten* [Principles of understanding foreign cultures] (Kyoto: Hōzōkan, 1995), 20ff.

19. In this regard see Nishitani's debate with Kobayashi Hideo, who argued for a rejection of modernity and a return to the premodern Japanese classics. See Kawakami Tetsutarō, Takeuchi Yoshimi et al., *Kindai no chōkoku* [The overcoming of modernity] (Sendai: Fuzanbō, 1979), 217ff.

20. See Bret W. Davis, "The Step Back Through Nihilism: The Radical Orientation of Nishitani Keiji's Philosophy of Zen," *Synthesis Philosophica* 37 (2004): 139–59.

21. See, for example, Kuki Shūzō's remarks in "Bergson in Japan," in Stephen Light, *Shūzō Kuki and Jean-Paul Sartre: Influence and Counter-Influence in the Early History of Existential Phenomenology* (Carbondale: Southern Illinois University Press, 1987), 74.

22. It is perhaps partly under the influence of the later Heidegger's turn to a radical critique of the will (see my *Heidegger and the Will* [Evanston, Ill.: Northwestern University Press, 2007]), but more directly on the basis of a Buddhist critique of egoistic craving, that Nishitani comes to see the concept of will as inherently problematic. See my essay in the present volume, "Nishitani after Nietzsche: From the Death of God to the Great Death of the Will."

23. For Nishitani's attempt to move through and beyond (Hegel's) reason to a Zen Buddhist standpoint of *prajñā*, see his "Hanya to risei" [*Prajñā* and Reason], in NKC 13.

24. I would argue, however, that this mutual openness to learning something new ("not yet known") is only half the legacy of Platonic dialogue. The other half is rooted in the doctrine of anamnesis and in Socratic irony, where the dialogical encounter is only an occasion for self-recollection and pedagogy. On this issue, see my "Taiho to kaikō."

25. See Bret W. Davis, "Provocative Ambivalences in Japanese Philosophy of Religion: With a Focus on Nishida and Zen," in James W. Heisig, ed., *Japanese Philosophy Abroad* (Nagoya: Nanzan Institute for Religion and Culture, 2004), 262ff.

26. On Nishida's conception of tradition, see Agustin Jacinto-Zavala, "Tradition and the Problem of Knowledge in Nishida Philosophy," *Dokyo International Review* 14 (2001): 91–118.

27. Elsewhere Nishida suggests that Asia's potential contribution to the world was to "shed new light on Western culture," and to add Eastern culture to the great Western meeting of Greek and Jewish cultures (NKZ 14: 407; and 12: 159–60). For a good account of these and other themes in Nishida's theory of culture, see Fujita Masakatsu, "Nihon-bunka, tōyō-bunka, sekai-bunka: Nishida Kitarō no Nihon-bunka-ron" [Japanese culture, Asian culture, world culture: Nishida Kitarō's theory of culture], in Fujita Masakatsu et al., eds., *Higashiajia to tetsugaku* [East Asia and philosophy] (Kyoto: Nakanishiya Press, 2003).

28. It is this ideal of a "nation of non-ego" that Nishitani points back to in 1946 as his attempt to resist and change from within Japan's wartime politics (NKC 4: 381).

29. Elberfeld, *Kitarō Nishida,* 209, 215.

30. Löwith, *Sämtliche Schriften,* 2: 536; *Martin Heidegger and European Nihilism,* 231. The second half of Löwith's text is quoted from Hegel's *Vorlesungen über die Geschichte der Philosophie I, Suhrkamp Theorie Werkausgabe* (Frankfurt: Suhrkamp, 1982), 18: 174, and we are also referred to ibid., 12: 237. The first part of this passage also contains a reference to ibid., 4: 320ff.

31. Löwith, *Sämtliche Schriften,* 2: 537; *Martin Heidegger and European Nihilism,* 232.

32. Löwith, *Sämtliche Schriften,* 2: 572.

33. G. W. F. Hegel, *Vorlesungen über die Philosophie der Geschichte, Werke 12* (Frankfurt: Suhrkamp, 1970), 134. Ōhashi Ryōsuke writes that Hegel did not foresee that the winds of imperialism would turn the tide of world history back to the East; and, more importantly, that this would not ultimately be a matter of the triumphant spread of the Western completion of history, but rather that it would become clear that the European world has a qualitatively different "outside" and can thus no longer be considered to be the entire world; *Uchi naru ikoku, soto naru Nihon* [The foreign inside and Japan outside] (Kyoto: Jinbunshoin, 1999), 160–61.

34. As Löwith writes elsewhere, according to Hegel's world history, it is first with the Greeks (as opposed to the Orient, where the world-spirit has not yet become self-consciously liberated) that "we feel at home immediately, because we are upon the ground of spirit, which independently *claims for itself everything alien*" (Karl Löwith, *From Hegel to Nietzsche,* trans. David E. Green [New York: Columbia University Press, 1964], 33; my emphasis).

35. Wilhelm Halbfass, *India and Europe: An Essay in Understanding* (Albany: State University of New York Press, 1988), 5–6.

36. Ibid., 96.

37. Gadamer, *Truth and Method,* 369.

38. Elberfeld, *Kitarō Nishida,* 213.

39. See note 27, above.

40. Edward Said, *Orientalism* (New York: Vintage, 1978). While Said focuses his critique on Western literature, a similar critique could be made against philosophers; although here the silence of indifference tends to be more deafening than the blasts of distortion. However, it is also necessary to supplement Said's critique of Orientalism by pointing out that since the Enlightenment a number of Western thinkers have self-critically affirmed Asian philosophies, or at least used them as a "corrective mirror" through which to engage in criticism of the West (see J. J. Clarke, *Oriental Enlightenment: The Encounter Between Asian and Western Thought* [New York: Routledge, 1997]).

41. For critical responses to such theories, see Fred Dallmayr, *Beyond Orientalism: Essays on Cross-Cultural Encounter* (Albany: State University of New York Press, 1996), chap. 7; and *Alternative Visions* (Lanham, Md.: Rowman & Littlefield, 1998), chaps. 9–10.

42. Francis Fukuyama, *The End of History and the Last Man* (New York: The Free Press, 1992).

43. Samuel Huntington, *The Clash of Civilizations and the Remaking of World Order* (New York: Simon & Schuster, 1996).

44. See, however, John C. Maraldo, "The Problem of World Culture: Towards an Appropriation of Nishida's Philosophy of Culture," *The Eastern Buddhist* 28, no. 2 (1995): 183–97. Maraldo argues that "Nishida took for granted that a single people formed the ethnic basis of a nation state and he foresaw *a multicultural world* of different ethnic nations. He did not [however] recognize or foresee multi-ethnic or *multicultural nations*" (194). Moreover, Maraldo writes, it is not just modern nations such as the United States that are multicultural, for even Japan's purported homogeneity is in fact an ideological construct laid over "long centuries of absorption and suppression of minority ethnic groups" (193). Yet this important criticism could be understood as an "immanent critique" which turns Nishida's insights back on his own blind spots.

45. On this notion, and for a more extensive critical treatment of the issues raised in this section, see Bret W. Davis, "Toward a World of Worlds: Nishida, the Kyoto School, and the Place of Cross-Cultural Dialogue," in James W. Heisig, ed., *Frontiers of Japanese Philosophy* (Nagoya: Nanzan Institute for Religion and Culture, 2006).

46. See Nishida's affirmative references to Heraclitus's saying that "*polemos* is the father of all things" in NKZ 8: 508, 516.

47. Also see Elberfeld, *Kitarō Nishida,* 223–27.

48. Maraldo, "The Problem of World Culture," 192.

49. See the often criticized characterization (or polemical caricature) of the Kyoto School in Tetsuo Najita and H. D. Harootunian, "Japan's Revolt against the West," in Bob Tadashi Wakabayashi, ed., *Modern Japanese Thought* (Cambridge: Cambridge University Press, 1998), 238–39.

50. Ōhashi, *Kyōtogakuha to Nihon-kaigun,* 20ff.

51. For an overview of this issue, see section 4 of my article on the "The Kyoto School" in the online *Stanford Encyclopedia of Philosophy.* For two excellent collections on this topic, see James W. Heisig and John C. Maraldo, eds., *Rude Awakenings: Zen, The Kyoto School, and the Question of Nationalism* (Honolulu: University of Hawai'i Press, 1994), and Chris Goto-Jones, ed., *Re-politicising the Kyoto School as Philosophy* (London: Routledge, 2007). Also see my "Toward a World of Worlds," and chapters 4, 13, and 14 in the present volume.

52. See Elberfeld, *Kitarō Nishida,* 61.

3

Tanabe Hajime's Logic of Species and the Philosophy of Nishida Kitarō: A Critical Dialogue within the Kyoto School

SUGIMOTO KŌICHI

As is well known, Nishida Kitarō and Tanabe Hajime are two of the most prominent philosophers in modern Japan. Tanabe, who succeeded Nishida as head of the Department of Philosophy at Kyoto Imperial University, began his philosophical career under the influence of Nishida. Gradually, however, he became aware of a gap between Nishida's philosophy and his own thought, and finally he dared to publish an article that, although titled "Looking Up to Professor Nishida's Teaching" (1930), criticized Nishida's philosophy in no uncertain terms. From that time forward, they continued a sharp exchange of opinions until Nishida's death in 1945, although in many cases they did not explicitly refer to each other's names in this exchange.

Tanabe criticized Nishida's philosophy for allegedly being based on a standpoint of religious or artistic "mystical intuition," whereas Nishida contended that Tanabe remained stuck in a standpoint of "abstract logic" or "morality" that did not grasp true reality. Because of this controversy, Nishida and Tanabe are sometimes represented as maintaining two sharply opposing philosophies. Hence many have the impression of Nishida's thought as a philosophy of religious experience based on his youthful practice of Zen Buddhism, an image which contrasts with that of Tanabe's thought as a philosophy restricted to the standpoint of logic and the relativity of the historical world.[1]

To be sure, these images embody some aspects of truth. But at the same time one should not forget that these two philosophies share many points in common. And this should not be surprising as they were formed in close relationship to each other, and emerge from a common foundation. In fact, several scholars have explored various aspects of this common foundation.[2]

In contemporary academic circles in Japan—where, generally speaking, Nishida's philosophy is more highly regarded than Tanabe's—it is often the case that scholars examine the common basis of Nishida and Tanabe in a manner that favors Nishida's philosophy. That is, scholars tend to find notions in Tanabe's philosophy that are similar to Nishida's philosophy, and then proceed to regard these notions as the common basis of both philosophies.[3] By contrast, a few inquiries have been made from the opposite direction, namely, the direction of determining the common basis of the two from the viewpoint of Tanabe.[4] This essay will take the latter approach.[5] In other words, the aim of this paper is to demonstrate that there are elements of Nishida's philosophy which correspond to the original philosophy of Tanabe, and that these elements can be regarded as another common basis for both philosophies. This demonstration will illuminate significant aspects of Nishida's philosophy that have not received enough attention.

For the purpose of this demonstration, the present essay shall focus especially on Tanabe's "logic of species" (*shu no ronri,* sometimes translated "logic of the specific") and Nishida's response to it. First, I will briefly describe the problems posed by Tanabe's "logic of species," based on his two articles: "The Logic of Social Existence" (1934–1935) and "The Logic of Species and the World Schema" (1935). In particular I will discuss Tanabe's implicit and explicit critique of Nishida in these articles. Second, I will consider Nishida's objections to the logic of species as articulated in his *Philosophical Essays II* (1937). And finally, I will show that, despite both Tanabe's frequent and unequivocal criticism of Nishida's philosophy and Nishida's seemingly irreconcilable objections to Tanabe's "logic of species," there in fact exists a common basis which underlies both philosophies.

Problems Posed by Tanabe's Logic of Species

THE PROBLEM OF SPECIES

One of the problems posed by Tanabe in his "logic of species" is the socio-ontological problem of "species" (*shu*). "Species" contrasts with "individual" (*ko*) and "genus" (*rui*). Expressed alternatively, "species" is "the particular" (*tokushu*) in contrast to the individual (*kobutsu*) and the universal (*fuhen*). As a practical problem of social philosophy, "species" refers to "ethnic nation" or "nation state," in contradistinction to the individual human being as well as the universal human race. In the historical context of his time, Tanabe confronted the irrational power of nations, which cannot be understood either from the standpoint of the individual human being or from the universal human race, but which nevertheless undeniably exist in actuality. With the aim of securing a rational ground for the blind power of species, one that would curb its volatile powers as much as possible, he took up the problem of species as his main philosophical theme.

Although he admits that previous philosophies did not entirely neglect the problem of species, Tanabe considered their treatment of the problem of species to be inadequate. According to Tanabe, previous philosophies have conceived of the relationship between genus, species, and individual in terms of continuity. In other words, they have conceived of the species as nothing other than the particularization of genus, and of the individual as that which is reached at the limit of this particularization. Tanabe insists that these conceptions cannot grasp the unique position of species, because in these conceptions, species is regarded as "only the middle or the mixture" (THZ 6: 54) of genus and individual, without any distinct characteristics of its own. An example of this is when the nation is conceived merely from the standpoint of the individual or from the standpoint of the universal. Nations are then either conceived with the individual as central, whereby the nation is formed by means of a "voluntary contract of individuals" (THZ 6: 54), or with humanity as central, whereby one stops at the thought that "the division of the real nation into many specific nations is no more than a negative limitation; for essentially it forms a nation of humanity as a whole" (THZ 6: 53). Here the irrationality of species, which cannot be reduced either to the individual or to the universal, is dissolved.

In opposition to these previous accounts, Tanabe stresses the unique significance of species as more than just the middle point between genus and individual. In particular, he pays attention to the role of species in "mediating" genus and individual. Tanabe's notion of "mediation," which is one of the central notions in his logic of species, is too involved a subject to be treated here in detail. Here I can only indicate the following two points: (1) Individual and species are thoroughly opposed to one another; species with its irrational power imposes controls on individual human beings, and the individual resists them and tries to negate the species. However, the individual in the real world exists only so long as it has species as its substratum, that is, as long as it is "mediated" by species. (2) If one thinks of the genus or the universal as something that underlies species and individual and embraces them completely, it is not the true universal. The true universal must be that which unifies the oppositions of species and individual without annihilating their respective specificity or individuality. Such a universal cannot be thought of as something apart from the oppositions between species and individuals.

Rather, it must be something that emerges only in accordance with such oppositions. In this sense, the genus must be "mediated" by opposing species.

From this point of view, Tanabe criticizes Nishida's philosophy. Tanabe interprets Nishida's logic of the "place of nothingness" (*mu no basho*) as follows:[6] The notion of the "place of nothingness" was originally introduced by Nishida with the intention of giving the individual a philosophical foundation. One cannot think of the individual as something in the "place of being" (*u no basho*)—that is, as something enclosed by the historical-social environment— because the true individual must be that which determines itself by itself and transcends historical-social determination, in other words, determination by the species. Therefore, one can think of the individual only by introducing the notion of the "place of nothingness" that transcends the place of being. In "arriving at the place of nothingness which returns the species as being to nothingness, that which is determined in the universal becomes the individual which is not a species" (THZ 6: 201). In this way, according to Tanabe's interpretation, Nishida's logic of the place of nothingness is none other than "the standpoint of the individual that neglects the species" (THZ 6: 202).

Based on this interpretation, Tanabe criticizes Nishida's logic of the place of nothingness. For Tanabe, who thought that the concrete individual which acts in the real world exists only as long as it is mediated by the species, an individual based on the logic of nothingness, namely, an individual apart from the determination by species, would be no more than an abstract notion of individual. In this sense, Tanabe asserts, although the logic of the place of nothingness was primarily introduced with the intent to provide a philosophical foundation for the individual, in this logic "both species as substratum and individual as subject get lost together" (THZ 6: 202). Moreover, Tanabe argues that the place of nothingness could not be the true universal, because it is assumed to be something given in an unmediated manner unrelated to species. Tanabe asserts that it is nothing but a "place that annihilates beings" (THZ 6: 204) or "the nothingness of mysticism" (THZ 6: 208). In short, the point of Tanabe's criticism of Nishida is that because Nishida unfairly slights the significance of species, his thought cannot offer a concrete theory, not only of species, but also of genus and individual.

THE PROBLEM OF MEDIATION

The range of Tanabe's logic of species is not limited to the problem of species as a problem of social philosophy. Tanabe argues that the notion of "mediation," which is the philosophical ground of the logic of species, has a wider significance that is also crucial to the method of philosophy in general. Tanabe formulates this thought as his "logic of absolute mediation" (*zettai baikai no ronri*).

Tanabe defines "absolute mediation" as follows:[7] "Absolute mediation means that the one could not be posited without the mediation of the other. . . . Absolute mediation means that any affirmation would be impossible without the mediation of negation. . . . Therefore, it rejects anything immediate" (THZ 6: 59). Tanabe criticizes the way of thinking inherent in many previous philosophies that assume some principle as something that is immediately given as the ground of the philosophical system. For example, he rejects both spiritualism and materialism; the former assumes spirit as the principle that exists by itself and from which matter is derived, and the latter, by contrast, assumes matter as its principle. Tanabe insists from the viewpoint of the logic of absolute mediation that spirit and matter depend on each other; each must be mediated by the other.

Still, it is not only to the relationship between two opposing elements that the logic of absolute mediation is applied. It is further applied to the relationship between opposing beings and what is supposed to transcend opposing beings, namely, between relative beings and the absolute. Tanabe states: "Even what is called the absolute cannot be posited in an immediate way, that is, without the mediation of the relative which negates it" (THZ 6: 59). In this way, Tanabe rejects "the One that is assumed to transcend the opposition between being and thought" and the "so-called absolute nothingness which negates being and thought from the transcendent standpoint and returns every act of positing into nothingness" (THZ 6: 173). It is clear that with the term "absolute nothingness" Tanabe is implicitly referring to Nishida's philosophy. The reason why Tanabe rejects the idea of an unmediated absolute (including "so-called absolute nothingness") is that it would entail that each event in the historical-relative world would become undifferentiated. This would be inadmissible for Tanabe, who maintains that philosophy must remain true to the differentiated world of historical reality.

The logic of absolute mediation is also applied to the relationship between "life" and "logic," which was one of the central issues in the controversy between Nishida and Tanabe. Tanabe disagrees with the following idea: "First of all there exist the contents of life which precede and transcend any kind of logic. The function of logic appears only when one fixes the flux of life, transforms the heterogeneous development of life into a homogeneous static mode and measures these abstract identical contents by means of comparison" (THZ 6:

179). Here Tanabe is criticizing the philosophy of life as represented by Bergson and at the same time the philosophy of Nishida who held an affinity with it. From the standpoint of the logic of absolute mediation, even "life" cannot be posited as something unmediated. For Tanabe, logic is not just an abstraction of life. Rather, he argues that in order for life to come to an awareness of itself, it must be mediated by logic. It is true that logic is the objectification and negation of life. However, according to Tanabe, "life comes rather to a higher stage of concrete self-awareness when it is negated." "Life cannot be aware of its acting without the mediation of objectification" (THZ 6: 185).

Nishida's Objections to the Logic of Species

CONCERNING THE PROBLEM OF SPECIES

In the preceding section we considered the problems posed by Tanabe's logic of species from two points of view: one is the problem of "species" and the other is that of "mediation." Nishida's reply (in *Philosophical Essays II*) to Tanabe's criticism corresponds to these two points.

First, I shall discuss Nishida's objection to Tanabe with regard to the problem of species. Nishida states: "As individuals of a species, we are born from this species. But we are not slaves of the species" (NKZ 8: 446). "Although we are born from a species, on the other hand we also go on to form the species ourselves. There we find our true life" (NKZ 8: 450). Against Tanabe, who stresses the restriction of the individual by the species, Nishida emphasizes that the individual is not one-sidedly determined by a species. As individuals, though born from the species, we break free of its restrictions. Furthermore, according to Nishida, the species is able to be a living species only insofar as it has the potential to be negated by the individual.

After emphasizing that the individual breaks beyond the species, Nishida questions the foundation on which the individual is grounded, and answers thus: "It must be grounded in the self-determination of the dialectical universal which determines itself as species. . . . Species and individual oppose and determine each other as long as the individual is the individual in the dialectical universal and species is the species in the dialectical universal" (NKZ 8: 451). Here Nishida posits the "dialectical universal" (*benshōhōteki ippansha*) as the foundation of individual and species.

The "dialectical universal" is Nishida's expression for the universal that unifies oppositions without annihilating them. In this sense, it occupies the position of genus as opposed to individual and species. Whereas Tanabe argues that genus cannot exist without mediation by species, Nishida insists here that the dialectical universal (genus) exists prior to the individual and the species as their ground. This notion is reflected in the following words of Nishida regarding "substratum" (*kitai*):

> From the standpoint of the logic of judgment, the particular may be considered to be the constant substratum of the individual, and the universal may perhaps be regarded merely as its negation. . . . However, I think that in the world of historical life, on the other hand, the particular is the particular in the universal and the universal has the meaning of substratum. (NKZ 8: 384)

Tanabe uses the term "substratum" exclusively with regard to species. Tanabe argues that species is the substratum that exists by itself and precedes individual and genus, which each in turn exist only insofar as they are mediated by species. But against Tanabe, Nishida asserts that it is rather the universal (genus) that is the substratum which exists immediately and concretely.

CONCERNING THE PROBLEM OF MEDIATION

Another of Nishida's objections to Tanabe is in regard to Tanabe's logic of absolute mediation. Nishida's thought on this issue is most clearly evident in his treatment of the relationship between "life" and "logic." Nishida's essay "Logic and Life" in *Philosophical Essays II* deals with this issue. But in this essay, while probably bearing Tanabe in mind, Nishida approaches this problem from his own standpoint—a standpoint which is different from, or in fact, the very opposite of Tanabe's standpoint.

Nishida's standpoint in "Logic and Life" is expressed in his claim that "rather than thinking of reality from the standpoint of logic, we should rethink logic from the standpoint of reality" (NKZ 8: 276). Against Tanabe who rejects the positing of "life" in an immediate fashion, Nishida argues that it is impossible to reach life as long as one starts from the standpoint of logic, and that life can thus only be presented in its self-evidence. Nishida states: "It is not by means of our thought that we know that we are alive, but rather we think insofar as we are alive" (NKZ 8: 296). In this manner Nishida takes life as the foundation of logic, and attempts to analyze the structure of life itself in order to demonstrate the emergence of logic as one abstract aspect of life.

From this standpoint, Nishida turns around to criticize Tanabe's logic of absolute mediation. According to Nishida, the standpoint of Tanabe, who treats life within logic, is merely a "logic of judgment" (NKZ 8: 381), a "logic of reflection" (NKZ 8: 393) or an "abstract logic" (NKZ 8: 476). What Nishida

calls abstract logic is Tanabe's position of "analyzing the concrete into opposite concepts, regarding what is thought in this way as if it were self-sufficient
reality, and attempting to reproduce the concrete as the mutual relationship
of these opposites" (NKZ 8: 475–76). Nishida argues that it is impossible to
grasp concrete life from this standpoint. The "life" that is considered only as
the negation of logic is merely something demanded from the side of logic,
and thus not real life in its actuality. Nishida repeatedly stresses that there exists a gap between abstract logic and concrete reality, and that it is impossible
to reach the latter from the former.

It is on the basis of this thought that Nishida regards the dialectical universal (genus) as a substratum that precedes the species. The dialectical universal refers to "the world wherein we are born, live, act and die" (NKZ 7:
217). In this sense it indicates the immediate reality that precedes the analysis
imposed via the logical schema of genus, species and individual. One cannot
grasp the dialectical universal by logical analysis, because the analysis is itself
based on it. Nishida starts from the dialectical universal as the immediate reality or the real world, and then aims to provide a foundation for species and
individual on the basis of it.

Tanabe's Logic of Species and Nishida's Later Philosophy

From Tanabe's standpoint, however, several critical questions need to be raised
in response to Nishida's thought, at least to the latter as it has been presented
here thus far. Assuming that Nishida exclusively emphasizes the precedence
of genus and individual over species, he will not be able to evade Tanabe's
repeated criticism of having neglected the significance of species. Assuming
that Nishida exclusively insists on the standpoint of immediate life, Tanabe
will criticize him once again for having fallen into a mysticism that presumes
the existence of something unmediated.

It is true that, on the surface, the standpoint presented in Nishida's arguments in *Philosophical Essays II* seems to directly conflict with that of Tanabe.
In fact, however, when one carefully examines Nishida's arguments, it becomes apparent that behind Nishida's seemingly irreconcilable objections to
Tanabe lay some notions that are surprisingly similar to those of Tanabe.

THE PROBLEM OF SPECIES IN NISHIDA

Although, contrary to Tanabe, Nishida insists on the precedence of genus and
individual over species, this does not mean that Nishida reduces species to ge-

nus or individual. First, one should note that Nishida's argument that the individual breaks through the species does not necessarily reduce the species to the individual. Nishida does not neglect to point out that the individual that is said to form the species at the same time never escapes being thoroughly determined by the species. He states:

> In any case, we possess our life as a life of the species that is fixed at present.
> ... When I refer to the individual that determines itself thoroughly by itself ...
> this does not mean the abstract individual that exists apart from species; on the
> contrary, it should be understood rather as the individual that is born from the
> species in reality and goes on in turn to form the species. (NKZ 8: 445)

And somewhat later: "For the individual to become creative as an individual does not mean that it becomes an isolated individual, but rather that it carries out the mission of the species as a specific instance of the universal" (NKZ 8: 453).

But the question is whether or to what extent this statement reflects the essence of Nishida's philosophy. Does his reference to the species have any positive meaning for his philosophy, or is it just a reluctant concession to Tanabe? In order to examine this question, we need to look closely at the concept of "individual" in Nishida.

In Nishida the word "individual" is used in two different senses. On the one hand, it means "individual determination" in contrast to "universal determination." In Nishida's view, the real world dialectically contains two contrary phases: "individual determination," which indicates that the individual determines itself by itself, and "universal determination," which indicates that the individual is determined historically and socially. It is in this sense that Nishida calls the real world the "dialectical universal." "Individual determination" is only one element of the real world, and if it is taken by itself apart from the element of "universal determination," it is only an abstraction.

On the other hand, in Nishida the word "individual" also refers to each of the beings that exist and act in reality. The "individual" in this sense is not an abstract element but a concrete entity in reality, which contains the two contrary elements that are contained in the real world: "individual determination" and "universal determination." Nishida sometimes (although not always) distinguishes the individual in the latter sense from that in the former sense by referring to it, not simply as "individual" (kobutsuteki), but as "uniquely individual" (koseiteki).[8] For example, he writes in one place: "What is uniquely individual is not equivalent to what is individual; much less too what is universal. The universal that is at the same time individual, or the in-dividual that is at the same time universal, is the uniquely individual" (NKZ 8: 506). When Nishida refers to "individual" as a concrete entity in reality, he means "the uniquely individual" entity that is dialectically at once both individual and universal.

The individual as a concrete entity in reality—that is, "what is uniquely individual"—is by no means "the abstract individual that exists apart from the species." It must rather be understood as the individual that is determined historically and socially (as well as, of course, at the same time actively determining itself by itself). For the individual as a concrete entity, to be born from the species and to break through the species are compatible. Or rather, to be more precise, the individual that is first of all able to negate itself and conform to the species becomes, as a concrete individual, capable in turn of forming the species itself. It is impossible for the abstract individual to act on the species and transform it objectively. Hence, we can conclude that, for Nishida, determination by the species is after all an essential moment of the concrete individual in reality.

Next, it should also be noted that Nishida's insistence on the precedence of the universal ("the dialectical universal") does not necessarily imply that Nishida reduces everything to the standpoint of the universal (genus). One can demonstrate this by examining Nishida's unique concept of "the dialectical universal."[9]

"The dialectical universal" is another expression of the "place" in which concrete entities exist. In regard to Nishida's concept of "place," what is often at issue among critics and commentators is the relationship between "the things that are in place" (*oite aru mono*) and "the place in which things are" (*oite aru basho*). Tanabe critically interprets Nishida's "place of nothingness" as a place that embraces everything and makes them indistinct. But the following quotation from Nishida indicates that this is not the case. "That one thing and another thing determine each other, or that one thing and another thing act on each other, is a matter of the place . . . determining itself. And that the place determines itself is a matter of one thing and another thing acting on each other" (NKZ 8: 16). Nishida argues here that the mutual activity of "things that are in place" and the self-determination of the "place in which things are" are not two different events. This means that there is no "place" which exists in itself apart from the action of "things that are in place." As is evident in Nishida's repeated use of the phrase "appearance qua reality" (see, for example, NKZ 9: 104), phenomena that appear in this world are for

Nishida the only reality; there is no metaphysical "place" in the sense of a substantial noumenal reality existing behind the phenomenal appearance of "things that are in place."

Tanabe interpreted "place" as something substantial to which the manifold of beings are reductively homogenized, but "place" in the context of Nishida's thought never functions in such a manner. The ultimate function of Nishida's "place" is rather only to let "things that are in place" be as they are, or to let them act as they act. This is precisely the reason why the place is called "nothingness." As we have seen, Nishida does, to be sure, assert that "things that are in place" are grounded in the place, in other words, species and individual are grounded in "the dialectical universal." But this does not mean that the place or the universal restricts the action of "things that are in place"; the place of nothingness rather brings them to their authentic existence. Thus, the species, as one sort of being in the real world, does not disappear in being reduced to the place of nothingness, but rather it attains its true reality by being grounded in that place. In fact, Nishida suggests that in the real world (that is, in the dialectical universal) "a species unreservedly asserts its own specificity from its own standpoint, and several species oppose and compete with one other within the same environment" (NKZ 8: 519–20).

As we have seen in this section, Nishida never slights the significance of species. Rather, Nishida insists, as does Tanabe, that there exists neither individual nor universal apart from species. In this respect, one can conclude that at bottom Nishida shares a common basis with Tanabe with regard to the problem of species,[10] in other words, with regard to the issue of the historicity and sociality of the real world.

IMMEDIACY AND MEDIATION IN NISHIDA

The disagreement between Nishida and Tanabe over the question of the "logic of absolute mediation" would appear to be even greater than their disagreement over the issue of "species." The rift between them here would seem especially severe given their apparently opposite views of "life." But a closer examination reveals that Nishida's standpoint of immediate life does not exclude an element of mediation.

Nishida argues: "Life should not be regarded as something merely irrational or direct and unmediated. A rational mediation, namely thought, must be included in our life. There is no human life that does not include some sense of rational mediation" (NKZ 8: 269). "To live is not simply a matter of emotion or mystical intuition, but involves objective poiesis" (NKZ 8: 270). In these passages Nishida clearly denies the idea of life as something "direct and unmediated" which can be grasped only by "emotion" or "mystical intuition."

In order to clarify Nishida's unique notion of life, and to show how it differs from the idea of unmediated life, it will be helpful to refer to the way in which he distinguishes between "historical life" (that is, human life) and "biological life." Nishida explains their difference by reference to their respective manners of making things: "In biological life, things that have been made are not free from the body; in other words, they are not free from the subject. . . . In historical life, on the contrary, things that have been made (*tsukurareta mono*) are independent from those who make them (*tsukuru mono*)" (NKZ 8: 501–502).

Nishida argues that when an animal makes something, the thing that has been made is not free from the subject that makes it. This means that with animals there is no genuine opposition between the self and the external world. With animals, the self as the subject of the making has not been established as an independent self. The self of an animal is nothing more than a part of an organic whole. By reason of the fact that animals exist within such a situation, making in the animal world is simply the self-development of an organic whole, which includes no negation or discontinuity. Therefore, the life of animals can be conceived of as a continual linear life, or a life that flows on without interruption. Such a life necessarily refuses any attempt at objective representation, and can thus be grasped only by way of immediate intuition. To put it another way, as long as life is thought in the sense of biological life, it cannot but be represented as something "direct and unmediated."

Yet Nishida distinguishes between biological life and historical life. In the historical world, a self emerges who is independent from the external world, and hence an opposition between self and external world is established. This enables human beings to make things in a genuinely objective manner. Human beings confront objective things that exist outside them and oppose them. And in negating themselves and submitting to things, human beings become all the more able to act on things and form them objectively. To quote Nishida, "Things that have been made make those who make them. When we make things, we ourselves are made" (NKZ 8: 502) Nishida refers to this genuine sense of "making," which takes place within the historical world, with the Greek term *poiesis*. According to Nishida, *poiesis* is nothing less than the essential characteristic of "historical life." The life of *poiesis* necessarily contains an element of "negation" of life's aspect of irrational immediacy by means of "rational mediation." Without this element, objective *poiesis* would be impossible. "Historical life" is therefore by no means something "direct and unmediated."

No matter how much Nishida emphasizes directness and immediacy, he does not, in the end, assert the kind of direct immediacy criticized by Tanabe. Nishida states: "The concrete or the immediate in the true sense must be that which mediates itself by itself" (NKZ 8: 434). As Nishida argues here, the concrete "immediate" must include "mediation" in itself. What is supposed to be immediate in the sense of excluding mediation is, after all, only an abstraction. It is simply that which is constructed by neglecting the element of mediation. This is also the case with Nishida's conception of the immediacy of life. It is true that Nishida regards life as immediate, but, strictly speaking, what Nishida calls immediate life is nothing other than the dialectical event of *poiesis* in the historical world. It is called immediate only in the sense that it is the concrete life of human being in its actuality. Nishida's thought would not allow the presupposition of an unmediated "life" that transcends or preexists each moment of concrete action within the historical world. Hence, it is reasonable to conclude that Nishida's philosophy also shares a common basis with Tanabe with regard to the problem of "mediation."

In this essay I sought to reveal the common basis of ideas underlying the philosophies of Nishida and Tanabe by way of considering the problems posed by Tanabe's "logic of species." This common basis, however, is not necessarily something that can already be found in the early stages of Nishida's thought. In fact, in his early texts Nishida hardly discussed these problems. In this sense, one could say that, with regard to the early philosophy of Nishida, Tanabe's criticism of Nishida was to a large extent justified. Yet over the course of his confrontation with Tanabe, Nishida developed his thought in significant respects. The result, as we have seen, is that Nishida's later philosophy was able to effectively deal with the problems posed by Tanabe's criticism.

Although in response to Tanabe's criticism Nishida did significantly develop his philosophy, his concern with the trans-historical religious world never weakened. In his refusal to remain content with the merely immanent realm of the historical and relative world, and in his relentless pursuit of a trans-historical religious dimension, the later Nishida continued the work of the early Nishida. However, unlike the early Nishida, the later Nishida pursued the trans-historical religious dimension in the very midst of the historical world rather than from the standpoint of a trans-historical religious experience. For the later Nishida, the trans-historical religious dimension is not some place separate from the historicity of human beings.[11] As I have attempted to show in this essay, by explicating his debate with Tanabe, the unfolding stages in Nishida's later thought lead to a dynamic and "immanently transcendent" form of religious philosophy.

NOTES

This essay is a slightly revised version of Kōichi Sugimoto, "Tanabe Hajime's Logic of Species and the Philosophy of Nishida Kitarō," *Synthesis Philosophica* 19, no. 1 (2004): 35–47, and is reprinted here with permission of the publisher.

1. The image of Tanabe's philosophy presented here may differ from the way he is perceived by most Western scholars. In the West, where research has centered on THZ 9 (1946), the only book of his translated into a Western language (*Philosophy as Metanoetics* [1986]), attention is mainly given to the religious aspect of Tanabe's philosophy (see, for example, Taitetsu Unno and James W. Heisig, eds., *The Religious Philosophy of Tanabe Hajime* [Berkeley, Calif.: Asian Humanities Press, 1990]). Western scholars tend to regard Tanabe's philosophy, like Nishida's, as an Eastern form of religious philosophy. In Japan, on the other hand, scholars tend to look at Tanabe's philosophy in terms of its opposition to Nishida's philosophy. Japanese scholars in general find the fundamental standpoint of Tanabe's thought expressed in his texts prior to *Philosophy as Metanoetics,* particularly his writings on the "logic of species" where his conflict with Nishida was most acute. Tanabe's philosophy is portrayed in the present essay according to this early but formative stage of his philosophy.

2. Nishitani Keiji discusses their common basis in terms of the idea of "absolute nothingness" (NK 161). This viewpoint has been passed on to scholars in the West. For example, James Heisig depicts three principal figures of the Kyoto School (Nishida, Tanabe, and Nishitani) as "philosophers of nothingness," and gives special attention to their notions of "the self-awareness of absolute nothingness" (*Philosophers of Nothingness: An Essay on the Kyoto School* [Honolulu: University of Hawai'i Press, 2001]).

3. Ueda Shizuteru, "Tanabe tetsugaku to Nishida tetsugaku" [The philosophies of Tanabe and Nishida], in Takeuchi Yoshinori, Mutō Kazuo, and Tsujimura Kōichi, eds., *Tanabe Hajime: shisō to kaisō* [Tanabe Hajime: thought and reminiscences] (Tokyo: Chikima Shobō, 1991). Ueda demonstrates that after *Philosophy as Metanoetics,* in the final phase of his career, "'the self-awareness of absolute nothingness' in Tanabe and that in Nishida came to correspond to one another through Tanabe's sudden turn of thought" (270).

4. A noteworthy study that analyzes how Nishida treats the problem of species posed by Tanabe is Kawamura Eiko, "Nishida tetsugaku to Tanabe tetsugaku" [The philosophies of Nishida and Tanabe], in Ueda Shizuteru, ed., *Nishida tetsugaku* [Nishida's philosophy] (Tokyo: Sōbunsha, 1994). But Kawamura, who regards Tanabe's criticism of Nishida as a result of the fact that "Tanabe did not completely open himself to the place of nothingness as an absolute and infinite openness" (280), does not pay attention to the significance of Tanabe's criticism as such.

5. The importance of this research is also pointed out in Heisig, *Philosophers of Nothingness*, 262.

6. Tanabe himself admits that this is not necessarily a faithful understanding of Nishida. He states: "Simplifying it [the philosophy of Nishida] to a type and pursuing its conclusion, I shaped it into a consistent ideal type, and then proceeded to confront it and criticize it. Accordingly, such a thought as I am criticizing could perhaps not be found in any actual philosophy" (THZ 6: 225).

7. Tanabe's "logic of absolute mediation" is formed under the influence of Hegel. But at the same time Tanabe asserts that the notion of mediation in Hegel is not thoroughgoing, and he remains suspicious of a kind of emanationism in Hegel's thought (THZ 6: 226–27).

8. The Japanese word *kobutsuteki* indicates the "individuality" of an individual thing taken as the limit point of the particularization of a genus (for example, this man, this apple, etc.). On the other hand, the Japanese word *koseiteki* refers to the "uniqueness" of a thing's identity in its difference from other things. It modifies not only individual persons or things but also species—for example, an age, a nation, or a state. *Individuell* as it is used in writings of the German Historical School—for example, in Ranke and Meinecke—is translated by *koseiteki* in Japanese. When Nishida introduced the term *koseiteki* into his thought, he perhaps had their thought in mind.

9. One should note that in Nishida not only "individual" but also "universal" has two different meanings. On the one hand, it means "universal determination" in contrast to "individual determination"; on the other hand, it signifies the "dialectical universal" which is at one and the same time both individual and universal—in other words, the real "world" in which concrete entities exist.

10. However, this does not mean that Nishida's and Tanabe's notions of "species" are the same. While Tanabe analyzes the structure of the world in terms of genus, species, and individual, Nishida does not place species within such a threefold structure. Nishida thinks that a species does not exist in the same sense or on the same level as "the world as dialectical universal" and "the unique individual," but rather only as a characteristic of "the world" and "the individual." He argues that species are the "forms" or "paradigms" according to which individuals shape themselves (NKZ 8: 455). As is evident in the very title of his essay "The Problem of the Emergence and Development of Species," for Nishida a species is not a "substratum," as Tanabe suggests, but rather something which emerges, grows, and disappears according to the actions of individuals in the world. Nevertheless, this idea of Nishida's does not necessarily weaken the significance of species in the real world. Although species exist in dependence on the actions of individuals, it is essential for individuals to be counter-determined by the very species they have formed.

11. One of the most remarkable common features of Nishida and Tanabe, which I have not treated here, is the compatibility of religiousness and historicity. On this point, see Kōsaka Masaaki, *Nishida tetsugaku to Tanabe tetsugaku* [The philosophies of Nishida and Tanabe]; repr. in *Kōsaka Masaaki chosakushū* [Collected works of Kōsaka Masaaki] (Tokyo: Risōsha, 1965), 8: 294.

In note 1, I distinguished the later philosophy of Tanabe, represented by *Philosophy as Metanoetics*, from his former philosophy, represented by the "logic of species." But one should note that even in his later religious philosophy, Tanabe maintained a central concern that he had had in the "logic of species," namely, a concern for the historicity of the real world. By remaining true to this concern, he was able to form a dynamic philosophy that includes both religiousness and historicity. The intimate connection between Nishida's religious philosophy and historicity is expressed in his notion of "the standpoint of ordinariness" (*byōjōtei*), which is discussed with reference to Zen Buddhism in his last essay, "The Logic of Place and the Religious World View" (1945) (NKZ 11; trans. Yusa Michiko, *The Eastern Buddhist* 19, no. 2 [1986]: 1–29; and 20, no. 1 [1986]: 81–119).

PART TWO

Self and
World

4

Philosophy as Auto-Bio-Graphy: The Example of the Kyoto School

Ōhashi Ryōsuke

A Preliminary Conception of the Kyoto School

In the following I would like to attempt to develop the idea of philosophy as auto-bio-graphy in three theses and to do so using the example of the philosophy of the Kyoto School, so that the conception of philosophy as auto-biography can be expounded along with some of the aspects of the philosophy of the Kyoto School.

Before doing this, a preliminary conception of the Kyoto School should be briefly explicated.[1] Somewhat like the Frankfurt School in Germany, the Kyoto School developed over several generations. Its "founder," Nishida Kitarō (1870–1945), certainly did not have the intention of founding a school, but his personality and philosophical thinking attracted many students, who then developed the thinking of their teacher in various directions, while sharing this common point of departure. This thinking can be characterized in the following way: One of its roots lies in European philosophy, while the other lies in the East Asian spiritual tradition. If one understands the so-called first philosophy in the Occident as ontology, that is, the philosophy of Being, then the Kyoto School developed the philosophy of absolute nothingness. On the one hand, Nishida incorporated the thinking of William James's pragmatism, Henri Bergson's life philosophy, Emil Lask's Neo-Kantianism, etc., but on the other hand he occupied himself intensively with Zen practice, without which experience his philosophizing would not have come about in the way that one knows it today.

The successor to his chair, Tanabe Hajime (1885–1962), was certainly with regard to philosophical thinking the greatest critic of Nishida, but despite all of his criticism of Nishida, for his part he likewise developed a philosophy of absolute nothingness, which was later influenced more and more strongly by the Buddhist body of thought. If one dubs Nishida and Tanabe the first generation of the Kyoto School, then one understands as the second generation several of their students such as Hisamatsu Shinichi (1889–1980), Kōsaka Masaaki (1900–1969), Nishitani Keiji (1900–1990), and Kōyama Iwao (1905–1991). The philosophers of this second generation were persecuted toward the end of World War II in the Pacific by the extreme right of the military regime, because their historical-philosophical thinking denoted a simultaneously latent but decisive critique of extreme nationalism. After the end of the War in the Pacific, however, they were repeatedly attacked by mainly left-oriented critics who passed themselves off as liberals. These critics attacked them on the grounds that Kyoto School philosophers had collaborated with the military regime.

The third generation of the Kyoto School consists of the disciples of the philosophers of the second generation. Their confrontation with European philosophy too takes place more or less in the direction that had been introduced by Nishida and Tanabe and assumed by the second generation of the Kyoto School.

The *Autō*

My first thesis reads: Philosophizing is the knowledge of *to autō*, that is, "the self." It is to know one's own self. Already at the beginning of the history of philosophy Plato understood the adage handed down in the Temple of Delphi, *gnōthi seauton* (know yourself), as an instruction for oneself. This thesis implies that my own self, as well as the self of the world, is indeed always somehow *familiar* to me, but not thereby *known* by me. Oneself must come to be known. As with all philosophical themes, one also finds here the starting point of aporia and astonishment: So long as I do not wonder at what my own self and the self of the world is, I know what it is—but as soon as someone asks me about it, I do not know anymore.

One's own self is neither identical with one's ego nor with the subject, although conversely this ego or subject, thematized again and again in modern philosophy since Descartes, is a modern name for the self. The development of modern philosophy is the development of the thinking about the ego, that is, the subject. *Ego cogito, ergo sum,* as Descartes said. This principle that he discovered was supposed to be the foremost certainty upon which the edifice of philosophy could first securely be built. Indeed, the Cartesian ego could not fully become aware of its own self. It certainly knew *that* it *is,* but it did not know *from where* it was supposed to have come. As is well known, Descartes further asked from where this otherwise self-secure ego came.[2] This "from where," the ground of one's own being, was in the end dubbed "God," upon which the ego could first be grounded.

I do not want to undertake here an historical tracing of the modern lines of development of the philosophical thinking that lead to the ego and the subject. It should suffice to indicate that philosophical terminology like Leibniz's monad, Kant's transcendental apperception, Fichte's and Schelling's absolute ego, Hegel's absolute, Husserl's transcendental ego, etc., despite all the distinctions that could be made among them, imply the same thing: Modern philosophy was the impulse to bring to full consciousness one's own self, as well as the self of the world, within the horizon of subjectivity.

The philosophy of the Kyoto School likewise involves this facticity of the self. In order to illustrate the experience of one's own self and the self of the world that is preserved and handed down in the Kyoto School, I will cite Nishitani Keiji, who in an autobiographical essay ("Waga shi Nishida Kitarō sensei wo kataru" [Memories of my teacher Nishida Kitarō]) describes a memory of his teacher, Nishida Kitarō: "For these essays of Nishida, I had a more intimate feeling than I had for any other essay I had read before, as well as for any other person that I had heretofore met. They gave me a qualitatively different impression, for it seemed as if they had originated from the innermost depths of my own soul" (NKC 9: 16).

The expression "out of the innermost depths of my soul" reveals the inborn affinity between the two thinkers. And beyond that, one can hear in it an appeal to Nishitani's conception of the "self," which he partially worked on in his study of Meister Eckhart. Furthermore, the appeal becomes clearer when one hears the following words: The encounter with Nishida would have been for him the encounter with a person "who is closer to me than I am to myself" (NKC 9: 16). The expression "closer to me than I am to myself" was very probably adopted from Meister Eckhart, who said God is "nearer than the soul is to itself," just like the Holy Spirit "is more immediately present to the soul than the soul is to itself."[3] The soul for Eckhart was not an objectively describable object, but rather the inside of "me." Eckhart would also have said that God is nearer to me than I am to myself. When Nishitani sees this relationship between God and the human also in the relationship between his teacher and himself, this does not mean a mystification of the teacher-student relationship, but rather an experience of what my own self is: the self of another is the same as the self of my own ego. When one understands by this "other" any other that is in the outer world, than this self is the same as that of the world. The question repeats itself here: What is this self?

Nishitani describes the core of the relationship between God and the human phenomenologically, as it were, and finds in it "the culmination of the noetic union." The union in the customary sense is that of present beings A and B in a higher being C. A noematic union of that kind concerns the present objects, but it is not the noetic union in Nishitani's sense, namely, different eyes uniting in their inexchangeable noetic act of seeing. In lieu of seeing one can also bring into play hearing, feeling, smelling, tasting, etc. In this simple act of perception, no one can take the place of the other. Even the person who is most intimately familiar to me can never perform *my* seeing, hearing, feeling, smelling, tasting, etc.; no one else can sense *in my place*. And the concern here is not at all with a mystical experience, but rather the experience that everyone constantly and without noticing makes in a quotidian fashion.

In this banal experience, everyone is actually someone in whose stead no one can enter. This uniqueness can be ascribed to everything that is—and is, indeed, the self of each thing. Yet humans first *know* this uniqueness. For them this means: Everyone is the other to everyone else. This otherness of the other shows itself in each sensation and each feeling, and, in the most extreme case, in death. Even humans who love each other cannot make the death of the other into their own experience. Yet precisely with regard to this noetic act that can never be exchanged with the other, everyone is the same manner of being like the other. In the noetic aspect of this otherwise utterly banal perception and sensation, everyone is the *other* to everyone else, and in this very respect everyone is the *same* as everyone else. Precisely at the point where everyone maintains their otherness and uniqueness in opposition to everyone else are they united with everyone else.

A remark is indispensable here. In this noetic union, mere egoity is breached. In a pure noetic act, one is without ego. An example: In play one forgets oneself, and precisely at the point where one forgets oneself can one play best. Even the sober supervision and calculation of the game demands this absence of an ego. In this ego-less dedication one is unified with the noetic that is likewise exercised in the game.

This lack of egoity is, to anticipate the following presentation, a name for the concept of the "nothing," and this nothing is a name for the "self" of the Kyoto School in the sense that it is preeminently used by Nishida and Nishitani.

The *Biōs*

Here my second thesis comes to bear: Philosophy always concerns the *biōs* of *to autō,* the life by which the otherwise ego-less self of my own ego express- es itself and maintains its egoity. In this self-expression one also recognizes the others, with whom the "world" forms an ego and is determined by this "world." The philosophy of the "self" as the philosophy of the "nothing" must develop itself as the philosophy of "life" and of the "world." Then again, this thesis is not new at all. The leading idea of Greek philosophy, "to live well," already refers to this idea. Whether the good life in the sense of eudaemonia is finally achieved through the acquisition of power and wealth and fame in this world or first in the world of the *eidos* as the state of the soul, was the crux of the confrontation between Socrates and the Sophists. After philosophy had achieved the position of a discipline within the university, around the time of the Enlightenment, and became more and more a drive toward scientific ac- tivity in the name of research, it lost this leading idea. But mere philologically oriented research alone cannot entirely depart from this objective as long as the good life is treated in the text.

Regarding the structure of life, we should first of all see what was just now glimpsed in the structure of the "self": My life is thoroughly my own life, and nevertheless it is united with that of the others. Indeed, no one can carry out my life in my place; but precisely in that by which I carry out my life, which is otherwise independent from that of all others, I stand in the same manner of being that the others bear. One is united with the others in the noetic im- mersion in this manner of being. This noetic unification can only be proved true in noetic transcendence, that is, in the immersion in one's own ego-less self. The biological connection of individual creatures that has been visually discernible in the evolutionary lines of all creatures since antiquity, but also in the ecological context of the natural world, is the reflection of this noetic unity. No creature has given birth to itself but was rather born from another. The death of an individual creature is seen precisely as Leibniz once described it in his mature treatise, *Principes de la Nature et de la Grace, fondés en raison* (*Principles of Nature and Grace, Based on Reason*): It is not the mere cessa- tion of life, but rather the "metamorphosis" of the components of the organic body, which always transform themselves into another life.[4]

The relationship of individual creatures to the organic whole—as to the greater life which is easy to see in the biological world—is similar to the projection of the infinite plenitude. From the perspective of the theory of the plenitude, each part *is* the whole. This relationship of biological life must also hold for social and historical life. But no: It first becomes clear in social and historical life that the individual life *is* not only the whole, but rather *also* a unique life opposed to other individuals, that is to say, that it is free and creative and that it cannot be substituted with another.

In the philosophy of the Kyoto School the self-consciousness of this historical life is expressed in the form of an historical philosophy. That the philosophy of absolute nothingness can be thematized as something like history, and the manner in which this could be done, would constitute quite a philosophical theme. For history is certainly the world of being and not the world of nothingness. But, as stated above, what is called nothingness is not a mere vacuous nothingness in the sense of a lack of objects, but rather the very self which cannot be objectified and thereby does not admit of predication—and is thus the genuine status quo of creation.

Incidentally, it was not the Kyoto School who considered history for the first time under the aspect of nothingness. Nietzsche already saw the Christian-European world under the aspect of the nihilism of the eternal return of the same. He saw that, in the world in which God is dead and/or has been murdered, a final answer to the question "why" is necessarily lacking. The historical world, which recurs without an answer as to why, has neither goal nor meaning. For Nietzsche the overcoming of this nihilism of the eternal return of the same did not entail a deception about this insignificance, but rather (as he narrates in the well-known allegory of the "Three Metamorphoses") the bearing and enduring of the heavy burden of this insignificance of the world, until the bearer, the camel, transforms into the lion, who affirms even this insignificance as "I will" in order to finally transform, in this great *Yes,* into the "child."[5]

When Max Scheler after World War I elucidated "absolute nothingness" as the point of departure for philosophizing, the spiritual situation of Europe had changed yet again. The doubt about the reliability of reason was still intensifying in the face of a world catastrophe which was thought to be a consequence of the Enlightenment and its respective civilizations. Furthermore, Scheler believed that he had seen that the place of Europe had been put into question in the face of Asia's drive to expand. He deemed World War I to be a "parity" between these East-West contraries.[6] The altogether unstable na-

ture of this parity soon showed itself over the course of the 1920s and 1930s
The ground of existentialism—angst before nothingness as the mood of the
times—was already under way. The philosophy of nothingness developed in
the Kyoto School was in any case not an isolated venture, but rather belonged
to the contemporary path of philosophy in the twentieth century.

The "nothing" of the Kyoto School is, as has been said, the formless self
of the subject, which never admits of reification. The "subject" was never conceived by the philosophers of the School in the direction of "subjectivity," but
rather in the direction of subjectlessness. The subjectless subject was simply
what the Kyoto School meant by "nothingness." The latter as the self of my
own ego does not form an egotistical center, from which the ego would be
individual and sovereign and rule the periphery. The Kyoto School wanted to
question the previous view of the conception of history, according to which the
world should be universal and whose center signified Europe. "Nothingness,"
otherwise understood exclusively as a thought belonging to the philosophy of
religion, was in this context conceived as the principle of the historical world
and dubbed the "universal of nothingness" ("Sekaikan to kokkakan" [World-
view and stateview], NKC 4: 319). Only insofar as one takes this nothingness
as one's point of departure, can the individual be creative and inwardly bound
with the state, which likewise takes this nothingness as its point of departure,
and which co-forms the "worldly world." The Kyoto School wanted to consider this worldly world as one in which the Eurocentric, Anglo-Saxon modern
world would have been overcome. The religiosity of the "nothing" should also
not only be realized in human interiority, but also in the worldly world.

As was mentioned in the beginning, far-right partisans attacked the
Kyoto School because the latter's views were contrary to ultra-nationalistic
views of the time. National Socialism *de facto* implies that one maintain the
self-consciousness of one's own nation so that all other nations and peoples
are seen only from the perspective of this minute angle, and never from the
perspective of intercultural togetherness. The plurality of the world was never as such envisaged. To defend this plurality meant, at the time, a critique
of the prevailing ultra-nationalism. When one thinks of the confrontations
with totalitarian or fundamentalist regimes of yesterday and today, one can
imagine how serious the jeopardy to one's life could be for those who uttered
such a critique. For its part, the Kyoto School had indeed not carried out any
explicit critiques of the regime at that time, with the exception of Nishida's
Marxist-oriented students such as Tosaka Jun (1900–1945) and Miki Kiyoshi
(1897–1945), who had to have died tragically in prison shortly before and

after the end of the Pacific War respectively. The other philosophers of the Kyoto School attempted with their philosophy of history to provide a new orientation for and justification of the Pacific War, which more or less meant an implicit critique. The imprisonment of Nishida by the military regime did not occur, in the end, but it had in fact been planned. Without the aid of the Japanese Navy, he would quite possibly have been arrested together with some of his students.[7] The tragedy of imprisonment could be avoided, but another, much longer-acting tragedy accompanied it: Their attempt at a new orientation of the political reality foundered in the end not on account of their efforts, but rather on account of the hardness of the political reality itself, which was in the hands of a monstrous will of the state. The capitulation of Japan aggravated, for some philosophers of the Kyoto School, the extreme living conditions, as it resulted in their losing their positions. Moreover, mentally, this capitulation signified the failure of their thinking about the Pacific War. However, it is therefore important to investigate whether their idealistic arguments were really in no respect sensible, or whether these arguments—liberated from the conditions of their time and seen anew from a contemporary standpoint—contain insights that can only be appreciated today.

The *Graphē*

We now come back to the theme of "auto-bio-graphy." Our third thesis is: Philosophy as the *biōs* of the *autō*, the life of the self, demands *graphē*, that is to say, the description of a particular meaning. Philosophy as the description of the life of the self is in accordance with its form an auto-bio-graphy.

The philosophy of history as it was pursued since Augustine and further pursued in a secularized form in Kant, Hegel, and Marx, and whose echo can still be heard in Kojève and Fukuyama, is essentially characterized as Christian-eschatological. That is to say, what experience shows to be the never-given whole of history is constructed in it, despite all of the variations, by the Christian-eschatological idea. As a consequence of this, it must have a metaphysical character. The writer (*grapheus*) of history in particular always contemplates it from a bird's-eye view that does not suit humans, and by which the writer constructs the historical world in accordance with an idea and predetermines it through this idea. The historical world represented in this way is not the brute fact that one encounters in immediate experience.

If one wants to liberate oneself from this kind of philosophy of history, one will be confronted with a question: How should one, in the description of all that is and happens (i.e., the world), describe it as how it is (and thereby as the world), in the way that it is encountered in immediate experience? If the claim "to the things themselves" may be understood as the leitmotif of phenomenology, then the question posed above is one of phenomenology.

The fundamental idea of the philosophy of the Kyoto School wants to propose an answer to this question. By way of example, an answer according to Nishida would be the self-determination of the world. The world, which in natural science is described and determined in a mathematically and physically objective fashion, is not yet the "primary world," as Husserl (for instance) understands it. This world stands *prior* to any objectification. The objective image of the world is basically subjective insofar as there cannot be an object without a subject. Even if this subject does not mean something merely individual, but rather a faculty for cognition that is common to all humans, or even intersubjectivity—this changes nothing with regard to objectivity as the flipside of subjectivity.

The "self-determination of the world," as Nishida put it, is the event that emerges in immediate experience which is prior to any subject-object division—before an object is reified, calculated, and analyzed by its beholder. The arising of the world-event in the particular immediate experience of an individual, seen from the perspective of that individual, means that it becomes ego-less, but in such a way that the description that "I" undertake, is indeed egoistic but nonetheless also ego-less, so that it counts as the self-determination of the world. Nishida elucidated this seemingly abstract formula with a simple example: "Not that 'this bird' flies, but rather the fact 'this bird flies' is what there is" ("Watashi no zettaimu no jikakuteki gentei to iu mono" [My sense of the determination of absolute nothingness becoming aware of itself], NKZ 6: 168). Neither is "this bird" perceived noematically as the subject of a proposition, nor does the noetic "ego" as a knowing subject see this bird. In the *there* of the factual world, the brute fact "this bird flies" arises and this arising belongs as much to the ego as it does to the bird. The dawning awareness of this fact is the realization of the self-determination of the world. The writer is not an egoistic subject, but is rather nothingness in the sense of the subjectless subject.

Another few words regarding the structure of this description: every *graphē*, every description, is the achievement of a subject. Yet this subject does not absolutely have to be egoistic. It can be subject-less so that her or his description can be grasped as the self-description of the world materializing through her or him. This relationship can be understood more easily in the realm of art. The work of an artist, who is somehow "inspired" and motivated by this inspiration, is surely the artist's work; and at the same time the artist is not simply their work. What the artist has created can be understood as the self-creation of the world as it happens through the artist. The term "gift" in relationship to "gifted," as in the expression "this artist is gifted," refers to this subject-less dimension of consciousness in the artist who otherwise wants to be strongly individualistic. Every focus of the self-determination of the world is always individualistic and unique.

The description of the world by a subjectless subject, who strives to know their own self and the self of the world, results in the knowledge of the *autō* as the performance of the *biōs*. It results in the auto-bio-graphy of the world. The philosophy of the Kyoto School was a special case of this auto-bio-graphy.

As is the case with every philosopher, the philosophy of the Kyoto School also finds itself in a historical becoming, which continues to this day. The question posed above, namely whether the argumentation of the Kyoto School concerning the Pacific War, which in part remains too idealistic, was in no respect sensible, or whether, liberated from its historical determinations and seen anew from a contemporary point of view, this argumentation contains insights that can only be appreciated today, also pertains to this historical becoming. That is to say, Kyoto philosophy can be understood as a question that is posed within the contemporary constellation. In the present intercultural times, one sees that the philosophers of the Kyoto School had anticipated and foreseen something which has only in more recent times been said explicitly, and should be made more lucid yet. This is the necessity of the "worldly world" in which every cultural world, precisely in the place where it maintains its creative subjectivity, co-determines this "world" without recourse to ego-centered domination, let alone to Orientalism or Occidentalism.

It is admittedly a further question as to how one would describe the self auto-bio-graphically in the contemporary world that is being molded through normalization and leveling by the world-drive that originates in Europe and goes by the name of "world technology." Having posed this question, I now provisionally conclude my considerations.

Translated from the German by Jason M. Wirth

NOTES

1. The following preliminary conception of the philosophy of the Kyoto School is based on my introduction to a volume that I edited, *Die Philosophie der Kyōto Schule: Texte und Einführung* [The philosophy of the Kyoto School: texts and introduction] (Freiburg: Alber Verlag, 1990).

2. René Descartes, *Meditationes de Prima Philosophia*, in Charles Adams and Paul Tannery, eds., *Oeuvres de Descartes* (Paris: J. Vrin, 1964–1976), 7: 48.

3. See Meister Eckhart, *Die lateinische Werke* [The Latin works], J. Koch et al., eds. (Stuttgart: Kohlhammer Verlag, 1956), vol. 4. The original in the sermon reads: "(Deus) intimior est animae quam anima sibi ipis" (356). The first sermon has: "Spiritus sanctus immediator est animae quam anima sibi ipsi" (3).

4. G. W. Leibniz, *Principes de la Nature et de la Grace, fondés en raison*, §6, in *Die philosophische Schriften* (New York: Hildesheim), 6: 601. Translator's note: The English passage can be found in *Philosophical Essays*, trans. Roger Ariew and Daniel Garber (Indianapolis: Hackett, 1989), 209.

5. Cf. Nietzsche, *Also sprach Zarathustra*, in *Sämtliche Werke (Kritische Studienausgabe)*, ed. Giorgio Colli and Mazzino Montinari (Munich: Deutscher Taschenbuch Verlag / Berlin and New York: de Gruyter, 1988), 4: 29–31. Translator's note: The English citation can be found in *Thus Spoke Zarathustra*, trans. Graham Parkes (Oxford and New York: Oxford University Press, 2005), 23–24.

6. Max Scheler, *Vom Ewigen im Menschen*, 4th edition, *Gesammelte Werke*, ed. Maria Scheler (Bern: Francke Verlag, 1954), 5: 430. Translator's note: The English citation can be found in *On the Eternal in Man*, trans. Bernard Noble (New York: Harper, 1960), 430.

7. For more on this, see Furuta Hikaru, "Sekai shin chitsujo no genri kō" [Considerations concerning the affair "Principle of a New World Order"], *Nishida Kitarō zenshū, furoku*, 107–110, 165–70.

5

Nishitani after Nietzsche: From the Death of God to the Great Death of the Will

BRET W. DAVIS

The Death of God and the Birth of Dialogue

CRISIS AS OPPORTUNITY

For many, Nietzsche's proclamation of the "death of God"[1] marks a rupture in the history of the West; or at least it exposes a fracture in the ground of Western culture that had been steadily widening since the dawn of modernity. The "God" whose "death" Nietzsche announced is not only the Christian God of revelation, the creator and judge that had stood at the center of Western civilization for one and a half millennia, but also the "God of philosophy," the rational ground of metaphysical truth and ethical goodness. Many of the central debates in post-Nietzschean European philosophy have accordingly concerned the "overcoming of metaphysics," the "deconstruction" of the Western tradition of "ontotheology," and various attempts at radically questioning and/ or rethinking our philosophical, religious, and cultural foundations.

In short, post-Nietzschean Western philosophy is characterized by a crisis of self-critique. Yet "crisis" (Gr. *krisis*) can also imply opportunity, a watershed or a turning point, as in a fever on the verge of breaking. It is indeed one of Nietzsche's insights that sickness can be a path to greater health.[2] As Heidegger suggests, a meditation on the "end of philosophy" as metaphysics or ontotheology may in fact enable a return to a more elemental "task of thinking."[3] Moreover, a deconstruction of the Western tradition of philosophy could be seen as a step on the way to what he calls at one point "planetary thinking,"[4] and specifically to what he refers to elsewhere as the "inevitable dialogue with the East Asian world."[5]

The crisis of Western philosophy may thus also be understood as an opportunity for opening up a dialogue with non-Western traditions. A loss of confidence in the ideology that equates modernization with Westernization with progress—an ideology that has always been much easier to calculate in terms of science and technology than in terms of philosophy and religion—may open a door through which we may "step back" into a realm of radical dialogical thinking, that is, into bilateral conversation between the roots of the Western and Eastern traditions, as well as between their modern and postmodern branches.

In fact, upon opening this door to dialogue with the East, what we find is that the Kyoto School of Japanese philosophy has, for several generations now, been passing through it from the other side.

THE PROBLEM OF THE WILL IN OVERCOMING NIHILISM

Nishitani Keiji, the central member of the second generation of the Kyoto School, has responded to the "death of God" and to the increasingly global problem of nihilism by developing a philosophy of Zen Buddhism.[6] In this essay I take up a central aspect of Nishitani's contribution to what he calls the task of "overcoming nihilism by way of passing through nihilism" (NKC 20: 192),[7] namely, his deeply sympathetic and yet ultimately critical interpretation of Nietzsche. Rather than pursuing an exploration of Nishitani's profound affinities with Nietzsche's thought,[8] I shall focus here more on unfolding a confrontation (Gn. Auseinandersetzung) with Nietzsche's central notion of "the will to power" (der Wille zur Macht) on Nishitani's behalf. In the process I shall also be concerned to show how Nishitani's thought develops certain philosophical implications of Zen Buddhism in a manner that resonates with significant post-Nietzschean responses to the crisis of nihilism in the West, that of Heidegger in particular.

A pivotal issue for post-Nietzschean philosophers is the relation between nihilism and the will. This issue can be expressed as a series of questions: Can the nihilism of the death of God be overcome only by accepting Nietzsche's hypothesis that the world and we ourselves are "the will to power—and nothing besides"?[9] Does the death of the "Will of God" leave us with the untrammeled will of man? Does it leave us with the goal of the "overman" understood as a figure of maximum will to power? Can nihilism be "willfully overcome" or, as Heidegger has argued, is the "will to overcome" itself a central component of nihilism?[10] Could a "recovery" (Verwindung) from nihilism perhaps come about only by way of a "step back" from willing into a composed releasement of letting-be (*Gelassenheit*)? Could there be a *radical* negation of the entire domain of the will that leads, *not* to what Nietzsche criticizes as a convoluted "will to nothingness," but rather to an affirmative and active "non-willing" manner of being-in-the-world?[11]

In the context of these questions, Nishitani's philosophy of Zen is significant for two reasons: First, in contrast to Heidegger's criticism of what he calls Nietzsche's "metaphysics of the will to power," by emphasizing the idea of *amor fati* (love of fate) Nishitani is able to give a more nuanced and sympathetic interpretation of the depth and reach of Nietzsche's thought. The second and most significant contribution of Nishitani's thought in this context lies in his development of a Zen Buddhist critique of all forms of will and intimation of a non-willing way of being: a radical reaffirmation of life made possible by first passing through a "great death" (*daishi*) of self-will.

Before turning to Nishitani's philosophy of Zen and his both sympathetic and critical interpretation of Nietzsche, let us first consider the debate between Nietzsche and his critics over the relation between nihilism and the will to power.

Nihilism and the Will: Nietzsche's Critique and Critique of Nietzsche

NIETZSCHE'S CRITIQUE: NIHILISM AS NEGATION OF WILL

According to Nietzsche, nihilism is "the devaluation of the highest values."[12] Life as such is a matter of willfully positing values. By positing values humans impose interpretations on the world; and, insofar as "interpretation is itself a means of becoming master of something,"[13] this interpretive positing of values is an expression of will to power. Nihilism is then understood to result from a weakness of will to power, from a lack of strength to impose an interpretive schema of values on the world. The "death of God" is the pronouncement of an inability to sustain the projection of a transcendent foundation for values—although it could also be said that, for Nietzsche, the history of nihilism begins already with the *birth* of God, since a transference of positive value to heaven implies a devaluation of life on earth, and since a deference to divine Will signifies a degeneration of human will.

According to Nietzsche, nihilism, which arises as the will to affirm life and impart meaning to the world wanes, is found in two forms: a Christian *ressentiment* and a Buddhist renunciation. "Among the nihilistic religions," he writes, "one may always clearly distinguish the Christian from the Buddhist." Buddhism is said to be "a religion for the end and the weariness of civilization," "the expression of a fine evening," a "hedonism of the weary" without bitterness, disillusionment, and rancor. Christianity, on the other hand, is said to be "a degeneracy movement . . . founded on a rancor against everything well-constituted and dominant," a revengeful movement which learned to use "barbaric concepts and values to become master over barbarians."[14]

Nietzsche's fundamental hypothesis, that the world and the self are nothing but the incessant fluctuations of the will to power, underlies his critique of both Christianity and Buddhism. The Western tradition of metaphysics and theology are said to have been built on denying this ineluctable character of all existence, often by way of positing an otherworldly hinterland (*Hinterwelt*) that transcends the willful egoism of this fallen world of becoming. This positing of a *Hinterwelt* is necessarily at the same time a devaluation of this world; it entails a rejection of the earth, even a hatred of life. The history of this devaluation is the history of Western nihilism. However, Nietzsche argues, the rejection of this world is in reality feigned; it is in fact a hypocritical assertion of will to power in disguise. Christianity is characterized as a religion of *ressentiment,* a "slave morality" that denounces the will to power of the strong in a revengeful attempt to posit a "kingdom of God" wherein "the meek shall inherit the earth." The will to power is not in fact transcended, but only disguised, sublimated, and covertly asserted. The "ascetic priest" gains power over others by feigning the negation of his will, and by purporting to serve and represent a higher will; the projected "Will of God" is thus in reality "the condition for the preservation of priestly power."[15]

The "Buddhist negation of the will,"[16] on the other hand, is in Nietzsche's view a more honest form of nihilism; it is a forthright attempt to renounce life as the will to power and the suffering it causes. A Buddhist "yearning for nothingness" (*Sehnsucht in's Nichts*)[17] is a direct confession of a weariness of life; it wills only an end to all willing, which, for Nietzsche, could only mean an end to life as such. Nirvana, as "the extinction of craving," would be the nothingness of sheer non-existence pronounced holy.

Nietzsche nevertheless praises Buddhism for its candid expression of a "passive nihilism."[18] He even asserts that it may be necessary to pass through a "European form of Buddhism" on the way to an "active nihilism" that would clear the ground for a complete overcoming of nihilism by means of a revaluation of all values.[19] A descent into a Buddhist passive nihilism, as a pessimism that acknowledges yet renounces life as the will to power, would prepare us for a radical volte-face to a revaluation that affirms life as the will to power and nothing besides. Nietzsche viewed his own mission in terms of a "self-overcoming of nihilism,"[20] that is, as a descent into the depths of passive ni-hilism in order to bring about a revitalization that would pass through active nihilism and ultimately leave nihilism as such behind. In this sense Nietzsche claims that he could be "the European Buddha" who is at the same time a "counter-image of the Indian Buddha."[21]

CRITIQUE OF NIETZSCHE: NIHILISM AS ASSERTION OF WILL

The force of Nietzsche's critical interpretation of both Christianity and Bud-dhism cannot be denied. And yet, it may be the case that Nietzsche's critique—for all its effectiveness in revealing existing hypocrisies and degenerate forms within these traditions—fails to take account of their most radical message. In particular, it fails to follow their indications of a radical step back from (or "trans-descendence" of) "the life of will to power," a path that would lead, not to a hypocritical "covert will" or to a pessimistic "renunciation of the will to live," but rather to a genuinely alternative way of life, a way of being in this world that is *other than willful or will-less.* Nietzsche's critique may, in fact, ironically serve to help us rediscover and develop the possibilities of a "non-willing" reaffirmation of life as intimated through these traditions.

As we shall see, for example, Nietzsche's critical interpretation of the Bud-dhist doctrines of "suffering" and the goal of "extinction of craving" as signs of pessimism or passive nihilism would be countered by the reaffirmation of a non-egoistic life of spontaneous activity intimated in such expressions as "dharmic naturalness" (Jp. *jinen-hōni*) and "the action of non-action" (Ch. *wei-wuwei;* Jp. *mu-i no i*).[22] Such intimations of the possibility of reaffirming a life of "non-willing" by way of a radical negation of the life of will would, of course, undermine Nietzsche's basic hypothesis that life is the will to power and nothing besides. And insofar as life could not be exclusively defined in terms of the will to power, the very meaning of "nihilism" would need to be rethought. One might even go so far as to redefine nihilism as the inability to see life as consisting of any possible way of being other than the willing of power.

In fact, Nietzsche's thought of the devaluation and revaluation of life as will to power is neither the first nor the last Western understanding of "ni-hilism" and its "overcoming." According to Heidegger, thinking in terms of "values" is itself a symptom of nihilism, insofar as it centers the world on the perspective of the subject and his evaluating will. Heidegger writes that "Nietz-sche's metaphysics is nihilistic insofar as it is value thinking, and insofar as the latter is grounded in will to power as the principle of all valuation."[23] In conclusion to his prolonged *Auseinandersetzung* with Nietzsche's thought, Heidegger goes so far as to claim that "Nietzsche's metaphysics is not an overcoming of nihilism. It is the ultimate entanglement in nihilism."[24] According to Heidegger's own thought of the "history of being," the will to power is the penultimate expression of nihilism, the ultimate stage of which is reached in the cybernetic "will to will" (*der Wille zum Willen*) that pervades the contemporary technological "Europeanization of the earth."

This linking of nihilism to a hubristic assertion of human will is not unique to Heidegger. In fact, Heidegger's post-Nietzschean interpretation of nihilism echoes in some respects a pre-Nietzschean critique. The first philosophical critique of nihilism is generally ascribed to Friedrich Jacobi, who in a famous letter criticized Fichte's idealism of the "absolute ego" as falling into nihilism insofar as it denies the transcendence of God over human reason and will.[25] In a recent study, *Nihilism before Nietzsche,* Michael Allen Gillespie traces the roots of modern nihilism back to the late-medieval reinterpretation of God as absolute and irrational Will. He argues that this inflation of God's absolute power over humans triggered a reactive assertion of human power in modern philosophy from Descartes to Fichte, which paved the way for the late-modern transference of this originally divine character of absolute, irrational will back onto human beings themselves. Gillespie concludes that Nietzsche's proposed "solution to nihilism," in the image of the overman as a figure of maximum will to power, is in fact a "turn to exactly that notion that previously was conceived to be the essence of nihilism."[26] Like Heidegger, Gillespie suggests that what is called for today is neither a regress to a submission to the Will of God, nor a progress toward an inflated human will to mastery of the earth, but rather a step forward beyond nihilism by way of a radical "step back from willing" as such.[27] In order to step back out of nihilism, what is necessary is not a revival of the God of Will, but rather a releasement from the reactive assertion of human will.

Nishitani and the Buddhist Critique of the Will

Nishitani also comes to see nihilism as essentially connected with the problem of the will. In this regard the significance of his contribution to the discussion on how to "overcome" or rather "step back through" nihilism is twofold. On the one hand, Nishitani sympathetically illuminates the path of a "self-overcoming of nihilism" in Nietzsche's thought itself. He finds this self-overcoming at work particularly in the idea of *amor fati,* which he sees as expressing the profoundest moment of affirmation in Nietzsche's thought,[28] and which he interprets in terms of a synthesis or "contradictory identity" of passivity (acceptance of necessity or fate) and activity (love of contingency and the "play" of the will) (see NKC 8: 77; SN 49). On the other hand, Nishitani goes beyond Nietzsche to develop the radical critique of the will which lies at the heart of the Buddhist tradition. In what follows, Nishitani's development of the Buddhist critique of the will, and then his sympathetic as well as his critical interpretations of Nietzsche's thought, will be discussed.

KARMA AND CRAVING: INCLUDING THE DRIVE TO EXPAND THE EGO

According the Second Noble Truth of Buddhism, the primary cause of suffering in the world is "thirst" or "craving" (Pali *tanhā*). Craving can be understood to be a "voluntaristic metaphor" that "attempts to capture the most pervasive affective characteristic of samsaric existence."[29] It is thus both a passion and a volition. In fact, craving is one of several such affective/voluntaristic concepts in Buddhist thought, another of which is *karma*. Karma originally meant "action" or "doing" in general, but in the *Upanishads* as well as in Buddhism it comes to take on the specific meaning of "volitional action" that stems from craving, that is, action that centers on and supports the persistence of the ego. "According to the Buddha's analysis," writes Walpola Rahula, "all the troubles and strife in the world, from little personal quarrels in families to great wars between nations and countries, arise out of this selfish 'thirst.'"[30]

Is Nietzsche's notion of the will to power subject to the Buddhist critique of craving? Nietzsche, to be sure, explicitly denies that his notion of the will to power could be understood as a mere "lust" (*Begierde*) or "drive" (*Trieb*).[31] The will, proclaims Nietzsche's Zarathustra, is not the mere will to exist, or the will to live, but the will to power—"the will to be master."[32] And yet, such a will to mastery and preservation and expansion of power is in fact implied in the Buddhist critique. Rahula explains that "the terms 'thirst,' 'volition,' 'mental volition' and 'karma' all denote the same thing: they denote the desire, the will to be, to exist, to re-exist, to become more and more, to grow more and more, to accumulate more and more."[33] A standard Buddhist dictionary in Japan accordingly defines *bhava-tanhā* not merely as the will to exist, but as "the will to expand the ego."[34]

It is true that, like Buddhism, Nietzsche denies the existence of a *substantial* ego or will.[35] Yet in stark contrast to Buddhism, he does affirm the will as a *process* of *constructing* the ego and expanding its realm of power. "The 'ego' subdues and kills," writes Nietzsche; "it operates like an organic cell: it is a robber and is violent." The "noble soul," he tells us, "accepts this fact of egoism without any question mark." Life, for Nietzsche, "*essentially* is appropriation, injury, overpowering what is alien and weaker; suppression, hardness, imposition of one's own forms, incorporation and at least, at its mildness, exploitation. . . . [Life] simply *is* will to power."[36] If such an attempt to radically affirm life as exploitative egoism and will to power is the starting point of Nietzsche's philosophy, the crucial first step on the path of Buddhism is rather the commitment to a path of radical negation of craving as the will to preserve and expand the domain of the fabricated ego.

INFINITE DRIVE AND MECHANIZATION: A DOUBLE LOSS OF AUTONOMY

Nishitani in fact rarely dwells on Nietzsche's cruder formulations of the will to power; indeed he is often more interested in its life-affirming character, and in general in pursuing—up to a certain critical point—the proximity of Nietzsche's thought to Zen.

Before turning to Nishitani's sympathetic and critical engagement with Nietzsche's thought, however, let us first examine how Nishitani interprets and develops the Buddhist critique of the will. He does so in terms of what he calls the "infinite drive" of "self-will" that manifests itself in an exacerbated form in the nihilism of secular modernity. Nishitani too traces the modern problem of the will in part back to the monotheistic attempt to overcome the problem of egoistic human will by positing a transcendent Will of God. He argues—in a manner not unrelated to Nietzsche's critique of the hypocrisies of the ascetic priest's feigned deference of will—that here "self-centeredness appears once again, only this time on a higher plane: as the will of self backed up by the Will of God" (NKC 10: 223; RN 203).

Yet the "death of God" at the hands of modern secularism leaves us in an ambivalent situation. On the one hand, freedom from religious teleology (that is, from time structured according to the Will of God) allows humans to recover their autonomy, to become "autotelic." On the other hand, the self-centered autonomy of the egoistic will is not yet a true autonomy, since the self ultimately finds itself subject to an aimless "infinite drive" from below. In an age of secularism, writes Nishitani, "every function of life, as something that is autotelic and therefore aimless, is given over to the unrestricted pursuit of itself. Is it is here that the infinite drive, or what may be termed 'self-will,' is to be seen" (NKC 10: 259; RN 236). The volitional "autonomy" of the ego is only apparent insofar as it remains driven by passions and cravings. Here we find that, just as the apparent "passivity" of a purported submission to the Will of God can conceal a sublated self-will, the apparent "autonomy" of secularism may conceal a tendency toward a reversion to heteronomous "animality."

Moreover, this usurpation of autonomy from within is compounded from without by an increasing mechanization of (human) nature. In modern industrialized societies we find ourselves subjected to a peculiar inversion whereby "the controller becomes the controlled." While science and technology are developed under the auspices of increasing human freedom and power over nature, at "the extreme of the freedom of the self in controlling the laws of nature, man shows the countertendency to forfeit his human nature and to mechanize it" (NKC 10: 95; RN 84). As Heidegger points out, the problem of technology is not just that of human agents reducing nature to "natural resources"; humans themselves are increasingly being reduced to "human resources" for the increasingly cybernetic capitalistic machinery of production and consumption.[37]

In short, we are confronted with *a double loss of autonomy* in an age of extreme secularism. Human self-assertion over against God and nature leads to a situation where "the emergence of the mechanization of human life and the transformation of man into a completely non-rational subject in pursuit of his desires are fundamentally bound up with one another" (NKC 10: 98; RN 87). In this sense, Nishitani understands the modern crisis of nihilism in terms of a *failed* assertion of human autonomy that paradoxically succumbs to the dual heteronomies of exterior technological mechanization and the interior infinite drive of self-will.

Nishitani interprets this paradoxical symbiosis of assertion and loss of will in terms of a "demythologized" notion of *karma* (NKC 10: 260; RN 237).[38] Behind the scientific rationality and technological will of modern human being, he writes, lurks the same "infinite drive" that the ancient Buddhist doctrine of *karma* sought to expose (NKC 11: 168). In the great yet ultimately ambivalent secular revolution, "at the bottom of the elevation of human reason to independence, we find hidden an important event: the 'being' of human being becomes a matter of will" (NKC 10: 258; RN 235; translation modified). Yet the standpoint of secular humanism still conceals the problematic heteronomous character of this will as an infinite drive. Here the notion of *karma* can help, Nishitani suggests, since it "implies this self-awareness."

CUTTING THE ROOT:

THE POSSIBILITY OF RADICAL FREEDOM FROM SELF-WILL

Nihilism can be understood, according to Nishitani, as the "great ball of doubt" (*daigidan*) of the modern age. Paralleling its role in Zen practice, this great doubt has the positive potential to lead us to a deeper "investigation of the self" (*kojikyūmei*). This investigation reveals first of all that we are accustomed to living on what Nishitani calls the "field of [subjective] consciousness" (*ishiki no ba*), which is also the "field of possession/being" (*u no ba*). Drawing on the dual meaning of the character for "being" (Ch. *you*; Jp. *u*), which can mean both "existing" and "having" or "possessing," Nishitani depicts life on this field in the following manner: "By 'having' something outside the self, one seeks to secure one's 'being'; one is held by what one holds, in other words, 'possession' and 'existence' are bound together in a primordial will [*konpon-iyoku*] as a basic state of mind." In the crisis of nihilism one finds this existence of possessing and being possessed by beings slipping away, and the abyss of the "field of nihility" (*kyomu no ba*) opens up around one. Here arises the final temptation of the will, namely, that of the nihilist who attaches himself to this experience of nihility and to acts of annihilation. Still here a "deep trace of the primordial will" can be found. It is only by "cutting the root" of this primordial will altogether, writes Nishitani, that one could step back through the field of nihility and hence beyond nihilism (NKC 11: 190–91).

For Nishitani, nihilism is a crisis (*kiki*) both in the sense of the greatest danger (*kiken*)—the reduction of human being to the infinite drive of self-will—and in the sense of a great opportunity (*kikai*); for here the roots of the "primordial will" lie exposed. By cutting these roots a conversion to "the standpoint of *śūnyatā*" is possible, for "the standpoint of *śūnyatā* is first established at a bottomless place that exceeds by way of absolute negation all standpoints of any kind related to will" (NKC 10: 276; RN 251; translation modified).

THROUGH NEGATION TO REAFFIRMATION:

PLAYFUL *SAMĀDHI* AND THE ACTION OF NON-ACTION

We can speculate that Nietzsche would have mistaken this "great death" or "absolute negation of the will" for a renunciation of life itself. Like many Western interpreters of Buddhism in the nineteenth century, he misunderstood *nirvāna* in terms of a doctrine of annihilationism.[39] Insofar as Nietzsche considered the will to power to be the essence of life as such, the "right effort" to attain *nirvāna* could only appear to him as a "will to nothingness." But from the beginning Buddhist teachings clearly and consistently rejected both the doctrine of "annihilationism" (Pali *ucchedavāda*) and the "craving for non-existence" (Pali *vibhava-tanhā*). The rejection of these nihilistic doctrines suggests that *nirvāna* is not mere "extinction": The negation of craving opens the door to a higher affirmation. In Mahāyāna Buddhism, and Zen in particular, it is clear that the great negation of the will leads not to an annihilation of life, but rather to a great affirmation of a non-ego-centered life of non-attachment, that is, to an active yet "non-willing" way of being-in-this-world.

According to Nishitani, the "great negation" entailed in the experience of emptiness or *śūnyatā* does not put an end to all activity, but rather clears the ground for a radically different kind of ceaseless activity, one no longer centered on the ego and producing karmic debt. On the ultimate field of the non-duality of *samsāra* and *nirvāna,* "constant doing is constant non-doing," and "all being-at-doing . . . takes the shape of non-doing." Now "all our work takes on the character of play," for here "working and playing become manifest fundamentally and at bottom as sheer, elemental doing," or what Zen calls "playful *samādhi*" (*yuge-zammai*) (NKC 10: 277–79; RN 252–53). Nishitani uses the image of the "child" to depict the "dharmic naturalness" (*jinen-hōni*) of innocent activity that is at once play and elemental earnestness; "for the child is never more earnest than when engaged in play" (NKC 10: 281; RN 255). The earnest play of the child serves as an analogy for the "radical spontaneity" that characterizes life after the great death of self-will.

Nishitani on (the Limits of) Nietzsche's Self-Overcoming of Nihilism

AMOR FATI: NIETZSCHE'S CHILD AT PLAY

Yet does not Zen's "playful *samādhi*" and Nishitani's child at "earnest play" remind us of Nietzsche's own metaphoric imagery?[40] And indeed, does not Nietzsche's "child," who appears as the third metamorphosis of the spirit in *Thus Spoke Zarathustra,* represent "a new beginning, a game, a self-propelled wheel, a first movement, a sacred 'Yes'"?[41] In his 1949 book, *Nihilism* (translated as *The Self-Overcoming of Nihilism*), Nishitani develops one of the most insightful interpretations of Nietzsche's thought, and of its proximity to Zen, by focusing on Nietzsche's ideas of eternal recurrence, *amor fati,* and play. It is in this context that Nishitani writes: "Ironically, it was not in his nihilistic view of Buddhism but in such ideas as *amor fati* and the Dionysian as the overcoming of nihilism that Nietzsche came closest to Buddhism, and especially to Mahāyāna" (NKC 8: 185; SN 180).

The experience of the eternal recurrence of the same, Nishitani points out, threatens to crush the will with the weight of fatalistic necessity. Only if the will is strong enough to affirm life—all of life—unconditionally can it withstand the test of this greatest weight; only then can it undergo a "turn of need" (*Wende der Not*) whereby necessity (*Notwendigkeit*) becomes one with freedom. Here the will turns into a love of fate, and fate is united with the self. Nishitani interprets Nietzsche's phrase *ego fatum* to imply that "the world moves at one with the self, and the self moves at one with the world." "This idea," he goes on to say, "could be thought of as close to the Buddhist idea of 'karma'; however, Nietzsche's standpoint is a fundamentally creative one" (NKC 8: 78; SN 50; translation modified). This "creativity" would mark a decisive difference, for *amor fati* would not be a matter of suffering an external compulsion, but would mean that the "world appears as the 'playful' activity of will to power and at the same time as fate" (NKC 8: 75; SN 148).

Commenting on Nietzsche's lines, "Fate, says the grumbler, the fool calls it—play," Nishitani writes: "To immerse oneself in the 'play' of the samsaric world and its groundless activity, and to live it to the utmost, is the 'pantheistic' life" of Nietzsche's new Dionysian "religion." *Amor fati* would be a matter of joyful participation in the "divine play" (*göttliches Spiel*) of the "worlding of the world." Here concepts of "necessity" and "will" would both be eliminated, suggests Nietzsche at one point,[42] and Nishitani interprets this to imply that "complete fate comes to be, just as it is, complete freedom," and "effort remains effort and yet becomes effortless" (NKC 8: 95; SN 62; translation modified). Nishitani concludes that this conversion to *amor fati* marks the point where one finds "the self-overcoming of nihilism itself in Nietzsche" (NKC 8: 103; SN 68). Here, after the destructive will of the lion has done its work, a new child of laughter is born.[43]

The child's innocent affirmation would thus lie beyond the negating "I will" of the lion. And yet, would the child's play then no longer be driven by the will to power? Nietzsche's answer, at least the answer we find in the text at this point, is No. The sacred Yes of the new game of creation, we are told, would inaugurate yet another will to power: "the spirit now wills his own will, and he who had been lost to the world now conquers his own world."[44]

REMAINING TETHERED TO A STANDPOINT OF WILL

Nishitani began writing on Nietzsche by comparing his thought to that of Meister Eckhart in a remarkable essay written in 1938, titled "Nietzsche's Zarathustra and Meister Eckhart" (NKC 1: 5–32). In this essay Nishitani sought to reveal the dynamic of a self-overcoming of nihilism at the heart of both this late-modern philosopher, who announced the death of God, and this late-medieval mystic-thinker, who spoke of breaking through the persona of God to a oneness with the divine Nothingness of the Godhead. Nishitani found a "dialectic of life"—a reaffirmation of human existence made possible only by way of its thorough self-negation—at work both in Nietzsche's radical atheism and in Eckhart's radical theism. He then pursued this interpretation of each thinker further in the two central works of his middle period, *God and Absolute Nothingness* (NKC 7) and *The Self-Overcoming of Nihilism*.

However, by the time of his magnum opus, *What is Religion?* (translated as *Religion and Nothingness*), Nishitani credits Eckhart with having pursued the path of negation-*sive*-affirmation further than did Nietzsche. According to Nishitani, "Nietzsche does not seem to have attained Eckhart's standpoint of an absolute nothingness that takes its stand on the immediacy of everyday life," and this is said to reflect "the difference between a nihility proclaiming that 'God is dead' and an absolute nothingness reaching a point beyond even 'God'; or between life forcing its way through nihility to gush forth and life as absolute death-*sive*-life." While Eckhart more nearly approaches the Zen Buddhist standpoint of *śūnyatā* or absolute nothingness, "the nihility of Nietzsche's nihilism should be called a standpoint of *relative absolute nothingness*" (NKC 10: 75; RN 66).

If Eckhart was able to pursue this path of "self-overcoming" in his trans-mystical theism more radically than Nietzsche could do so with his trans-nihilistic atheism, for Nishitani this was possible only because Eckhart clearly speaks of breaking through and standing emptied of *both* self-will *and* the Will of God (NKC 10: 73; RN 64).[45] For Nishitani, only by letting go of *both* assertion of self-will *and* subservience to a higher Will can we step back through nihilism to "the field of emptiness" as a groundless ground of earnest play. While Nietzsche's notion of the *Unschuld des Werdens* approaches this "pure activity beyond the measure of any teleological gauge," in the end it remains still tethered to a "standpoint of will" (NKC 10: 285, 292; RN 258, 265).

Nishitani explicitly criticizes the doctrine of the will to power from the standpoint of emptiness (Sk. *śūnyatā*; Jp. *kū*) as well as from the standpoint of non-ego (Sk. *anātman*; Jp. *muga*). Insofar as the will to power ultimately remains "something conceived of in the third person as an 'it,' it has yet to shed the character of 'being something,' that is, of being a *Seiendes*" (NKC 10: 237; RN 216; translation modified). Graham Parkes rightly points out that this criticism is invalid if it implies that Nietzsche reified the will to power; for "Nietzsche characterizes will to power as a force (*Kraft*) rather than a 'thing.'"[46] Yet I think Nishitani's main concern here is heteronomy rather than reification. As long as the will to power does not "completely lose its connotation of being an other for us" (NKC 10: 257; RN 234), we remain bound to a desire, determined by a drive which remains outside the indeterminable freedom and abyssal openness of what Nishitani calls the "radical subjectivity of non-ego [*muga*]" as a "subjective Nothingness" (*shutai-teki mu*) (NKC 1: 88). Nietzsche, as a matter of fact, writes that even those who command must obey the will to power, as even the greatest soul cannot help but "risk life for the sake of power."[47] The freedom of the self is thus for Nietzsche limited by its inability to step back beneath and beyond the purportedly fundamental drive of the will to power.

Nishitani, to be sure, never succumbed to the temptation to reduce the subtleties of Nietzsche's thought of the will to power to a simple affirmation of a biological drive or a brute "lust for authoritative power" (*kenryoku-yoku*).[48] In fact, Nishitani never lost his appreciation for a positive sense of the will to power as a creative life-force that wells up after a great negation (NKC 1: 26; 15: 338). In *Religion and Nothingness,* Nishitani still affirms that "for Nietzsche, it was the will to power that appeared in the conversion from a great death to a great life" (NKC 10: 254; RN 232; translation modified). In the end, however, the radicality of both Nietzsche's negation and his reaffirmation of life are said to remain limited insofar as the "standpoint of will" is not cast off. A "cutting the roots of the will" is what ultimately distinguishes Nishitani's "standpoint of Zen" from Nietzsche's philosophy of will to power.

Only by way of a great death of the will to power could Nietzsche's *amor fati* and the innocence of becoming, twisting free of self-will no less than the Will of God, reach the standpoint indicated by Zen expressions such as playful *samādhi* and the doing of non-doing. Such expressions are said to articulate a "true freedom that is not simply a matter of the freedom of the will" (NKC 10: 314; RN 285). This is the standpoint of Mahāyāna Buddhism that Nishitani had claimed "cannot yet be reached even by a nihilism that overcomes nihilism, even though the latter may reach in that direction" (NKC 8: 185; SN 180; translation modified).

Conclusion: Overcoming Nietzsche by Way of Passing through Nietzsche

Nietzsche's provocative thought, and in particular his critical exposure of the will to power that hypocritically operates beneath the surface of many traditional doctrines and practices, has helped to expose the roots of modern Western—and increasingly, global—nihilism. After Nietzsche's announcement of the death of God, traditional answers to ultimate questions often appear much less convincing. Submissive obedience to the Will of God, for example, no longer simply appears as an innocent and viable answer to the problem of egoistic self-will. Indeed, in an age that is threatened by a regressive tendency to religious wars, appeals to the Will of God often appear to be desperate and hostile expressions of communal self-will.

Nietzsche forcefully uncovered a pervasiveness of the will to power in our lives. Yet we may accept Nietzsche's critique without simply accepting either his affirmation of the will to power as the ultimate fact of the world and ourselves, or his embrace of an active nihilism that would prepare for the overman as a figure of maximal will to power.

The dynamic subtleties of Nietzsche's thought, to be sure, are multifaceted and many-layered; and certain provocations such as "master morality" have often been misunderstood and interpretively abused, by his enthusiasts no less than his critics. Moreover, as Nishitani helps reveal, the ultimate message of Nietzsche's thought lies not in his "no-saying" polemics against the past and present, but in his future-oriented intimations of a profound "yes-saying": for example, Zarathustra's teaching of a "gift-giving virtue" that forces "all things to and into yourself that they may flow back out of your well as the gifts of your love."[49] The ultimate figure of this yes-saying is not the infamous "blond beast" of violent destruction and egoistic revelry, but rather "the over-hero" (*der Über-Held*) who, at the end of an arduous path of *self*-overcoming, "unlearns even his heroic will" and is thereby elevated as "the will-less one" (*der Willenlose*).[50]

Nevertheless, it must be said that such intimations of what I would call a "self-overcoming of the will to power" in Nietzsche's *Denkweg* remain at least underdeveloped, and perhaps irredeemably ambivalent.[51] To the end, Nietzsche's thought remains torn between a resolute affirmation and a self-overcoming of egoistic will to power.[52]

Nishitani's deeply sympathetic yet ultimately critical interpretation of Nietzsche from the standpoint of Zen Buddhism makes a significant contribution to thinking through nihilism and the problem of the will. Nishitani's style of thought in general can be characterized as an "overcoming by way of passing through." A major avenue on his path of "overcoming nihilism by way of passing through nihilism" is his interpretation of Nietzsche, which could indeed be characterized as an overcoming of Nietzsche by way of passing through Nietzsche. Nishitani takes seriously not only the critical impact of the doctrine of the will to power, but also its "reaffirmative" aspect, that is, its expression of a great affirmation by way of a great negation. And yet, in the end, Nietzsche's reaffirmation is found to remain limited insofar as residues of heteronomy as well as of egocentricity inevitably remain in a philosophy of will to power. It is necessary not only to unblinkingly accept the death of the transcendent God of Will, but also to undergo the "great death" of human will to power. Only by thoroughly cutting off the roots of self-will could *amor fati* truly intimate a conversion to a spontaneous love of life and life of love. Only then would the great affirmation of life entail a dharmic naturalness or an action of non-action freed from the cycle of karmic debt, together with a compassionate gift-giving that springs, not from a guilty conscience, but from a realization that the true self is the non-ego of the "self that is not a self," the self that ek-statically exists in the world with others.

Nishitani's philosophy of Zen entails an unflinching acceptance of the death of the transcendent God of Will and also the modern pervasiveness of the will to power—without giving these or other forms of nihilism the last word. It suggests a way toward being in the world in a manner "other than" *either* regressive submission to God's Will *or* reactive assertion of human self-will, a way that passes through a radical negation to a radical reaffirmation of life beyond both deference and assertion of will.

NOTES

An earlier version of this essay was written and published in Japanese as "Kami no shi kara ishi no daishi e: posuto-Niiche no tetsugakusha toshite no Nishitani Keiji" [From the death of God to the great death of the will: Nishitani Keiji as a post-Nietzschean philosopher], in Fujita Masakatsu and Bret W. Davis, eds., *Sekai no naka no Nihon no tetsugaku* [Japanese philosophy in the world] (Kyoto: Shōwadō, 2005), and the present English version is printed here with permission of the publisher. Material has also been incorporated from my more encompassing article on this topic, "Zen after Zarathustra: The Problem of the Will in the Confrontation between Nietzsche and Buddhism," *Journal of Nietzsche Studies* 28 (2004): 89–138, and is reprinted here with permission of the publisher.

1. *Nietzsche Kritische Gesamtausgabe*, ed. Giorgio Colli and Mazzino Montinari (Berlin: Walter de Gruyter, 1967ff.), div. 5, 2: 145, 159, 255; *The Gay Science*, trans. Walter Kaufmann (New York: Vintage, 1974), §§108, 125, 343. In general, references to Nietzsche's works will hereafter be given according to title followed by part and section numbers. I have in all cases consulted the original German text in the *Kritische Gesamt-ausgabe* and in *Der Wille zur Macht: Versuch einer Umwertung aller Werte* (Stuttgart:

Alfred Kröner Verlag, 1996). With occasional modifications, I have generally adopted the translations by Walter Kaufman in *The Portable Nietzsche,* ed. Walter Kaufmann (New York: Viking Penguin, 1982) and *Basic Writings of Nietzsche,* ed. Walter Kaufmann (New York: Random House, 1968), and by Walter Kaufman and R. J. Hollingdale in *The Will to Power,* ed. Walter Kaufmann (New York: Random House, 1967).

2. See Nietzsche, *Nietzsche Contra Wagner,* Epilogue, §§1–2.

3. Martin Heidegger, "Das Ende der Philosophie und die Aufgabe des Denkens," in *Zur Sache des Denkens,* 3rd edition (Tübingen: Max Niemeyer, 1988); "The End of Philosophy and the Task of Thinking," in *Basic Writings,* ed. David Farrell Krell (New York: Harper & Row, 1993).

4. Martin Heidegger, *Wegmarken* (*Gesamtausgabe* 9) (Frankfurt am Main: Vittorio Klostermann, 1985), 424; *Pathmarks,* ed. William McNeill (Cambridge: Cambridge University Press, 1998), 321.

5. Martin Heidegger, *Vorträge und Aufsätze,* 7th edition (Pfullingen: Neske, 1994), 43; *The Question Concerning Technology and Other Essays,* trans. William Lovitt (New York: Harper & Row, 1977), 158.

6. For an introduction to Nishitani's philosophy of Zen and his treatment of nihilism, see Bret W. Davis, "The Step Back Through Nihilism: The Radical Orientation of Nishitani Keiji's Philosophy of Zen," *Synthesis Philosophica* 37 (2004): 139–59.

7. Unless otherwise indicated, all translations from Japanese are my own.

8. In this regard see the pioneering works by Graham Parkes: "Nishitani on the Self Through Time," *The Eastern Buddhist* 17, no. 2 (1984): 55–74; the translator's introduction to Nishitani Keiji, *The Self-Overcoming of Nihilism,* trans. Graham Parkes with Setsuko Aihara (Albany: State University of New York Press, 1990); "Nietzsche and Nishitani on the Self-Overcoming of Nihilism," *International Studies in Philosophy* 25, no. 2 (1993): 51–60; and "Nietzsche and East Asian Thought: Influences, Impacts, and Resonances," in Bernd Magnus and Kathleen M. Higgins, eds., *The Cambridge Companion to Nietzsche* (Cambridge: Cambridge University Press, 1996). While Parkes reports that Nishitani admitted in conversation that "the parallels between Nietzsche's thinking and his own run farther than he was prepared to allow in *Religion and Nothingness*" ("Nietzsche and East Asian Thought," 381), Parkes nevertheless concludes elsewhere: "While I remain confident that Nietzsche's ideas come closer to certain types of Zen thinking than Japanese philosophers are willing to admit, I still believe that Nishitani's mature thought . . . may indeed comprehend and in some respects go beyond what Nietzsche has wrought" ("Nietzsche and Nishitani on the Self-Overcoming of Nihilism," 59).

9. Nietzsche, *The Will to Power,* §1067; also see *Thus Spoke Zarathustra,* II, §12, and *Beyond Good and Evil,* §38.

10. Martin Heidegger, *Nietzsche,* 5th edition (Pfullingen: Neske, 1989), 2: 389; *Nietzsche Volume IV: Nihilism,* trans. Frank A. Capuzzi (New York: Harper & Row, 1982), 243.

11. Heidegger's later thought is characterized by a radical critique of the will and a search for a "non-willing" way of being that would lie beyond the traditional dichotomy of activity and passivity. See Bret W. Davis, *Heidegger and the Will: On the Way to Gelassenheit* (Evanston, Ill.: Northwestern University Press, 2007).

12. Nietzsche, *The Will to Power,* §132.

13. Ibid., §643.

14. Ibid., §§154–55; and *The Antichrist,* §22. It should be born in mind that Nietzsche claimed that Christ himself had transcended the spirit of revenge: "there was only one Christian, and he died on the cross" (*The Antichrist,* §39).

15. Nietzsche, *The Antichrist*, §26. Also see *The Genealogy of Morals*, I, §7.

16. Nietzsche, *The Birth of Tragedy*, §7.

17. Nietzsche, *The Will to Power*, §1.

18. In *The Will to Power*, §§22–23, Nietzsche writes that "nihilism" is ambiguous; "*active* nihilism" refers to an "increased power of the spirit," whereas "*passive* nihilism," which he equates with Buddhism, is a "sign of weariness" and a "decline and recession of the power of the spirit."

19. Ibid., §132.

20. Friedrich Nietzsche, *Grossoktavausgabe*, ed. Nietzsche Archive (Leipzig: Kröner, 1894–1912), 16: 422. Nishitani refers to this note in NKC 8: 98; SN 64.

21. Nietzsche, *Kritische Gesamtausgabe*, div. 7, 1: 111.

22. Nietzsche's knowledge and critique of Buddhism is evidently restricted to the so-called Hīnayāna schools, such as Theravāda. For two studies that respond to Nietzsche's critique from a Theravada perspective, pointing out the "ironic affinities" between Nietzsche's thought and Buddhism, see Freny Mistry, *Nietzsche and Buddhism: Prolegomenon to a Comparative Study* (Berlin: Walter de Gruyter, 1981); and Robert Morrison, *Nietzsche and Buddhism: A Study in Ironic Affinities* (Oxford: Oxford University Press, 1997). However, it must be said that the Buddhist reaffirmation of life is generally more explicit and indeed more radical in Mahāyāna, and in schools such as Zen in particular.

23. Heidegger, *Nietzsche*, 2: 342; *Nietzsche Volume IV: Nihilism*, 204.

24. Ibid., 340; 203.

25. *Friedrich Heinrich Jacobis Werke*, ed. J. F. Köppen and C. J. F. Roth (Leipzig: Gerhard Fleischer, 1816), 3: 49; repr. Darmstadt: Wissenschaftliche Buchgesellschaft, 1968. For Jacobi, a reassertion of faith in the absolute transcendence of God over man is the answer to the nihilism of an absolutization of the human ego. Nietzsche in effect turns the tables on Jacobi by claiming that it is in fact the absolute transcendence of God that nihilistically negates the immanent value of this world. Nishitani's thought suggests, however, that a Buddhist dialectic of "absolute negation-*sive*-absolute affirmation" offers a radical "middle path" beyond *both* versions of nihilism.

26. Michael Allen Gillespie, *Nihilism before Nietzsche* (Chicago: University of Chicago Press, 1995), xx.

27. Gillespie criticizes Heidegger for not having investigated the origins of nihilism in late-medieval theological voluntarism, and even claims that Heidegger falls back into the same trap of attempting to overcome human will by hypostatizing a "will of Being" (xxii). However, this critique does not take account of the fact that Heidegger explicitly distinguishes his notion of *Gelassenheit* from a "letting self-will go in favor of divine will," and in general his attempt to think the relation between humans and being outside "the domain of activity and passivity." See Martin Heidegger, *Country Path Conversations*, trans. Bret W. Davis (Bloomington: Indiana University Press, 2010), 70; and Davis, *Heidegger and the Will*, chaps. 5 and 8.

28. Nishitani Keiji and Abe Masao, "Taidan: Sekai-aku to nihirizumu" [Conversation on world-evil and nihilism], in Abe Masao, *Kyogi to kyomu* [Falsity and nihility] (Kyoto: Hōzōkan, 2000), 193.

29. See Morrison, *Nietzsche and Buddhism*, 138–39.

30. Walpola Rahula, *What the Buddha Taught*, rev. edition (Bedford: Gordon Fraser, 1967), 29–30.

31. See Nietzsche, *The Will to Power*, §84.

32. Nietzsche, *Thus Spoke Zarathustra*, II, §12.

33. Rahula, *What the Buddha Taught,* 31.

34. *Iwanami Bukkyōjiten* [Iwanami dictionary of Buddhism] (Tokyo: Iwanami, 1989), 53.

35. See Nietzsche, *Beyond Good and Evil,* §§16–17; and *The Will to Power,* §715.

36. Nietzsche, *The Will to Power,* §768; *Beyond Good and Evil,* §§259, 265.

37. See Martin Heidegger, *Vorträge und Aufsätze,* 7th edition (Pfullingen: Neske, 1994), 21; *Basic Writings,* ed. David Farrell Krell (New York: Harper & Row, 1993), 323.

38. Nishitani is more concerned with the doctrine of *karma* as an account of our existential manner of being in the world than as a cosmological doctrine of rebirth.

39. See Roger-Pol Droit, *Le Culte du néant: Les Philosophes et le Bouddha* (Paris: Éditions de Seuil, 1997); *The Cult of Nothingness: The Philosophers and the Buddha,* trans. David Streight and Pamela Vohnson (Chapel Hill: The University of North Carolina Press, 2003).

40. See Ueda Shizuteru's interpretation of Nietzsche's "child" in Ueda Shizuteru and Yanagida Seizan, *Jūgyūzu: Jiko no genshōgaku* [The ten ox pictures: the phenomenology of self] (Tokyo: Chikuma, 1992), 146–49. According to Ueda, on the one hand Nietzsche's image of the child expresses a "forgetting" or "dropping off" (*datsuraku*) of the will to power for the sake of a more originary natural playfulness. On the other hand, the innocence of the child is said to fall short of the "old man" found in the final stage of Zen's *Ten Ox Pictures,* who has not only "forgotten power" but who compassionately reaches out to help others.

41. Nietzsche, *Thus Spoke Zarathustra,* I, §1.

42. See Nietzsche, *The Will to Power,* §1060.

43. And yet, does Nietzsche's Zarathustra himself ever learn to laugh this radiant, over-human laughter? Nietzsche writes rather that a "thirst" and "yearning [*Sehnsucht*] for this laughter" gnaws on Zarathustra (*Thus Spoke Zarathustra,* III, §2). Could perhaps the future laughter that Zarathustra yearned for be found echoing from the distant past of the East? See Ōhashi Ryōsuke, "'Hi' to 'kōshō': *Tsuaratosutora wa kaku katatta* to Zen" ["Compassion" and "laughter": *Thus Spoke Zarathustra* and Zen], in Ōhashi Ryōsuke, *Hi no genshōron josetsu: Nihontetsugaku no roku teeze yori* [Prolegomenon to a phenomenology of compassion: from six theses of Japanese philosophy] (Tokyo: Sōbunsha, 1998), 161–77.

44. Nietzsche, *Thus Spoke Zarathustra,* I, §1.

45. See *Meister Eckehart: Deutsche Predigten und Traktate,* ed. and trans. J. Quint (Munich: Hanser, 1963), 308.

46. Parkes, "Nietzsche and Nishitani on the Self-Overcoming of Nihilism," 58. Parkes refers here to *Beyond Good and Evil,* §36.

47. Nietzsche, *Thus Spoke Zarathustra,* II, §12.

48. See Nishitani's comments in a 1949 dialogue with Watsuji Tetsurō and others, reprinted in NKC 15: 348.

49. Nietzsche, *Thus Spoke Zarathustra,* I, §22.

50. Ibid., II, §13.

51. For a more extensive and nuanced treatment of the ambivalence of Nietzsche's "self-overcoming of the will to power," and of the problem of the will in Buddhism, see my "Zen after Zarathustra."

52. A number of noteworthy Nietzsche interpretations have reached similar conclusions. See for example Wolfgang Müller-Lauter, *Nietzsche: His Philosophy of Con-*

tradictions and the Contradictions of his Philosophy, trans. David J. Parent (Chicago: University of Illinois Press, 1999); Karl Löwith, *Sämtliche Schriften,* vol. 6: *Nietzsche* (Stuttgart: J. B. Metzlersche, 1987), 426; Ōkōchi Ryōgi, *Niiche to Bukkyō: Kongenteki Nihirizumu no Mondai* [Nietzsche and Buddhism: the problem of radical nihilism] (Kyoto: Hōzōkan, 1983), 207–208, 214; and Ryōgi Ōkōchi, "Nietzsches amor fati im Lichte von Karma des Buddhismus," *Nietzsche-Studien* I (1972): 86, 88.

6

Empty Soul, Empty World: Nietzsche and Nishitani

DAVID JONES

In *Nishida Kitarō*, a collection of essays written about his teacher from 1936 to 1968, Nishitani Keiji provides a portrait of Nishida's most important work, *An Inquiry into the Good*. For Nishitani, to arrive at the Good entails the deployment of the non-differentiating love of *agapē*. To deploy *agapē* is to "empty oneself." This emptying of the soul first shows itself as a flowing-over beyond the field of the ego into the indifferent realm of the non-ego. For Nishitani, this *kenōsis* is more than the self-emptying of Christ—it is an emptying of God himself into the world. Thinking *agapē* in the sense of *kenōsis* differentiates Nishitani from those heterodox Christian thinkers who would see Jesus' entering the world as a forfeiture of his divine qualities (which reinforces the dualistic and transcendent nature many Christians see in their religion), and aligns him with those who view *kenōsis* as a hypostatic union where Jesus "takes the form of being a servant," as stated in *Philippians* 5:2, "in the likeness of man."

Such a metaphor of *kenōsis* is found prior to Nishitani, in modern philosophy, in Nietzsche's *Thus Spoke Zarathustra*: "I love him whose soul is overfull, so that he forgets himself, and all things are in him: in this way all things, come to be his going-under."[1] Zarathustra, the advocate of the circle, the advocate of life, declares that his "cup . . . wants to overflow, that the water may flow from it golden and carry everywhere the reflection of [the star's] delight [*Wonne*]. Behold, this cup wants to become empty again, and Zarathustra wants to become human again."[2] This self-emptying is the perfect mode of being constituted by *karuna*, or Buddhist compassion. The lack of selfishness is ultimately what is meant by non-ego, or emptiness, and constitutes the *mahākaruna*, or Great Compassion, of Buddhism. Although not obvious in the works of Nietzsche, this sense of compassion is nevertheless present;

it is through the lens of Nishitani's writings and Buddhism that the idea of compassion becomes more visible in Nietzsche. This is perhaps the reason Nishitani thinks Nietzsche has not quite realized that emptiness is even more profound than his nihility.

The implications of such views and practices are radical in nature: All visible forms of the experienced world are radically transformed by losing their substantiality, and a fundamental conversion of the human way of being in the world requires a new religiosity. This new religiosity implicates the world and its inhabitants in a sweeping and deep-seated ontological and ethical egalitarianism of occasion that is apparent in both thinkers, notwithstanding Nishitani's reluctance to see his work as being overly close to Nietzsche's. Such implications are radically *ecological,* in that human nature and what constitutes a self are fundamentally and vitally redefined.

The Channel Forms as the Water Flows

In the chapter "What is Religion?" in his *Religion and Nothingness,* Nishitani attempts to plumb the fundamental religiosity of religion. In spite of the apparently fundamental differences underlying Christianity and Buddhism—most notably, Christianity's transcendent orientation and Buddhism's inherently immanent dimensions—Nishitani insists on bringing together the "Buddha's Vow of Compassion" as "the name for the unity of the Buddha and all things" (RN 26) with Christianity. In this process he invokes Christian scripture and the Christian philosopher Kierkegaard by earlier discussing Christian agapic love[3] through a discussion of the ego self: "The ego represents the subjectivity of the individual, but as the standpoint of 'ego' it can be universalized into the standpoint of everyone else" (RN 27). This universalization of the self, however, will not ultimately prevail for Nishitani (as it would in some form of Upanishadic monism). To universalize the self in this fashion is to fall prey ultimately to egoism, since the "characteristic of [this] ego is already apparent in . . . the Cartesian *cogito ergo sum.*" The self of the ego is for Nishitani (as for Kierkegaard) "incapable of the true self" (which is the solitary self in Kierkegaard) (RN 27).

However, it is Nietzsche and not Kierkegaard who is closest to Nishitani, for of all Western thinkers it is Nietzsche who was most aware of the dangers of defining self as ego. Not only is it the self of the self-centered individual in a psychological sense, that Nietzsche and Nishitani wish to do away with, but even more radically it is the sense of any self—be that the *cogito* or a sense of the self as free agent. Nietzsche and Nishitani thus target whatever underlies the psychological, cognitive, and volitional senses of what constitutes a self. In one of the most famous passages on the topic, Nietzsche writes that

> a thought comes when "it" wishes, and not when I wish, so that it is a falsification of the facts . . . to say that the subject "I" is the condition of the predicate "think." *It* thinks; but that this "it" is precisely the famous old "ego" is, to put it mildly, only a supposition, an assertion, and assuredly not an "immediate certainty."[4]

The quest for certainty, beginning with Plato and culminating in Descartes, was a reaction to the fear of becoming. Hypothesized Being became life's *pharmakon,* for we needed a cure for the deadly disease of change and movement—a cure for this deadly disease we call life. And now our crisis of faith in the West, which is given witness to in fundamentalism and literalism, cries out for a new *pharmakon* against the deadly diseases of will, ego, and spirit. Such a crisis of faith is manifested in the ways in which we treat the earth, view others as other, and so on—and was recognized as such by both Nietzsche and Nishitani.

Historically in the West we see that with the advent of the ego comes its handmaid monotheism, and she has served us well from time to time; or conversely put, with the advent of monotheism, egoism is its handmaid that is born through the literalization and reduction of all the many divinities into one great economical God. This god is omniscient, omnipotent—and everything the human is not. Nietzsche announces that this god must die since he is the product of some grave philosophical error, bad faith, and anxious psychology:

> Man projected his three "inner facts," that in which he believed more firmly than in anything else, will, spirit, ego, outside himself—he derived the concept "being" only from the concept "ego," he posited "things" as possessing being according to his own image, according to his concept of the ego as cause. No wonder he later always discovered in things only *that which he had put into them!*—The thing itself, to say it again, the concept "thing" is merely a reflection of the belief in the ego as cause.[5]

For Nietzsche, as for Buddhist and Kyoto School thinkers such as Nishitani, we became so comfortable and secure in this ego zone that we develop a profound attachment to it and have become content with its great lie that the "soul [is] something indestructible, eternal, indivisible . . . a monad . . . an *atomon,*" and have failed to realize that such a "belief ought to be expelled from science!"[6]

This great lie we live lulls us into a religious, ethical, and existential slumber; and we are now living out its very real consequences with our nearly global inability to realize our interconnectedness to the world and its creatures. This lack of interconnectedness manifests in our failure to design human habitats and food production systems in equitable and meaningful ways, to use land and other resources responsibly and justly, to build human communities that integrate with the planet's macroclimate and microclimates, and to live harmoniously with each other. Nietzsche and Nishitani challenge us not to just focus on the elements of the world themselves such as plants, animals, rocks, soils, and water as if they are somehow out there, but rather to assemble ourselves within the matrix of multitudinous relationships created by those plants, animals, rocks, soils, and water. To become synergetic with the various forces of nature is to learn how to mimic emerging patterns as enhanced by the interactions of those elements found in nature. To accomplish all of this, the ego that underlies our sense of self mush be abolished (Nietzsche) or broken through (Nishitani). This ground of being will, however, always be a groundless ground.

It is a qualified "faith" that moves us beyond this bad faith and anxious psychology that gives rise to the consequences outlined above since it is faith that "marks the point at which the self is really and truly a *solitary* self, and really and truly becomes the self itself" (RN 27). This realization of an existential self brings about the presencing of the religious moment, the emergence of a time wherein we can experience that "this faith is not simply a thing of the self, but takes on the shape of a reality" (RN 27). The absolute negation of *this* ego-self, its purchase and hold on a soul of substance, is the original sin of both Christianity and Buddhism that cuts off the authentic self, the true self, the non-self, from the "very ground of its being" (RN 27).

For Nishitani, this absolute negation of the self is also an affirmation of the solitary self. The negation recognizes, and perpetually re-cognizes, the fundamental aloneness of a solitary self in the presence of its always present other, but also simultaneously places this acknowledging existential self into the flowing reality that unifies all things. In response to the ancient saying, "The channel forms as the water flows," Nishitani explains that the "water does not flow into a ready-made waterway called 'man' but flows along freely its own way, and so makes its own waterway called 'new man'" (RN 28). The movement of water, its flowing and rushing, is central to Nietzsche as well. His current rushes as a torrent through a narrow canyon after an early spring melt. One must love one's fate in order to become what one is. The suffering and nausea of the deepest depths and their truth of the eternal recurrence are necessary conditions for becoming, for our love of our fate brings chaos to our souls; this chaos is as a necessary condition for the soul's subsequent bliss of overflowing into the world, of ensouling the world. Zarathustra, the prophet of the *Übermensch* and eternal recurrence, must know his suffering and it must be affirmed—for it too must be a joy! "My formula for greatness in a human being is *amor fati:* that one willed nothing to be otherwise, not forward, not backward, not in all eternity. Not merely to suffer what is necessary, but to *love* it."[7] The *Übermensch* must even love the chaos of his soul and affirm that he is not created in the image of God for "water does not flow into a ready-made waterway called 'man' but flows along freely its own way, and so makes its own waterway called 'new man.'" Zarathustra (and the *Übermensch*) must love the suffering and nausea that the eternal recurrence brings, because it is necessary; Zarathustra's suffering must be known and cultivated. The overhuman needs to know and experience suffering and nausea because they are the requisite routes back into the waterway of world, and willing "nothing to be otherwise, not forward, not backward, not in all eternity" is of the essence in understanding eternal recurrence not as a cosmological theory, but as a profound thought of and challenge to the self.

The New Sense of Soul in Nature

To be this "new man" is to be the empty soul of all things. To be this "new man" is to become the Great Compassion of Buddhism and Christian *agapē*, for Nishitani; to become this "new man" is to be reborn into the divine Dionysian undifferentiated flow, for Nietzsche.[8] The rebirth of the self, however, should not become literalized, stripped of existential and religious meaning. This rebirth is always a continuous re-birthing in a world that is born anew in each moment; this rebirth as the "new man" is also concomitantly the rebirth of the "new world"; and this "new world" is the world of nature, the natural world. In many ways, the Japanese language lacks an equivalent to the English word "nature," seen as an entity somehow outside the world of human beings. The Japanese word most commonly used to express nature is *shizen*. This is the word typically adopted to render Greek *phusis*, Latin *natura*, German *Natur*, and the "nature" of other Western languages.[9] Nishitani tells us in his essay "On Nature" that Japanese *shizen* is the same as the Chinese word *ziran*,[10] which typically gets translated as "spontaneous" and less elegantly (but more correctly) as "self-so-ing" or "self-so." As we unpack the multiple senses of *shi-*

zen, this relationship to the Chinese *ziran* will be interesting and instructive to appreciate more fully the connection between self, nature, *mahākaruna*, and the Good, as envisioned by Nishitani.

The last part of *shizen* (*zen*) means "the state of" or "the condition of being," and as a suffix it is employed in many Japanese words. One meaning of the word *shi* (or *ji*—pronunciation is determined by what follows) curiously means "self,"[11] and hence the state of *ji* (*shi*), or *ji*'s (*shi*'s) being, is the state or being of the self. In other words, the self when in its being as a true self is natural or is equated even to nature itself. Nishitani writes, "with the word *shizen* we have to ask just what kind of *Zustand* [Gn. 'condition'] it refers to and what it means. In that case this *ji* comes after all to resemble the 'natural' of Western languages."[12] Nishitani continues by saying that in "Japanese the *ji* occurs in the expression *mizukara* [where the ideograph *ji* is read as *mizuka*] which means 'oneself,' as in 'one [does something] oneself.' Another example concerns the Japanese *onozuka* [where the ideograph *ji* is read as *onozuka*], meaning 'naturally.'"[13] These examples—and Nishitani lists more such as *jikaku* (self-awareness), *jiai* (care of oneself), *jiga* (ego), and *jiyū* (freedom)—point to something philosophically significant concerning the Japanese perception of nature and the relation of the self to the natural world.

Nishitani makes use of this linguistic analysis to reveal the underlying relations of East Asian religious sensibilities to the natural world. These sensibilities are also part of the original Buddhist project that inspired a more vigorous reaction against aspects of the Pali and Sanskrit languages which share the same syntactic seductions that Nietzsche warned against in his preface to *Beyond Good and Evil*: "any old popular superstition from time immemorial (like the soul superstition which, in the form of the subject and ego superstition, has not even yet ceased to do mischief) [is] some play on words perhaps, a seduction by grammar, or an audacious generalization of very narrow, very personal, very human, all too human facts." The pertinent Buddhist doctrines here are interdependent arising (Pali *paticca-samuppada*), the impermanence of all things (*anicca*), and the no-self (*anatta*). Ultimately the true self, the self that emerges from *shizen*, is the no-self, which is a requisite state of being for the great compassion (*mahākaruna*), for it is the self emerging from *shizen* that is linked to all things in the world (RN 149).

The no-self doctrine of Buddhism is a doctrine of the non-permanence of the self. This doctrine denies an abiding self that is separate and distinct from the impermanence of all natural things. Such a doctrine denies the idea of an enduring soul, one that survives its body in some kind of heavenly realm beyond the physical. Although he does not state explicitly the *anatta* doctrine, Nishitani suggests this when he points out the etymological relation of heaven to the natural:

> [In] the case where the Chinese ideograph *zen* is attached, forming the compound *shizen*, I think the aspect of *onozukara* [naturally] that was already included in the word *ji* becomes central. There are many examples, but it often appears in the expression *tennen shizen* (naturally given), when the first part of the ideograph *ten* (heaven) is combined with *nen* (*zen*).[14]

In other words, that which is naturally given is a matter of heaven and/or is heavenly. This conception of heaven is very unlike Western transcendent conceptions and their hopes of a perfect hereafter, and is equivalent to the Chinese *tian* wherein the focus is more on the here and now. This is true of Buddhist thought in general and especially true of Zen, where the primary focus is placed on the interrelatedness and mutual emergence of all things. But there are further religious implications here: That which is spiritual is to be found within the naturally given; however, it is important to note this given is not a *kenōsis* from a godly above, but rather the givenness that naturally, spontaneously (*ziran*) is from *tennen shizen*, heavenly nature. This givenness is an emergent given from within the dynamic process itself. The "Pure Land" is just that—its purity is devoid of human value; its value is grounded in the land itself, that is, in its flowing nature.[15] The character of this land is value neutral; it is just-so. Therefore, to accentuate the sacred dimension of the natural in light of typhoons, tsunami destruction, and other natural disasters is an existential and ethical challenge of the highest order. In other words, to bring ourselves to affirm the process of the natural as being the highest Good and to develop the great compassion toward it is as challenging as the Abrahamic tradition affirming that such a good God allows so much indiscriminate suffering in the world.

The person of no rank, the *mui no shinjin* or "true human of no rank," in Buddhism fits into this greater landscape of things with *jikaku* (self-awareness) of being *onozukara* (natural). In this way, the *ningen* (human being) becomes the *maningen* (genuine person), "which has the connotation of an honest, sincere human being."[16] This sincerity is a requisite condition for the *mui no shinjin* because "to say that a human being becomes human means that he becomes what he ought to become, a *maningen* in the genuine sense, or *shinjin*."[17] What one ought to become is an integrated self—that is, a nondual self that realizes itself as an emergent condition in the continuing flow of becoming. This self is one that has forfeited its ego-sense of being as a socially constructed entity and a function of language that has claimed a persistent place for itself through the progression of time. In other words, this self has relinquished itself as a "narrative self" for an enhanced narrative for which there is ultimately no listener, reader, or evaluator as a "world-self." The psychological and ontological urbanization of the self that is yet-to-be the enhanced no-self of the Buddhist project creates a border of the human from the natural world and its self-so-ing. Not only do we urbanize nature initially through fences, walls, and the city proper, we then encroach upon it by further extension of the sub-urban. This suburban encroachment persists until other species are forced to interact with the brainy bipeds who have created an alterity of "nature" and treated other species as "naturally" subaltern.

The Place of Emptiness and Nothingness

The implications emerging from Nishitani and Nietzsche are significant for developing more intimacy with the natural world. I wish to suggest this is something both thinkers have in mind, at least as an undercurrent in their thinking. To get to this undercurrent and its implications for an ecological philosophy—that is, for a philosophy of a self more intimately related with the world—it is worthwhile to visit Nishitani's thinking on time and emptiness. In the "*Śūnyatā* and History" chapter of *Religion and Nothingness,* Nishitani's most direct engagement with Nietzsche bears abundant fruit.

Religion and Nothingness may just be the first real example of doing comparative philosophy because it moves well beyond the "debits and credits" of comparison to a new movement of philosophy, a triangulation of approaches that yields a new understanding and level of inquiry. *Religion and Nothingness* is a new moment in the time of philosophy. It is in its last chapter that Nishitani engages his greatest Western influence, and serves this influence well by following Nietzsche's advice in *Thus Spoke Zarathustra:* "One repays a teacher poorly if one always remains only a student."

Having said this, one still wonders in what way or ways Nishitani thinks he has somehow gone beyond one of his most significant Western influences, and how it is that Buddhism somehow trumps the insights of Nietzsche. He thinks this too even of Heidegger and the Western philosophical project when he announces that *Śūnyatā,* or emptiness, "is another thing altogether from the nihility of nihilism" (RN 95), for it is from "the very standpoint of *Śūnyatā* itself that enables such a viewpoint to come about" (RN 94). Nishitani in some sense sees this "nihility of nihilism" as being characteristic of the Western philosophical orientation toward metaphysics that still has a trace of some kind of substantial self lurking in the background. This is the case even though for "the self-existence of man, nihility became a field of ecstatic self-detachment" and nihilism "had become existential" (RN 95) with "the representation of nothingness in nihilism still show[ing] traces of the bias of objectification, of taking nothingness as some 'thing' called nothingness" (RN 95).[18] Nishitani's point is simply that "nihility is always a nihility *for self-existence,* that is to say, a nihility that we contact when we posit ourselves on the side of 'existence' of our self-existence" (RN 96). Therefore, he can conclude that the "longstanding Western view of nothingness has yet to divest itself of this way of thinking. The *śūnyatā* we speak of points to a fundamentally different viewpoint" (RN 96). But is this assessment true of Nietzsche as well? Is this an accurate understanding of Nietzsche and his project?

Nishitani allows *śūnyatā* to trump the Western engagement of nothingness on its own terms because emptiness is seen as being more fundamental than nothingness. For Nishitani, and this will be his critique of Nietzsche: "Emptiness in the sense of *śūnyatā* is only emptiness when it empties itself even of the standpoint that represents some 'thing' that is emptiness" (RN 96). Emptiness can empty itself; this self-emptying is "its original Form" and is "united to and self-identical with being" (RN 97). Hence, we have the Buddhist equation that "form is emptiness and emptiness is form." Nishitani moves along to discuss how Mahāyāna thought is concerned with the overcoming of dualism that emerges from logical analysis, but this, of course, is the mutual concern of both Nietzsche and Heidegger as well. Although there is admiration for both of these thinkers, there seems to be an implicit criticism that they are still in the throes of some concealed dualism or dualistic posture in the world. But is this perception accurate? We will leave Heidegger out of the discussion that follows and focus on Nietzsche since he is even closer to Nishitani than Nishitani thinks. The closeness of these two thinkers brings us to the "home-ground" of a philosophical ecology or a philosophy of ecology; Nietzsche and Nishitani bring us to the same place, to the same *basho,* but from different cultural orientations: One's step back is the other's step forward.

Nishitani takes some issue with Nietzsche's sense of time and history as it is portrayed in his "theory" of eternal recurrence. In his reading of *Religion and Nothingness,* especially the chapter titled "*Śūnyatā* and History," Thomas P. Kasulis reads Nishitani's trouble with the eternal recurrence in more cosmological terms, that is, as presenting an actual theory about the nature of time and history's relation to time. Although Kasulis does recognize the place of values in Nietzsche's pronouncement of the eternal recurrence, he places more emphasis on its cosmological side:

> Based on his insight into the value theory hidden within the Enlightenment's view of history, Nietzsche believed the linear, diachronic view of each event as happening once-and-for-all was no longer tenable. Such a view died with God. . . . Since the valuing process is renewed in each moment, Nietzsche claims time does not progress but instead continuously turns back on itself. This is the theory of eternal recurrence. Historical time collapses into the present, where the arc of the past and future merge. For the nihilist, time is a circle, not a line.[19]

Others such as Arthur Danto and Walter Kaufmann have seen the eternal recurrence in a similar cosmological light, while still others such as Bernd Magnus look to eternal recurrence less as actuality and more as possibility.[20] It is not always clear the way in which Nishitani understands Nietzsche's "greatest weight," but he does seem to use this weight to cast Nietzsche as the last nihilist—as one under the last grip of nihility, and as one not yet liberated to emptiness. Nishitani's discussion of Nietzsche in *The Self-Overcoming of Nihilism* is certainly sympathetic, even to the point of being like-minded, but it is in *Religion and Nothingness* where we sense his criticism that Nietzsche just does not go far enough:

> But when time spoken of in terms of an unlimited past and an unlimited future becomes a single, circular whole; when this circle of time is depicted as a meaningless repetition on the canvas of nihility; and when all being in time is nullified from the ground up and turns into an endless, pure becoming; then the optical illusion or confusion of dimensions that tries to ask about the home-ground of time and being with time, is awakened from its illusion and refocused on what Nietzsche calls a "radical nihilism." There is no home-ground at all to be sought in the world of that pure becoming, that circular world-time turning eternally within itself. And where all things are to be repeated endlessly in exactly the same fashion, where everything is nullified and rendered meaningless, any search at all for the elemental loses its significance. (RN 226)

Nishitani's reasons behind this criticism stem from Nietzsche's conception that the will somehow remains a thing. For Nishitani, "Nietzsche's standpoint of Eternal Recurrence and Will to Power was not able fully to realize the meaning of the historicity of historical things. And the fundamental reason for this lies in the fact that the Will to Power, Nietzsche's final standpoint, was still conceived as some 'thing' called 'will'" (RN 234). Nishitani understands the will to power's returning to itself as still being a matter of a willing its will to return, that is, as a will *that wills* or a will *to will*.

It is when Nishitani turns to his concluding discussion on play in *Religion and Nothingness* that we begin to see even more clearly where Nietzsche fails. After discussing the "standpoint of elemental play" in Heraclitus and Nietzsche, Nishitani shows his hand: "They cannot be said to have arrived at the authentic self-centeredness of absolute emptiness that holds all dharmas in its grip, that, master wherever it is, makes wherever it is true. However one looks at it, theirs remains a standpoint of 'will,' not the standpoint of *śūnyatā*" (RN 265). But is Nishitani's assessment reflective of Nietzsche's underlying project—namely, a total reintegration into the process of world?

The Greatest Weight

If eternal recurrence and will to power are thought in light of the *Übermensch,* the "ideal" self for Nietzsche, it becomes clearer why we should not interpret the eternal recurrence in cosmological terms. These three great thoughts of Nietzsche's—the overhuman, will to power, and eternal recurrence—should always be taken together, never taken literally, and never viewed in isolation. To take any of these thoughts in isolation would violate the spirit of inter-relatedness that is the indispensable foundation of Nietzsche's unique project in the West. Viewing eternal recurrence in cosmological terms will amount to a desecration of Nietzsche's religious call to redeem the earth as a spiritual movement of inextricably interrelated *loci* of will to power. Although Nietzsche did indeed muse on various theories in physics, he is much more preoccupied with the metaphor of writing and seeing the world as text; in this light, humans are viewed as characters in that text and construct themselves as authors of their own worlds in relation to their encounter with other *loci* of will to power. The "self" for Nietzsche is nothing but a field of forces, and concomitantly things in the world are *loci* of the will to power: "*This world is will to power*—and *nothing besides!* And you yourselves are also this will to power—and nothing besides!"[21] Things for Nietzsche are not isolated substances or essences or subjects, but interrelated affects and effects, actions or events, which are part of a greater unfolding of the drama of life and death in the world's text:

The world . . . [is] a play of forces and waves of forces, at the same time one and many, increasing here and at the same time decreasing there; a sea of forces flowing and rushing together, eternally changing, eternally flooding back, with tremendous years of recurrence, with an ebb and flood of its forms; out of the simplest forms striving to the most complex . . . and then again returning home to the simple out of abundance, out of the play of contradictions back to the joy of concord.[22]

These interrelated affects and effects, actions and events are inter-implicated with each other in a mutually influencing onrush of amplifications and diminutions in and through an open sea of will to power.

The will to power *interprets* (—it is a question of interpretation when an organ is constructed): it defines its limits, determines degrees, variations of power. Mere variations of power could not feel themselves to be such: there must be present something that wants to grow and interprets the value of whatever else wants to grow. Equal *in that*—In fact, interpretation is itself a means of becoming master of something. (The organic process constantly presupposes interpretations.)[23]

It is only from particular perspectives that we see these interrelated events and their effects as *not* being a part of the greater self-same activity of this organic process, which has already presupposed our interpretations of its flowing process where every event in the world is intimately connected to every other event. Hence, the will to power will always include interpretation as its fundamental *modus operandi* for understanding the world.

The self for Nietzsche is a locus no different from other "things" in the world. The self (and reflections of the self on "itself") is nothing more than the continuing narrative of the totality of its experiences, drives, actions and nonactions, affects and effects, and so on of a will to power. The self is an interpretation; and is even an interpretation and constant reinterpretation of itself. As Graham Parkes aptly puts it: "The will that would then hold gentle sway over the monstrously powerful drives no longer operates only through the conscious ego, but rather works and plays as 'will to power'—a configuration of the interpretive energies that constitute *life* in the widest sense."[24] The eternal recurrence of the same is not so much a theory of time or a cosmological theory of physical causation as it is a theory of self, for the self is nothing more than a configuration of the same drives, forces, affects, effects, and processes of the will to power situated in the open field of the world. For Nietzsche's ideal self of the *Übermensch* to be approached (realized), overhuman *discipline* must be imposed to order the psyche politic so that one can understand and respond appropriately to and indeed re-enter this worlding we call world; the idea of eternal recurrence helps initiate such a discipline.

One is always involved in interpreting the past, as has been noted, and this reinterpretation is often a reinvention or recreation as the self revisions itself as a character in the greater drama within which it finds itself unfolding. Nietzsche's thought of the eternal recurrence is not a doctrine of cosmology, but rather a challenge and guide to experience oneself cosmologically:

> We are buds on a single tree—what do we know about what can become of us from the interests of the tree! . . . *Stop feeling yourself as the phantastic ego!* Learn gradually *to jettison the supposed individual?* Discover the errors of the ego! Realize that *egoism is an error.* . . . *Get beyond* "me" and "you"! *Experience cosmically!*[25]

For Nishitani, the self too is beyond any self-enclosure and is the field of all the insubstantial being-becomings (things) of the world:

> All things that are in the world are linked together, one way or the other. Not a single thing comes into being without some relationship to every other thing. . . . To say *that a thing is not itself* means that, while continuing to be itself, it is the home-ground of everything else. . . . It serves as a constitutive element of their being so that they can be what they are, and thus provides an ingredient of their being. *That a thing in itself* means that all other things, while continuing to be themselves, are in the home-ground of that thing; that the roots of every other thing spread across into its home-ground. This way that everything has of being on the home-ground of everything else, without ceasing to be on its own home-ground, means that the being of each thing is held up, kept standing, and made to be what it is by means of the being of all other things; or, put the other way around, that each thing holds up the being of every other thing, keeps it standing, and makes it what is. In a word, it means that all things "are" in the "world." . . . This is what we mean by speaking of beings as "being that is in unison with emptiness," and "being on the field of emptiness." (RN 149)

The self then, as a home-ground, is ultimately a "cosmic self" and must be realized as such in order to be enlightened and serve meaningfully and appropriately as a home-ground for the "being of all other things." But this is not some kind of slushy monism; it is rather a sophisticated and profound view of the dynamic process of all things stripped of conceptual and psychological projections onto its open field of manifested expression and representation. Nishitani calls this field of interpenetrating relationships "circuminsessional" (RN 148), and clarifies that "this circuminsessional system is only possible on the field of emptiness or *śūnyatā*" (RN 149).

If we view the kind of self that is hereby suggested as a momentary narrative at work and at play in the macrocosmic field of will to power, we soon see that eternal recurrence is more about redemption *in* time than any theory *of* time. As Nietzsche states in the *Anti-Christ*: "The profound instinct for how one would have to *live* in order to feel oneself 'in Heaven', to feel oneself 'eternal', while in every other condition one by *no* means feels oneself 'in Heaven': this alone is the psychological reality of 'redemption',—A new way of living, *not* a new belief."[26] This "new way of living" requires that we understand the eternal recurrence as a realization of a cosmic self, that is, a self in nature since for Nietzsche this world is "a monster of energy, without beginning, without end; a firm magnitude of force that does not grow bigger or smaller, that does not expend itself; as a whole, of unalterable size, a household without increase or income; enclosed by nothingness as by a boundary."[27]

Redemption in Nietzsche's eyes is not so different from redemption in Nishitani's, as is indicated in the above quotes from Nishitani. So is nihility in the manner of Nietzsche's thought, as Nishitani suggests, ultimately superseded by Buddhist emptiness? Is "emptiness, or *śūnyatā* . . . another thing altogether from the nihility of nihilism," which remains only "existential" (RN 95)? Will emptiness in the sense of *śūnyatā*, as that emptiness out of which it empties itself even of the standpoint that represents some "thing" that is emptiness, be an unexplored horizon for Nietzsche (see RN 96)? Is Nietzsche unaware that emptiness can empty itself and does so continually as some kind of self-emptying original form that is "united to and self-identical with being" (RN 97)?

If some key passages in Nietzsche's work are identified (as shown above), we soon find the closeness in their thinking. Nietzsche states: "We need 'unities' in order to be able to reckon: that does not mean we must suppose that such unities exist. We have borrowed the concept unity from our 'ego' concept—our oldest article of faith. If we did not hold ourselves to be unities we would never have formed the concept 'thing.'"[28] Nietzsche was well aware that this form of unity is just "our oldest article of faith" and that it is void of any reality and is something we most certainly need to discard and get beyond. For both Nietzsche and Nishitani, we can no longer redeem ourselves through such self-deceptive acts of bad faith. We must find a new redemption in the process of utter insubstantiality, where all is characterized by emptiness. But what could this emptiness mean if not the radical interrelatedness of the very constitutive forces of self and world that are constantly under way?[29]

In *Nietzsche: Life as Literature*, Alexander Nehamas has argued persuasively that eternal recurrence should be understood in the general way outlined above. Nehamas also discusses the relationship between the creative act of writing and life itself:

> And if we consider that every human action, not only a book, is in some way or other the cause of other actions, decisions, and thoughts; that everything that happens is inseparably connected with everything that is going to happen, we recognize the real *immortality*, that of movement—that which has once moved is enclosed and immortalized in the general union of all existence, like an insect within a piece of amber.[30]

Movement is our immortality, and our redemption is diving into the Dionysian flow of Being and making it our home—this is the floating and mutually influencing home-ground of all beings. This is Being and this being is a becoming; it is what Nietzsche refers to as "primal unity" in *The Birth of Tragedy*. This flow of being, I suggest, meets Nishitani's criterion that "water does not flow into a ready-made waterway called 'man' but flows along freely its own way, and so makes its own waterway called 'new man'" (RN 28). For the new man and woman who can enter this flow is to enter the groundless ground of the overhuman; this groundless ground is the floating place where resentment is overcome by redemption in time and movement in the dance of life and death, and death in life. This is the challenge of eternal recurrence: For if the self is indeed a microcosm of the greater matrix of will to power, then to will one's life differently is to will the world to be different. For Nishitani, the true self that is not self is cast as a natural self, for

> the term "nature" was assigned to the force that acts to gather all things together and connect them to one another. In karma, nature in this sense can be conceived as the elemental force by which the self connects all things while gathering them together into the self in the manner of self-enclosure; and the force by which the self itself then enters into incessant becoming without beginning or end while so engaged in connecting all things to one another. (RN 249)

For Nietzsche, and I take it for Nishitani, to will things *differently* is simply bad faith, the height of hubris; it is fundamentally philosophically wrong, and gives rise to an impoverished way to live and die. Even more significantly, however: To deceive ourselves religiously has greater implications for how we treat "others" in our shared home-grounds, for these shared home-grounds are where *agapē* and *mahākaruna* open up from the loving and compassionate soul. There can be no *agapē* or Great Compassion without the Great Death of the ego, the atomized self—and this death is a precondition for reintegration into the home-ground of all that is, and was, and will be. This is the direction in which both Nishitani and Nietzsche point our ways. And their gestures point toward and direct us to return to our homes, which are now and always the shared, and thus selfless, homeless-and-groundless home-grounds of everything in the world.

NOTES

1. Friedrich Nietzsche, *Thus Spoke Zarathustra*, trans. Graham Parkes (Oxford: Oxford University Press, 2005), "Prologue," §4.

2. Ibid., "Prologue," §1. Also see David Jones, "Crossing Currents: The Overflowing/Flowing-over Soul in *Zarathustra* and *Zhuangzi*," *Dao: Journal of Comparative Philosophy* 4, no. 2 (Summer 2005): 235–51.

3. On the previous page, Nishitani discusses the issue of faith and its relation to nothingness. Here he writes: "The acceptance of divine love is called faith. Although this faith remains throughout a faith of the self, it is fundamentally different from the ordinary sense of faith which posits the self as agent. . . . In religion, however, faith comes about only on a horizon where this field has been overstepped and the framework of the 'ego' has been broken through" (RN 26). For Nishitani, *agapē* is only possible when the ego "has been broken through" and the singularity of the existing self is affirmed vis-à-vis the generalizability of the *res cogitans*.

4. Friedrich Nietzsche, *Beyond Good and Evil*, trans. Walter Kaufmann (New York: Random House, 1966), §17.

5. Friedrich Nietzsche, *Twilight of the Idols*, in *Twilight of the Idols and The Anti-Christ*, trans. R. J. Hollingdale (Middlesex: Penguin, 1968), §3.

6. Nietzsche, *Beyond Good and Evil*, §12.

7. See, for instance, Friedrich Nietzsche, *Ecce Homo*, trans. Walter Kaufmann (New York: Random House, 1969), "Why Am I So Clever," §10.

8. Although Nietzsche will have none of this *agapē* talk, Nishitani does not hesitate to invoke such discussion in the spirit of *kenōsis*; Nietzsche may be more reluctant given his immediate project and historical context. God as a symbol for all metaphysical absolutes that override particularity, context, relationality, and the ongoing interpretation of the constituent forces of becoming is for Nietzsche something that must quite simply be done away with. Perhaps Nishitani wishes to find religious resonances between the two traditions in order to set up his arguments for the superiority of *śūnyatā* over nihility (hence the appeal to Kierkegaard in this regard), but he devotes far more time to Nietzsche in *The Self-Overcoming of Nihilism*, which indicates that Nietzsche is a stronger influence. Nietzsche must reject *agapē* since "pity," an emotion

he abhors, involves an active sympathy for the weak and arises from *agapē*. Nishitani seems to agree with Nietzsche, where he discusses pity in *The Self-Overcoming of Nihilism*. But we often forget that the word that most often gets translated as "pity" is the German *Mitleid*, which is the word Nietzsche has at his disposal to rail against that preeminent Christian-Schopenhauerian virtue. Literally, however, *Mitleid* means to "suffer with," and this literal sense comes closer to the Buddhist notion of "compassion." Given the direction of Nietzsche's thought, the latter is something I do not think he would find so objectionable. See especially chapter 4 of Nishitani's *The Self-Overcoming of Nihilism*, trans. Aihara Setsuko and Graham Parkes (Albany: State University of New York Press, 1990).

9. Nishitani Keiji, "On Nature," trans. Aihara Setsuko and Graham Parkes, in William Ridgeway and Nobuko Ochner, eds., *Confluences: Studies from East to West in Honor of V. H. Viglielmo* (Honolulu: University of Hawai'i Press, 2005), 61.

10. Ibid., 61.

11. Ibid.

12. Ibid., 62.

13. Ibid., 63.

14. Ibid.

15. I am not attempting a reinterpretation of Pure Land Buddhism or any of its practices or tenets in relation to other forms of Buddhism. I do, however, invoke its spirit in the sense of the Pure Land being a rich and fertile place of harmonious relations.

16. Nishitani, "On Nature," 69.

17. Ibid., 69.

18. Heidegger also falls into this because "even in Heidegger's talk of self-existence as 'held suspended in nothingness,'" and "despite the fundamental standpoint from other brands of contemporary existentialism or nihilism," the "very fact that he speaks of the 'abyss' of nihility already tells as much" (RN 96). There is a beautiful irony present here in that Heidegger calls Nietzsche the "last metaphysician" (perhaps so that he can himself become the first philosopher of the future), and Nishitani seems to repay Heidegger in kind. Whether Nishitani is correct in this assessment is beyond our scope here, but has been addressed previously by Fred Dallmayr in "Nothingness and *Śūnyatā*: A Comparison of Heidegger and Nishitani," *Philosophy East and West* 42, no. 1 (1992): 37–48.

19. Thomas Kasulis, "Whence and Whither: Nishitani's View of History," in Taitetsu Unno, ed., *The Religious Philosophy of Nishitani Keiji* (Freemont, Calif.: Asian Humanities Press, 1989), 266.

20. For this view, see Bernd Magnus, *Nietzsche's Existential Imperative* (Bloomington: Indiana University Press, 1978).

21. Friedrich Nietzsche, *The Will to Power*, trans. Walter Kaufmann and R. J. Hollingdale (New York: Random House, 1968), §1067.

22. Ibid., §1067.

23. Ibid., §643.

24. Graham Parkes, *Composing the Soul: Reaches of Nietzsche's Psychology* (Chicago: University of Chicago Press, 1994), 359.

25. Quoted from Parkes, *Composing the Soul*, 300. *Beyond Good and Evil*, §265 seems to run contrary to this proclamation of egoism being an error, where it is asserted that "egoism belongs to the nature of the noble soul—I mean that unshakable faith that to a being such as 'we are' other beings must be subordinate by nature and

have to sacrifice themselves. The noble soul accepts this fact of egoism without any question mark." This type of "egoism" is first and foremost not a proclamation of a besotted ego that is granted justification to wield its power as it desires. Rather, it seems to be a necessary phase, stage, or step toward realizing that "we are buds on a single tree." In this regard, egoism is a necessary condition, in this qualified sense, to realize that "egoism is an error." In fact, Nietzsche calls this type of egoism "justice itself." By doing so, he does not wish to dispense with the Apollonian ability, which is crucial in Nietzsche's earlier work (especially *The Birth of Tragedy*), to differentiate between those who are potentially capable of moving toward the overhuman and those who are locked into the security of their ready-made perspectives. Such inability would render the self helplessly adrift without the possibility of any kind of knowing or realizing. Not to realize this fact would be to engage in self-deception, for the noble soul simply "knows itself to be at a height."

26. Nietzsche, *The Anti-Christ*, in *Twilight of the Idols and The Anti-Christ*, trans. R. J. Hollingdale (Middlesex, U.K.: Penguin, 1968), §33.

27. Nietzsche, *Will to Power*, §1067.

28. Ibid., §635. This passage supports my argument in note 25, above, for accepting *Beyond Good and Evil*, §265 as an evolutionary phase toward the unitary realization that all (including this phase of egoism) is will to power.

29. See Elizabeth Gallu, "*Śūnyatā*, Ethics, and Interconnectedness," in *The Religious Philosophy of Nishitani Keiji*, 181–200.

30. Friedrich Nietzsche, *Human, All Too Human*, "From the Souls of Artists and Writers," §208; cited in Alexander Nehamas, *Nietzsche: Life as Literature* (Cambridge, Mass.: Harvard University Press, 1985), 164.

7

Ueda Shizuteru's Phenomenology of Self and World: Critical Dialogues with Descartes, Heidegger, and Merleau-Ponty

STEFFEN DÖLL

No account of the Kyoto School is complete without reference to Ueda Shizuteru, the central figure in the School's current third generation. A direct student of Nishitani's and the successor to his academic post, Ueda is one of today's leading authorities on the philosophy of Nishida as well as an expert in Zen Buddhist literature. It was Ueda's original work on Christian mysticism—especially his comparative studies on Meister Eckhart and Zen—that first earned him recognition in the West, and his numerous publications illustrate how engaging in a critical dialogue with other patterns of thought and experience is essential to the formation of his philosophy.[1] This is apparent, for example, in his masterful interpretations of Otto Friedrich Bollnow and Martin Buber.[2] Ueda consistently manages to highlight and clarify the central issues at stake in the philosophies of his dialogue partners, while relating these to his own central concern with developing a phenomenology of self and world.

Ueda's philosophical standpoint is characterized (1) by a severe critique of the modern understanding of the self as subject; (2) by a logic of locus (*basho no ronri*) which he develops in reference to Heidegger's topological ontology; and (3) by an endeavor to lay a philosophical foundation for the soteriology of Zen practice.[3] These three characteristics find their paradigmatic formulation in Ueda's core concepts of "being-in-the-twofold-world" and "self as not-self." Also crucial is his original understanding of the central Kyoto School notion of "absolute nothingness" or "absolute negation." Following Ueda's own accounts, we can give the following preliminary sketch of the core concepts of his thought (see USS 9: 22–23):

- The world is essentially and primordially a twofold world. The self always finds itself in a specific "world" (*sekai*), that is, in a concrete situation. But at the same time, this world is in turn located in an "infinite openness," an "invisible *nihilum*" as the locus of all loci. And so the self and its specific world are surrounded and permeated by nothingness.
- In accord with this invisible twofold structure, Ueda formulates the notion of a "self that is not a self," or more concisely, a "self as not-self." Such a "true self" has its identity in constantly negating itself. Being within a specifically determined world, the aspect of "self" dominates; in nothingness, the aspect of "not-self" does. That being so, we can state that "the invisible twofoldness of the world is incarnated in a visible twofoldness" (USS 9: 22), insofar as the aspect of "self" is, in fact, visible.
- When the underlying deeper dimension of world and self is forgotten, the invisible twofold structure seems to collapse into a superficial onefoldness; the world is mistaken as being merely "the (specific) world," the self as merely "the ego."
- The position of authentic twofoldness then is usurped by fictitious dualities (subject/object, self/other, etc.), which are taken to be constituted by mutually independent substances. These fictitious dualities rule our everyday thought and conduct.
- When these illusions of duality and the underlying misconception of self and world are given up, that is, negated, the twofold structure of the world self-actualizes itself in the self-awareness of the self as not-self and as "being-in-the-twofold-world." This transition from delusion to truth is the vector along which Ueda's philosophy is projected. Negation, for Ueda, first and foremost holds soteriological possibilities.

This essay attempts to clarify these central concepts of Ueda's philosophy by focusing on his dialogue with two major figures in modern European philosophy: Maurice Merleau-Ponty and Martin Heidegger. These philosophers' at-times strikingly similar criticisms of Descartes's conception of the self will provide us with a starting point for our inquiry.

The first part of this essay (sections 1–3) is devoted to explicating Ueda's concept of self, and it moves from the Cartesian cogito to Merleau-Ponty's tacit cogito and finally to Nishida's theory of pure experience and its spontaneous self-unfolding. The second part (sections 4–7) is concerned with Ueda's conversation with Heidegger's thought. The idea of being-in-the-twofold-world will emerge more clearly via an analysis of the concepts of world, nothingness, anxiety, and releasement. The essay comes to a close with a look at the self as not-self and the dynamic structure of negation as the essential basis of the true self. Along the way, I will demonstrate how Ueda gleans elements of his soteriological phenomenology of self and world from his sympathetic yet critical and distinguishing dialogues with Descartes, Heidegger, and Merleau-Ponty.

The Self as Pure Reflection:
Ueda's Critical Interpretation of Descartes's Cogito

Descartes posits an "actively pursued methodical doubt" (USS 10: 84) as the principle of his thought. By submitting to radical doubt not only that which appears doubtful, but everything that is in any way doubtable, he finally arrives at a fact which is supposed to be impervious to doubt. Descartes discovers this fact in the axiomatic truth of his own thinking:

> Finally, as the same precepts which we have when awake may come to us when asleep without their being true, I decided to suppose that nothing that had ever entered my mind was more real than the illusions of my dreams. But I soon noticed that while I thus wished to think everything false, it was necessarily true that I who thought so was something. Since this truth, *I think, therefore I am,* was so firm and assured that all the most extravagant suppositions of the skeptics were unable to shake it, I judged that I could safely accept it as the first principle of the philosophy I was seeking.[4]

I who doubt can only recognize myself to truly be (*sum*) in the fact of my own thinking (*cogitans*)—that is, as the one (*ego*) who doubts. Recursivity is thus the decisive characteristic of the Cartesian method. Not the existence of the self as such, but reflective thought is certain: "On the basis of the reflection of thought, the certainty of reflective thinking is discovered, and along with it the existence of the 'I' ('I think') as subject of reflective thought is proved for the 'thinking I'" (USS 10: 86). Unabbreviated, Ueda claims, Descartes's formulation should read: "I think (cogito B) that I am, because I think (cogito A)," or, "I think: I think, therefore I am" (USS 10: 87). Thought is in its foundation once more supported only by thought; thought tries to reach being, but in fact only revolves around itself in a *regressus ad infinitum*. Thought thinking itself "arrives at the admission that the discovering cogito is more certain than the 'cogito ergo sum' it had discovered as certainty. It does not stop at discovering truth but, as that which discovered truth, includes the tendency to elevate itself to be truth as such" (USS 10: 87). In its cogito as pure reflection, the self discovers its axiomatic, indubitable foundation solely in itself. It is statically self-identical, and in this hermetical condition, this autistic self-enclosure, it cannot but become conscious of itself in the form of circular reasoning: "I am, because I am" or, more precisely, "I am I because I am I."

One might want to object to Ueda that Descartes was, in fact, not really interested in the existing individual, but rather in the theorizing subject. Then, Ueda's criticism would operate on a completely different level than that where the Cartesian argumentation was located. But Descartes, in fact, goes beyond his strictly theoretical considerations in order to show that also our everyday conduct (exemplified by perception) is based on reflection. In the *Second Meditation* he writes:

> Finally, I am the same being which perceives—that is, which observes certain objects as though by means of the sense organs, because I do really see light, hear noises, feel heat. Will it be said that these appearances are false and that I am sleeping? Let it be so; yet at the very least it is certain that it seems to me that I see light, hear noises, feel heat. This much cannot be false, and it is this, properly considered, which in my nature is called perceiving, and that, again speaking precisely, is nothing else but thinking.[5]

With reference to this important passage, Ueda breaks down the Cartesian theory of perception into three parts: (1) "I hear a noise"—this sensation might be an illusion, a dream, or a hallucination. (2) "It seems to me that I hear a noise"—the abstraction of the direct sensation allows for certainty. It must be true that it seems to me that I hear a noise. Ueda terms this certainty, "semi-cogito." And (3), on closer scrutiny, this abstraction reveals itself to be thought: "I think (cogito) that I hear a noise." At this point, the subject has completely left the level of perception and has become indubitable in its rationality. Perception (and with it every event, every action) is a fact only insofar as it is thought (see USS 10: 89–90).

Descartes achieves consistency between theory and practice by subjugating every conceivable function of the subject to the cogito. The self exists by thinking, it understands itself as final reality within and based on its thought; it exists only insofar as it reflects.

> I am, I exist—that is certain; but for how long do I exist? For as long as I think; for it might happen, if I totally ceased thinking, that I would at the same time completely cease to be. I am now admitting nothing except what is necessarily true. I

am therefore, to speak precisely, only a thinking being, that is to say, a mind, an understanding.[6]

In the cogito, Descartes links existence directly to thought. Solely the thinking existence *is*. Every other mode of being is dubitable; it may be a false conclusion or mere supposition, and thus in the end is to be devoured by methodical doubt. The world as such may be an illusion and can only become certain by being thought of by the self. Thus the self claims to be not only the basis of its own existence, but the basis of existence as such. The self thereby tends toward fulfilling all the metaphysical conditions of an absolute existence (even if Descartes's ego still requires the proof of God's existence to ground the existence of the world). As Ueda puts it, the absolute "metastasizes onto the side of the human subject" (USS 10: 86). But for Ueda that is only one side of the coin: In the perfectly autarkic solitude of the indubitable cogito, in which neither world nor others could exist as such, "hollowness spreads and before long even a reversal to nihilism occurs" (USS 10: 90).

The Self as Perception: Merleau-Ponty's Tacit Cogito

Merleau-Ponty refuses to acknowledge the ontological primordiality of the Cartesian cogito.[7] In our living experience, perception (what Ueda calls the "semi-cogito") and action function together "in the body as mediator of a world"[8] without having to be linked together by recursive reflection. For example, the actions of an experienced soccer player are not guided by his cogito's reflection but by his active perception on the playing field. "Perception" for Merleau-Ponty cannot be understood as the process of a subject receiving sense data, for it calls into question the very dichotomy of subject and object, self and world: The ball as well as the playing field in its totality are located along with the body of the player in a continuum of active perception. But this also means that our selves are variables of specific situations. The epistemological and ontological primacy therefore lies not with the reflexive cogito but with the activity of perception: "Consciousness is in the first place not a matter of 'I think that' but of 'I can.'"[9]

Before all reflection, before any philosophical endeavor, there has to be a "primordial I," "the presence of oneself to oneself, being no less than existence."[10] This immediacy is neglected in the Cartesian cogito, which Merleau-Ponty calls the "verbal cogito" in light of its total dependence on the medium of language. The primordial I turns out to be the basis for this verbal mediacy in that it signifies a more fundamental perception: "Behind the spoken cogito, the one which is converted into discourse and into essential truth, there lies a tacit cogito, myself experienced by myself."[11]

However, the tacit cogito is in no way a substance antithetical to the reflexive cogito, but rather its complementary counterpart. Tacit and explicit cogito are mutually dependent:

> though it is true that all particular knowledge is founded on this primary view [of the tacit cogito], it is also true that the latter waits to be won back, fixed and made explicit by perceptual exploration and by speech. . . . The tacit cogito is a cogito only when it has found expression for itself.[12]

Explicating this aspect of complementarity, Ueda writes: "If it was not for the 'verbal cogito,' the 'tacit cogito' would not have become a problem in the first place" (USS 10: 188). Nonetheless, there is a qualitative difference: Merleau-Ponty bases the explicit cogito on the tacit cogito and thus opens up previously unreachable depths for the total structure of the cogito.

> To the question "What is the I?" Descartes's cogito, that is, the "*cogito ergo sum,*" was able to offer an extreme and powerful answer. But we can state that the "tacit cogito" is preparing another answer of greater depth under the feet of Descartes. When we can sense the possibility of a pre-cogito (thus a "without ego") becoming apparent together with a silence—not a mere "tacit cogito," but the transcendence of [the tacit cogito's] wordlessness into [a primordial] "wordlessness"—the "tacit cogito" can point towards Nishida's "pure experience." (USS 10: 189)

By "wordlessness" Ueda is not referring to Merleau-Ponty's prereflexive cogito as counterpart of the explicit cogito; he is not talking about a self that at times renounces speech. Rather, he aims at a more primordial dimension of the self, which he finds in Nishida's theory of pure experience. And it is by means of the latter that he attempts to detach himself from the standpoint of subjectivity that still underlies Merleau-Ponty's *Phenomenology of Perception.*

Pure Experience: Nishida's Non-Dual Origin of Self and World

According to Nishida, "pure experience" is the dimension in which "there is not yet a subject or an object, and knowing and its object are completely unified" (IG 3–4). He illustrates this as follows: "The moment of seeing a color or hearing a sound, for example, is prior not only to the thought that the color or sound is the activity of an external object or that one is sensing it, but also to the judgment of what the color or sound might be" (IG 3).[13]

Ueda stresses that Nishida does not rest content with simply claiming the possibility of such pure experience; he attempts rather to make it the origin and starting point of his philosophy: "I wanted to explain all things on the basis of pure experience as the sole reality" (IG xxx). In his own analysis of Nishida's philosophy of pure experience, Ueda develops a framework of three interrelated layers.[14]

First, the event of true experience as such presents the concrete experiential dimension. There, "the framework of subject and object, in which consciousness was enclosed, is broken through, opening up a [field of] disclosedness." This is an original fact (*koto*), namely, the awareness (*kaku*) that forms the "origin of self-awareness [*jikaku*]" (NKY 250).

Second, out of this experiential fact of awareness unfolds a primordial "self-articulation," an "*Ur-Satz*" in the form of the "words of 'self-awareness' in which 'pure experience' becomes aware of itself" (NKY 250) and articulates itself. Nishida's *Ur-Satz* here is: "pure experience is the only real reality." This is the first reappropriation and mediating expression of that which was initially experienced existentially. Awareness and articulation of the primordial event arise from the undividedness of the event itself by means of a fundamental creativity. Here, we see ourselves confronted with an elemental poetic language (*koto*), found for example within the Zen tradition in its pointed couplets and sharp retorts.

Third, proceeding from originary immediacy and building on its elemental poetic expression, the philosophical dimension of the *Grundsatz* or philosophical principle is disclosed. By way of increasing abstraction, experience and self-awareness are made accessible through and beyond the intimately personal relation so that now the realm of discourse is opened up. In the process of a "self-objectification of pure experience" (NKY 252), the ego and the world come into being out of pure experience and its self-articulation. The methodological project Ueda inherited from Nishida—"I wanted to explain all things on the basis of pure experience as the sole reality"— leads invariably to a "self-understanding of the self as being-in-the-world" (NKY 252).

It is possible to retrospectively disclose the "spontaneous self-unfolding" of pure experience, the "dynamic connection that makes up the layering of (1) awareness, (2) self-awareness, and (3) understanding 'self and world'" (NKY 250). The self[15]—in its initial appearance as Cartesian reflection, deepening into Merleau-Ponty's self-perception[16] and even further into the non-self of pure experience and the non-ego of Zen meditation—can retrace the self-unfolding of itself by descending through its own formative layers and eventually reaching the unbroken facticity of pure experience.

Insofar as in pure experience self and world are not yet constituted in their illusory independence from one another, self-awareness discovers itself to be grounded in a field embracing not only the latent self, but also the latent world. The structure of this self/world-complex is what will concern us in the following sections of this essay.

World and Dasein: Heidegger's Critique of Descartes

Heidegger also finds profound difficulties with the structure of consciousness implied by the *cogito ergo sum*. Descartes's certain and unshakable foundation of all philosophy remains a mirage as long as the ontological status of the *sum* is not thoroughly clarified. But that is exactly what Descartes had not done: The "unexpressed ontological foundations of the '*cogito sum*'"[17] still remain unexamined. Heidegger attempts to examine the "being" of the Cartesian *sum* as part of his fundamental ontology, and this project continues to determine his thought, as is obvious from the following quote from the "Seminar in Zähringen 1973": "subjectivity itself is not questioned in respect to its being; for since Descartes it has been the *fundamentum inconcussum*. In all of modern thought arising from Descartes subjectivity accordingly forms the obstacle to bringing the question of being on its way."[18] The reason that Cartesian subjectivity not only ignores, but positively obstructs and forestalls the question of being, lies in the fact of its essential self-enclosure. This self-enclosure determines the "immanence" of all objects in consciousness: The moment I am conscious of something, it is present to me as the content of my consciousness; it is immanent to my subjectivity. Raising the question of being anew, by way of radically questioning the meaning of the *sum,* allows us to step out of the immanence of the *cogito* and to abandon the standpoint of consciousness. Thus, Heidegger calls the world as content of consciousness into question and locates the subject "*in the world* (which in turn is not immanent to consciousness)."[19] He understands subject and world on the basis of existence (ek-sistence) and Da-sein (being-there).

> In contrast to the immanence of consciousness that was expressed by the "being" in *being*-conscious [*»sein« im Bewußt-sein*], the "being" in *being*-there [*»sein« in Da*-sein] designates the being-outside-of. . . . The realm in which everything that can be called a thing can encounter [*sic*] as such is a district that gives room to

the possibility of this thing becoming manifest "out there." Being [*Sein*] in being-there [*Da-sein*] has to preserve an "outside." That is why Da-sein's mode of being is characterized in terms of ek-stasis in *Being and Time*. Strictly speaking, Da-sein therefore means: being ek-statically there. Immanence is thereby broken through. Da-sein is essentially ek-static.[20]

Freeing the self from its solipsistic immanence, Heidegger accords it a new position that is characterized by "being-in-the-world" and "Dasein." The autonomous position of the subject is abandoned in favor of a larger frame of reference. And thus, in order to clarify the situation of the self, a phenomenologically sufficient description of the world is also necessary.

World and Nothingness: Ueda's Interpretation of the Early Heidegger

Ueda calls our attention to two closely related aspects of the concept of "world" in Heidegger's fundamental ontology. First, insofar as we exist, we interact: "We exist by discovering ourselves within a disclosed locus, and from the start we exist by associating with others and relating to things within this locus. This relational totality is nothing other than our existence" (USS 9: 28). We disclose hermeneutically that which we encounter in a specific situation, that is, within a certain locus. Heidegger terms the space that renders this hermeneutical disclosure possible "the world"—whether disclosure takes place analytically by means of our "understanding" or intuitively and comprehensively by means of our "disposition" (*Befindlichkeit*). In its disclosedness the world is established as a sphere of significance; it is meaningful.

Second, according to Ueda, the totality of all loci within which we exist is called world: "If the inclusive disclosedness of the loci that contains the respective concrete loci within itself is called 'world,' then [it must be said that] from the start we can exist only by stepping out of ourselves toward the world. Dasein is in its fundamental structure 'being-in-the-world'" (USS 9: 28). The disclosedness of the world thus unifies the two aspects of openness and understanding: The world is disclosed as an open space which we hermeneutically disclose by our ek-sistence. But as our innerworldly existences relate to other innerworldly beings (the entirety of which Heidegger in *Being and Time* calls our "totality of involvements"), for the most part our view of the world as such is obstructed. Nevertheless, we can catch a glimpse of the world as world in anxiety.

In anxiety, "the totality of involvements . . . discovered within-the-world is, as such, of no consequence; it collapses into itself; the world has the character of completely lacking significance."[21] In this anxiety-ridden lack of significance, everything within the world loses its meaning, and, "on the basis of this *insignificance* of what is within-the-world, the world in its worldhood is all that still obtrudes itself. . . . Being-anxious discloses, primordially and directly, the world as world."[22] Ueda explicates this thought as follows: "The 'nothingness of the world' (the insignificance), in which the disclosedness (significance) that constitutes the worldhood of the world submerges into nothingness, reveals the world as world" (USS 9: 30–31). In the nothingness of the world, then, one aspect of disclosedness—namely, understanding—is destroyed and solely the world in its own open disclosedness remains.

Therefore, in Heidegger the term "world" has a double meaning: On the one hand it designates the "world as relational totality of the connection of significances," and on the other hand the "world as world revealed in the nothingness of the world" (USS 9: 31). The former world of significance is based on the latter world of nothingness, and yet Ueda will go on to question whether even these two together provide a sufficient account of the phenomenon of world. "The totality of beings as a whole (the world) that is spread open by the connection of significances constitutes . . . the disclosedness (meaningfulness) of the totality of involvements, and the totality (the world) that initially formed its basis is as such a totality limited by nothingness" (USS 9: 35). Accordingly, the meaningfulness of the world is given only insofar as nothingness permits it to be meaningful. The world reveals itself as being limited and conditioned by nothingness. "Although being becomes apparent as being within nothingness and as limited by nothingness, nothingness is at the same time concealed by the appearance of being. For, seen from being, nothingness is nothing more than nothing" (USS 9: 36). Following Ueda we may add: Solely out of nothingness is being in fact being. A more thoroughgoing inquiry into nothingness thus becomes necessary if we are to finally elucidate the phenomena of the world and our being-in-the-world.

Heidegger attempts such an inquiry into nothingness (or "the nothing")[23] in his 1929 lecture, "What is Metaphysics?" The initial, naive as well as obvious attempt to question nothingness—"What is the nothing?"—falls abruptly into logical contradiction. For in this question, nothingness is posited as something; but nothingness, being nothing, is of course *not* a being. Yet for Heidegger, the question rather immediately gives rise to a doubt as to whether logic is really in a position to pass judgment on nothingness. That would only be the case if nothingness was subordinated to negation in the logical sense, that is, to "a specific act of the intellect." Against this "reigning and never challenged doctrine of 'logic,'"[24] Heidegger is convinced that "the nothing is more original than the 'not' and negation."[25]

Heidegger substantiates his claim by referring to the fundamental mood of anxiety, which he had discussed at great length in *Being and Time*. Anxiety is contrasted with other moods, for example with profound boredom, in which, precisely by our being led before "beings as a whole,"[26] nothingness is concealed. Furthermore, anxiety is distinguished from common fear. Whereas fear depends totally on its object, anxiety is characterized by the absence of an object. More precisely, anxiety does not simply lack an object; it is essentially impossible to determine its object. For in anxiety, all beings slip away: "We can get no hold on things. In the slipping away of beings only this 'no hold on things' comes over us and remains. Anxiety reveals the nothing."[27] Then, when beings as a whole slip away in anxiety, nothingness discloses itself.

However, in anxiety beings do not suddenly cease to exist, and no more are we able to voluntarily become anxious (and thus catch a glimpse of nothingness as such) by way of negating beings as a whole. Structurally speaking, beings obstruct our view of nothingness, and nothingness is revealed only when beings slip away in anxiety. Beings as a whole find themselves invariably before the backdrop of nothingness, which in its nihilation, its withdrawal, makes room for the being of beings: "The nothing does not merely serve as counterconcept of beings; rather, it originally belongs to the essential unfolding as such. In the being of beings the nihilation of the nothing occurs."[28]

The withdrawal of nothingness opens up the space in which beings can be. Dasein can thereby relate to these beings in terms of its ownmost possibility of being: "since existence in its essence relates itself to beings—those which it is not and that which it is—it emerges as such existence in each case from the nothing already revealed. Da-sein means: being held out into the nothing."[29] Dasein's being held out into nothingness is the fundamental rendering possible of being-in-the-world. Dasein is, in its being held out into nothingness, first and foremost being-in-the-world. But then, Ueda concludes, nothingness is also characterized by a latent double structure:

> On the one hand, nothingness lets beings as a whole slip away in the manner of "having no hold on things"; it reveals itself for Dasein and drives Dasein about in nothingness. But, on the other hand, nothingness inversely makes existence possible in that, by transcending beings as a whole, existence relates to beings.... We can say that the ambivalence of the world in *Being and Time* here becomes, with slight changes, the ambivalence of nothingness (nihilation). (USS 9: 32)

Fourfold and Releasement: Ueda's Assimilation of the Later Heidegger

Ueda accepts Heidegger's analyses as a step in the right direction.

> "Dasein is within nothingness and within the world," or "The Dasein that is within the world is, by being within the world, at the same time within the nothingness within which the world is." . . . With Heidegger as a guide, it has become apparent that our existence is a twofold "within." (USS 9: 36)

At the same time, however, Ueda does not hesitate to offer a critique: Contrary to Heidegger's statements, anxiety is ultimately not able to disclose nothingness primordially and as such. While anxiety does permit the "inauthentic" self—absorbed in its everyday interactions and forgetful of being—to enter into a more profound dimension in which the nothingness of the world becomes apparent, anxiety cannot yet detach itself from this inauthentic mode of being. The nothingness revealed in anxiety is nothing more than the irruption of a still alien nothingness into inauthenticity. "The fact that the manifestation of nothingness is brought about by anxiety has its ground in nothingness, but more fundamentally it has its ground in the fact that we have forgotten nothingness" (USS 9: 37). A radical disclosure of nothingness thus cannot take place in anxiety. Moreover, "the fundamental ontology in which a transcendental character was in fact still retained, as well as metaphysics which questions nothingness on the basis of 'beings as a whole,' were not yet able to make the mutual belonging of being and nothingness as such the issue of their thought" (USS 9: 44). Therefore, Ueda demands a "fundamental turn in our relation to nothingness" (USS 9: 37). He finds this fundamental turn under way in Heidegger's later thought of "releasement" (*Gelassenheit*). It is to this idea that the next step shall take us.

Looking back, a more radical formulation of the idea of "being held out into nothingness" can be found already toward the end of "What is Metaphysics?" There Heidegger writes: "we release ourselves into the nothing, which is to say, . . . we liberate ourselves from those idols everyone has and to which he is wont to go cringing."[30] With Dasein's voluntary acceptance (*Sicheinlassen*) of itself as being conditioned by nothingness, the idea of releasement (*Gelassenheit*) is anticipated, and anxiety as the fundamental mood gradually yields to releasement. "From the anxiety disclosed in nothingness to the releasement that lets itself go into nothingness; from the nothingness of anxiety to the nothingness of releasement" (USS 9: 45)—in this movement Dasein and world step into their utmost possibilities. For in releasement, the human subject is transformed into the "mortal," and to "die means to be capable of death as death. Only man dies, and indeed continually."[31] At the same time, the invariably anthropocentric world of the "totality of involvements" is transformed into the "fourfold" world of earth and sky, divinities and mortals. In a released acceptance of their proper finite essence as "mortals," human beings take part in the "mirror play" of this fourfold and surrender their presumed position of preeminence as "subjects."

According to Ueda, when anxiety gives way to releasement, and the early "being-toward-death" is transformed into a "being-from-death," there lies the possibility of a new disposition (*Befindlichkeit*): Releasement *beyond* anxiety reveals itself to be the moment in which "being able to die" proves to also genuinely entail "being able to live." This willingness to die an "existential death"[32] hints at a breakthrough beyond every kind of subjectivity, toward Ueda's true self as not-self. But in Heidegger this breakthrough is not yet completely carried out, and thus his nothingness—even in its released form—is not the most fundamental nothingness Ueda is looking for.[33]

"Being-in-the-Twofold-World" and "Self as Not-Self": Ueda's Standpoint of Zen

Ueda is aware of the resistance his method of reading Heidegger might evoke. Heidegger's thought-path traverses a considerable time span and its complexity is impossible to reduce to any single term. Ueda nevertheless holds that his trans-chronological interpretation of Heideggerian "nothingness" is justified:

> The fact that it is not impossible to consider together [the earlier and the later Heidegger's thought] is illustrated in the fact that both include, each in its respective manner, a relation to nothingness. In this nothingness lies concealed the connection between the two. Of course, as we have already seen, they do not have the same manner of relating to nothingness. We might even say that it is not the same nothingness. These differences in respect to nothingness, however, make possible a synchronization [of Heidegger's thought] with precisely this nothingness in question as its locus. . . . (USS 9: 47)

And Ueda ventures even further: His reading Heidegger under the aspect of "nothingness" is not only possible and justifiable as an interpretation, but more importantly it is *necessary* if one is to realize the truth of the matter at stake.

According to Ueda, in a layering of the "world" explicated in *Being and Time* with the later Heidegger's "fourfold," one upon the other, "the true shape of the world is disclosed for the first time" (USS 9: 28). Only then does a view become possible that was formerly obstructed by our constant forgetting of nothingness. "First and foremost, we understand (or rather misunderstand) the world and the self in a prejudiced way in that we find ourselves within the world" (USS 9: 36). Submerged—or as Heidegger would say, "fallen"—into our dealings with things within the world, we do not recognize the world in its essential twofold structure. But when we take up a position in nothingness, the actuality of the world becomes visible. This point is nicely summarized by Nishitani: "Our existence is an existence that is one with nonexistence; incessantly disappearing into nothingness, incessantly returning to itself, it oscillates over nihility" (NKC 10: 6; RN 4). In its totality, the world is a twofold one: (1) the world as the gathering of all loci; and (2) the world "within" nothingness, which thereby has to be acknowledged as the locus of the world, the ultimate locus of all other loci.

Accordingly, the self as being-in-the-twofold-world, in its true form, must be essentially ek-static. In contrast to the Cartesian cogito, we have already seen that the self cannot be simply and statically self-identical. The disclosure of world and the letting oneself go into nothingness—that is, the ekstasis into the interpenetration of world and nothingness—is only possible on the basis of the self negating itself. In this self-negation, the self-enclosed subjectivity of deluded self-certainty is abandoned.

For Ueda, this negation is of enormous consequence: Not only is negation a crucial element of the self, but negation itself possesses a reflexive structure. Negation has to negate itself. Out of simple self-negation then arises an absolute negation with a twofold structure, a "pure movement in two directions at the same time: (1) the negation of negation in the sense of a further denial of negation that does not come back around to affirmation but opens up into an endlessly open nothingness; and (2) the negation of negation in the sense of a return to affirmation without any trace of mediation."[34] The movement of stepping out of the self and into the twofold world is necessarily accompanied by a movement of returning to the self; and precisely in this double movement the true self turns out to be the "self as not-self."

We are in a position now to define the main difference between Heidegger's and Ueda's conceptions of nothingness and negation: In Heidegger, negation is treated as one among many kinds of nihilating behavior, and by no means as the most fundamental nihilation. For Ueda, in contrast, negation is not a subfunction of nothingness; negation is the action that necessarily results when nothingness takes place in self-awareness. In absolute negation, the true self corresponds to the twofold structure of the world. Through the self's self-negation, the unending openness of world/nihility is actualized, and in negation turning back upon itself, the concrete self manifests itself within a concrete locus, yet without losing touch with its "unground" of nothingness.

A deconstruction of the Cartesian concept of subjectivity has shown us that the true self cannot be simply self-identical. For Ueda, Merleau-Ponty makes an initial attempt at a more profound response to the question of the self, and, with his prereflexive cogito, he offers a pathmark pointing toward Nishida's thought. Yet the tacit cogito is unable to grasp (even the possibility of) the most fundamental layer of unfragmented unity. In that the self unfolds spontaneously out of pure experience, a phenomenology of self necessitates a phenomenology of world, since a pure experiential unity disallows an original differentiation between the two. Ueda's reflections on Heidegger's thought have demonstrated clear parallels to Ueda's thinking (above all the twofold structure of the world and the self's being-in), but have also revealed issues (namely, nothingness and negation) where Heidegger stops short of Ueda's aim.

Ueda's readings of Descartes, Merleau-Ponty, and Heidegger may at times appear questionable, especially when he rethinks their central concepts from his own point of view. This questionable nature of his readings, however, is counterbalanced by the enormous fertility and fresh authenticity of his original interpretations and critical developments. And this is one of the reasons his texts will continue to be found compelling, certainly by many existentially engaged readers if not by every specialist.

Ueda's relation to Nishida is somewhat different. He acknowledges Nishida's philosophy as the basis of his own thought, while attempting to pursue its implications more methodically. Pure experience provides him with an irreducible touchstone of reality, which he never once abandons. The whole of Ueda's thought is deeply rooted in and unfolds as the reappropriation of pure experience in Zen practice, and the ultimately soteriological character of his interpretations and critical dialogue with other thinkers locates him squarely within the tradition of Zen.

This essay has attempted to show how significant a critical dialogue with Western thinkers has been in the formation of Ueda's thought. Yet his intrinsic willingness to commit himself to dialogue—not only to philosophical dialogue, but also to interreligious, intercultural, and interdisciplinary dialogue—is based precisely on the fact that Zen Buddhism is Ueda's constant touchstone. Indeed, for him it is ultimately from this standpoint of Zen that other standpoints are to be measured and evaluated.

Notes

1. Ueda's numerous publications in Western languages include "Der Zen-Buddhismus als 'Nicht-Mystik' unter besonderer Berücksichtigung des Vergleichs zur Mystik Meister Eckharts," in Günter Schulz, ed., *Transparente Welt: Festschrift zum sechzigsten Geburtstag von Jean Gebser* (Bern and Stuttgart: Hans Huber, 1965); "'Nothingness' in Meister Eckhart and Zen Buddhism: With Particular Reference to the Borderlands of Philosophy and Theology," trans. James W. Heisig, in Frederick Franck, ed., *The Buddha Eye: An Anthology of the Kyoto School* (New York: Crossroad, 1982); "The Concept of God, the Image of the Human Person and the Origin of the World in Buddhism," in Peter Koslowski, ed., *The Concept of God, the Origin of the World and the Image of the Human in the World Religions* (Dordrecht: Kluwer, 2001). For a study explicitly concerned with Heidegger, see "The Place of Man in the Noh Play," *The Eastern Buddhist New Series* 25, no. 2 (1992): 59–88.

2. See USS 9: 59–104 and USS 10: 101–23, respectively. All translations from foreign languages, unless indicated otherwise, are my own.

3. This characteristic is most explicit in Ueda's authoritative interpretation of the *Ten Ox-Herding Pictures*. See USS 6 and my *Wozu also suchen? Zur Einführung in das Denken von Ueda Shizuteru* (Munich: Iudicium, 2005).

4. René Descartes, "Meditations on First Philosophy," in *Philosophical Essays,* trans. Laurence J. Lafleur (New York: Bobbs-Merrill, 1964), 24.

5. Ibid., 86.

6. Ibid., 84.

7. For the following argument see the chapter titled "The Cogito" in Maurice Merleau-Ponty, *Phenomenology of Perception,* trans. Colin Smith (London: Routledge & Kegan Paul, 1962), esp. 398–404.

8. Ibid., 145.

9. Ibid., 137.

10. Ibid., 404.

11. Ibid., 403. Merleau-Ponty assures us: "This silent cogito was the one Descartes sought when writing his *Meditations*" (ibid., 402), but we may doubt whether Descartes would have accepted perception—be it ever so fundamental—as the certain principle of his philosophy.

12. Ibid., 404.

13. After a decade of intense practice, Nishida was apparently not fully satisfied with his experience and gave up at least the formal practice of Zen. Nonetheless, Ueda takes the *satori* of zazen to be the basis for the theory of pure experience; see USS 1.

14. For the following see also "Watakushi no shisaku: kenkyūreki ni sotte," in *Tōzai shūkyō kenkyū* 4: *Ueda Shizuteru-shi no shisō* (Nagoya: Japan Society for Buddhist-Christian Studies, 2005), 4–20. Also see John C. Maraldo's critical comments

on the issue of language and pure experience in "An Unedited Recapitulation of the Problem of Experience and Language," presented at the 1990 American Academy of Religion seminar on Process Thought in New Orleans, Louisiana.

15. For Ueda, the true, authentic self (*jiko*) contrasts sharply with the superficial ego (*jiga*), and correspondingly the common, objectifying self-consciousness (*ji'ishiki*) is shown to be a mere degeneration of self-awareness (*jikaku*).

16. It is noteworthy that Ueda's considerations seem to doubt whether the pre-verbality of the tacit cogito—as the point of greatest profundity in the compound structure of the reflexive and prereflexive cogito—could even claim the "fundamental creativity" that belongs to the *Ur-Satz*. Rather, the tacit cogito seems to be located somewhere between (2) and (3) and thus is only slightly more primordial than Descartes's semi-cogito.

17. Martin Heidegger, *Being and Time*, trans. John Macquarrie and Edward Robinson (New York: Harper & Row, 1962), 46.

18. Martin Heidegger, *Vier Seminare: Le Thor 1966 1968 1969 Zähringen 1973* (Frankfurt am Main: Vittorio Klostermann, 1977), 120.

19. Ibid., 120.

20. Ibid., 121.

21. Heidegger, *Being and Time*, 231.

22. Ibid., 231–32.

23. Martin Heidegger, "What is Metaphysics?" in *Basic Writings*, rev. edition, ed. David Farrell Krell (New York: Harper & Row, 1993). In the following, Krell's translation for *das Nichts*, "the nothing," and the somewhat more commonplace term, "nothingness," are considered to be interchangeable. The word "being" (*Sein*) has not been capitalized here.

24. Ibid., 97.

25. Ibid. Heidegger continues: "Does the ostensible absurdity of question and answer with respect to the nothing in the end rest solely in a blind conceit of the far-ranging intellect?" (ibid., 98). Heidegger's footnote from the fifth edition of 1949 specifies the blind conceit, rather, as "the *certitudo* of the ego cogito, subjectivity" (Martin Heidegger, "Was ist Metaphysik?" in *Wegmarken*, *Gesamtausgabe* 9 [Frankfurt am Main: Vittorio Klostermann, 1976], 108). See above, for his critique of Descartes. Ueda's interpretation will suggest that the "rambling intellect" (this translation seems to do more justice to the original, *schweifender Verstand*) is opposed by calm releasement in which the "ostensible absurdity" is dissolved and nothingness becomes approachable.

26. Heidegger, "What is Metaphysics?" 100.

27. Ibid., 101.

28. Ibid., 104. Nothingness becomes the cipher of ontological difference, since in nothingness the difference between being and beings is revealed. "The essence of the originally nihilating nothing lies in this, that it brings the Da-sein for the first time before beings as such" (ibid., 103), and Heidegger's 1949 footnote specifies: "expressly before the being of beings, before the difference" ("Was ist Metaphysik?" 114).

29. Heidegger, "What is Metaphysics?" 103.

30. Ibid., 110.

31. Heidegger, "Building, Dwelling, Thinking," in *Basic Writings*, 352.

32. See Bret W. Davis, *Heidegger and the Will: On the Way to Gelassenheit* (Evanston, Ill.: Northwestern University Press, 2007), 56–59.

33. Ueda's translation of the German term *Gelassenheit* as *hōge shite byōjōshin* is noteworthy here. This Japanese phrase can be roughly retranslated in a literal fashion as "unmoved everyday heart-mind in letting-go." This "everyday heart-mind" signifies, in the Zen tradition, the state of utmost awakening (*kaku*), imperturbable by all dualities, that has grown in constant concentration beyond even enlightenment itself and into nothingness as such. Heidegger's releasement, for Ueda, serves to describe a detached self-awareness that can let itself go into being as well as into nothingness, that, having "no hold on things," tends neither toward the one nor the other.

34. Ueda, "'Nothingness' in Meister Eckhart and Zen Buddhism," 160–61.

PART THREE

God and Nothingness

8

Nothing Gives: Marion and Nishida on Gift-giving and God

JOHN C. MARALDO

The Christian philosopher Jean-Luc Marion and the Buddhist philosopher Nishida Kitarō, as vast as their differences may be, have both proposed alternatives to thinking of God in terms of being and thinking of being in terms of ground. They both offer a way out of onto-theology that is markedly different from Heidegger's. Marion presents the alternative of God revealed as gift and giving rather than as a being. Differing from Derrida, Marion places this alternative within the scope of phenomenology and affirms the possibility of an unconditional gift unrelated to any potential recipient. Nishida offers the alternative of a self-negating absolute to which we inevitably relate and which necessarily relates to us. His name for that relation in Japanese is *gyaku-taiō*, "inverse correlation"; it draws upon but expands the Buddhist notion of co-dependent origination, and differently envisions the possibility of giving. The following reflections investigate the issues underlying these assertions, from the question of the possibility of the gift in Derrida and in Buddhism, to Marion's critique of onto-theology and offer of God as gift, to Nishida's alternatives. In the end I suggest that Marion's notion of God as giving needs a notion like Nishida's absolute nothing to make it work.

Derrida, the Impossibility of the Gift, and Two Responses

We begin with the notions of gift and gift giving, which are crucial to Marion's thinking of God. Marion is in contention with Derrida regarding the thought of the gift. Derrida of course thinks against the possibility of the gift—not simply of any gift or any gift giving, but more precisely the possibility of the appearance of an unconditionally given gift—the only gift worthy of the name. Any other kind of "gift" would really be a form of exchange and not a gift at all. We may recapitulate his argument in phenomenological terms, for it is also against the possibility of phenomenology that Derrida frames his argument: The gift is impossible as a phenomenon, that is, the gift can never be present as such, for the intention of unconditioned giving can never be fulfilled. Such a gift—the gift as such—can never be "given" in the phenomenological sense, as fulfilling an intention. It can never appear or manifest or be present as a phenomenon. And here's why: When I give to you, I leave you in debt, and therefore I take something from you, and therefore what I give is no longer (and never really was) truly given as a gift. In a conversation with Marion in 1997 at Villanova University, Derrida elaborates on this aporia and even insinuates that in giving to you I inevitably both congratulate myself and elicit gratitude from you; so I have not freely given at all. The problem is not simply that we must describe every actual gift as an exchange and inscribe it within "the circle of economy." In fact, Derrida claims to want to free the gift from the "horizon of exchange and economy,"[1] namely by recognizing that there is such a "thing" (such an intention?) as a freely given gift, one that is not an implied request for something in return, but that it can never "appear as such," for its manifestation or givenness cancels out the intention. As soon as one tries to give a gift, it enters into the circle of economy and the expectation of something in return. The intention of giving a gift interrupts the economy of exchange, and the intention of exchanging something for the gift annuls it. Like a ghost, the gift disappears before one can grasp it. It is its appearance, its givenness, that is impossible.[2] In other words (not Derrida's words), the condition for the possibility of the gift is an impossibility—yet again, not its "absolute impossibility" but its impossibility as a phenomenon. How then can we even speak of a gift? Derrida does not defer: "through the experience of the impossibility."[3] And such an experience, of the impossibility of the full presence of something, once again and more generally vitiates the very possibility of phenomenology. We are left once again with a promise of something always to come but never present. If I may be allowed a double pun, recalling that *Gift* in German means poison and "present" in English also means gift, then for Derrida the gift received poisons the giving, a present poisons the future.[4]

Even before we offer Marion's own novel alternative, two more traditional responses are possible. The first, from within the phenomenological tradition, addresses the possibility of phenomenology, which Derrida sees (in the 1997 conversation at least) as limited to a description of phenomena, those things that are supposed to be given, that is, supposed to be fully present or presentable: Classical phenomenologists have had a way of describing much more than what is given in Derrida's limited sense of the word. Husserl took great pains to demonstrate how an absence can be manifested as such, how something can be given precisely as absent, and how things are given in a blend of presences and absences. There are three features to notice here. First, when something is actually present to us, or "intuited" in Husserl's sense, it may be so in contrast to our intending it in its absence. But it may still be given in a mixture of absences and presences, as for example a Rubik's cube is inevitably given to one's perception as a presence of some sides and aspects of the cube together with an absence of the sides and aspects that are presently hidden to one.[5] The cube is nevertheless intuited precisely as a cube. Secondly, I can see that something is absent or missing: I can for example notice that the Rubik's cube that was just there on my table is now gone; I present the cube as a missing object. Thirdly, my focus can turn to and see the absence as such. I can manifest the absence. The absence itself is not merely intended, in contrast to being intuited; it is given precisely as an absence. All three examples make the point that the given cannot simply be equated with what is fully present, without remainder. For Husserl, the given is not simply what is bodily present. Indeed, the identity of an object like this particular Rubik's cube is itself given only "across the difference of [its] presence and absence."[6] Heidegger also addressed the issue of givenness and absence, albeit in his own terms. He emphasized what he ironically calls *the* phenomenon of phenomenology, namely, that which does *not* (at first and for the most part) show itself,[7] which in early Heidegger is the prior world that remains hidden and absent with respect to what is present to us. Or in later Heidegger, the opening or clearing which itself does not appear but by which all (other) phenomena do appear.[8] Or throughout Heidegger, Being (*das Sein*)—which can never appear as such.

We need not have recourse to the treatment of absence in classical phenomenology, however, to indicate how it can account for the phenomenon of the gift. For a gift to be given, what must be presented along with the given item is the intention, in the conventional sense of the word—the intention that nothing be given back in return. Indeed, for the item to appear as a gift, the item itself recedes behind the intention presented with it. Derrida's contention would seem to be that such an intention is never given: Either it is missing in the first place on the part of the giver, or no sooner than it shows up, it is cancelled by the recipient's inevitable anticipation that something in return is expected, and so on. Once given, the intended gift becomes an item of exchange that is really not a gift at all. It is as if Derrida imagines only one or another of these two scripts:

> "Here's a present for you . . . {and you'd better give me back something I want}."
>
> Or,
>
> "Here's a present for you!"
> {"Oh oh, now I guess I owe you something in return in the future."}

But why not imagine the following sincere exchange instead?

> "Here, a present for you."
>
> "Thank you."
>
> "Not at all."

Sometimes "not at all" is merely a thoughtless response. Sometimes "not at all" expresses the insignificance of the gift, which would make it not much of a gift at all ("it was no bother at all"). Sometimes, however, the "not at all" expresses that no "thank you" is needed or has even been expected. Consider then this third sense of the expression. Does "not at all" deny that a gift has been given in order to preserve (the secrecy of) the gift, as Derrida might say? And if so, does such a denial annul the gift? A denial presumably would not mean that the giver takes back the intended gift. Would it mean that the giver's intention of receiving nothing in return is now annulled because something—an expression of gratitude—has in fact been returned? But has something been returned? Perhaps the "not at all" is a refusal of the return, and the denial pertains to the offer of gratitude rather than to the giving of the gift. Yet would it not seem harsh to turn back an expression of gratitude offered by the recipient? No, that is not it at all: these proposals do not capture the sense of gift-giving and thanks-giving at all. The "not at all" is not a rejection of the gratitude expressed, and when no thanks are called for, a "thank you" is not a gesture of return. The difference between gratitude and a commodity or article of trade is the utter gratuitousness of gratitude. One is especially grateful for what one can never return. We might suppose that gratitude, like the gift, is impossible, that it never appears as such, but this would be already to grant Derrida what he assumes: that we find no giving outside the circle of exchange. Derrida's intention to free the gift from the "horizon of exchange and economy" presupposes the link (the imprisoning chain) between gift and economy. Derrida's intention here cannot be fulfilled. On the other hand, there is no phenomenological reason that an intention to give unconditionally cannot itself be given, and hence no evident reason why such a gift cannot be given.

The second response to Derrida's aporia of the gift comes from within the Buddhist tradition. The Buddhist virtue of *dāna*, giving or generosity, is instructive here. In both practice and conception, *dāna* would seem to work precisely in the economy of exchange. For example, lay people give to monastic communities and receive merit or good karma in return; in addition they receive from the monks: the Dharma or teaching, the gift that excels all gifts.[9] Some texts suggest that in giving to the monks and dedicating the gift to the local gods, the gods will look favorably upon the donors but the gods too will share the karmic benefits.[10] Even beyond the conception and practice of giving and getting something in return, there is undoubtedly the economic motive of the monks who write the texts and recommend that lay people give generously to them: They want to stay in business, as it were, and they need others to give because they are not self-sufficient. This rather realistic, economic interpretation of *dāna*, however, makes assumptions that are questioned by Buddhist philosophy, which presents the phenomenon of giving in a different light. Buddhist ontology proposes that no beings are self-sufficient in any way; all are interdependent and co-arise. Following this premise, there cannot be any giving which does not affect all—that is, the donor as well as the recipients. In a sense, giving effects or brings about the donor and the recipient. As one Buddhist pamphlet says, "*Dāna* means simultaneously giving and receiving"—a receiving that is not a taking away of someone else's possessions, and a giving that is not a giving away of any possession, because there is no possession in the first place. *Dāna* is a recognition of our interdependence. What, if anything, is given up is attachment to things and to the very idea of possession. Thus, to reduce actual giving to a circle of exchange and cast it solely in economic terms is to presuppose an ontology of pre-possession and self-possession, of beings who could be self-sufficient and intend to give unconditionally, even if in practice they need or want what others have, and even if in performance their intention can never be fulfilled. Derrida's critique of giving, and his attempted rescue of the gift from the circle of exchange by proclaiming its givenness to be impossible, alike presuppose an ontology of radically independent beings. Within Buddhist theories and practices, to be sure, there is a conflict of interpretations regarding gift-giving, as self-interested exchange or as affirmation of interdependence. Nevertheless, we need not try to resolve that conflict in order to recognize the ontological presupposition of Derrida's critique.[11]

Marion for his part uses the phenomenon of the gift to reveal certain other presuppositions, namely, onto-theological assumptions that take God to be a being, and indeed, a causal being. Working his way out of these presuppositions, Marion has attempted to alter and to expand phenomenology by showing how the gift need not be given "as such," as a gift with an identifiable giver or recipient or given thing. He has attempted to show further that the phenomenological notion of givenness can dispense with the notion of "as such"[12]—a description suggesting perhaps the essence that a being can have. We turn next to these attempts.

Onto-theology and Marion's God as Gift beyond Being

Consider first the connection between the gift and the critique of *onto-theology*. Heidegger used this word for what he believed to be the predominant tradition of philosophy, what he called "Occidental metaphysics." Onto-theology designates discourse or reasoning (*logos*) that takes God (*theos*) to be the supreme being and first cause of all other beings, yet also understands all beings as grounded in Being and thus, in a confused manner, takes God as Being. Heidegger's analysis recalled the forgotten difference between Being and beings, the "ontological difference." Heidegger's project was to free Being from its delimitation as ground and so to disentangle God and Being.

Marion's *Dieu sans l'être* (*God Without Being*), first published in 1982, challenged the notion that God must be or should be thought of as a being. It further questioned the more philosophically sophisticated notion that God functions as the ground or first cause of all beings. This work clearly posed itself against both onto-theology and Heidegger's treatment of it. It uncovered historical exceptions to the onto-theology that Heidegger found to be pervasive in metaphysics, and thus disputed Heidegger's claim that onto-theology defines the dominant tradition of philosophy. Marion also made a case that Heidegger's diversion from this tradition—that is, his insistence on the ontological difference—does not offer the dimension wherein God would become thinkable: "Being says nothing about God," namely, the God of biblical revelation, "that God cannot immediately reject."[13] Most importantly, Marion's early work developed its own theology of God without being. Later, less theological and more phenomenological works such as *Étant donné* (*Being Given*)[14] shift from an account of God as gift to accounts of gift as a paradigm of givenness; Marion would not only save God from the onto-theological tradition, but also save phenomenology from challenges to its very possibility.

Phenomenologists might indeed be inclined to read Marion's early accounts, in *God Without Being* and other essays, as an almost desperate attempt to rescue God from oblivion in contemporary philosophy. The God that is rescued is perched on the brink of the collapse of thought, at least from a human perspective. Several of Marion's works interpret Anselm's famous definition of God as *id quo majus cogitari nequit*, "that than which a greater cannot be thought." For Marion, God posits a transcendental limit to thought or the power to conceive. In one essay that presents Anselm as an exception to the onto-theological tradition, Marion suggests that we "experience" God only "when thought thinks that it cannot think what it cannot think and that what it cannot think surpasses it by being not only outside its understanding but beyond what it will ever understand."[15] A phenomenology of God, then, would seem to require a phenomenology of the unthinkable, of what cannot be given even to thought, much less to experience.[16] Marion's radicalized phenomenology of the gift and of givenness will attempt a way out of this aporia.

For Marion, the God who (is) not a being is also not thinkable within an ontological difference from beings, and thus (is) not a differend of Being. The implied "not this, not that" structure of Marion's God easily elicits, for readers of Nishida at least, thoughts of another naught, the absolute nothing of Nishida. Could Marion possibly be talking about the same sort of thing—or rather the same sort of no-thing? I will return to that question later. First we must see how Marion replaces being not with nothingness, a *negativum*, but rather with giving, a *positum*. God, it will turn out, is neither being nor not-being.

To de-ontologize God and yet indicate how his unthinkableness saturates our thought, Marion does eventually cross out the word *God*. He leaves us with more than a blank space, however, and more even than a thought crossed out. There is a sign, he says—but one only—that is feasible for the unthinkable thought of God, and that sign or concept is love, *agapē*. Divine giving, synonymous with love or *agapē*, is unconditional (and could be unrequited); it is pure bestowal.[17] In this discussion the giving that (is) God does not presuppose that there be recipients, that we are already there to receive—or reject—the gift. One could phenomenologically interpret this implied presuppositionlessness and say that *we* are what is given, and given precisely through the act of divine creation. It might be a stretch to call us human creatures a gift, if not to use that word for the created world, but in any case it is clear that phenomenological givenness does not necessarily entail a giver or a recipient. Yet Marion's *God Without Being* does not equate the given with creation, presumably because such an equation would identify God with a first cause or creator being—a notion that remains captive to onto-theology.[18] Marion's later works continue to avoid talk of creation as the given, and even disassociate the given—that is, phenomena in general—from the necessity of a giver.[19] What then is the sense of God as the giving we call love?

In *God Without Being* it seems that Marion speaks of God, the crossed-out God, as the giver, the gift, the giving, and in a sense even the given. The seemingly deliberate web of conflations and distinctions that Marion suggests permits only a tentative interpretation here. The discussion that first suggests *agapē* as the sign for God seems to identify God (crossed-out) with pure giving. "Love . . . postulates its own giving, giving *where the giver strictly coincides with the gift* without any restriction, reservation, or mastery."[20] A later passage states that giving "must be understood by reference to the giver," and places a necessary distance between the giver and the gift. From our side, Marion says, this distance allows the giver to be seen or read in the gift. Indeed, the self-withdrawal of the giver in the gift is what makes our reference to the giver possible.[21] Clearly there is a distinction between giver and gift here, although the giver, God crossed-out, is not a being. Being belongs to this (our) side of the giving—apparently not because being or existence constitutes what is given us, but because being is thinkable or graspable, and God is not.

So far this discussion implies distinctions between giver, act of giving, and gift or what is given. Marion goes on to imply the necessity of recipients and response. But the response he has in mind is necessary only if and when we attempt to think God/love, which would indeed require a response of love, a loving response.[22] God himself is under no restriction to love only when he is loved in return; much less does God need to be thought or conceived by us. And the respondents or recipients needed for the thought of God's love are not receivers of the gift, for if the gift is unconditional love they are unneeded. Rather the recipients are diviners of the gift's source. Marion speaks both of reading or seeing the giver through the gift, and of the trace of the giver in the giving.[23] His discussion, however, avoids the questions, *for whom* is the gift given, *who* reads the sign or finds the trace?

God also appears as a "pure given"—namely in the guise of the gift—but without justification or rationalization, "with neither deduction nor legitimation,"[24] without reason, irreducible to logic, to onto-theological thinking. The gift, moreover, is never exhaustively given, is never done with its deliverance. That is because (if I may use that word), "the gift gives the giver to be seen . . . [in] a ceaseless play of giving."[25]

So despite the appeal to a giving "*where the giver strictly coincides with the gift,*" it seems we have several distinct components: a giver, a giving, a gift or given, and a recipient. And here this means: A giver who is not a being and is not thinkable within the ontological difference, a giving which does not give any thing, a gift which is not directed at anyone, a given which is never fully delivered, and a recipient who is unneeded. If there is a problem with this conceptuality, perhaps it is belied by my wording, "we have" (these various distinctions). After all, we are talking about a God (crossed-out) who can never be a matter of our conceptual possession.

Perhaps Marion's later work, focusing on the possibility of a phenomenology of the gift rather than the conceptuality of God, can provide some clarification. In the book *Being Given* and the 1997 conversation with Derrida, Marion is concerned with the variable phenomenon of the gift in general but makes remarks that might pertain to the idea of God as gift. He argues that we can "bracket" or give up in our description one or more seemingly essential components of an enacted or actually performed gift. We can imagine a gift given without any giver—for example, some useful thing that Robinson Crusoe happens to find on his island. We can imagine a gift where nothing, no thing, is given—when for example what is given is time, or power, or one's word or promise. And we can imagine a gift with no receiver—that is, a gift given with no recipient in mind, no one who is actually known to the giver. Notice that in Marion's imaginative variations any one and even two of the distinct components mentioned above (giver, given, and recipient) can be absent—with the exception of the giving.[26] Notice also that the bracketed component in each case is a qualification or specification of what can count as a giver, a given, and a recipient. We can, Marion asserts, make sense of a gift without an *identifiable* giver, a *known or anticipated* recipient, or a given *as a concrete thing*. He does not, however, dispense with *some* sense of a giver, given, or recipient in the phenomenon of the gift; much less does he bracket the notion of giving. Indeed he seems to imply that givenness is the manifestation/presentation of giving; thus the active, verbal reformulation of givenness as "being given." He explicitly wants both to establish that there is no such thing as the gift "as such," and "to reduce the gift to givenness," but not to reduce givenness or phenomenality (which makes phenomenology possible) to the gift.[27] These reflections are consistent with Marion's earlier efforts to free the notion of God from the onto-theological idea of a creator/giver whose given is creation itself. They differ from the earlier discussion of God as gift only in this manner: In the case of God, from the more general phenomenological vantage point, we are dealing with a kind of gift (a phenomenon of dispensation?) in which not one or two but all of its components are bracketed—in which, to repeat, we have a giver who is not a being, a giving which does not give any thing, a gift which is not directed at anyone, a given which is never fully delivered, and a recipient who is unneeded. Is this expansive bracketing the reason that the entire notion of God seems to be bracketed in the later phenomenology of *Being Given*? Neither it nor the 1997 conversation resolve the tension between the distinct components of the gift on the one hand and the idea of a giving "*where the giver strictly coincides with the gift*" on the other.

We might try to give Marion a more charitable reading by finding a way to unify these various distinctions in one notion. Might we appeal to Nishida's famous "self-identity of absolute contradictories"? Marion himself notes that his model of the gift "unites only to the extent that it distinguishes," and this may remind one of Nishida's logic.[28] Unless Nishida's notion were itself explained, however, it would be a mere *deus ex machina* here, or perhaps worse, the substitution of one inexplicable idea for another. Marion's own notion of course is *love*. Can the idea of unconditional love unify these different distinctions? Marion states that *agapē* "is not—but gives (itself)."[29] The qualification "is not" removes God as *agapē* from being; the description "gives (itself)" implies that divine love is at once the giver, the giving, and the given. The parentheses around "itself" subvert the expectation that something different is what is given, that there is a separate transitive object. *Agapē* gives (itself) as unity of giver, giving, and the given, if not of recipient as well—but then, we should not expect to find a recipient named here for unconditional love requires no reception and no response. Yet there is an opening for the unnamed recipient in the mention of distance that is shortly to come. Marion follows this statement with the metaphor of a flowing current, "too violent to go back up, too profound for one to know its source or valley," everything flowing along the giving which leaves an ungraspable wake traced in the water. "[E]verything indicates the direction and meaning of distance," he writes, which suggests not a distance between giver and giving and given, but a remove from them of those standing downstream, of us recipients.[30]

It would seem that the torrent of love effaces any definitive difference between giver, giving, and gift, but also pushes against and frustrates the grasp of any expecting recipient. And not only can no one stand in its way, but there is no One that stands unmoved at its source. Marion's earlier discussion that first suggested love as the only feasible sign for God, that spoke of a giving "where the giver strictly coincides with the gift," goes on to say that "love gives itself only in abandoning itself . . . love holds nothing back, neither itself nor its representation . . . it transcends itself in a critical movement where nothing—not even Nothingness/Nothing—can contain the excess of an absolute giving."[31] I am unsure of Marion's intent in stressing Nothingness/Nothing here; perhaps he is anticipating his later discussion of Pseudo-Dionysius's proposal that God (is) the Requisite (*aitia*) of non-being as well as of being, and thus is not defined by either.[32] In any case this passage does suggest that a God who (is) love or absolute giving cannot be thought as an agent-being who is separate from his activity. Marion's God is not only crossed-out but swept-away, as it were, in his doing, his giving (Marion strangely continues to use the masculine pronoun).

Does the idea of unconditional love, then, unify the distinctions between giver, giving, and gift? Yes, but only by invoking a kind of self-negation, a self-abandoning, of their difference.

Nothing Gives: A Nishidan Perspective on Giving

Marion's themes of self-negation and God as love find resonance in Nishida's last completed essay, "The Logic of Place and the Religious Worldview," written in 1945. In its discussion of how the absolute and relative relate, Nishida appropriates the language of God as love. "It is said that God created the world out of love, but what we call God's absolute love is essential to God as absolute self-negation" (NKZ 11: 399).[33] God's being consists in God's self-negation; God (is) not God and therefore God (is) God. The classical source of this formulation, although without referring to God of course, is the Buddhist *Diamond Sutra*.[34] An example used by Nishida's follower Nishitani Keiji helps explain its logic. Nishitani writes, "Fire does not burn fire,"[35] and by extension we could say, "Fire is not fire and therefore it is fire." If I may be allowed to repeat an explanation I have offered elsewhere,[36] think of fire not as some thing, but as activity, as what fire does, what it is by be-ing fire. What is it that only fire does, that defines its singular being? Fire burns; it exists, it is, by burning. But it cannot burn itself. Of everything in the physical universe, only fire (at least in a broad metaphorical sense) is exempt from burning. It is itself only by negating what it is. Now apply this logic to the notion of God as love. To take love as the nature of God is to say God (is) loving, where "loving" functions as God's identity and not as an attribute of God. To say God loves is analogous to saying fire burns. And as fire cannot burn itself, so too God cannot love Godself.[37] Fire cannot be fire except in terms of what it is not, in terms of the not-fire that burning is and the not-fire that is the thing burned.

Analogously, God cannot (be) God without be-ing not-God, and without that which is loved and which is not God.

Notice that the talk of God loving but not Godself, like the talk of fire burning but never itself, implies an Other already there, or at least something else arising contemporaneously. "Burning" and "loving" function as transitive verbs in this logic: Fire means burning something that is not fire; God means loving and creating God's other, God's creation. This difference between the verb and its transitive object could indeed be bridged by the Buddhist idea of co-dependent arising (*pratītya-samutpāda*), which would collapse any separate appearance of the two and undermine any notion of an agent preexisting an object. The idea of co-dependent origination could indeed be in the back of Nishida's mind, but then this would also mark an unbridgeable difference between him and Marion. Whatever his alternative to the onto-theological notion of creation, Marion would still abide by "the Christian distinction," as some philosophers have called it: This is the conviction that God is in no sense whatever dependent on His creation, that His creating is absolutely gratuitous, that the created world plus God is in no way greater than God alone and that God minus the world is in no way lesser.[38] Marion's notion of love giving (itself) would seem in no way to require a created recipient. As we have seen, Marion does not take creation itself as the gift, or as what is given. God (is) absolute love, unconditional loving that needs no other.[39] Marion's kind of self-negation or self-abandonment seems quite different from Nishida's.

Another word for God in Nishida's essay is the absolute. An elaboration of absolute and relative may throw light on the difference between Nishida and Marion. There are two strands in this issue, the relation between absolute and relative and the relation that defines the absolute itself. Nishida's neologism for the relation between absolute and relative is *gyaku-taiō*, "inverse correlation" or, we might say, "contrary respondence." *Gyaku* denotes inverse or reverse; *tai* means "overagainst." *Gyaku-tai* indicates the asymmetry between absolute (*zettai*) and relative (*sōtai*); and the ordinary word *taiō* indicates a correspondence or relation between them. The relation between the truly absolute and the relative, or God and human self, is exceptional. The two do not mutually oppose one another, for mutual opposition literally describes *sōtai*, the relation between relative and relative. Absolute and relative are not opposites. Indeed, Nishida reminds us that the term *zettai* which we translate as "absolute" literally means "breaking through opposition" (*tai wo zessuru koto*) (NKZ 11: 396). The expression *gyaku-taiō* (contrary respondence) that names the relation between the absolute or God and the relative or human self, serves to deny both ultimate identity and ultimate difference. It implies that the absolute or God and the relative human self are inseparable yet never dissolve into one another.[40]

Nishida also insists that the true absolute is not *merely* something that breaks through opposition. If the function of the absolute were only to go beyond oppositions, he implies, it would merely name an all-inclusive total-ity, a passive harmony or, in his own words, a God without creative power, not really God at all. The absolute neither stands in mutual opposition to its other nor merely severs opposition to go beyond it. Rather, a kind of internal relation defines the absolute. The true absolute stands overagainst nothing but itself. This formulation implies a self that relates to itself in a certain way. In general, Nishida writes, "[W]hat opposes itself must negate itself. . . . what has no relation to itself cannot negate itself" (NKZ 11: 397).[41] But the self-relation of God or the absolute that Nishida struggles to define is not simply that of the classical being-for-itself. The "being" of the absolute[42] requires a space or place within which it can relate to itself by way of self-negation. In the case of God the self-negation is so complete that God embraces all (other) beings. God is truly nothing in itself. By expressing nothing, God allows all relative beings to be themselves, mutually opposed to one another, and to relate to God in contrary respondence. In this sense God as the absolute is the expres-sion of absolute nothing. The two are not identified, but brought together in a relation called absolute self-negation—a relation not between God and noth-ing but between God and Godself. Absolute nothing, in a sense, is the place-holder that allows self-negating.

What does this sense of the absolute bring to the notion of God as pure-ly self-giving love? How can God's giving be unconditional, from Nishida's standpoint? In giving and as giving, God negates Godself; God as the absolute opposes nothing. There is no need to reify *nothing* here: God does not oppose any other, but embraces all, even while all else differs from God, for all else is mutually opposing. Nishida's contrary respondence suggests a different kind of alterity for the absolute.[43] Extrapolating from Nishida, we can envision the difference in the kind of relation that obtains between giving and receiving.

The absolute gives in giving itself away to the relative. There can be no such giving without the relative as recipient, even though the absolute is not dependent on the relative in the way that relative beings are co-dependent on one another. In receiving, we relative beings oppose or stand over against God; we face God, which for Nishida entails our dying to self, our self-negation.[44] The absolute's giving of itself is unconditional in that it could not receive back at all, much less expect to receive.[45] When relative beings give to one another, on the other hand, they enter into a relationship of mutuality, and their giving is conditional—even if not necessarily a matter of economic exchange. (Why cannot there be moments of selfless giving, as in a parent-child relationship, and so much so that such selfless giving defines oneself because it negates one's self?) A giving that cannot receive in turn is contrary to the kind of giving in relationships of mutuality. It is a relation of contrary respondence, *gyaku-taiō*. Nishida's notion adds a new dimension to the traditional Buddhist concept of co-dependent origination, *pratītya-samutpāda*, which typifies the relation between all beings. Nishida's notion specifies these interdependent beings as relative beings and contrasts the relation among them with the relation between any self-aware being and the absolute, the relation of contrary respondence. Although the notion of the absolute has troubled precedents in Buddhist philosophy,[46] I suspect that Nishida deliberately looked to Christian ideas of God to formulate a contrary notion—a notion of a self-negating absolute which necessarily relates to us, and to which we inevitably relate.

Does this kind of self-negation bring Nishida and Marion any closer together? Marion's God or absolute love ostensibly moves against nothing as much as against being: "Love gives itself only in abandoning itself . . . love holds nothing back, neither itself nor its representation. . . . it transcends itself in a critical movement where nothing—not even Nothingness/Nothing—can contain the excess of an absolute giving."[47] Here God's manner of self-negation or self-abandon knows no bounds. It is indeed unknowable, ungraspable, conceptually unthinkable, as Marion says over and over again. If there were ever a word that bespeaks the inconceivable, it is absolute nothing. Marion's self-abandon and Nishida's self-negation seem to approximate each other; both undermine self-subsistent being. Nishida's nothing may be too negative for Marion, however. Marion wants God purely as the gift, the self-giving, of love; and he imagines nothingness as something that can hold God back. Yet it is precisely absolute nothing that is entailed by taking the thought of absolute giving as self-abandoning to its limit. At this limit, nothing gives: Nothingness allows the total self-negation that defines the kind of love we call God. Nishida's thought would also imply that, in a certain sense, nothing receives; he has said that for the relative to face the absolute is to die, a death that negates the self and opens it to the absolute. The relative nothing that receives, if we may use a nominal expression, is the place opened by the self-negating of the relative self. For his part Marion has left the recipient end open; whether or not the gift is received is inconsequential to the giving. Could that gift and that giving be relayed by the relation called "contrary respondence," and indeed, perhaps only by that kind of relation?

Contrary respondence, as I have suggested, describes the relation between God and relative human selves; both are necessary to that relation. Marion has implied that we relative human selves are not necessary—neither as being the recipients of love, nor as being creatures of a gratuitous creation. Yet I find the notion of gift and giving truly inconceivable without the supposition of a potential recipient. Moreover, this is not the kind of inconceivability that Marion wants to retain in thinking of God. I can make sense of a notion of unconditional love that requires no response in kind. This is precisely the kind of asymmetry captured in Nishida's converse respondence, where God or the absolute embraces and never excludes the human or relative, but where the human never coincides with or melts into God. Absolute love or giving may be the province solely of God, but the human or relative recipient is the necessary condition for the presencing of the gift. Nishida and Marion can agree that absolute giving is not reciprocal; it is not like the gift that Ralph Waldo Emerson has in mind. That gift, "to be true, must be the flowing of the giver unto me, correspondent to my flowing unto him."[48] If contrary respondence and not reciprocity describes the relation of absolute giving, then the distance between Marion and Nishida reduces to the place of nothing—the nothing that gives, for Nishida, and the nothing that holds back, for Marion.

NOTES

1. Economic exchange of course is the horizon that has defined gift-giving for generations of scholars ever since Mauss's *Essai sur le don* (1925). See Marcel Mauss, *The Gift: The Form and Reason for Exchange in Archaic Societies*, trans. W. D. Halls (New York: W. W. Norton, 1990).

2. Aside from my analysis in terms of intentionality and the analogy of the ghost, the formulations of the gift's impossible appearance are from "On the Gift: A Discussion between Jacques Derrida and Jean-Luc Marion, Moderated by Richard Kearney," in John D. Caputo and Michael J. Scanlon, eds., *God, the Gift, and Postmodernism* (Bloomington: Indiana University Press, 1999), 59.

3. Derrida's full statement reads: "I never said that there is no gift. No, I said exactly the opposite. What are the conditions for us to say there is a gift, if we cannot determine it theoretically, phenomenologically? It is through the experience of the impossibility; that its possibility is possible as impossible" ("On the Gift," 60).

4. For Derrida, part of the impossibility of giving a gift, fully and without expectation of return, is a necessity for this giving to be repeated in the future. I fail to

see such a necessity. In his 1997 dialogue with Marion, Derrida remarks on the ideal uniqueness but future commitment entailed by the (actually impossible) gift: "I would associate the singularity of the gift as an event with the necessity for it or the promise for it to be repeated. When I give something to someone, in the classical semantic of the gift . . . I already promise to confirm it, to repeat it, even if I do not repeat it. The repetition is part of the singularity" ("On the Gift," 67).

5. Robert Sokolowski eloquently clarifies this point, as well as phenomenology's attention to absences, in his *Introduction to Phenomenology* (Cambridge: Cambridge University Press, 2000), 35–39.

6. Ibid., 37.

7. Martin Heidegger, *Sein und Zeit* [1927] (Tübingen: Max Niemeyer Verlag, 1963), 35.

8. See James Hart's formulation, inspired by Thomas Prufer: "The claim that the clearing is *the* phenomenon of phenomenology therefore struggles against the 'myth of the given' and the pervasive teleology of presencing of language as the gathering out of hiddenness and absence into presence and manifestation. The phenomenon of phenomenology is an emptiness . . . that absence within which all presencing and absencing occurs. This absence withdraws itself in all acts of presencing" (Martin Heidegger, *The Piety of Thinking*, trans. with notes and commentary James G. Hart and John C. Maraldo [Bloomington: Indiana University Press, 1976], 94).

9. The classical statement of the *Dharma* (Pali *Dhamma*) as the gift of gifts is found in verse 354 of the *Dhammapada*, an anthology of verses attributed to the Buddha. There are many English translations; one is *The Dhammapada: A New Translation of the Buddhist Classic with Annotations*, trans. Jack Kornfield and Gil Fronsdal (Boston: Shambhala, 2005).

10. Peter Harvey, *An Introduction to Buddhist Ethics* (Cambridge: Cambridge University Press, 2000), 64.

11. A different and much more detailed analysis of the complex approach of Buddhists to gift-giving is found in Reiko Ohnuma, "Gift," in Donald S. Lopez, ed., *Critical Terms for the Study of Buddhism* (Chicago: University of Chicago Press, 2005), 103–23. Ohnuma recognizes another possible answer to Derrida in Buddhist ideals: "[For Derrida] the gift can only be a gift *when there is no gift at all*—when it is not recognized as a gift, when there is a radical 'forgetting' of it, and no remembrance of the gift or obligation to repay it, for either donor or recipient—and this, Derrida maintains, is impossible. But in the Buddhist tradition, perhaps we find precisely this impossible ideal expressed in the notion of the gift given by one liberated person to another. Here, the wholly detached and liberated mind of one who has attained *nirvāna* might, in some sense, be seen as equivalent to Derrida's 'radical forgetting.' Having eradicated all desires, interests, and expectations, the liberated mind can give or receive a gift without recognizing it as such, without setting into motion the entire cycle of desires and interests that normally accompany all gifts. Thus, the impossible ideal of the pure gift exists, but is possible only among Buddhism's most highly exceptional beings" (112). In the end, however, Ohnuma finds that Buddhism "confirms one of Mauss' most basic points—that the gift, as a 'total phenomenon,' is always a complicated combination of interest and disinterest, freedom and constraint" (120).

12. In the conversation of 1997, Marion explains that, unlike Derrida who claims to work outside the bounds of phenomenology, he wants to retain the title of phenomenology while releasing it from the limited notion of the gift as such, indeed of any phenomenon "as such," and hence of any givenness as such. Further, there can be

givens that are not necessarily intuited. We shall see how he attempts this release with respect to the gift ("On the Gift," 64–68).

13. Jean-Luc Marion, *God Without Being*, trans. Thomas A. Carlson (Chicago: University of Chicago Press, 1991), 45.

14. *Étant donné* (Paris: Presses Universitaires de France, 1997) was published prior to Marion's conversation with Derrida at Villanova University, and translated several years later by Jeffrey L. Kosky as *Being Given: Toward a Phenomenology of Givenness* (Stanford, Calif.: Stanford University Press, 2000). For an exemplary clarification of the entire problematic, see Robyn Horner, *Rethinking God as Gift: Marion, Derrida, and the Limits of Phenomenology* (New York: Fordham University Press, 2001).

15. Jean-Luc Marion, "Is the Argument Ontological? The Anselmian Proof and the Two Demonstrations of the Existence of God in the *Meditations*," in *Cartesian Questions: Method and Metaphysics* (Chicago: University of Chicago Press, 1999), 149–50; originally published as *Questions cartésiennes: Méthode et métaphysique* (Paris: Presses Universitaires de France, 1991). Compare the statement: "Concerning God, let us admit clearly that we can think him only under the figure of the unthinkable, but of an unthinkable that exceeds as much what we cannot think as what we can" (Marion, *God Without Being*, 46).

16. One might be tempted here to venture a comparison with the Buddhist notion of the inconceivable, *acintya* (Jp. *fukashigi* or *fushigi*), used to indicate the marvelous, unfathomable nature of *nirvāna* for example. An interesting contrast to the conceptual limitation, on the other hand, would be with the practice enjoined by Zen master Dōgen, following Yüeh-shan, to "think of not-thinking." See Dōgen, "Lancet of Seated Meditation," in Carl Bielefield, *Dōgen's Manuals of Zen Meditation* (Berkeley: University of California Press, 1988), 188–89.

17. "Love does not suffer from the unthinkable or from the absence of conditions, but is reinforced by them. For what is peculiar to love consists in the fact that it gives itself. Now, to give itself, the gift does not require that an interlocutor receive it, or that an abode accommodate it, or that a condition assure it or confirm it" (Marion, *God Without Being*, 47). The "divine abode" alludes to Heidegger's notion of the abode of the Holy.

18. In *God Without Being* (109–110) Marion does, to be sure, claim that in appropriating the language of creation, the *creatum* would encompass not only the *ens* or beings, but also Being and thus the ontological difference itself.

19. See for example the remarks in the 1997 conversation with Derrida: "It is very important to understand that you can describe a phenomenon as given without asking any question about the giver. And in most of the cases, there is absolutely no giver at all . . . there are many situations where phenomena appear as given, that is, without any cause or giver. When they appear to us as given, of course, we have to receive them, but this does not imply that we should claim God as the cause of what we receive" ("On the Gift," 70).

20. Marion, *God Without Being*, 48; my emphasis.

21. Ibid., 104–106.

22. Ibid., 49.

23. Ibid., 104–105.

24. Ibid., xxiv.

25. Ibid., 104.

26. After mentioning Robinson Crusoe and other examples of how a component can be missing, Marion notes that it is "within the horizon of such absences that the pos-

sible phenomenon of the gift may appear, if it appears" ("On the Gift," 63). Sections 9–11 of *Being Given* treat of these bracketings, and section 8 presents a "triple epokhē" that reduces the gift to givenness and thereby releases it from the circle of economic exchange.

27. Marion asserts this reversed reduction to counter Derrida's reading of him ("On the Gift," 70).

28. Marion, *God Without Being*, 104. Elsewhere I elaborate Nishida's expression "self-identity of absolute contradictories" as a relation of two items that is all the closer the stronger the contrariety between them. See John C. Maraldo, "Rethinking God: Heidegger in the Light of Absolute Nothing, Nishida in the Shadow of Onto-theology," in Jeffrey Bloechl, ed., *Religious Experience and the End of Metaphysics* (Bloomington: Indiana University Press, 2003), 38.

29. Marion, *God Without Being*, 106.

30. Ibid., 106.

31. Ibid., 48.

32. Ibid., 75–78. Of *aitia*, Marion notes that it "defies categorial expression since [as Dionysius says] 'everything is at once predicated of it and yet it is nothing of all these things'" (Marion, *God Without Being*, 216 n. 55, quoting Pseudo-Dionysius's *Divine Names*, V, 9, 824b).

33. I limit my analysis primarily to this essay—Nishida's last, and the consummation of his thinking on God. Michiko Yusa's complete translation is "The Logic of Topos and the Religious Worldview," *The Eastern Buddhist* 19, no. 2 (Autumn 1986): 1–29 and *The Eastern Buddhist* 20, no. 1 (Spring 1987): 81–119.

34. The formulation Nishida cites is: "The Buddha is not the Buddha, therefore the Buddha is the Buddha" (NKZ 11: 399). Nishida adapts here a Japanese translation of section 8 of Kumārajīva's Chinese version of the *Vajraccchedikā-prajñapāramitā-sūtra*. The context makes clear that Nishida would substitute God or the absolute for the Buddha in this formulation.

35. Keiji Nishitani, *Religion and Nothingness*, trans. Jan Van Bragt (Berkeley: University of California Press, 1982), 116ff., 125ff.

36. Maraldo, "Rethinking God," 39–40.

37. I use the expression *Godself* to avoid gendered locutions such as *himself.*

38. See James G. Hart, "Aspects of Intentionality Within the Christian Distinction," in Guy Mansini, O.S.B. and James G. Hart, eds., *Ethics and Theological Disclosure: The Thought of Robert Sokolowski* (Washington, D.C.: Catholic University of America Press, 2003), 69–101.

39. James G. Hart makes a case that love or *agapē* does not reduce to incomparable generosity; love, unlike generosity, is necessarily directed toward a particular, personal recipient; see Hart's *Who One Is*, vol. 1: *Meontology of the "I": A Transcendental Phenomenology* (Dordrecht: Springer, 2009), 206–38.

40. In my "Rethinking God," I note that Nishida draws examples from the Neo-Platonists and Christian mystical, apophatic traditions, but the quote that best illustrates the term for him is from the fourteenth-century Zen master Daitō Kokushi, in which he says that he and the Buddha are "mutually distinct for an eternity, and yet not apart even for a moment; mutually opposed the whole day, yet not opposed even an instant." The quotation is from NKZ 11: 399, and is repeated at NKZ 11: 409.

41. The metaphors of facing and standing overagainst only approximate the Japanese verb *tai suru*, whose cognate form *ni tai shite* commonly functions like the English prepositions "to," "toward," "vis-à-vis," "for" or "against," depending upon the idiom and context.

42. Nishida occasionally writes *zettai u*, "absolute being," as well as *zettai sha*, "that which is absolute," to refer to God. Both are contrasted with *zettai mu*, "absolute nothing."

43. Alterity for Marion's God seems to be purely optional, never necessary, insofar as the gift is not other than God "himself" and the giving does not require an other who accepts the gift, and of course insofar as creation does not pose as an other to a creator being. Nishida's contrary respondence here suggests that a different kind of alterity obtains in the case of the absolute.

44. "Only through death does our self contact God, and in the manner of contrary respondence" (NKZ 11: 396). The context makes it clear that such death means the dying of the ego-self, not the nihilation of the person.

45. A theology premised on this notion, where God cannot expect anything in return, would of course preclude the possibility of divine reward or punishment.

46. Various Buddhist accounts of *dharmas*, in the sense of elements or entities, emphasize that none has self-subsistent being (Sk. *svabhāva*) but rather all arise, exist, and perish causally and inter-dependently. These correspond to Nishida's relative beings who interrelate mutually, with the proviso that Nishida is concerned primarily with self-aware relative beings or selves. Buddhist accounts also sometimes contrast the conditioned *dharmas* with unconditional qualities including "suchness" (Sk. *tathatā*), or with "emptiness" (Sk. *śūnyatā*) itself. The difficulty that Buddhist philosophers faced was to avoid hypostatizing the unconditional quality or emptiness. Taken as qualifiers, emptiness and suchness simply indicate the lack of substantial being and the conditioned nature of all things. As such there is no need to posit an absolute to which things relate, but the pervasive temptation was to take emptiness as a noun that referred to something to which things could relate. A similar difficulty lies in the danger of hypostatizing Nishida's absolute nothing (Jp. *zettai mu*). Understood as the place of self-negation, however, absolute nothing is clearly distinct from absolute being, as Nishida's formulations imply, and yet is not another thing.

47. Marion, *God Without Being*, 48.

48. Ralph Waldo Emerson, "Gifts," in *Essays, Second Series* [1844] (Boston and New York: Houghton, Mifflin & Co., 1975), 163.

9

Language Games, Selflessness, and the Death of God: A/Theology in Contemporary Zen Philosophy and Deconstruction

GEREON KOPF

Zen discourses and postmodern philosophy are frequently suspected of being inherently anti-theistic. Their subversive methodologies as well as their non-substantial metaphysics seem to be at odds with anything religion is supposed to stand for. But this is not the case. They may "cause," as John D. Caputo suggests, "a lot of well-deserved trouble to a faith or a religious institution that has frozen over into immobility," but definitely do not constitute "the sworn enemy of faith or religious institutions."[1] The difference between their philosophical approaches and the modernist vision lies in the metaphysical frameworks underlying their conceptions of religion. Most contemporary Zen thinkers and postmodern philosophers reject the notion that god, self, history, and *logos* possess a substance and constitute discrete and persisting metaphysical entities. A rejection of these ideas has of course far-reaching implications for the religious project but does not preclude it. Rather, to paraphrase Geoffrey Bennington, while theology "cannot fail to be a theme or an object of deconstruction,"[2] subversive philosophies[3] "will have *specific* interventions to make in the traditional metaphysical vocabulary" of theology;[4] they disclose what Bennington may call the "archi-theological," and a theology that "survives deconstruction."[5] One example of such an archi-theology is, to use Mark C. Taylor's term, the "a/theology" based on the non-substantial metaphysics of Zen philosophy and the thought of deconstruction. In this essay, I would like to suggest such an "a/theology" based on a comparative reading of Nishida Kitarō's[6] "The Logic of Basho and the Religious Worldview" (NKZ 11: 370–464; LW 47–123) and Mark Taylor's *Erring: A Postmodern A/Theology.*[7]

Philosophy of Subversion

I use the term "subversive philosophy" to denote philosophical approaches that share with the philosophers of the Kyoto school and the deconstructionists three fundamental commitments: First, a reduction of modernism *ad absurdum* and the subsequent "revelation of the inner vacuity of the much touted 'modern' outlook";[8] second, a rejection of any form of dualism; third, a non-substantial philosophy that radically redefines our notions of god, self, and history. The first two criteria apply to much of postmodernism as well as contemporary Buddhist philosophy. It is the third criterion that pertains more concretely to the development of a postmodern and Zen Buddhist a/theology.

Derridean deconstruction, which parodies the Cartesian quest for certainty and first truths, rejects what Jacques Derrida calls "metaphysics of the presence," challenges the belief in an onto-theological essence, and destabilizes the notion of an independent subject. No other term illustrates the deconstructionist project as well as Derrida's notion of *différance*. *Différance,* which evokes the dual meaning of the French word *différer,* denoting both "to defer" and "to differ," exposes the ambiguity of signs and their inability to reveal metaphysical structures. "Every concept is inscribed in a system within which it refers to the other, other concepts, by means of a systematic play of differences."[9] Concepts reveal first of all the intertextuality by which they are determined and the multiplicity of differences embodied by the sign; as Martin Heidegger pointed out, they simultaneously disclose and conceal meaning. For this reason, the deconstructionist *crosses out* signs such as "is" as well as "Being" and puts them "under erasure"[10] to read "~~is~~" and "~~Being~~." But there is another aspect to deconstruction: Notwithstanding its hermeneutical preoccupation, deconstruction reveals what Bennington would call an "archi-metaphysics" that "survives deconstruction," not because deconstruction can be completed, but rather since the way in which we use signs has far-reaching (even metaphysical) implications and is, in some sense, indicative of our worldview. In other words, it is not without metaphysical significance whether I write "Being" or "~~Being~~." In this sense, Jin Y. Park takes Derrida's notion of *différance* to the next logical step when she suggests that it is "a Derridean term for devoid-ness of the self-nature of being, when identity is understood as non-identity,"[11] and thus implies a non-substantial and non-dual metaphysics where "the two poles of binary opposites [such as the ontic and the ontological] sustain their position through mutual *inclusion* and dependency instead of mutual *exclusion*."[12]

This is where the most obvious similarities between deconstruction and Kyoto School philosophy can be found. Kyoto School philosophy is not only known for its critique of modernism and dualism, but this critique is based on what Park calls the "mutual inclusion" of binaries. Fujita Masakatsu suggests that "Nishida pioneered for these people"—Maurice Merleau-Ponty, Michel Foucault, and Richard Rorty—"and pointed into a direction to overcome the aporia of modernity's[13] knowledge."[14] The key to this project lies, for Fujita, in Nishida's "critique of the dualism between subjectivity and objectivity."[15] Similarly, John C. Maraldo describes Nishida's project as the "systematic deconstruction of logical relations." Maraldo suggests that Nishida's philosophical method directly aims at the subversion of "a positive determination of any foundation," the subversion of "anthropocentric assumptions about the nature of knowledge," and the subversion of "many logical and metaphysical categories."[16] He even likens Nishida's subversive method to Nāgārjuna's logical deconstruction. I would like to add to Maraldo's analysis that in many cases Nishida performs his subversion of the commonly accepted concepts, assumptions, and commitments, not unlike Nāgārjuna, as a rejection of two allegedly mutually exclusive positions. As I have argued elsewhere,[17] Nishida categorizes all philosophical positions as forms of either objectivism or subjectivism. With regard to each philosophical dilemma, Nishida then demonstrates that both positions are equally untenable since they, ultimately, are reduced *ad absurdum,* and thus must be replaced with a new inclusive philosophical position—namely, Nishida's own.

However, it is not only Nishida's overall project to subvert the substantialist and dualistic paradigms that can be compared to Derridean deconstruction; in addition, his approach to the terminology of the philosophical traditions he inherits reveals some similarities with Derrida's deconstructive method. Where Derrida uses the terminology of *différance,* Nishida employs phrases that incorporate the Japanese word *soku.* One of the most famous examples of this phraseology is his notion of "affirmation-and-yet-negation" (*kōtei-soku-hitei*). Phrases of the form A-*soku*-not-A are designed to shatter the dualistic paradigm without, however, implying a unity of the opposites in particular or a monism in general. As Maraldo says rather succinctly, *soku* indicates "not merely a juxtaposition . . . not merely a relativity . . . not a transformation . . . Rather a simultaneous co-habitation of a space . . . a place itself hidden by the terms and revealed by following their self-negation."[18] *Soku* does not signify an equation of opposites; rather it indicates that a term cannot be conceived of independently of its opposite and, even stronger, that a concept obscures what it is supposed to signify and that the signified can be only illuminated in light of the self-negation of the signifier. By using the phrases of the form A-*soku*-not-A, Nishida *de facto* puts his metaphysical terminology under erasure and intimates the existentially ambiguous nature of that which is signified by his concepts. It seems to be Nishida's intention to show that "the two poles of binary opposites sustain their position through" a "mutual determination" (*sōgo-gentei*) in the form of the "self-identity of absolute contradictories." The result is, as with Derrida, a non-substantial metaphysics.

Non-Substantial Metaphysics

The first concept that falls victim to the subversive potential of any non-substantial philosophy is the notion of the ground of being; in the theologies of monotheistic religions this position is usually assigned to god. "God," conceived of as "creator," "sustainer," "first principle," "unmoved mover," etc., even if formulated in the language of a negative theology, constitutes nothing but an object of human thought and imagination. A standard claim of some theologians is that god constitutes the absolute other and thus cannot be objectified. While it is definitely possible to define god in such a way, this position does not solve the fundamental problem of theology, but rather illustrates it: The very concept of god, even if god is defined as ineffable, constitutes an objectification of whatever is signified. It is the goal of subversive philosophies to expose this fundamental predicament of theology and to replace monotheistic theology with a non-substantial a/theology. But what does it mean to postulate an a/theology or to proclaim the "death of God"?[19] Why does Nishida reject pantheistic as well as theistic terminology (NKZ 1: 175; IG 155; NKZ 11: 398; LW 69) and destabilize the definition of god as the "absolute transcendent" (NKZ 11: 398; LW 69)? In some sense Taylor and Nishida do not so much reject god-talk *per se* as suggest that "god" has to be put under erasure in the Derridean sense, and be written as ~~god~~ instead. Any ontological categorization of "god" is ambiguous at best and untenable at the worst: ~~God~~ neither exists nor does not exist. Robert P. Scharlemann explicates this predicament when he suggests that a "deconstruction of the theistic picture . . . obliges one to rethink that origin . . . at the point where the contradiction is discovered . . . I have suggested that the formula for reconstructing that appearance is 'the being of god when god is not being god.'"[20] This description of ~~god~~ in the ambiguity of is/is-not or, as Nishida would say, "affirmation-and-yet-negation" is the beginning of postmodern a/theology. The refusal to designate an ontological status for god does not indicate, as Park has argued convincingly, a rejection of metaphysics itself but rather of a metaphysics of substances in particular and of essentialism in general. Ultimately, non-substantialist a/theology maintains that god neither exists nor does not exist because "both being and non-being anchor themselves in the idea of substantial existence of an entity [expressed] either through affirmation or negation."[21]

So how is it possible to think about god in a philosophically responsible way? In what could be considered a manifesto of non-substantial a/theology, "The Logic of Basho and the Religious Worldview," Nishida defines god as the "self-identity of the absolute contradictories" (NKZ 9: 317; 11: 405). By this he means that god "includes the absolute self-negation of itself within itself" (NKZ 11: 405) or, more concretely, that "the sentient beings are Buddha and Buddha the sentient beings; the created world god the creator and, vice versa, god the world of creation" (NKZ 11: 398; LW 69). "Because there are no Buddhas there is Buddha. Because there are no sentient beings there are sentient beings. . . . Since god is transcendent to a certain degree and, at the same time, immanent to a certain degree, it must be a truly dialectical god" (NKZ 11: 399; LW 70). And finally, "the truly absolute god must be devilish in some respect" (NKZ 11: 404; LW 74) and "the true absolute negates itself until it becomes the devil" (NKZ 11: 435; LW 100). These comments cover quite an array of topics within traditional Christian theology and are not without shock value for any reader steeped in the traditional terminology and *imaginaire* of monotheistic theologies. What these phrases have in common, however, is that they are fundamentally designed to collapse the traditional polarities of absolute-relative, creator-creation, divine-human, transcendence-immanence, and god-devil—and subsequently, the fundamental dualism inherent in the monotheistic project. Most of these statements, with the possible exception of the binary god-devil, explore the relationship of the absolute to the relative. But even the juxtaposition of god and devil assumes the exclusivity of the *tertium non datur*. Yet Nishida does not simply equate the polarities of these oppositions; rather, he postulates that they are "mutually determined" through an act of "self-negation" (*jiko-hitei*). This relationship between what seem to be mutually exclusive opposites may be more intelligibly rendered as "internal negation" or, following Park's terminology, "mutual inclusion." While monotheistic theologies for the most part frown at the possibility of the mutuality of, for instance, creator and creation and assign god a privileged position in a radically asymmetric relationship, Nishida does hint at some kind of mutuality when he suggests that "in self-negation and inverse correlation,[22] we always touch the absolute" (NKZ 11: 429; LW 94). Nevertheless, Nishida never seems to completely dissolve the primacy of the absolute. In the end, the relationship between god and its self-negation remains, to appropriate one of his favorite phraseologies, asymmetric-and-yet-symmetric. Be that as it may, the key to Nishida's a/theology is his conviction that each term is irreducible yet not privileged; each has integrity and yet relates to its other in an "internal relationship" in the sense that "it is part of the essential nature of relatents that they are connected as they are; they are interdependent, not independent."[23]

Such a non-substantial a/theology, which postulates the mutual relationship between god and its self-negation, has far-reaching implications for the fields of ontology, epistemology, and soteriology. Most obviously it inverts the so-called ontological proof of the existence of god. Anselm of course (in)famously argued that "God cannot be conceived not to exist. God is that, than which nothing greater can be conceived. That which can be conceived not to exist is not God."[24] God as envisioned by the ontological argument thus formulated constitutes the pure and supreme being, that is, Being in the metaphysical sense. Baruch Spinoza thought God consistently as Being and defined God as "an absolutely infinite being, that is, substance consisting of infinite attributes, each of which expresses eternal and definite essence."[25] Inspired by Thomas J. J. Altizer's "death of God" theology, Mark C. Taylor observes that such a "transcendent deity appears to be completely self-enclosed, totally self-identical, and absolutely self-present. . . . As the full realization and original ground of selfhood, God is wholly other, is absolute alterity."[26] If God is defined as Being, every relationship between creator and creation—be it ontological, conceptual, or logical—is severed; what is more, to assert the existence of God, a theology of Being, if thought consistently, has to deny creation any ontological status and reduce it to nothing. In a theology of Being, the ontico-ontological difference morphs into an unbridgeable abyss; monotheism thus passes over into a *de facto* monism. In either case, Being itself is self-identical, isolated, wholly other; God reveals itself only to itself, relates itself only to itself, and exists only for itself. Ultimately, so the conclusion, any theology of Being either results, as in the case of Spinoza, in a monism that assimilates or dissolves the creation into God or in a dualism that stratifies God as *deus absconditus* who is, from the perspective of creation, at best irrelevant and at worst non-existent.

This is where Nishida comes in. Nishida agrees that the absolute is self-identical, but to be truly absolute, it has to constitute a self-identity that does not dissolve difference. Monism denies difference, theism externalizes otherness and, if thought consistently, negates that which is not divine. Both positions are equally untenable and reject the possibility of a human-divine relationship; the former denies the existence of the immanent, while dualistic theism postulates an infinite abyss between creator and creation. To counter both positions, Nishida argues for an a/theology that conceives of god as simultaneously transcendent and immanent, absolute and relative. Nishida explains:

> [I]t (the absolute) does not face something outside itself as an object, but what we call "facing absolute nothingness" implies that it faces itself as self-contradiction. That which faces itself negates itself. . . . Insofar as it negates itself outside itself and opposes itself, it is not the absolute. The absolute contains its own absolute self-negation inside itself. (NKZ 11: 397–98)

Nishida argues that to be truly self-identical and self-present, the absolute has to face itself. But this moment of "facing itself" requires a moment of negation and an internal rupture. The absolute must contain its own negation, that is, relativity, inside itself; in other words, the absolute is always under erasure and thus necessarily appears always in the form of the ~~absolute~~. However, if the ~~absolute~~ contains its own self-negation, it constitutes the "mutual inclusion" of the absolute and the relative. In other words, in a given context the ~~absolute~~ appears as absolute and in another as relative. Scharlemann comes to a similar conclusion regarding the nature of god when he critiques monotheistic conceptions of creation: "What cannot be thought, in the tradition of this picture, is that the world itself is a moment of the being of God; what cannot be thought is that the world is itself the being of God when God is not being deity." He concludes that "to be God is both to be deity and to be other than deity."[27]

There is yet another aspect to non-substantial a/theology. It takes into account that, form the perspective of humanity, G/god always exists, as Taylor argues following Martin Luther's *pro nobis* theology: G/god exists "for us."[28] A monotheistic theology that interprets the relationship between creator and creation as one of "mutual exclusion" or "external negation" over-emphasizes the integrity of "God" to such a degree that it denies any relationship with or significance for humanity which god might have. This is of course problematic for two reasons. First, the *deus absconditus* must remain, however "omnipotent" as it may be, without any soteriological relevance for humanity. Second, any theology is always necessarily anthropocentric insofar as the knowing subject constitutes the center and anchor of all human knowledge.

As Taylor aptly observes: "If man is defined as subject, everything else turns into object. This includes God, who now becomes merely the highest object of man's knowledge."[29] Thus objectified, god "is only to the extent that it is *for* the subject."[30] Furthermore, every soteriology, even a soteriology that assigns the source of justification to an absolute "other power" (Jp. *tariki*) as the rhetoric of Pure Land Buddhism suggests, is inherently and undeniably anthropocentric. The remedy to anthropocentrism, however, does not lie in the postulate of an absolute other, but rather in the recognition that ~~god~~ and ~~nature~~ are neither identical nor different, but that they relate to each other in the form of a "mutual inclusion" and "internal negation." Thus, the existential attitude of the human subject is not "twofold" (Gn. *zwiefältig*),[31] as Buber suggests, but rather, threefold. In this sense, Nishida adds to Buber's "comportments" of objectification (I-It) and intersubjectivity (I-Thou), the relationship of "mutual inclusion" and "internal negation" when he suggests that to break the objectification of and by the other one has to "see to other inside the self" (NKZ 6: 389). He continues, "it is not that self and the other are one, but that one sees the absolute other inside the self" (NKZ 6: 390); "the absolute other dwells hidden in the depth of our self itself." When "the absolute other dwells hidden in the depth of our self itself," the "absolute Thou" (*zettai no nanji*) (NKZ 6: 420) expresses itself through self-negation. In the end, ~~god~~ constitutes the "mutual inclusion" of god and humanity in theology and religious practice.

The same principle that subverts the conception of god also destabilizes the concept of self. Overall, the self suffers a fate not unlike that of god. As Taylor observes, the subject of modernity having celebrated the death of God loses itself similarly in the futile attempt to be self-identical and to eliminate alterity. "In order to secure its propriety, the Neoplatonic self attempts to expropriate the other by appropriating its propert(y)ies. Apparent success is really failure. The appropriation of the other exprorpriates the self."[32] The self's obsession to be self-identical by appropriating and possessing the other results in its own undoing and, ultimately, in the postmodern fragmentation of the self. Despite the similarities between the fate of god and that of the self, there is one fundamental difference: While God dies on his escape from the alterity and, ultimately, the nihility of creation into the self-reflexivity of its own Being, the self suffers its own inability to face "the uncanny" (*das Unheimliche*) as revealed by Sigmund Freud's psychoanalysis, and to bear the ambiguity of what Michel Foucault calls the "empirico-transcendental doublet";[33] both of which the subject tries to sublimate, if not repress, through an infinite expansion of itself to name, possess, and dominate the external world. Nevertheless, like God the self has to learn, as Altizer puts it, that "we can evoke an actual or real identity only by embodying difference, a real and actual difference, a difference making identity manifests, and making it manifest as itself."[34] Taylor adds to Altizer's observation: "There is always difference *within* identity and absence *within* presence. . . . Presence/present and identity are forever fugitive—they disappear in the very act of appearing."[35] The self's inability to dissolve the ambiguities of identity/difference, presence/absence, affirmation/negation, and, since it can be conceived of as the "point where the absolute reflects itself" (NKZ 10: 409), absolute/relative reveals its radically ambiguous nature. The self does not oppose god but relates to him/her in a relationship of "mutual inclusion"; in short, it constitutes the self-negation, self-reflection, and self-expression of god. While "god" symbolizes the transcendent dimension of god, the self marks the immanence thereof. Therefore, non-substantial a/theology puts the self under erasure and re-writes and re-thinks the self as self.

As the immanent dimension of the absolute, the self is radically historical. Nishida, for example, defines "our self" alternately as a "historical body" (*rekishi-teki shintai*) (NKZ 8: 498; 10: 352), as "that which creates and is created" (*tsukuri tsukurareta mono*) in "expressive action" (NKZ 10: 450), and as "the productive particular of history" (NKZ 10: 396). Immersed in history, the self is torn vertically between the "I of yesterday and the I of today" (NKZ 6: 343) and horizontally between the "I and Thou" who "have to be thought as individuals who mutually determine each other" (NKZ 7: 125; FP 63) to the point where the "I" is "both desubstantialized and deindividualized."[36] In more positive terms, the self embodies the intersection between the "I of yesterday and the I of today" and the encounter of "I and Thou." Firmly grounded in the spatial and temporal reality of history, it ceases to be the transcendental subject envisioned by modernism and is reduced to a "this," which "is made up of a temporal and spatial component. The 'This,' in other words, is 'Here and Now.'"[37] This is an important point to note: The self of non-substantial a/theology should not be confused with the transcendental subject, the immortal soul, or even a personal identity in the sense of a psycho-physical continuity. Rather it comprises the antithesis to God's infinity and inhabits the infinitely small "*hic et nunc.*"[38] Nishida identifies the self of non-substantial a/theology as the "basis of individuality" (NKZ 10: 378) precisely because it discloses particularity not only in the spatial but also in the temporal sense. The self eschews duration and exists solely in the moment. Ironically, it is the conception of the self as "person-in-the-moment" rather than that of an essence or a person-over-time that assigns to the ~~self~~ an existentially temporal character; the ~~self~~ does not constitute an essentially atemporal entity which is located in time but discloses what Dōgen calls "being-time" (*uji*) as its authentic existential modality. Thus, the ~~self~~ loses the integrity, independence, and self-identity of the transcendental subject *beyond* and of an unchanging substance located *in* time; in turn, it finds its identity as the "self-identity of absolute contradictories," that is, an identity that does not reject differences in the interspatial encounter of the self and other and the intertemporal intersection of "the I of yesterday and the I of today" characteristic of what Nishida calls the "historical world" (Jp. *rekishi-teki sekai*). As "historical body," the ~~self~~ temporalizes (Gn. *zeitigt*) itself, in the Heideggerian sense. It is thus possible to say that while God dies in the face of the transcendental subject's alterity, the self disappears along the unrelenting course of history in a single, infinitely small *moment of time*. As Nishida observes laconically: "If we think the present to be a moment, one point, on a continuous line, it will disappear" (NKZ 9: 149). In other words, the self qua *hic et nunc* falls victim to history. However, this is not where the story ends. History neither escapes the ambiguity that is characteristic of human existence, nor is ontologically or temporally primary to the ~~self~~. That is to say that history itself is under erasure. ~~History~~ does not simply determine the self, but the ~~self~~, as that which creates and is created, *makes* and transforms history.

Here at the end of this introduction to non-substantial metaphysics, I would like to briefly discuss the conception of "history." According to non-substantial a/theology, ~~history~~, not unlike the ~~self~~, evolves within the present. As Taylor suggests, ~~history~~ is eternally suspended "between the *archē* and the *telos*"[39] and implies the "death of the Alpha and the Omega."[40] Yet, not only is ~~history~~ bereft of beginning and end, it even lacks past and future; "there is but one tense of time, present."[41] In other words, nothing exists outside of the present; even past and future exist but in the present: "In the present the past simultaneously has come to pass and has not yet passed. The future has not yet come, but in the present it is already present" (NKZ 9: 149). While it seems commonsensical to locate the self in the "here and now," is it not rather counterintuitive to restrict history to the present? Does history vanish in the present? What does it mean to call in, as Taylor does, the "end of history"? For Taylor, a history without *archē* and *telos* loses its "firmly fixed center" and dooms the human subject to a "nomadic existence" of "endless erring."[42] But it seems to me that a non-substantial a/theology of the present does not cause the "*radical* purposelessness"[43] that Taylor laments. Is it not the linear conception of time wherein the present self disappears into the dark crevices of history that condemns its own origin to an unattainable and unknowable past while it also defers its final fulfillment infinitely into a future that will always escape us? A non-substantial a/theology, on the contrary, replaces the hegemony of one center with the democracy of an infinity of centers since the "Now is 'plurality of Nows,'"[44] and "the concrete present comprises the simultaneity of innumerable moments" (NKZ 9: 149). The notion of a plurality of centers is best illustrated by the analogy of "Indra's net" from the *Avatamsaka Sūtra*. Indra's net consists of an infinite number of jewels, each of which reflects and is reflected in every other. Nishida's terminology strongly echoes this image when he describes the present using the Huayan phrase, albeit without admitting its origin, "one-and-yet-many" (Jp. *issokuta*): In every moment the infinity of all moments past, present, and future is reflected. In the end, a non-substantial a/theology that locates history in the present ruptures the assumed linearity of history which deceives us into believing in an *archē* and which promises us a *telos*. It mercilessly exposes the undeniable ambiguity of history, which is neither exclusively archeological nor exclusively teleological; rather, it is simultaneously continuous and discontinuous and forms what Nishida calls the "continuity of discontinuity" (*hirenzoku no renzoku*); it evolves, as Nishida (in)famously suggests, from the "present to the present" (*genzei kara genzai e*).

The Divine Milieu

The preceding exploration has demonstrated that non-substantial a/theology does not eliminate the notions of god, self, and history, but rather discloses the radical existential ambiguity of what is signified by the *markers* "god," "self," and "history." What remains after a philosophical subversion is not nihilistic atheism but an a/theology which announces (not unlike Siddhartha Gautama did, some twenty-five hundred years ago) a middle path between eternalism and annihilationism, and (as every dialectical philosophy has also suggested) a middle path between affirmation and negation. Caputo calls this middle path "ankhōral religion."[45] *Khōra* "constitutes a third species"[46] insofar as it "belongs neither to the sensible nor the intelligible, neither to becoming nor to non-being . . . nor to Being";[47] it constitutes "neither Being nor Nothing, God nor Man, Nature nor History, Matter nor Spirit."[48] *Khōra* marks the place where the polarities of binary oppositions intersect and relate to each other in "mutual inclusion." This place—and it is interesting to note that Nishida develops his conception of *basho* as that which includes "being and non-being" (NKZ 4: 218) from Plato's *Timaeus* as well—is most fittingly described in Taylor's terminology as the "divine milieu." Taylor prefers the terminology of the "milieu" over that of the "middle" since the latter implies a center, whereas the former discloses a world wherein the infinity of centers as illustrated in the image of Indra's net eliminates the privileged position and hegemony of any particular present as the center. As Taylor remarks: "If *die Mitte is überall, die Mitte* is not so much the center as it is the milieu."[49] Taylor calls this milieu "divine" because it marks the religious terrain where god appears in the "mutual inclusion" of the opposites.

The term "divine milieu" thus marks the "mutual inclusion" of the various polarities within binary oppositions, but it should not be misunderstood as the "external relation"[50] of "mutual exclusion." What, then, are the characteristics of the absolute? Nishida coins the term "inverse correlation" (Jp. *gyaku-taiō*)[51] to designate the relationship between the absolute and the relative. This is an interesting term, which Nishida introduces only at the very end of his career. While Ueda Shizuteru suggests that "inverse correlation" signifies "the religious relationship,"[52] I believe that Nishida introduces the term "inverse correlation" to shift the focus of his discussion from the terminology of god as the non-dual principle to the discussion of two terms that express the relationship between the transcendent and the immanent; and thus that the new term indicates, as Kosaka Kunitsugu suggests, an "expansion and development"[53] of Nishida's "self-identity of the absolute contradictories." Kosaka's observation is right on target. If one investigates the relationship between god and humanity in Nishida's writings, one can detect an apparent development from the rather theocentric conception of this relationship in his *Inquiry Into the Good,* where god is defined as "that which unifies nature and spirit" (NKZ 1: 96; IG 79), to the stratification of the "inverse correlation" as the (almost) mutual relationship between divinity and humanity on the last fifty-eight pages of his last completed essay. I inserted the modifier "almost" here, since while the notion of "inverse correlation" is not only bilateral but also implies mutuality—Kosaka claims rightly that the "inverse correlation . . . indicates that the absolute and the individual touch each other mutually in self-negation"[54]—some of Nishida's phrases do imply a certain asymmetry in favor of the transcendent.

A quick analysis of Nishida's "The Logic of Basho and the Religious Worldview" reveals that the majority of passages that include the term "inverse correlation" thematize the relationship between the divine and the human individual (NKZ 11: 409, 421, 423, 442–43; LW 78, 87, 89, 105) or relate that the human self "touches" god or the absolute (NKZ 11: 396, 427, 429–30, 435, 454; LW 68, 93–95, 99, 115). Another set of passages suggests that the activity of the "inverse correlation" is located in the present (NKZ 11: 423, 425; LW 89, 91). The remaining passages indicate that the "inverse correlation" ruptures the relationship between god and self insofar as they maintain that the absolute/god negates itself (NKZ 11: 398; LW 69, 83), the self transcends itself (NKZ 11: 435; LW 99), "god hides inside the heart of evil people" (NKZ 11: 405; LW 75), and that "the self responds to the absolute in the depth of itself" (NKZ 11: 448; LW 110), yet "exists within the absolute" (NKZ 11: 449; LW 111). This moment of negativity is important since it is indicative of Nishida's conception of the "inverse correlation" as "internal negation" and "mutual inclusion"; this moment further identifies Nishida's approach as a non-substantial alternative to monotheism and pantheism. A few passages that do not fall into any of these categories simply identify the "inverse correlation" with "everydayness" (byōjōtei) (NKZ 11: 450; LW 111) or remind the reader that the "inverse correlation" constitutes the "world of the absolute" (NKZ 11: 423; LW 89) and/or the "world of the self-identity of the absolute contradictories" (NKZ 11: 409; LW 78).

This has been a quick summary of Nishida's usage of the term "inverse correlation" where his new terminology "advances one step"[55] over the "logic of basho." I think it is possible to identify three basic characteristics of the "inverse correlation" as defined by Nishida's "Logic of Basho and the Religious Worldview." First, the "divine milieu" is dynamic. The absolute and the relative are not static but are constantly engaged in an interaction of "mutual determination" and transformation. Taylor echoes this sentiment when he observes that the "divine milieu" constitutes the "wavering vibration piercing force and irresistible medium (Mitte or milieu) in which everything arises and passes away but which does not itself arise or pass away is the 'ever-never-changing-same.'"[56] In the "divine milieu" the standoff between the substances of traditional theology gives way to the interaction of forces characteristic of non-substantial a/theology. Second, Kosaka identifies four basic dimensions of the "inverse correlation," which, while different in sequence and terminology, are rather reminiscent of the "fourfold worldview" of Huayan Buddhism: "The relationship of self-negation and self-contradiction between the absolute and relative individuals"; "the relationship of self-negation and self-contradiction wherein the absolute opposes itself"; "the relationship of self-negation and self-contradiction wherein the relative opposes itself"; and "the mutual relationship of self-negation and self-contradiction among innumerable relative (individuals)."[57] While Kosaka sticks to the heavy-handed terminology reminiscent of the writings of German Idealism, which Nishida had appropriated in part, the parallel to Huayan Buddhism is warranted not least because Nishida himself evokes similarities between his thought and the third and fourth of the fourfold worldview, namely, the "non-interference of noumenon and phenomena" (Ch. *lishi wuai*, Jp. *riji-muge*) and the "non-interference among phenomena" (Ch. *shishi wuai*, Jp. *jiji-muge*) (NKZ 10: 414). Be that as it may, it is worth noting that Nishida assigns four dimensions to the "inverse correlation": the interaction between god and the human individual, the self-determination of god (that is, the interaction of god with itself), the self-determination of the human subject (or the interaction of the self with itself), and the interaction among human individuals. Each of these constitutes a dynamic interaction (in the case of the self-determination of god, god faces its own alterity, while the self confronts its own fragmented self in its act of self-determination) and the "mutual inclusion" of opposites. A "mutual exclusion" or "external negation," on the other hand, would create an absolute other and lead to alienation.

So how can this moment of "mutual inclusion" be understood? In his commentary on Nishida's conception of the "inverse correlation," Takemura Makio juxtaposes the observation that "if we make the absolute the absolute, it becomes the relative; if we make the relative relative, it returns to the absolute itself"[58]—or alternatively, "the more we exhaust the individual we transcend it and touch god"[59]—with the *dictum* that "(the self-negation of the) absolute and (the individual affirmation of the) relative should neither be separated nor identified."[60] He adds elsewhere that "the relationship between god and humans can neither be dissolved, collapsed, nor reversed."[61] These comments assert the irreducibility of each of the polarities, god and the human individual, and at the same time suggest a "transgression" of the one into the realm of the other. Since a relationship of "mutual inclusion" implies that god enters inside the self and vice versa, the divine transgresses onto secular terrain and the human individual onto divine territory. These transgressions result in a rupture of both immanence and transcendence, which alters both realms irrevocably and transforms the heretofore immaculate and clearly defined provinces into shape-shifting targets without either identifiable borders or a center. This tension between irreducibility and transgression is, according to Park, the key to understanding the principle of "mutual inclusion." In a recent essay on Wŏnhyo (617–686) and Derrida, she explains that the

> transgression theme in Wŏnhyo's life . . . offers not a vision of harmony, but of an inevitable tension between the provisional and the ultimate reality. . . . And this tension between the provisional and the ultimate reality, or that between the finite and the infinite, is the faith which Wŏnhyo reads as the beginning of the Bodhisattva precepts.[62]

Transgression here constitutes an essential ingredient in the relationships between the opposites. In Wŏnhyo's case, the act of transgression consisted of violating the precepts and indicates what Park calls an "ethics of tension." Others, such as the Japanese monk Ikkyu (1394–1481), transgress the boundaries between the sacred and the secular. Zen Buddhist discourses revel in the latter form of transgression and are known for notorious statements such as: "The Buddha dharma is not useful nor does it accomplish anything; it constitutes nothing but the everyday and the ordinary; have a shit, take a piss; put on your clothes, eat and drink, retire when tired" (NKZ 9: 333; 11: 424, 446).[63] The motivation for this kind of comments is, so it seems, to destabilize and subvert our preconceptions of what constitutes the divine and the secular without resolving the tension between them. This, I think, comprises the most fundamental characteristic of the principle of "mutual inclusion." While the divine and the secular maintain their integrity, their boundary is radically indeterminate. As Taylor observes,

> this milieu marks a middle way that is thoroughly liminal. At this threshold, opposites cross. The margin itself, however, is not reducible to the extremes whose mean it forms. . . . consequently, the milieu is always para-doxical. . . . It is also the boundary itself, the screen which is a permeable membrane connecting inside and outside.[64]

Non-substantial a/theology thus shifts the focus of god-talk from the polarities that comprise the existential ambiguity of human existence to the dynamic tension between them, from the center to the boundaries, from god to the "divine milieu."

So where does this leave us? What does the notion of the "divine milieu" reveal about the nature of religion? In order to answer these questions, I would like to briefly recapitulate the previous discussion so far: A philosophy of subversion strips theology of its most fundamental conceptions such as god and self, *archē* and *telos,* and thus eliminates any trace of substantial metaphysics. In its place, it renders a non-substantial a/theology that centers on the border-region of the "divine milieu." The "divine milieu" does not signify any place in any geographical or ontological sense—Caputo cautions that *khōra* is a "placeless place" "without being,"[65] while Nishida unapologetically identifies his *basho* as "absolute nothingness" (*zettai-mu*)—but rather marks the tension between the opposites of absolute-relative, transcendent-immanent, and infinite-finite which are frequently embodied in monotheistic theology as the conceptual pair creator-creation, and in Buddhism as buddhas–sentient beings. At the same time, a non-substantial a/theology cautions us that these polarities should not be understood as entities but rather as *forces*. Shinran, for example, uses the term "other-power" to describe god, and "self-power" (Jp. *jiriki*) to designate the self. However, these two terms do not imply two separate entities or even two essentially different religions. Rather, as Nishida asserts, the religions of self-power and other-power not only share "the same standpoint" (NKZ 11: 411) but also the same vision of the "ultimate" (NKZ 15: 330).[66] In this sense, the terms "self-power" and "other-power" indicate the possibility that the absolute transgresses into the territory of the relative and vice versa. For this reason, and this brings us the questions I asked at the beginning of this paragraph, a non-substantial a/theology does not proclaim the simple collapse of the sacred and the profane but rather proposes a conception of religion that is dynamic and that possesses neither a center nor a determinate boundary, but rather implies that the religious encroaches on and penetrates into the realm of the irreligious and that the irreligious trespasses on the religious domain. Ultimately, so Takeda, "within the irreligious, we touch the essence of religion."[67] Only a theory of religion that refrains from dissolving the inherent existential ambiguity of the human predicament as well as the tension between the absolute and relative can do justice to the religious phenomenon as religion, and can theorize a reality that is incontrovertibly divine-and-yet-secular.

NOTES

1. John D. Caputo, *The Prayers and Tears of Jacques Derrida: Religion without Religion* (Bloomington: Indiana University Press, 1997), 18.

2. Geoffrey Bennington, *Interrupting Derrida* (London: Routledge, 2000), 34.

3. Bennington focuses on "deconstructive thought" (ibid., 34), but I use the term "subversive philosophy" to indicate that while Zen discourse and deconstruction differ in method, they agree in their criticisms of essentialism and dualism.

4. Ibid., 35 (italics in original).

5. Ibid., 34.

6. I choose the thought of the later Nishida as one possible example of how traditional Zen discourses can be integrated into contemporary philosophical discourse. Nishida writes clearly in the traditions of Continental philosophy; yet in his later work he strongly emphasizes a kinship between his philosophy and a variety of Zen classics such as the *Records of Linji* and the *Gateless Barrier*. My usage of the term "Zen philosophy" follows that of Ueda Shizuteru, introduced in *Zen to sekai* [Zen and the world] (USS 5: 11–181). Fujita is more generous when he defines as one criteria for membership in the Kyoto School the commitment to use "Western philosophy" and "Buddhist, especially Zen Buddhist, thought." Fujita Masakatsu, "Hajime ni" [Introduction], in Fujita Masakatsu, ed., *Kyoto gakuha no tetsugaku* [The philosophy of the Kyoto School] (Tokyo: Shōwadō, 2001), iii.

7. Mark C. Taylor, *Erring: A Postmodern A/theology* (Chicago: University of Chicago Press, 1984).

8. Carl Raschke, "The Deconstruction of God," in Thomas J. J. Altizer, Max A. Meyers, Carl A. Raschke, Robert P. Scharlemann, Mark C. Taylor, and Charles E. Winquist, *Deconstruction and Theology* (New York: Crossroad, 1982), 2–3.

9. Jacques Derrida, *Margins of Philosophy,* trans. Alan Bass (Chicago: University of Chicago Press, 1982), 11.

10. Heidegger introduces the method of "crossing out" signs such as "is" and "Being" to indicate the inconceivability and primacy of "Being." Derrida, in comparison, puts the trace under erasure to indicate the ambivalence of signs and to critique Heidegger for assigning "Being" a privileged position and thus suggesting a metaphysics of presence. When I write terms such as "god" and "absolute" under erasure in this essay, I do so in the Derridean sense of "crossing out" the sign as well as the erasure itself and denying the signifier any privileged position in the system of signs called "metaphysics." See Gayatri Chakravorty Spivak, "Translator's Preface," in Jacques Derrida, *Of Grammatology,* trans. Gayatri C. Spivak (Baltimore, Md.: Johns Hopkins University Press, 1974), ix–lxxxvii.

11. Jin Y. Park, "Transgression and Ethics of Tension: Wŏnhyo and Derrida on Institutional Authority," in Youru Wang, ed., *Deconstruction and the Ethical in Asian Thought* (London: Routledge, 2007), 202.

12. Jin Y. Park, "Naming the Unnameable: Dependent Co-arising and *Différance,*" in Jin Y. Park, ed., *Buddhisms and Deconstructions* (Lanham, Md.: Rowman & Littlefield, 2006), 11.

13. *Overcoming Modernity* (*Kindai no chōkoku*) is also the title of a collection of papers given by Japanese intellectuals, including Nishitani Keiji, at a symposium organized by the magazine *Literary World* (*Bungakkai*) in 1942. For more information see James W. Heisig, *Philosophers of Nothingness: An Essay on the Kyoto School* (Honolulu: University of Hawai'i Press, 2001), 208–11; also see Minamoto Ryōen, "The Symposium on 'Overcoming Modernity,'" trans. James Heisig, in James Heisig and John Maraldo, eds., *Rude Awakenings: Zen, the Kyoto School, and the Question of Nationalism* (Honolulu: University of Hawai'i Press, 1994), 197–229.

14. Fujita Masakatsu, *Gendai tetsugaku toshite no Nishida Kitarō* [Nishida Kitarō as a contemporary philosopher] (Tokyo: Kōdansha, 1998), 113.

15. Ibid., 73, 76.

16. John C. Maraldo, "Nishida Kitarō (1870–1945)," in *Routledge Encyclopedia of Philosophy* (New York: Routledge, 1998), 13r.

17. Gereon Kopf, "The Ethical and the Non-ethical: Nishida's Methodic Subversion," in *Deconstruction and the Ethical in Asian Thought*, 129–48.

18. John C. Maraldo, "Rethinking God: Heidegger in the Light of Absolute Nothing, Nishida in the Shadow of Onto-Theology," in Jeffrey Bloechl, ed., *Religious Experience and the End of Metaphysics* (Bloomington: Indiana University Press, 2003), 40.

19. Taylor, *Erring*, 19.

20. Robert P. Scharlemann, "The Being When God is not Being God: Deconstructing the History of Theism," in *Deconstruction and Theology*, 107.

21. This wording is taken from Jin Y. Park, *Buddhism and the Politics of Postmodernity: Zen, Huayan, and the Possibility of Buddhist-Postmodern Ethics* (New York: Lexington Books, 2008), chap. 1.

22. David Dilworth translates *gyakutaiō* variously as the "paradox of god," the "relation of the simultaneous presence and absence" (LW 89), "God's own mirror image and opposite" (LW 93), the "paradoxical structure of inverse polarity and biconditionality" (LW 99), and as the "relation of inverse polarity" (LW 111). His translation of *gyakutai* as "contradictory identity" (LW 69) not only obscures the fact that the original implies a "correlation" if not a "relationship," but also renders it indistinguishable from Nishida's *mujunteki jikodōitsu* ("contradictory self-identity" or "identity of contradictories").

23. Thomas P. Kasulis, *Intimacy and Integrity: Philosophy and Cultural Difference* (Honolulu: University of Hawai'i Press, 2002), 36.

24. Anselm, "The Ontological Argument," in G. Lee Bowie, Meredith W. Michaels, and Robert C. Solomon, ed., *Twenty Questions: An Introduction to Philosophy* (Orlando, Fla.: Harcourt Brace, 1996), 56–57.

25. Baruch Spinoza, *The Ethics and Selected Letters,* ed. Seymour Feldman, trans. Samuel Shirley (Indianapolis: Hackett, 1982), 31.

26. Taylor, *Erring*, 23.

27. Scharlemann, "The Being When God is not Being God," 90.

28. Taylor, *Erring*, 21

29. Ibid., 22.

30. Ibid., 26.

31. Martin Buber, "Ich und Du," in *Das dialogische Prinzip* (Heidelberg: Verlag Lambert Schneider, 1984), 7.

32. Taylor, *Erring*, 30.

33. Michel Foucault, *The Order of Things: An Archeology of the Human Sciences* (New York: Pantheon, 1970), 322.

34. Altizer is cited in Taylor, *Erring*, 49.

35. Taylor, *Erring*, 49.

36. Ibid., 135.

37. Ibid., 46.

38. Ibid., 47.

39. Ibid., 64.

40. Ibid., 73.

41. Ibid., 43.

42. Ibid., 156.

43. Ibid., 157.

44. Ibid., 48.

45. Caputo, *Prayers and Tears of Jacques Derrida*, 154.

46. Jacques Derrida, "How to Avoid Speaking: Denials," in Harold Coward and D. Foshay, eds., *Derrida and Negative Theology* (Albany: State University of New York Press, 1992), 104.

47. Ibid., 105.

48. Caputo, *Prayers and Tears of Jacques Derrida*, 156.

49. Taylor, *Erring*, 116.

50. Kasulis, *Intimacy and Integrity*, 36.

51. While Nishida himself suggests an affinity, if not an etymological link between his *gyakutaiō* and Buddhism (NKZ 11: 449; LW 111), it is, as Ueda and James Heisig have pointed out, one of Nishida's neologisms. Cf. Ueda Shizuteru, *Nishida Kitarō to wa dare ka* [Who is Nishida Kitarō?] (Tokyo: Iwanami Gendai Bunko, 2002), 249; and Heisig, *Philosophers of Nothingness*, 103. Kosaka Kunitsugu painstakingly traces the origin of the term back to the inspiration Nishida received from Mutai Risaku's *The Logic of Basho* (*Basho no ronrigaku*) and Tanabe Hajime's *Philosophy as Metanoetics* (*Zangedō toshite no tetsugaku*). Cf. Kosaka Kunitsugu, *Nishida tetsugaku to shūkyō* [Nishida philosophy and religion] (Tokyo: Daitō Shuppansha, 2000).

52. Ueda, *Nishida Kitarō to wa dare ka*, 251.

53. Kosaka, *Nishida tetsugaku to shūkyō*, 324.

54. Ibid., 305.

55. Ibid., 324.

56. Taylor, *Erring*, 113.

57. Kosaka, *Nishida tetsugaku to shūkyō*, 335.

58. Takemura Makio, *Nishida Kitarō to bukkyō* [Nishida Kitarō and Buddhism] (Tokyo Daitō Shuppansha, 2002), 199.

59. Ibid., 198.

60. Ibid., 200.

61. Ibid., 204.

62. Park, "Transgression and Ethics of Tension," 212.

63. Cited from Linji, *Linjilu* [Record of Linji], T47.1985.498.

64. Taylor, *Erring*, 115.

65. Caputo, *Prayers and Tears of Jacques Derrida*, 156.

66. Also see Takeda Ryūsei, *Shinran jōdōkyō to Nishida tetsugaku* [Shinran's Pure Land Buddhism and Nishida philosophy] (Tokyo: Nagata Bunshōdō, 1997), 368–76.

67. Ibid., 367.

10

Buddha and God:
Nishida's Contributions to
a New Apocalyptic Theology

Thomas J. J. Altizer

Nishida Kitarō is the most distinguished and influential philosopher in the history of modern Japan, and as a founding member of the Kyoto School he has had a great impact upon religious thinking throughout the world. Throughout most of his philosophical career, Nishida was shaped primarily by his response to German philosophy from Leibniz through Husserl. He only centered upon Buddhist philosophy in his final years, yet it is his final thinking that has had the greatest impact. His last essay, "The Logic of the Place of Nothingness and the Religious Worldview" (1945), is the most comprehensive formulation of his philosophy, and it has become known as a pivotal, fundamental text of the Kyoto School. This is above all true in its centering upon an absolute nothingness, giving us our most modern understanding of *śūnyatā*, and yet this nothingness is here called forth as the primal center and ground of both thinking and of human existence itself. Nowhere in the West has such an absolute nothingness been so comprehensively understood, but Nishida unveils it as the center of both Eastern and Western thinking, although he believed that it is only in the Japanese spirit that there occurred an integral realization of the identity of absolute nothingness with actuality itself, as most openly realized in Zen Buddhism and a uniquely Japanese Pure Land Buddhism.

Speaking as a Christian theologian whose work is grounded in an absolute nothingness, I acknowledge that Nishida and the Kyoto School have been a fundamental ground of my work, but this has entailed an enormous struggle to realize a uniquely Christian absolute nothingness, and uniquely Christian if only because of its apocalyptic actuality. While Nishida and the Kyoto School have been most challenging to me in their correlation of Buddha and God, and of a uniquely Buddhist Buddha and a uniquely Christian Christ, this occurs through a deeply kenotic or self-emptying thinking—one which has no parallel in the history of Christian theology, although it is the center of a uniquely Hegelian thinking. This is the thinking which has been my primary philosophical ground, so that pale as my thinking is in the perspective of Nishida and the Kyoto School, I think that it is nevertheless the fullest Christian counterpart to their thinking, and certainly one which has been deeply affected by their work. I shall always be grateful for the rich dialogues that I had with Nishitani and Abe Masao, who seemed to be able to enter my thinking spontaneously, and who ever prodded me to prosecute it more radically—a radicalness surely realized in the Kyoto School, and embodied there as it nowhere is in any body of Christian theologians. Not insignificantly, Buddhist thinking is deeply grounded in meditation, or in what the West understands as contemplation as opposed to meditation; and just as a deeper mystical thinking in both East and West has called forth an absolute nothingness, this is a critical point at which Eastern and Western thinking coincide. Buddhist scholars have initiated the West into the fundamental role of an absolute nothingness in Eastern art, but so too we are now coming to understand a parallel role of an absolute nothingness in modern or late-modern Western art, literature, and music, even if at this point Western philosophical and theological understanding lag behind Western art.

Absolute nothingness or an absolute Nihil has only very peripherally entered into Western philosophical thinking. Although this is fundamental in crucial sections of Hegel's *Science of Logic,* as in Heidegger's *Being and Time* and *Beiträge,* neither Heidegger nor Hegel fully explored an absolute nothingness. Among our theologians, only Barth and Tillich have openly confronted the Nihil, and even if this is crucial to their deeper thinking, it only gave way to strictly limited confrontations with absolute nothingness in their theologies. Perhaps at no other point are we in deeper need today of a truly new theology; and if we are now being overwhelmed by the dominance of orthodox theologies, it could well be that they would best be challenged by a new theological thinking of absolute nothingness—and thus, the Kyoto School might be more contemporary now than ever before. Indeed, we are keenly aware of the power of nihilism in our world, a nihilism that is more universal now than it has ever previously been. But nihilism cannot be understood without understanding an absolute nothingness, even if a truly nihilistic nothingness is the very opposite of a Buddhist nothingness. Now if Satan is that symbolic figure who most embodies a nihilistic nothingness, it is fascinating that Nishida can affirm that the true absolute must negate itself even to the extent of "being Satan," here employing the Mahāyāna concept of expedient means (Sk. *upāya*), a means whereby the absolute mediates itself into the depths of illusion and evil. Only thereby is a genuine redemption possible for us, and this occurs only by way of an absolute self-negation of the absolute itself, a self-negation that Nishida can name as both God and Buddha.

If it is only in the Kyoto School that there has been a genuine correlation of God and Buddha, this occurs in a truly kenotic thinking, a thinking of self-emptying or self negation as the deepest depths of the absolute itself, and only thereby does *nirvāna* realize itself as *samsāra,* or does Godhead realize itself as itself. Hence absolute nothingness is here inseparable from both God and Buddha, and one inevitably wonders if there can be any final distinction between Buddha and God, or even any final distinction between East and West. Nishida appears to go beyond even Hegel in understanding the true absolute as an absolute self-contradiction, for it is truly absolute by being opposed to nothing, and it is absolute being only if it is opposed to absolutely nothing. Yet nothing at all can objectively or actually oppose the absolute, therefore the true absolute can only be opposed to nothing by being opposed to itself, and this can occur only by way of an absolute self-contradiction. Therefore, the absolute can only truly or actually express itself by negating itself, but by negating itself it is paradoxically at one with itself, so that the absolute being of the absolute is an absolutely self-negating being, and it is that self-negation which *is* the absolute.

Underlying this understanding is the Mādhyamika identification of "is" and "is not," but the Kyoto School has been criticized by many Buddhist thinkers for its transformation of a genuinely Mādhyamika ground, accused here and elsewhere of importing Western categories into Buddhism, and above all of engrafting a Western understanding of actuality upon Buddhism. Perhaps this is most true of its understanding of self-negation, and just as self-negation is the very center of Nishida's thinking, its uniquely Buddhist ground may well reside in its understanding of absolute nothingness. A uniquely Western Nihil may be most distant from an Eastern absolute nothingness in terms of its brute actuality, or its actuality in the modern world, and just as that is the actuality which has been the primary mode of a Western opening to Buddhism, this has surely been a decisive source of the power of the Kyoto School's impact upon the West, one rivaled in late modernity by no other form of Buddhism. Only in late modernity does a human existence or *Dasein* fully stand forth, which is a consequence of an encounter with the Nothing, one inducing that *Angst* which *Being and Time* can understand as our deepest call. We could understand that this is the very call which has opened so many of us to Buddhism, and thereby we could know Buddhism as addressing our deepest existence.

Despite its Buddhist horizon, Nishida's later thinking is in large measure addressed to a specifically Western human existence, hence its substantial employment of Kierkegaard, and its continual evocation of the deep individuality of human existence. Perhaps this is where Nishida's thinking is most paradoxical to his Western reader, as when he affirms that it is because death entails that a self enter into eternal nothingness that the self is historically unrepeatable, unique, and individual. Or when he maintains that the absolute Buddha and the individual person are one in the paradoxical bi-conditionality of the Mādhyamika "is" and "is not," for the true individual arises as a unique, momentary self-determination of the absolute present. Thus, that absolute present is all in all, but if so it is extraordinarily difficult to understand how such an absolute present could actually be the individual person, or how an absolute presence which is an absolute absence could possibly be anything which a Kierkegaard could recognize as the concretely existing individual. Is it actuality itself that is most elusive in these formulations, and does this actuality have both an Eastern and a Western ground, even a Buddhist and a Christian ground, and above all so in its understanding of an absolute death and an absolute nothingness?

Perhaps Nishida is closest to Christianity in his understanding of an absolute death, an absolute death which the Christian or the Western Christian knows as the one source of redemption; and while the orthodox Christian refuses the Crucifixion as the death of God or the Godhead, Nishida knows the true absolute as undergoing an absolute death or an absolute self-negation, and an absolute self-negation realizing an absolute emptiness or an absolute nothingness. Obviously self-negation—an absolute self-negation—is truly primal for Nishida and the Kyoto School, but what is its relation to a truly Christian self-negation, or to what the Christian most deeply knows as the Crucifixion? Some Christians have been deeply enlightened by the Kyoto School at this crucial point, for when the Crucifixion is understood as an absolute self-negation in this sense it even thereby is understood as what the Christian knows as Resurrection. Here, it is vital to understand that while both Paul and the Forth Gospel enact or call forth the Crucifixion as Resurrection, this never occurs in Christian theology, and above all not in orthodox Christian theology. Indeed, the Resurrection has been the most controversial category in modern Christian theology, in large measure because our established theological language about resurrection is so distant from what critical scholarship has unraveled as its New Testament ground, but equally because biblical language about resurrection and eternal life is so discordant with all of our established conceptual and logical categories. Apparently no such problem exists in Buddhism, so that the Buddhist thinker can here realize a clarity and coherence that is denied the Christian thinker, and this has inevitably had a real impact upon the critical Christian thinker, who can sense the possibility here of a fundamental theological liberation.

Noteworthy here is how Nishida can pass so immediately and so spontaneously from an absolute death to an absolute liberation, or from an absolute self-negation to that absolute nothingness which is *śūnyatā;* it is as though each simply is the other, or "is" and "is not" its other. This is another crucial point at which the Mādhyamika ground of Nishida's thinking is in question: Can a genuinely Mādhyamika dialectic sustain such thinking? If this is to be a dialectic that dissolves all possible dualism or all possible otherness, then is it even possible to speak of an absolute death as death or an absolute nothingness as nothingness? One could imagine that in a truly Mādhyamika dialectic there could be no movement at all, and not even an immediate and a spontaneous movement, between death and liberation, or between *samsāra* and *nirvāna,* for not only does nothing happen in the realization of *nirvāna,* but finally nothing happens at all. Here, one suspects that Nishida truly is under the impact of the West, and if he spent most of his life in assimilating German philosophy, that is the most theological of all modern Western philosophies, and the one most grounded in the very center of Christianity. Surely that is a center which profoundly affected Nishida, and perhaps affected him more than it did any German philosopher, and most so in his centering upon an absolute self-negation. As opposed to Hegel, who is our greatest Western philosopher of an absolute self-negation, Nishida's is not a comprehensive or systematic understanding of self-negation; it is far rather a pure understanding of self-negation alone, and a self-negation which has no reverberations whatsoever beyond itself. This is doubtless a fundamental ground of that transition which Nishida effects. But in being such an immediate transition, does it thereby lose everything which Hegel understood as the "labor of the negative," a labor which is the ultimate source of both history and consciousness, or everything which the West knows as actuality?

In this perspective, Nishida both is and is not open to that actuality, and perhaps the crucial problem here is the actuality of that absolute death which Nishida knows. Is this a death which actually occurs, and actually occurs to the absolute itself, or as an absolute death is it simply the epiphany or manifestation of absolute life to us? Does a real transfiguration of the absolute occur in absolute death—a transfiguration which is a transformation, and a transformation occurring in the actuality of time itself, so that there is an ultimate and even absolute difference both between the absolute life and the absolute death of the absolute and between that original or primordial absolute which knows no death and that absolute which has undergone an absolute death? Seemingly, a pure Mādhyamika thinking would allow no difference or otherness whatsoever between an absolute life and an absolute death—but could this be Nishida's position? Or is absolute death for him an absolute self-negation in which the true absolute does actually negate itself, and negate itself so that it is now the very opposite of an absolute life? If no such opposite is possible, then how could this be an actual self-negation, or even a real self-negation at all? Perhaps Nishida unintentionally reveals himself when he speaks about the absolute's becoming Satan, and doing so in order to mediate redemption to us. Surely such a Satan is only a mask of the absolute—and could that be what Nishida finally means by an absolute death?

No, this is surely not possible. But it is possible that Nishida is deeply ambivalent at this point, or even that he is simultaneously Buddhist and Christian; Buddhist in knowing and only knowing an absolute emptiness, and Christian in knowing an absolute self-emptying of God. That self-emptying is what the Christian knows as an absolute sacrifice, the sacrifice of the Crucifixion, and it is possible that Nishida knows that sacrifice more purely than any Christian theologian, and even knows it as totality itself, a self-emptying totality that is all in all. Could it be that this is the very totality that the Christian knows as apocalypse? While apocalyptic language is alien to Nishida, it is possible that he realized a Buddhist counterpart to that language, and did so in his understanding of absolute nothingness itself, an absolute nothingness that is wholly distinct from a Neoplatonic absolute nothingness, and wholly distinct as an actually self-emptying absolute nothingness. A truly and finally self-emptying absolute nothingness could be apocalypse itself, for Christianity has never realized a truly and fully apocalyptic theology; thus apocalypse is a deep mystery to us, and no doubt is far distant from our common or given understanding of apocalypse. Yet we do know that both Paul and the

Fourth Gospel could call forth or enact the Crucifixion as apocalypse itself, and if the Crucifixion is an absolute sacrifice or an absolute self-negation, it perhaps could be understood as the realization of an absolute nothingness, if an absolute nothingness is known as an absolute self-emptying or an absolute self-negation.

We imagine apocalypse as an absolute plenitude, but is it possible to imagine it as an absolute emptiness, or as an absolute emptiness that is an absolute plenitude? Once again "is" is a crucial word here, but if here "is" is identical with "is not," in what sense could that be true: simply in the sense that there is no difference whatsoever between them, or in the sense that this "is" affects or realizes "is not," and in such a way as to realize a truly new "is" and a truly new "is not"? If the former is true, and there is no difference at all between "is" and "is not," it is extraordinarily difficult if not impossible to understand how this could be actual in any Western sense, for the West understands actuality as a fully active as opposed to a wholly passive state or condition. But if this "is" truly realizes an "is not," then it would be actual in a Western sense, and so, too, an absolute nothingness would be a truly actual nothingness, and a truly actual absolute nothingness which could be manifest and real as the Nihil. An Hegelian *das Nichts* is generated by a negation of Being or *Sein;* that negation is a real or actual negation, so that *das Nichts* is truly real by way of that negation, and wholly unreal or non-actual apart from an absolute negation. Could this be true of that absolute nothingness known by Nishida and the Kyoto School, or must it be known as non-actual in any Western sense, and thereby known within any Western horizon as an absolute passivity or an absolute quiescence?

The crucial theological problem here is the relation between Buddha and God, and more particularly the relation between the self-negation of Buddha and the self-negation of God: Does Nishida understand this as one and the same self-negation, or is there a fundamental difference between them? Here, God is the crucial category, at least from a Western perspective, and if the Westerner commonly and even critically understands that God is absent from Buddhism, is the Kyoto School here perhaps unique in Buddhism, and is that the major reason why it has had such an impact upon Western theology and thinking? Certainly God is a fully actual God in Western thinking, and is so even in a uniquely Western thinking of the death or self-negation of God—a self-negation or death which is a fully actual one, and in Nietzsche and Hegel that death or self-negation is the ultimate source and ground of actuality it-self. Could what Nishida understands as the self-negation of God be actual in this sense? And is this actuality identical with the self-negation of Buddha, or is there an ultimate difference between them? Now if the Christian knows the full actuality of the absolute death of the Crucifixion, does the Buddhist know the full actuality of the absolute self-emptying or the absolute compassion of the Buddha, even if the Buddhist knows an absolute death in a very different way than the Christian knows an absolute death?

Nothing is more alien to Buddhist iconography than the cross, but is the bodhisattva or the absolute compassion of the Buddha fully parallel to what the Christian knows as the Christ of Passion or the Crucified God? And does each realize a redemption which is a fully actual redemption—a redemption absolutely transforming existence itself? Thereby totality itself would undergo an absolute transfiguration, as the depths of *samsāra* are transfigured into the depths of *nirvāna,* or the depths of sin transfigured into the depths of grace, but only insofar as an absolute reversal occurs. Such a reversal surely could be understood as apocalypse. Is a uniquely Christian apocalypse profoundly illuminated, though, by a uniquely Buddhist self-emptying, and is there finally an ultimate identity between that apocalypse and this self-emptying? If so, this could account for the inability of Christian theology to become an apocalyptic theology; and so, too, could it account for the apocalyptic ground of Hegel and Nietzsche, who are our fullest Western philosophers of an absolute self-emptying. Is it because we have known apocalypse as a plenitude that is absolutely other than an absolute nothingness that apocalypse is so unthinkable in Christian theology? And if profoundly imaginative visions of apocalypse do indeed occur in the uniquely Christian epic, is that occurrence inseparable from the horizon of absolute darkness or absolute self-annihilation or absolute chaos itself?

Christian epic visions of apocalypse from Dante through Joyce are visions of an absolutely actual apocalypse, one which is both the consequence of a full and total movement of history and consciousness, and the consequence of the absolute actualization of Godhead itself, and here Godhead is fully correlated or fully integrated with consciousness and history, a history and a consciousness that is actually embodied in apocalypse. Thus far we have continued to be unable to decisively understand that apocalypse, but could it be illuminated by a Buddhist absolutely emptying or by a Buddhist absolute nothingness? If a Buddhist absolute nothingness is itself an absolute plenitude, and is so as absolute nothingness itself, could apocalypse be an absolute plenitude which we could only know as an absolute nothingness, and not because of its apparent or manifest transcendence, but far rather because of its absolute immanence? Yet this is an absolute immanence which is the consequence of an absolute sacrifice of absolute transcendence—a sacrifice which has actually and totally occurred. If that sacrifice is finally apocalypse itself, then apocalypse is an absolute transfiguration, and an absolute transfiguration of actuality itself. That transfiguration could only be known to us as an absolute nothingness, but an absolutely actual absolute nothingness, one releasing an ultimate and even absolute Nihil, which could be recognized as the very signature of apocalypse.

Is Buddhism closed to such a Nihil, or does it know it in a way that is the very opposite of any possible Western way? If we know *Angst* in response to the Nihil, the Buddhist might well respond with an integral calm, for here the Nihil is not a wholly negative nothingness, but far rather a wholly positive one, as one which the Buddhist can name as *śūnyatā*. Yet if it is possible to know apocalypse as an absolutely positive negativity, or an absolutely positive absolute nothingness, and one which is the consequence of an absolute death, then that death would be the realization of that negativity, a negativity which can genuinely be named as resurrection. Hence crucifixion *is* resurrection, and when resurrection is understood as eternal life alone, it becomes the very opposite of that resurrection which is crucifixion, thereby ushering in that Gnosticism or that Christian paganism which radical Christians understand as dominating virtually all expressions of historical Christianity. Can Buddhism liberate Christianity from that paganism, and above all so in its realization of absolute emptiness or absolute nothingness, an absolutely self-negating absolute nothingness, and therefore an absolute nothingness that is the absolute reversal of itself? Such a reversal could be understood as a consequence of absolute sacrifice, an absolute sacrifice which is an absolute self-negation. If that is the sacrifice of Godhead itself, then it is realized as an absolute transfiguration of the Godhead, a transfiguration which can be named as an absolute apocalypse.

Such a transfiguration could only be a fully actual transfiguration, and a transfiguration realizing an absolutely new absolute nothingness, or a new absolute self-emptying. If it is Buddhism—and most decisively for us Nishida and the Kyoto School—which most purely understands an absolute self-emptying as the self-emptying of the Godhead, could that self-emptying be an apocalyptic realization of Godhead itself? Classical Christian theology has fundamentally understood Godhead as an absolutely primordial Godhead. This theology, however, arose only after a negation or reversal of Christian apocalypticism had occurred, and that negation can be understood as a reversal of a forward-moving apocalyptic movement into a backward-moving primordial movement. Western thinkers commonly understand Buddhism as a backward movement to a primordial absolute nothingness, but Buddhist thinkers insist that this is a fundamental misunderstanding, for in Buddhism there is no distinction at all between backward and forward, and hence there cannot possibly be a genuinely backward movement. If there can be no denying the ultimacy of the backward movement of eternal return in the dominant expressions of Christianity; and if it is true that such a movement is alien to Buddhism, so that a Buddhist self-emptying is not a primordial movement; then a Buddhist self-emptying could open the possibility for the Christian of a dissolution of every possible primordial movement, and hence a dissolution of the dominant conception and the dominant realization of the Christian God.

Only thus could Christianity once again become open to apocalyptic Godhead. And if Christianity has been virtually closed to apocalyptic Godhead throughout its history—a primal consequence of its reversal of an originally apocalyptic Christianity—when apocalypticism returns in late modernity it is inevitably a profoundly heterodox apocalypticism, as in Hegel, Nietzsche, and Heidegger, but no less so in Blake and Joyce. Hence a genuinely apocalyptic theology could now only be an absolutely radical theology—one truly inverting and reversing orthodoxy; and just as orthodoxy came into existence by reversing apocalypticism, an apocalyptic theology can now come into existence by reversing orthodoxy. One decisive way by which this could now occur is by a theological absorption of Nishida and the Kyoto School: Already these thinkers employ Christian theological language, and above all so in speaking so purely of the absolute self-negation of God—a self-negation and self-emptying which is the very opposite of the orthodox dogma of the absolute sovereignty and absolute transcendence of God, and a self-emptying which could only be a pure reversal of that transcendence and sovereignty.

The apocalyptic theologian could understand that this is just what occurs in the Crucifixion, and in that Crucifixion which is apocalypse; and if, thereby, the Crucifixion truly is Resurrection, that resurrection could be understood as an absolute self-emptying that becomes all in all in apocalypse. Blake envisioned this apocalypse in his vision of the "Self-Annihilation of God," and if Blake is our most revolutionary visionary, he can be understood as being closer to Buddhism than any other Christian visionary, and most so in his apocalyptic enactment of "Self-Annihilation." That self-annihilation or self-negation reverses Godhead itself, just as does Hegel's absolute self-negation, and if this self-negation truly parallels a Buddhist self-negation, then perhaps this is the very point at which Nishida and the Kyoto School realized a universal philosophy. If so, we stand profoundly in their debt, but a debt that can be honored theologically only by incorporating their thinking into our own. And if that promises a truly new theology, such a theology has never been more necessary than it is today.

PART FOUR

Ethics and
Politics

11

Other-Power and
Absolute Passivity in
Tanabe and Levinas

BRIAN SCHROEDER

Nishida Kitarō's project was, in part, to provide a rational ground for the phi-losophy of Zen. His junior colleague and successor, Tanabe Hajime, departed however from his focus on Zen and embraced instead the approach of Shin-ran (1173–1262), the founder of True Pure Land (*Jōdo Shin-shū*) Buddhism.[1] This is most evident in Tanabe's major work, *Philosophy as Metanoetics*, which was written at the end of World War II and published in 1946. Tanabe did remain faithful though to Nishida's desire to explicate Buddhist thought in a rational manner, thereby conjoining more fully the disciplines of philosophy and religious thought in an effort to generate a genuine world philosophy. A distinguishing aspect of many associated with the Kyoto School was the adop-tion of a decidedly religious orientation at a time when the major currents of European thinking, such as existentialism and phenomenology, were moving away from such a stance.

On Nishida's advice, Tanabe went to Germany from 1922 to 1924 to study with Husserl. It was there that he fell under the influence of the young Heidegger. Despite his early attention to Heidegger's philosophy, however, Tanabe ultimate-ly moved away from hermeneutic phenomenology, in part no doubt because his study of Hegel led him to think in a more dialectical manner, culminating in his original development of a "logic of species,"[2] which he then deployed in support of the Japanese state during World War II; but perhaps also—we may specu-late—because Heidegger did not experience, or reveal at any rate, the profound sense of repentance and remorse that Tanabe did following the end of that war, and certainly did not develop a full treatment of the question of "the other."[3]

The European thinker who emerged from that era with the most conse-quential view of otherness for recent thinking was Emmanuel Levinas, who was also a student of Husserl's and Heidegger's during the late 1920s and early 1930s. Levinas's first major original work, *Totality and Infinity*,[4] was published in France in 1961, and it is highly unlikely that Tanabe, who died in 1962, would have been familiar with his work. Also, like many other Europeans, Levinas indicated neither acquaintance with nor interest in the comparative work being done in Japan. Yet despite their pronounced differences, and perhaps more than that of any other contemporary thinker, the philosophy of Levinas stands closest to the heart of Tanabe's metanoetic thinking.[5]

One of the difficulties that ensues in constructing a dialogue between works such as Tanabe's *Philosophy as Metanoetics* and Levinas's *Totality and Infinity* results from their remarkably similar composition. Neither is written, as are most philosophical essays, with the intention of putting forth a set of arguments to defend a particular thesis. Jacques Derrida's suggestive 1963 description of Levinas's text is pertinent for Tanabe's own work. Both *Totality and Infinity* and *Philosophy as Metanoetics* pursue a "thematic development that is neither purely descriptive nor purely deductive. [They proceed] with the insistence of waves on a beach: return and repetition, always, of the same wave against the same shore, in which, however, as each return recapitulates itself, it also infinitely renews and enriches itself." Being more of a "work of art than a treatise," such texts are "beyond rhetorical abuse," protecting them as well from any structured critique.[6] Given the Buddhist predilection for paradox, this may not be such a problem for the reception of a work like *Philosophy of Metanoetics*, but for one such as *Totality and Infinity*, which implies from the start a radical self-critique on the part of reason or philosophy itself, to the degree of having to relinquish its attempt to render the meaning of ethical metaphysics theoretically graspable, it is a significant hurdle to surmount. This is, however, what arguably distinguishes ethical-religious discourse from the purely philosophical, and what leads both thinkers to dissociate the former from the latter on the foundational level. Each appeals to an *experience* of the Other which occurs prior to and remains beyond the total grasp of a theoretical reason. The critical difference that determines this relationship is that between the ineffable absolutely other, in Levinas, and absolute nothingness in Tanabe.

The present essay brings together the thinking of Tanabe and Levinas in order to assess their respective interpretations of alterity in light of their respective efforts to establish a fundamental conception of social ethics and religion. Central to the philosophies of both is the possibility of the ethical transformation of the self in response to the imperative imposed by the passive power of the other. This self-transformation is a necessary condition for confronting the problem of evil, a perennial issue that becomes all the more pressing in the wake of recent world terrorism. Given the need for an effective, constructive, and not solely retaliatory response to terrorism, widening the space for comparative cross-cultural dialogue is increasingly important. And since recent terrorist activities around the world have been repeatedly cast by many as a matter where religion takes center stage, it follows that a religious-philosophical response is vital toward reaching a long-term resolution of this crisis.

The notion of self-transformation, or *metanoesis*, has resonances with Nietzsche's and Nishitani's respective conceptions of self-overcoming, but differs from these in that for Tanabe and Levinas such transformation is predicated on the relationship between the self and the other, rather than on the self's relation to itself. The concept of *breaking through,* employed by both Tanabe and Levinas, attends this self-transformation and will be examined in order to acquire an adequate understanding of the dialectic between good and evil, power and passivity, response and reconciliation, mediation and proximity, self and other, humanity and divinity, and God and absolute nothingness.

The thinking of Tanabe and Levinas share a similar dimension of absolute resoluteness in their insistence on the primacy of the ethical relationship for philosophy and lived existence. Tanabe frames the issue in a way that determines the course of what follows in this essay, posing a question that seems almost made for Levinas:

> Unless we undertake the new way of *zange* [metanoesis], free ourselves of the evil institutions of the past, and collaborate in carrying out whatever changes are necessary in the social system, there is no possibility of reconstruction. The only course open to us at present is metanoetics, not culturalism. Does not the Old Testament prophet Jeremiah show us the way? (PM lxi)

In constructing a dialogue between Tanabe and Levinas, the following questions will serve as a guide: Does Levinas's conception of the other's absolute passive alterity coincide with Tanabe's interpretation of absolute Other-power? How does ethical passivity translate into ethical responsibility in light of the possibility of radical evil? Is metanoetics the standpoint that allows the self to respond to the ethical demand of the Other?

Metanoesis and Religious Philosophy

The Kyoto School was criticized by the emerging political left in the post-Meiji era for having aligned itself during World War II with certain ideals of Japan's imperial nationalism.[7] But it is important to note that Tanabe's metanoetic philosophy was developed prior to the end of the war, and not in response to later critics on the left. Tanabe's metanoetic philosophy, or rather his conception of "philosophy *as* metanoetics" (*zangedō;* way of repentance, change of heart), was determined by his own particular "self-awareness" (*jikaku*) of the extremely violent injustice done to others in the name of nationalistic identity and pride. This led him to confront a problem that even so great a thinker as Kant did not fully take up—despite his introduction of the problem—namely, radical evil.

The importance of *jikaku* cannot be overstated, and in many respects this concept connects the various Kyoto philosophers as a whole. A modern Japanese term used early on to philosophically translate the Western concept of "self-consciousness," the meaning of *jikaku* was extended by Nishida to serve as a "philosophical equivalent for Buddhist 'enlightenment,'" reaching beyond the standard meaning of self-consciousness to designate an essentially *religious* transformative event that is able to be grounded through philosophical reason.[8] This event of self-awareness is the fundamental insight of awakening—namely, non-ego or no-self (Sk. *anātman;* Jp. *muga*);[9] that is, the realization that the everyday self or ego is not the "true" self, and that this is "a *self*-awareness, not an achieved one," such as one encounters in the Hegelian dialectic.[10]

Standing on common ground regarding the priority of religion over philosophy, Levinas and Tanabe each formulate a religious philosophy as the heart of their thinking, and abandon ontological philosophy as the principal means to realize the ethical in existence. For each there occurs a *conversion* from philosophy to religion. Levinas teaches that the meaning of religion *is* ethics: Religion is neither theology nor liturgy nor belief, but rather the practice or exercise of ethical responsibility to the point of non-reciprocal substitution. For Tanabe, the relation between ethics and religion first denotes a passage from the former to the latter, but also vice versa:

> In mediating the absolute through the metanoetic confession of its own finitude and powerlessness, the relative ethical subject cooperates to make manifest the absolute nothingness of religion. . . . Metanoesis is both the gate through which ethics passes over into religion and the axis around which religion converts into ethics. Thus metanoesis is really a *kōan* mediating a dialectical transformation between ethics and religion. (PM 190)

Moreover, "metanoetics views ethics as the '*kōan* of reality'" (PM 131). Ethics, which is never fully absolved of its connection to the standpoint of self-power, is mediated by Other-power, and converted into metanoesis.

Self-Power and Other-Power

For Tanabe, religious metanoesis is a process that implies both conversion and repentance. Repentance or self-surrender (*zange*) "should be infinitely continuous as conversion and should, therefore, envelop within itself the infinite repetition of 'eternal return.' Conversion, however, is transformed negativity, the negativity of metanoesis turned into affirmation through the transforming act of the absolute" (PM 6).[11] In metanoesis the self "dies" to Other-power. This is Tanabe's hermeneutic of the "great death" in Buddhist thinking.[12]

Tanabe's own metanoetic experience, his self-proclaimed "conversion" (*tenkan*), led him to move beyond the position of "self-power" (*jiriki*)—characteristic of the philosophy of Zen adopted by Nishida and his student Nishitani—and more toward the standpoint of self-transformative "Other-power" (*tariki*). This standpoint is precisely what enables the self to realize a "breakthrough" (Gn. *Durchbruch*)[13] to its true nature, such as conceived by Shinran, whom Tanabe credits with having led him to the realization of *zangedō*. Tanabe, however, does not fully abandon the concept of self-power; rather, he tries to think *jiriki* and *tariki* in terms of a new dialectical unity that opens one to the realization of absolute nothingness.

Self-power and Other-power are perhaps best interpreted respectively as internal-affectivity and external-affectivity. In other words, self-power is the becoming-external of the interior egoistic will which manifests itself as action. Conversely, Other-power is the affectivity exerted on the ego-self to the point of shattering the unity of the individual will, thereby calling the self to question the extent of its own sovereign freedom. This is the realization of "self-awareness" (*jikaku*) on which is predicated metanoesis (*zange*). It is critical to note that Other-power is not to be construed in terms that might suggest the voluntaristic imposition of a divine will on the self. While Other-power is Tanabe's name for the absolute, this has nothing to do with a transcendent other, or a being such as God. Rather, "since this absolute is the negation and transformation—that is, conversion—of everything relative, it may be defined as absolute nothingness" (PM li). Other-power is radically *passive* and real only insofar as it is perceived by the I-self and allowed to destabilize or break through the resistances of the egoistic will.

According to Tanabe, "what is impossible with *jiriki* becomes possible with *tariki*, though both *tariki* and *jiriki* remain complementary to one another" (PM 9, cf. 25). Thus it is not a matter of deciding for either Zen or Pure Land Buddhism, or whether both Zen and Pure Land are correct interpretations of the Buddha-dharma. Metanoetics constitutes rather a third position, one that is neither Zen nor Pure Land. "Logically speaking, absolute Other-power means absolute mediation, which is simply an absolute reciprocity in which all things form a dynamic, transforming unity of opposites in terms of a mutually mediating relationship of *neither/nor*: neither one nor two, neither identity nor difference" (PM 257). Tanabe is not advocating, however, a standpoint that seeks to balance Zen and Pure Land, a dialectic of reciprocity between self and other such as one finds in Tendai (Ch. *Tian-tai*) Buddhism. Rather, paralleling Levinas in an important respect, Tanabe's metanoetics connotes an *asymmetrical* dialectic between Other-power and self-power.[14]

With respect to the Western tradition, writes Tanabe, metanoetics seeks a middle path between existentialism, exemplified primarily in the philosophies of Nietzsche and Heidegger, and the philosophy of freedom, as found in Schelling (PM 151). Unlike Zen, which "differs from the transformation of Other-power of metanoetics insofar as it agrees with the self-power doctrines based on a theory of freedom" (PM 192), metanoetics is a fundamentally *religious* philosophical response to both critical philosophy—that is, philosophy understood as the autonomous power of reason for critique—and atheistic existentialism.

Evil and Absolute Responsibility

Both Tanabe and Levinas were initially drawn to phenomenology but ultimately abandoned that philosophy on similar grounds—namely, that it perpetuated the primacy of the ontological standpoint of egoity; that is, the tendency of subjectivity to absolutize itself in the name of freedom. Tanabe recognizes this as the locus of moral evil, on the order of a Kantian radical evil that lies at the constitutive base of human existence: "the self-assertion and rebellion of the relative vis-à-vis the absolute" (PM 23). But "it is utterly important," he states, "to realize that it is not the subject of evil but the subject of goodness that comes to awareness of the structure of evil" (PM 152). The radical nature of evil means that evil is not the mere lack or absence of goodness, as one finds for instance in Augustine. Levinas would agree with Tanabe insofar as the transcendence of goodness is revealed in the contact with evil. In a startling passage from "Transcendence and Evil," Levinas writes:

> [Evil] would reach me in a wounding in which there arises a meaning, and is articulated in a saying which recognizes this someone that is thus revealed. . . . In any case, it is an interpellation of a you, and a glimpse at the Good behind

evil. A first "intentionality" of transcendence: someone is seeking me out. A God that does evil, but a God as a you. And, through the evil in me, my awakening to myself.[15]

Earlier in the same essay, Levinas goes so far as to describe evil in terms of "excess" and "transcendence," comparing this apprehension of evil's "pure quality" to the "rediscovery" of phenomenological intentionality.

> In the appearing of evil, in its original phenomenality, in its *quality*, is announced a *modality*, a manner: not finding a place, the refusal of all accommodation with . . . a counter-nature, a monstrosity, what is disturbing and foreign of itself. *And in this sense transcendence!* The intuition that consists in catching sight, in the pure quality of a phenomenon such as evil, of the *how* of a break with immanence is a view that seems to us to be intellectually as rich as the rediscovery of intentionality appeared at the beginning of phenomenology.[16]

What is most important here with respect to dialogue between Levinas and Tanabe is the meaning of this "break with immanence." In abandoning any traditional interpretation of transcendence as situated in a classically construed metaphysical beyond, each of them locates the *movement* of a transcendence that radically transforms the self in the relation that the self has with the concrete, human other. This is why Levinas will claim: "The you in God is not an 'otherwise than being,' but a 'being otherwise.'"[17] What cannot be thematized, grasped through one's own power, is the absolutely other (Fr. *l'absolument autre*), which is also to say, the other person (*l'autrui*).[18] Similarly, as noted earlier, Tanabe will also identify Other-power as the absolute conversion of everything relative, as absolute nothingness, recognizing that while this standpoint is reached dialectically, it resists the positive, thematizing knowledge of the other that characterizes, for instance, German absolute idealism.

The evil of human violence, according to Levinas, expresses itself in the positing of freedom over justice as the highest ideal or value, which results in an "imperialism" of theory that totalizes the Other (*l'Autrui*) and thus renders the formation of genuine ethical community impossible. Being, or the totality, is essentially violent, and at base humanity is fundamentally "hypocritical."[19] According to Tanabe, human existence is "evil and untruthful by nature" (PM 3). The self is imbued with radical evil in its absolute self-affirmation. Though he initially applied the notion of radical evil to only the individual, in a revised version of his 1946 essay on the "logic of species," he subsequently included society as a whole in this critique.[20] Despite their shared negative appraisal of the "human condition" (to borrow Hannah Arendt's phrase), both Tanabe and Levinas allow for the possibility of transforming the self into an ethical agent, though only by realizing the demand that the Other places upon the self to be responsible not only for its own freedom but for the *Other's responsibility* as well. Levinas is fond of citing Dostoyevsky's character the Elder Zossima[21] in support of this position: "We are always guilty before the other and none more than I."[22] Similarly, writes Tanabe: "I feel responsible for all of the evils and errors committed by others, and in so doing find that the actual inability of my philosophy to cope with them compels me to a confession of despair over my philosophical incompetence" (PM 26).

This last point is critical. If philosophy is incompetent to the task, then how is responsibility to be assumed? Put another way, how does this confession of despair translate into praxis? Given the enormity of this question, the following remarks will be confined to that which arguably alone renders praxis viable in any universal way—namely, dialectical mediation; and specifically, with respect to Tanabe, the mediation of being by nothingness and the relative by the absolute. Such mediation is the focal point for grasping the truth of metanoetics: "Other-power is *absolute* Other-power only because it acts through the mediation of the self-power of the relative that confronts it as other" (PM 18). Likewise, for Levinas, the other is absolute in that it also confronts the self experientially in the totality of being as the ethical imperative conveyed through the face-to-face relationship. But for Levinas, mediation actually constitutes the very problem, as it always carries with it the possibility of violence, being a product of theory and thereby inherently ontological.

Is it possible to adjudicate these seemingly polar positions? The issue revolves around the status of the *absolute*. Briefly stated, in Levinas the absolute is the Infinite, the wholly other—utterly transcendent in the sense of being beyond all conceptuality. Yet this absolutely other is experienced *pre*-conceptually as the "trace" of the absolutely other in the "face" (*visage*) of the concrete Other. This point cannot be overemphasized, as it is precisely this that signals for Levinas the break from onto-theology, or what he collectively terms "ontology." The absolute is not being; it is "otherwise than being." Hence, the absolute is beyond the reciprocity of an idealist dialectic between *relative* conceptions of being and nothingness and, by extension, of the relative good and evil that ultimately negate, or at best as in the case of Heidegger, neutralize being's complicity in violence and injustice.[23] On Tanabe's interpretation, the absolute is only realized as such through a reciprocal negation of beings which entails a self-negation of relative beings. The absolute is thus absolute nothingness because it is absolute transformation by way of absolute mediation. "This, and none other," Tanabe flatly asserts, "is the only absolute that can really be considered absolute" (PM 158).

Absolute Nothingness and the Absolutely Other

Tanabe borrows from Nishida the important concept of "absolute nothingness" (*zettai mu; mattaku mu*), refining and extending its meaning and application in various ways. This concept derives from and is practically synonymous with the key Mahāyāna, especially Mādhyamika, Buddhist term *śūnyatā* (Jp. *kū*). The various forms of Buddhism that flowered in East Asia, particularly Ch'an and Zen, were in large measure the result of the interaction between Indian Mahāyāna and Chinese Daoism. The standpoint of absolute nothingness reflects the movement of *Dao:* "doing nondoing" or "acting nonacting" (Ch. *wei wuwei*), the spontaneous, unconditioned way of natural existence. The simultaneous unity and difference of all entities, absolute nothingness (or emptiness) does not mean "nonbeing" in the sense of the conceptual opposite of "being." Absolute nothingness is not the negation that ushers in nihilism but rather, to use a key term employed by Nishida, the "place" or "locus" (*basho*) wherein there is nothing that is not present; in other words, wherein everything exists on its own as it is. There is thus neither a temporal nor spatial disjunction expressed in the difference between absolute nothingness and being, nor between absolute nothingness and the relative nothingness of nonbeing. Absolute nothingness is the "standpoint" (Jp. *tachiba*)—not the ground (Gn. *Grund*)—from which all that is and is not emerges as it is grasped by the non-egocentric self. Absolute nothingness signifies the fundamental unity of existence that non-dialectically encloses all differentiation.

According to Tanabe, the standpoint of absolute nothingness can only be reached dialectically. However, it is precisely the standpoint of dialectics, and hence of mediation, that Levinas refuses in understanding the ethical relationship between the self and the Other. It would appear, then, that Tanabe and Levinas reach an impasse here: If dialectically grasping the signification of absolute nothingness is fundamental toward a realization of the metanoesis of self that opens one to a genuine ethical relationship, as Tanabe maintains, how can this perspective be reconciled or brought into meaningful dialogue with the infinite of Levinas's ethical metaphysics? Though religious in orientation, both thinkers are decidedly non-theological, that is, they eschew theistic conceptions of the absolute wherein God, to use Tanabe's language, is conceived as "an absolute existence transcending absolute nothingness and a unified will embracing the mediation of dialectics" (PM 94). Both appeal instead to the Platonic notion of the *epekeina tēs ousias* as that which stands closest to their interpretation of transcendence. Tanabe rejects, however, the Platonic Good's later reformulation by Plotinus as the One, on the grounds that this is ultimately an affirmation of being that remains closed to the notion of absolute nothingness. Tanabe succinctly spells it out: "The absolute One that Plato deals with in the *Parmenides,* and from which the One of Plotinus derives, corresponds exactly to the transcendent One of absolute nothingness which mediates the transformation of the relative one (the individual self). It is not merely contemplated as self-identical Being, like the One of Plotinus, but is always 'practiced' in action" (PM 89). And while Levinas explicitly correlates his interpretation of the absolutely other with Plato's Good, his relation to Plotinus is far more complex;[24] yet Levinas can share Tanabe's concerns about the One, and for many of the same reasons, and he too ultimately breaks with Neoplatonist metaphysics on the grounds that it remains an affirmation of *absolute being.*

There is a significant difference, however, between Levinas and Tanabe with respect to the idea of creation.[25] Levinas's thinking is both philosophically and biblically grounded, and his notion of the trace is predicated on a quasi-Lurianic kabbalistic withdrawal of the *En Sof* from creation, albeit to the extreme point of near disappearance *as such.* In this sense, Levinas would not contest the Hegelian moment of beginning as necessary (it is rather the negative totalizing movement of *Geist* that poses the difficulty). Whereas, according to Tanabe, Hegel's dialectic is flawed in that it fails to fully realize the depths of absolute mediation. Despite its pantheistic overtones, the Hegelian system remains fundamentally theistic insofar as it is a personal God that created the world through unmediated, absolute volition. From the standpoint of metanoetics, on the other hand, God is synonymous with absolute nothingness, that is, with the infinitely mutually mediated "dependent origination" (Sk. *pratītya-samutpāda*) of all opposites. Hegel does not fully move away from the theism of onto-theology, which has the Idea or God as "an absolute existence transcending absolute nothingness and a unified will embracing the mediation of dialectics" (PM 93–94). The danger is the risk of either a coercive transcendent being that undermines the freedom and autonomy of individual existence, or the loss of individuality in an all-encompassing pantheism. "Even the absolute we term God," writes Tanabe, "cannot in principle exist apart from this absolute mediation of nothingness" (PM 98).

Mediation and Transformation

Tanabe's metanoetic philosophy is dialectical in its approach and bears many affinities with Hegel's speculative dialectics, especially the concept of mediation, although Tanabe refuses the teleology of absolute knowing (PM lvi–lvii). Still, it is only through dialectical thinking, Tanabe argues, that one can arrive at the standpoint of absolute nothingness:

> When we speak of Other-power [*tariki*], the Other is absolute precisely because it is nothingness, that is, nothingness in the sense of absolute transformation. It is because of its genuine passivity and lack of acting selfhood that it is termed absolute Other-power. Other-power is *absolute* Other-power only because it acts through the mediation of the self-power [*jiriki*] of the relative that confronts it as other. Only to that extent is genuine, absolute Other-power mediated by self-power. In this way, the absolute becomes absolute mediation. (PM 18)

Absolute nothingness is absolute transformation as well as the necessary condition for absolute transformation. Simply and forcefully stated: "Nothingness means transformation" (PM 22). For Tanabe, self-transformation is possible via the mediation of Other-power, which in turn is absolute only because of its mediation by the relativity of self-power.

Despite what he views as Hegel's failure to grasp the concept of mediation in an absolute manner, Tanabe's dialectical philosophy nevertheless parallels Hegel's in several distinct ways. For instance, in the *Science of Logic* Hegel writes of the totality of the infinite and the finite, which is nothing less than an infinite totality insofar as it is the infinite becoming of finite being— that is, the unity of being and nothingness. That is why he characterizes the true infinite as a circle, even a "circle of circles"[26]—there is no beyond, no radical difference, no absolute alterity. The finite and the infinite are connected by the very negation that separates and distinguishes them from each other. Each term acts as the limitation of the other; but at the same time, each term dissociates itself from the other as its limit, as its nonbeing, and "as qualitatively separate from it, posits it as another being outside it."[27] The absolute is disclosed to consciousness as totality only in the realization of the equiprimordiality of each term in every dialectical opposition. Thus is the comprehension of the totality the recognition of that which is already present in the immediacy of the natural consciousness, namely, the *identity* of identity and difference, the *unity* of unity and multiplicity, the *sameness* of sameness and otherness.

In a similar vein, Tanabe states: "precisely because nothingness is mediated by being, and the absolute is mediated by the relative, absolute nothingness is able to be both absolute and nothingness" (PM 19). But Tanabe parts from Hegel's analysis in that the latter's logic is predicated on an irreversible forward movement of consciousness that does not necessitate the reciprocal dialectic that Tanabe maintains is essential for metanoesis. In other words, despite Hegel's famous contention that the dialectic is driven by the "power of the negative," from Tanabe's standpoint Hegel's logic is not "radical" enough to realize metanoesis (PM lvi–lvii, 55): "Metanoetics is a philosophy that has to be erected at the very point that all prior philosophical standpoints and methods have negated in their entirety" (PM lv). This total negation does not, precisely because it cannot, happen in the absolute knowing of dialectical logic. Mediation is not absolute in Hegelian philosophy; it remains but a touchstone, in Tanabe's construal, to something beyond it—that is, according to Hegel, to absolute knowing, or philosophy proper. This is the point at which both Tanabe and Levinas depart from Hegelian dialectics: Philosophy, which is to say reason, does not have the final word with respect to the meaning of being; metanoetics or ethics does.

Hegel is the first thinker to philosophically realize the death of God and, depending on one's interpretation, he consequently advances either a pantheistic or atheistic perspective. Both Tanabe and Levinas also acknowledge their philosophies as fundamentally atheistic, though not because they are predicated on the death of God.[28] The difference between them is a matter of how the absolute is approached by relative being. From the standpoint of absolute nothingness, there is no question of coercion; but one may object that there is a similar loss of individuality that is associated with the more obvious being-only position of pantheism. In Levinas, the opposite is the case. Though pantheism is here clearly not an issue, a recurrent concern is whether the infinite other poses the risk of an oppressive coercion. This irresolvable tension does not so much indicate, however, the impossibility of forming a dialogue between Tanabe and Levinas, as rather it serves to point out the irreducible difference signified by the absolute's refusal to be encapsulated by theory. This difference makes ethics possible for both to begin with, and furthermore designates the neither/nor standpoint governing their discourse that rejects both the either/or logic of onto-theology and the both/and logic of dialectical idealism.

Dialectic and Critique

Philosophy *as* metanoetics situates itself *between* the logical positions of either/or and both/and, acknowledging the seemingly contradictory role of self-power in arriving at the repentant standpoint necessary for "a philosophy founded on action-faith-witness (*gyō-shin-shō*) mediated by the transformative power of *tariki* (Other-power)" (PM 2–3). Other-power is the *passive* "disruption" of the conscious rational subject by absolute nothingness. Other-power is thus not an ontological but an existential principle, founded on the primacy of *social* mediation that leads to an absolute affirmation of the self as an individual-in-community. For Tanabe, this results in the development of a new "logic of absolute critique," which, in effect, is tantamount to contemporary deconstruction—the turning of reason upon itself, thereby revealing reason's own self-referential, totalizing ground.[29] The logic of critique is a critique of reason itself which "needs to be pressed to the point of an absolute critique through 'absolute disruption' and absolute crisis, which constitute the abandonment of reason" (PM 20). But what exactly does the "abandonment of reason"—or as he poses it elsewhere, in contrast to Nietzsche's absolute affirmation of being as will, the "absolute negation of reason" (PM 233)—mean for Tanabe? From the standpoint of metanoetics, it can only mean the complete submission of the self to Other-power. As Tanabe emphasizes time and again, self-power *qua* Other-power necessarily entails Other-power *qua* self-power. The dialectic is fundamentally reciprocal; moreover, this is necessitated by the standpoint of absolute nothingness.

In Levinas, philosophy is also construed as critique, wherein the very freedom of the self is called into question, a freedom that in its autonomy refuses the other as infinitely different from itself. Idealist mediation subsumes alterity as an object for selfsame consciousness, thereby grounding violence conceptually and paving the way for more concrete violence, such as war. The labor of the negative that drives the Hegelian Spirit is a purely active (as opposed to passive, not to reactive) force operating solely in the interest of self-consciousness or, in Tanabe's terminology, from the standpoint of self-power, which is also to say, from the standpoint of freedom. The reciprocity denoted by idealist mediation nullifies the *asymmetry* of the ethical relation, absolving the self of the perpetual infinite demand imposed on it by the Other. But the reciprocity that Levinas critiques is not that espoused by metanoetics, which, according to Tanabe, is not that of "a matter of a causal relationship in the temporal order, according to which a preceding cause produces a succeeding effect, but of a reciprocal relationship in which each element mediates and influences the other" (PM 30). In other words, metanoetic mediation is not an exchange based on recognition, but an internal dialectic that occurs solely within the self and only thereafter is converted into ethics and religion. Ethics is thus neither contingent on any legalistic dialectic of mutual and fair exchange, nor the result of an all-encompassing logic. "Absolute criticism" is the logic that functions in metanoetics; it is the "self-surrendering" of reason, that is, of self-power.

Proximity and Absolute Mediation

If the self-power of philosophy is incapable of coping with the radical evil of human existence, then how does the self realize the infinite sense of responsibility that, depending on the perspective, either *is* religion (Levinas) or *makes possible* religion (Tanabe)? Such realization is contingent on one's being open to a breaking-through the self by Other-power. Metanoetics is not simply a "thinking afterward" or repentance based on recognition of one's past sins.[30] This would confine *zange* to the stance of *jiriki*. The breaking-through of the self is predicated on both the self-power of repentance and the transformative power of the Other, though it is neither one nor the other. In biblical Hebrew, the word *qadosh* also means a breaking-through or, more precisely, a breaking-in, a rupture of the spatiotemporal order by divinity, or what Levinas refers to as the face (*visage*), the trace of the absolutely other, which signifies both divine and human alterity. Levinas writes:

> The other who manifests himself in a face as it were *breaks through* his own plastic essence, like a being who opens the window on which its own visage was already taking form. His presence consists in *divesting* himself of the form which does already manifest him. His manifestation is a surplus over the inevitable paralysis of manifestation.[31]

Are both the absolute criticism of metanoesis and the possibility of the ethical relationship subsequent to a breaking-through?

Levinas's deep suspicion toward Hegelian mediation is based in part on what he sees as the attempt to coalesce the same (*le même*) and the other (*l'autre*) into a theoretical whole or negative universal that, despite Hegel's claims to the contrary, dissolves the critical difference between the terms, and delivers being out of nothingness—that is, renders the absolute solely as being: "Idealism completely carried out reduces all ethics to politics . . . [in which] language loses all social significance; interlocutors renounce their unicity not in desiring one another but in *desiring the universal.*"[32] The idealist desire for universality is construed by Levinas not as transcendence, but as a lack or need (Fr. *besoin*) that ultimately refuses social or communal difference, the difference of otherness on which ethics is predicated. Still, it is a mistake to assume that Levinas repudiates any and all notions of mediation. "Mediation (characteristic of philosophy)," he says, "is meaningful only if it is not limited to distances."[33] Levinas counters, rather, the concept of mediation with that of *proximity,* a non-mediated intersubjective positioning that maintains the separation of subject and object, self and other, as necessary for realizing an ethical, just community.[34] The *paradox* attending proximity lies precisely in that it signifies the concrete personal nature of the face-to-face encounter (that which makes relationships possible to begin with) while simultaneously signifying the absolute *distance* that remains between the self and Other.

The passivity of the Other, destitution and exposure, constitutes the very signification of the ethical relationship for the self in the Levinasian understanding. This meaning is, however, neither conveyed through the devices of reason nor is it known as such. Reason only grasps this after the fact of the initial face-to-face encounter that opens this up to consciousness. The passivity of the other is paradoxically the other's very activity or "power." Tanabe's own analysis also reveals this to be the case. The terms "activity" and "passivity" are not contradictory but complementary in the sense of their role in transformative mediation (PM 162). Though the term "mediation" is generally employed in the context of the power of reason, Tanabe's "*absolute* mediation," wherein there exists a *mutual* mediation between *jiriki* (self-power) and *tariki* (Other-power), is also paradoxical since metanoesis both is and is not one's own action. Surrender to Other-power in metanoetics is possible because of the passivity that subtends relative beings, who, though imbued with radical evil, are also "pure passivity presupposing no substantial agent other than themselves" (PM 25). In a passage reminiscent of the mutual mediation one finds in Theodor Adorno's "negative dialectic,"[35] which contests the positivity of idealist dialectic that always returns to the object, even if infinite, as a modality of possession, Tanabe writes:

> The fact that metanoesis is going on within me is not to the credit of self-power. Indeed, I have to admit that even the self-power implied in my practice of *zange* [metanoesis] is itself already mediated by Other-power, which effects the absolute transformation of my self-surrender and self-negation into self-affirmation. Self-power and Other-power converge here and thus penetrate each other. (PM 27)

In other words, metanoesis is neither a once-and-for-all event nor something akin to Zen *satori*, but rather a continual process, and absolute insofar as it is the realization of the absolute nothingness of reality.

Ethics, Religion, Universality

Levinas claims that a "truth is universal when it applies to every reasonable being. A religion is universal when it is open to all."[36] But if it is the reasonable being that grasps the universality of truth, then how is it that, in this formulation, ethics need to be predicated on the relinquishing of the sovereignty of reason? Is this contradictory? In attempting an answer, it is necessary to distinguish between the truth claims of religious and philosophical discourse. From the perspective of religion, reason is the servant of ethics; it is ethics which alone connects us to the absolutely other and makes possible the universality that seduces and frustrates pure thought. This religious universality, while open to the phenomenological powers of the subject, is not constituted by that self-power. In this sense, Levinas stands quite close to Tanabe. But the subject or relative being which is capable of philosophy is reasonable in the service of ethics and religion to the effect that the self-power of reason necessarily becomes critique, "a tracing back to what precedes freedom. . . . To welcome the Other is to put in question my freedom."[37]

Metanoesis is arguably just such a questioning, but with the important proviso that it is "realized only according to the prompting of Other-power" (PM 8). Since this "prompting" is only actualized in social mediation, it assumes the form of responsibility, so much so that Tanabe is "deeply convinced of the fact that, in the last analysis, everyone is responsible, collectively, for social affairs. Once one assumes this standpoint of responsibility, there can be no doubt that metanoetics is indispensable for each person at each moment. Therefore metanoetics, like morality, can provide the way to a universal philosophy" (PM liv–lv). In sum, metanoetics is not identical with ethics, but rather is its complement.

Notes

1. On Tanabe's relationship to Shinran and Shin Buddhism, see the following essays in Taitetsu Unno and James Heisig, eds., *The Religious Philosophy of Tanabe Hajime* (Berkeley, Calif.: Asian Humanities Press, 1990): Hase Shōtō, "The Structure of Faith: Nothingness-*qua*-Love," trans. Jan Van Bragt, 89–116; Taitetsu Unno, "Shin Buddhism and Metanoetics," 117–33; Ueda Yoshifumi, "Tanabe's Metanoetics and Shinran's Thought," trans. Taitetsu Unno, 134–49.

2. See, in this volume, Sugimoto Kōichi, "Tanabe Hajime's Logic of Species and the Philosophy of Nishida Kitarō: A Critical Dialogue within the Kyoto School."

3. It is interesting to note that despite his own subsequent condemnation by the political left for his uncritical stance toward the Imperial Japanese government, in an article dated 5 September 1933, Tanabe criticized both Heidegger and other German academics for resigning themselves to a sense of fate and blind obedience to the state, and in 1941 he and others intervened to save Karl Jaspers and his wife from Nazi persecution (James W. Heisig, *Philosophers of Nothingness: An Essay on the Kyoto School* [Honolulu: University of Hawai'i Press, 2001], 135).

4. Emmanuel Levinas, *Totality and Infinity*, trans. Alphonso Lingis (Pittsburgh: Duquesne University Press, 1969).

5. To my knowledge, the only published study to date on the relation between Tanabe and Levinas is an untranslated essay in Japanese by Hase Shōtō, "The Philosophies of Tanabe and Levinas: Ontology and Ethics as Philosophical Positions" (1994).

6. Jacques Derrida, "Violence and Metaphysics: An Essay on the Thought of Emmanuel Levinas," in *Writing and Difference*, trans. Alan Bass (Chicago: University of Chicago Press, 1967), 312 n. 8.

7. For an alternative viewpoint, see the essay by Graham Parkes in the present volume, "Heidegger and Japanese Fascism: An Unsubstantiated Connection." For an overview of Tanabe's political writings, criticisms of them, and his response to the criticisms, see Heisig, *Philosophers of Nothingness*, 122–51. Also see John Maraldo, "The War Over the Kyoto School," *Monumenta Nipponica* 61, no. 3 (Autumn 2006): 375–401.

8. James Heisig, "The Religious Philosophy of the Kyoto School," in *The Religious Philosophy of Tanabe Hajime*, 19–20.

9. Buddhism does not deny the existence of the ego-self, but only that it is originary in its individuated manifestation, or is the transcendental condition for the possibility of knowing. All beings are interconnected and therefore exist in a state of contingent mutual co-dependency (Sk. *pratītya-samutpāda*). The teaching of *anātman* expresses this nonhierarchical state of differentiated unity.

10. Heisig, "The Religious Philosophy of the Kyoto School," 21.

11. For a developed treatment of the relationship between metanoesis and the eternal return, see my "Dancing on Nothing: Nietzsche, the Kyoto School, and Transcendence," *Journal of Nietzsche Studies* 37 (2009): 44–65. Part of this essay was published in Italian translation as "Trans-discendenza estatica: Religione e metanoesi in Nietzsche, Tanabe e Nishitani," trans. Silvia Benso, *Annuario Filosofico* 23 (2007): 397–420.

12. On the notion of the great death, see in the present volume Bret W. Davis, "Nishitani after Nietzsche: From the Death of God to the Great Death of the Will."

13. This term is borrowed by Tanabe and Nishitani from Meister Eckhart.

14. See Whalen Lai, "Tanabe and Dialectics of Mediation: A Critique," in *The Religious Philosophy of Tanabe Hajime*, esp. 263–65.

15. Emmanuel Levinas, "Transcendence and Evil," in *Collected Philosophical Papers*, trans. and ed. Alphonso Lingis (Dordrecht: Martinus Nijhoff, 1987), 181.

16. Ibid., 180.

17. Ibid., 182.

18. Levinas, *Totality and Infinity*, 39.

19. Ibid., 24.

20. See Tanabe Hajime, "The Logic of the Species as Dialectics," trans. David Dilworth and Satō Taira, *Monumenta Nipponica* 24, no. 3 (1969): 273–88. This is a partial translation of "Dialectics of Logic of Species" (THZ 7: 251–372).

21. During his last days, Zossima remarks that one is "not only worse than others, but . . . responsible to all men for all and everything, for all human sins, national and individual . . . every one of us is undoubtedly responsible for all men and everything on earth, not merely through the general sinfulness of creation, but each one personally for all mankind and every individual man" (Fyodor Dostoyevsky, *The Brothers Karamozov*, trans. Constance Garnett [New York: Random House, 1950], 194).

22. Emmanuel Levinas, *Time and the Other*, trans. Richard A. Cohen (Pittsburgh: Duquesne University Press, 1987), 108; also see *Ethics and Infinity*, trans. Richard A. Cohen (Pittsburgh: Duquesne University Press, 1987), 98, 101; "God and Philosophy," in *Collected Philosophical Papers*, 168.

23. Heidegger qualifies the "peculiar neutrality" of Dasein in his 1928 lectures on logic and transcendence as the "primordial positivity and potency of the essence of Dasein," and insists that this neutrality refers to the question of *origin* and not to Dasein in its factical concretion as the egocentric individual (Martin Heidegger, *The Metaphysical Foundations of Logic*, trans. Michael Heim [Bloomington: Indiana University Press, 1984], 136–37). Nevertheless, on Levinas's interpretation, Heidegger's early project of a fundamental ontology remains within the boundaries of the very metaphysics he seeks to displace or overcome insofar as it affirms the primacy of individual freedom over the ethics of the face to face. This results in a neutralizing conception of being, denoted by Heidegger's later concept of "letting-be" or "releasement" (*Gelassenheit*), a seemingly positive and liberating movement that actually reveals itself in Levinas as a neutralizing mode of interaction with a secretly threatening and oppressing other. See *Totality and Infinity*, 43, 67–68; also Emmanuel Levinas, "Is Ontology Fundamental?" trans. Peter Atterton, *Philosophy Today* 33, no. 2 (1989): 121–29; "Martin Heidegger and Ontology," trans. Committee of Public Safety, *Diacritics* 26, no. 1 (1992): 11–32.

According to Tanabe, Heidegger does not realize "how absolute nothingness, as the principle of absolute transformation, functions as ground. . . . In other words, Heidegger is not yet aware of the fact that only absolute nothingness can transform it into the free project of the self by means of a conversion in action" (PM 78–79).

24. On the relation between Levinas and Plotinus, which also takes up the problem of evil, see my "A Trace of the Eternal Return? Levinas and Neoplatonism," in Brian Schroeder and Silvia Benso, eds., *Levinas and the Ancients* (Bloomington: Indiana University Press, 2008), 210–29.

25. For a perspective on Tanabe's views on creation particularly with regard to *kenōsis*, see Hase Shōtō, "The Structure of Faith: Nothingness-*qua*-Love," in *The Religious Philosophy of Tanabe Hajime*, 99–105.

26. G. W. F. Hegel, *Phenomenology of Spirit* (Oxford: Oxford University Press, 1977), §18; also, *Science of Logic*, trans. A. V. Miller (New York: Humanities Press, 1969), 842.

27. Hegel, *Science of Logic*, 140.

28. Tanabe qualifies his atheism thus: "Given my high regard for science, I can find no basis for belief in either the Pure Land or the Kingdom of Heaven, nor can I believe in the continuation of a disembodied soul after death" (PM 157).

29. For an overview on the logic of absolute critique, see Heisig, *Philosophers of Nothingness*, 157–62.

30. On this point, see Jean Higgins, "Conversion in Shinran and Tanabe: Undergone or Undertaken?" in *The Religious Philosophy of Tanabe Hajime*, 150–60.

31. Emmanuel Levinas, "Meaning and Sense," in *Collected Philosophical Papers*, 96; my emphasis.

32. Levinas, *Totality and Infinity*, 216–17.

33. Ibid., 44.

34. See Emmanuel Levinas, *Otherwise than Being*, trans. Alphonso Lingis (The Hague: Martinus Nijhoff, 1981), 81–98; also, "Language and Proximity," in *Collected Philosophical Papers*, 109–26.

35. Theodor W. Adorno, *Negative Dialectics*, trans. E. B. Ashton (New York: Continuum, 1987). On the relation between Levinas and Adorno, see my *Altared Ground: Levinas, History and Violence* (New York: Routledge, 1996), 61–64. On the relation between Adorno and Hegel with allusion to Levinasian ethics, see Drucilla Cornell, *The Philosophy of the Limit* (New York: Routledge, 1992), 13–38.

36. Emmanuel Levinas, *Difficult Freedom: Essays on Judaism*, trans. Seán Hand (Baltimore, Md.: Johns Hopkins University Press, 1990), 21.

37. Levinas, *Totality and Infinity*, 85.

12

Beyond the Binary:
Watsuji Testurō and Luce Irigaray
on Body, Self, and Ethics

ERIN McCARTHY

Both Watsuji Tetsurō and Luce Irigaray critique the concepts of selfhood, body, and ethics as they have appeared in traditional Western philosophy. They both argue that Western philosophy has predominately seen self and ethics in binary, limited ways, providing us with theories that do not reflect the fullness of human experience in the world. Critiquing this individualist view of self that seems to dominate in Western philosophy—a self that is an isolated, autonomous individual whose relations with others are only contingent—they each provide us with alternative, non-dualistic models of selfhood. Nevertheless, on my reading, neither sacrifices the notion of the individual. Rather, in rejecting the binary structures that permeate Western philosophy, they opt for a model according to which *both* individuality *and* relationality are equally fundamental to human being-in-the-world.

Watsuji and Irigaray also agree that the body is not merely a contingent aspect of selfhood but integral to identity. For them, body cannot be thought of as separate from mind; the body is thus an ethical and epistemological site. Hence ethics, for both philosophers, starts from a different point than ethics in much of the Western tradition. Rather than starting from the standpoint of the isolated individual, the ethical subject for both Watsuji and Irigaray is in relation: The ethical lies in the "betweenness" of human beings whose identities include the body. For these thinkers then, self, body, and ethics are intimately interrelated.

There are important differences, however. Whereas Irigaray's focus is on the reimagining of selfhood, body, and ethics for the female subject, gender concerns do not appear in Watsuji's work. Irigaray wants to not only make a place for the feminine subject but to de-universalize the male subject so that there can truly be a place for both subjects—that is, a recognition of difference. Reading Watsuji's work in light of Irigaray enriches Watsuji's view of self, as we will see; however, Watsuji's work can also illuminate Irigaray's since it provides a model of selfhood that is not based on a binary starting point. Irigaray has herself encouraged this sort of comparison, having looked at models of the self in the Indian tradition in her 2002 book *Between East and West: From Singularity to Community.* In this essay, I will pursue this theme by drawing on Watsuji's work. Reading Watsuji in light of Irigaray reveals, I believe, implications of his work that he did not foresee; and these ideas are important because they can help foster understanding across and within genders, nations, and cultural and philosophical traditions in the way that Irigaray suggests, yet perhaps in ways she too did not foresee. Bringing these two philosophical voices together, then, should allow us to further reconceptualize selfhood, body, and ethics.

The Body in Philosophy: East and West

In most Western philosophy, the body has not historically been considered as a site for knowledge, properly speaking, if it has been considered at all. As far back as Plato, the body was seen as something that kept us from the highest, most certain knowledge. In the *Republic,* for example, we learn that we must control the body with the mind—keep it in check lest it overtake us and drag us down. Elizabeth Spelman notes: "According to Plato, the body, with its deceptive senses, keeps us from real knowledge; it rivets us in a world of material things which is far removed from the world of reality; and it tempts us away from the virtuous life."[1] The soul, and not the body, is that which attains certain knowledge. Self too is situated in the soul, if not simply identified with it, while the body is regarded as merely contingent.

The conception of the body that much modern philosophy inherited from Descartes shares this aspect of Platonic thought: for Descartes the body as such is an inert object; it is animated and known by the mind, but is not something active in itself. It is not a *knowing,* but rather a *known* body. As Drew Leder suggests in "A Tale of Two Bodies: The Cartesian Corpse and the Lived Body," modern medicine is based "first and foremost, not upon the lived body, but upon the dead, or inanimate body."[2] This dead, inert body serves as a model for the living body. Descartes's fascination with automatons further influences this Cartesian view of body as machine—as driven by strictly mechanical forces—which leads him to maintain, at least on certain registers, that the "living body is not fundamentally different from the lifeless;

it is a kind of animated corpse, a functioning mechanism."[3] It was not until the recent advents of phenomenology and existentialism, and then feminist philosophy, in the last century, that the concept of the lived body began to be given real prominence in various schools of Western philosophy.

In Japanese philosophy, however, a different picture of the body has long held sway. In this tradition, the body is viewed as necessary for attaining knowledge, and there is an emphasis in much of Japanese philosophy on lived experience, in which the body is included as philosophically significant. Watsuji, in fact, illustrates just this point in his critique of the mind-body separation in Western philosophy when he states: "What is not in accord with the concrete facts of experience is the view that something psychological, accompanied by no bodily events, and a process of the physical body entirely unrelated to bodily experiences subsist in the form of an opposition between body and mind existing independent of each other" (WTR 65). For Watsuji, this opposition simply doesn't reflect our lived experience. Furthermore, as David Shaner explains, in Japanese philosophy and particularly in Zen Buddhism, expressed through the concept of "bodymind,"[4] there is a very strong feeling of the interdependence of the mind and body—in fact, that they are "inseparably connected"—and as a result "the body serves as a vehicle for, not a detriment to, the direct experience of . . . truth."[5]

The Western philosophical view of body as hindrance or detriment to knowledge has thus, for the most part, kept the body from being accorded a significant place in philosophy. As Elizabeth Grosz explains, the Western tradition's opposing viewpoint associates man with the mind and woman with the body and she points out that, coupled with philosophy's definition of itself as concerned with the mental—that is, the conceptual, the ideal, the theoretical, the abstract, and the rational as opposed to the body—philosophy has "surreptitiously excluded femininity, and ultimately women, from its practices through its usually implicit coding of femininity with the unreason associated with the body."[6] She goes as far as to state that since "the inception of philosophy as a separate and self-contained discipline in ancient Greece, philosophy has established itself on the foundations of a profound somatophobia."[7] What we end up with in most of the history of philosophy in the West, then, is the dichotomy of male/female and the homologous hierarchical dichotomies that follow wherein the second term in the pair is always devalued—mind/body, reason/emotion, and so on.[8] In these dichotomies, each side is set up in opposition to the other. We are left with a logic of either/or and there is no room for one of both-and.

In Japanese philosophy, this is not the case for the mind/body pair nor even, necessarily, for male/female. This can be most clearly seen in the above-mentioned Buddhist concept of bodymind. From the nondual perspective of bodymind, "mind is not necessarily higher than body." In fact, from this perspective "all diverse phenomena are identical as to their constituents within; all are in the state of constant transformation; no absolute difference exists between man and nature; body and mind are non-dual."[9] In other words, body and mind work integrally and any thought of them as separate, hierarchical or oppositional, is a false abstraction. Japanese philosopher Yuasa Yasuo recognizes this historical lack of both body *and* the feminine in Western thought. Referring to the Daoist body in his discussion of body-mind cultivation of *ki* energy and the importance of the balance of *yin-yang* in Chinese philosophy, Yuasa notes first that in this system, "femininity and masculinity do not signify a *physiological* distinction between man and woman." He then goes on to explain that

> To put it from a depth psychological point-of-view, a mature, all-round personality cannot be formed unless the power of femininity, rooted in the unconscious, complements the masculine tendency that surfaces in consciousness. When seen from this vantage point, the history of modern thought and philosophy initiated in the West discloses a situation, we might say, in which the power of masculinity has been a solo runner, fortifying rationalism as well as promoting the opposition and competition between "I" and "other," while the power of femininity has failed to function.[10]

So for Yuasa, in a certain sense, even the male/female dichotomy is false: Every well-balanced bodymind is feminine as well as masculine.

In her analysis of Greek philosophy, Grosz notes how far back this emphasis on rationality and the mind goes: "In his doctrine of the Forms, Plato sees matter itself as a denigrated and imperfect version of the Idea. The body is a betrayal of and a prison for the soul, reason, or mind. For Plato, it was evident that reason should rule over the body and over the irrational or appetitive functions of the soul." Woman, as we saw earlier, was associated with the body and hence: "The binarization of the sexes, the dichotomization of the world and of knowledge has been effected already at the threshold of Western reason."[11] In Japanese philosophy we find an alternative model. Rather than being ignored or devalued, as is evident through the very term "bodymind," the body works with or even *as* the mind, and thus the body-mind relationship should be cultivated rather than fled from or avoided. Zen master Dōgen, for example, "says that 'learning through the mind' must be united with 'learning through the body' (*shinjitsunintai* . . . 'truth' + 'reality' + 'human body,' literally 'the real human body')."[12] Yuasa states, regarding the difference between Eastern and Western philosophy, that the "most fundamental difference is that the cultivation method does not accept the mind-body dichotomy that Descartes elevated to the status of a principle."[13]

Subjects in Betweenness

Luce Irigaray characterizes her philosophy as having developed through three stages: "the first a critique, you might say, of the auto-mono-centrism of the western subject; the second, how to define a second subject; and the third phase, how to define a relationship, a philosophy, an ethic, a relationship between two different subjects."[14] Here I explore the third stage, comparing Irigaray and Watsuji in an effort to clarify the idea of an embodied ethic between subjects. Irigaray finds the cultivation of body-mind in her exploration of predominantly Indian thought. Like Grosz, she critiques the West for elevating the mind (thus the male subject) over the body (and thus female subject): "Separating body and spirit, he has valorized the one, as the result of a disincarnated speech, making of the other a vehicle, necessary but cumbersome, during existence said to be earthly."[15] The body (and more specifically, the female body) is a necessary evil, and there is certainly no cultivation of any relationship between the two. Implicitly also criticizing Descartes's model in a manner similar to Leder's critique, cited above, Irigaray states that a "cultivation of breathing, of energy maintains life and health better than abandoning a body-cadaver-animal to medical science and its diverse types of operations."[16] Throughout Irigaray's work, we find this recognition that body and mind must be cultivated together if there is going to be understanding between genders, and if we are to ever live ethically in the world.

In *Sexes and Genealogies,* Irigaray maintains that a proper understanding of the feminine "consists in the systematic nonsplit of nature and spirit, in the touching together of these two universals."[17] In other words, Irigaray sees the need for a philosophical recognition of mind (spirit) and body (nature) as integrated in the female subject so as to make questions of the body, and thus of women, central to philosophical reflection. Irigaray challenges Western philosophy to re-imagine a concept of self that is not bound by patriarchal or Western frameworks—one that is open and nonbinary in nature, one that is not built on opposition but rather on openness to the other and continual becoming, all the while retaining difference. In her philosophy, even though difference is retained, identity is not fixed, for Irigaray is a philosopher of change.[18] Irigaray's philosophy aims to reveal a truly different subject (woman) and bring her into the philosophical (and political) dialogue. As Tamsin Lorraine writes in *Irigaray and Deleuze: Experiments in Visceral Philosophy*, "the implicit assumption of Irigaray's project is that it is more ethical to work toward a cultural imaginary that would support the subjectivity of all through active recognition of our interdependence and mutually constitutive activity than to allow the silencing of an other (or group of others) in order to maintain one's own subjectivity."[19] As Irigaray has shown throughout her work, however, the frameworks of Western, patriarchal philosophies do not provide us with a vocabulary or philosophical framework that is inclusive of female subjectivity (not to mention other marginalized or non-Western philosophical voices which have been left out of the dialogue due to a search for sameness and a silencing of difference). We need a framework that allows for difference without being dualistic, that provides equal space to *parler-femme* without silencing other voices; a framework that disrupts the traditional notions of what is masculine and what is feminine and that allows for dialogue between the sexes that supports their mutual growth.

Watsuji Tetsurō's notion of self and ethics as *ningen*—the Japanese word for "human being" which, however, literally means "between persons"— points us to a framework that can be used to re-imagine and support such growth and a nondual subjectivity. Synthesizing Irigaray's concepts and the directions she points us in with the philosophical vocabulary and concepts of Japanese philosophy can help us, I believe, move even further beyond the binary oppositions informing the received (and still-current) patriarchal ways of thinking and seeing the world, to a place in which dialogue can support the mutual growth of human beings, both male and female, and hopefully move us, as a result of understanding between people, out of a culture of violence. As far back as *Sexes and Genealogies* in 1987, Irigaray notices the link between violence and a culture that denies sexual difference:

> We are driven to compete in the rat race of modern life—so maddened and overwhelmed by the pace of existence that we embrace war as a means of regaining some measure of order and opening some new space onto the future. This was often true in the past. It will continue to be so if we fail to set up an ethics of the couple as an intermediary place between individuals, peoples, States.[20]

In the opening pages of his *Ethics,* similar to Irigaray's call for an ethics of betweenness, Watsuji states that the "essential significance of the attempt to describe ethics as the study of *ningen* consists in getting away from the misconception, prevalent in the modern world, that conceives of ethics as a problem of individual consciousness only" (WTR 9). The core of Watsuji's ethical theory is his concept of human being understood as *ningen.* The locus of ethical problems, he tells us, "lies not in the consciousness of the isolated individual, but precisely in the in-betweenness of person and person" (WTR 10). In other words, ethics is the study of human beings or *ningengaku,* human beings not only as individual but also as social in the betweenness (*aidagara*) among selves in the world. So Watsuji's view of human being as *ningen* is nondualistic in at least two aspects. One such aspect is the nondualism of body-mind; another is nondualism of self and other, as expressed through his concept of betweenness. His definition of human being as *ningen* includes self not only *as both* individual and relational, but also as embodied. Conceptualizing human being as *ningen* argues against the Western concept of self as *purely* individual, while relationships with others are contingent. The very terms used to designate "self" in the West, he argues, indicate that it is conceived of in terms of the isolated individual; and any such concept, he further argues, is merely an abstraction, for as *ningen* we are always in relation with other human beings. This Japanese word *ningen* is composed of the characters for "person" and "between," signifying the individual and social *at the same time.* It is "the public, and, at the same time, the individual human beings living within it. . . . What is recognizable here is a dialectical unity of those double characteristics that are inherent in a human being" (WTR 15).

Ningen is a dynamic concept of self, one that John Maraldo has suggested be understood, not as a metaphysical entity, but rather as an interrelation.[21] For Watsuji, one cannot be fully human or ethical (and if one is a human being in one's fullest potential, one is also ethical) unless one is, as well as being an individual, also in relation with other human beings. As Maraldo puts it, for Watsuji "the concrete reality of being human lies in the midst of the two more abstract poles, the individual and the social,"[22] and this "subjective and dynamic structure does not allow us to account for *ningen* as a 'thing' or 'substance'" (WTR 19). *Ningen* has, as part of its structure, this sense of reciprocity—a refusal to be a fixed, static object. Its very structure is nonbinary and this betweenness within it mirrors a betweenness with the mind-body complexes of others. The dynamic nature of *ningen* is such that there is a constant movement back and forth between the poles of individual and social.

When Irigaray, in *Sexes and Genealogies,* explains that we need an ethics of the couple, it is a model of interrelationship—or might we say of betweenness, of *ningen?*—that she has in mind.[23] In *Why Different?*, critiquing the traditional logic of personal identity as self-identity, she articulates her alternative notion of relational identity:

> Relational identity goes counter to this solipsistic, neuter, auto-logical ideal. It contests the cleavages sensible/intelligible, concrete/abstract, matter/form, living/dead. It also refuses the opposition between being and becoming, and the fact that the plural of the one would be the multiple before being the two. Relational identity considers the concrete identity which is always identity in relation. As such, it is always metastable, becoming. What I try to think is the articulation between the constant transformation required by a living connection to nature and a return to self which permits a being- and a remaining-self in the process of becoming.[24]

Irigaray offers a concept of self that does not reinforce the identity of sameness. The self—as *ningen* for Watsuji and as seen above for Irigaray—is dynamic, continually becoming; the self is not an entity. It is a work in process that is never completed because it is not based on sameness. Watsuji puts it this way: "The subject is not something static like a mirror, whose only business is to contemplate objects, but includes within itself the connections between oneself and the other. And these connections operate subjectively and practically, prior to contemplation" (WTR 31). If the subject were static, then relations would be outside of the subject. Human being as *ningen,* however, precludes this. We do not have a notion of our constitutive living relations being merely additive, grossly cumulative, or numerically discrete (1 + 1 + 1); rather relationality, such connections, are an integral part of human being. Thus, for Irigaray and Watsuji, to study human being is to study ethics, as ethical problems are found between people.

Bodies in Betweenness

For both Watsuji and Irigaray, such connections between people also include corporeal connections, and in fact, they call us to re-think our usual understanding of the corporeal. Irigaray introduces the idea of the skin or mucous membrane to challenge corporeal boundaries and give us a different way of thinking about just such connections between oneself and the other. Attacking binary frameworks that focus on identity as sameness—much like Watsuji, but foregrounding that sameness as a reflection not just of the subject but of the male subject—Irigaray contrasts the notion of the mirror with mucosity. The mirror, she argues (again much like Watsuji) separates and constitutes a screen between self and other—it serves to create a static image, a reflection of whoever looks into it. In *Speculum,* this is made clear, for the male subject,

> in order to assert his own subjectivity . . . must forever distance himself from a feminine and corporeal reality, through a process of deliberate miscognition. Thus, "mother-matter" must only be "apprehended by her mirage, not by her dazzling radiance," in other words, by an image of sameness rather than one of difference: an image that unproblematically *mirrors* masculine identity.[25]

And in *Sexes and Genealogies,* she comments: "In a way quite different from the mucous membranes or the skin that serve as living, porous, fluid media to achieve communion as well as difference, the mirror is a frozen—and polemical—weapon to keep us apart."[26] Binary, polemical frameworks serve to keep us looking outward at the world for sameness, for images that reflect our worldview, for images that reflect our selves. And Irigaray argues, on the Western philosophical model, regardless of who is looking in the mirror, the self that is both sought and reflected is that of the male subject. The mirror is passive reflection, while the mucous membrane which is porous allows for interaction, for relationality, for coming together. Bringing the idea of *ningen* in here, I believe, gives us a way of thinking of selfhood that is useful for working through what Irigaray proposes with the idea of the mucous membrane or skin as providing a way of achieving communion or betweenness.

Even though, as Yuasa points out, there is no explicit account of the body in Watsuji, it is clear that it permeates his concept of *ningen* and is central to some of his most evocative examples of betweenness (*aidagara*) and ethics—which is, after all, "concerned with those problems that prevail *between* persons" (WTR 12).[27] Watsuji does not believe that it is possible to have *only* a mind-connection between people *or* only a body-connection. Rather, such "connections are neither merely physical nor merely psychological or physical/psychological" (WTR 66). For Watsuji, the body is an inherent part of human being-in-the-world—which encompasses human spatiality *and* being-with, being in the betweenness with other human beings, for he says: "Insofar as betweenness is constituted, one human body is connected with another" (WTR 68). So we have a connection, it seems, for *ningen* between bodyminds—connections which go beyond either/or dichotomies and challenge what we normally conceive of as limits of both self and body. Watsuji maintains:

> Activity inherent in the consciousness of the "I" is never determined by this "I" alone but is also determined by others. It is not merely a reciprocal activity in that oneway conscious activities are performed one after another but, rather, that either one of them is determined by both sides; that is, by itself and by the other. Hence, so far as betweenness-oriented existences are concerned, each consciousness interpenetrates the other. (WTR 70)

Watsuji and Irigaray come together here, as both argue for this communion of bodyminds, a concept that is not found in a philosophical system where rationality is privileged and the body is ignored or fled. The body ought to be understood as rich, complex; as a site for knowledge and for ethics; and as involving not just the mind or the body, but both as intimately interconnected: "When we are aware of something in our mind, this experience already involves the human body as an element within it" (WTR 66). In other words, again we see the concept that we know not just with our minds, but also with our bodies. For Watsuji and Irigaray both, then, to be fully human is to be an integrated human being, a mind-body complex, and furthermore to see others as such also.

As Tamsin Lorraine puts the goal: "A theory of embodied subjectivity can help us map corporeal connections among people and thus indicate how different forms of subjectivity are interdependent and mutually informing. Challenging traditional boundaries among bodies and among minds as well as between bodies and minds allows us to rethink the interdependent nature of subjectivity."[28] Lorraine points to what I think we find in Watsuji and Irigaray. In bringing together the ideas of Irigaray and Watsuji here we begin to think selfhood in a broader manner—in a way that connects us ever more deeply to other human beings on every level. Thinking in this way, we realize the potential for broader communion and communication. The work of Irigaray, and I contend, that of Watsuji give us new ideals of human interconnectedness that often get lost in theories of self that focus on the rational and individual. Watsuji's model of human being as *ningen* gives us a structure with which to challenge those boundaries and think, rather, about the permeability or porosity of boundaries as one of the very structures of what it is to be human. We see here also Irigaray's idea of the preservation of self and other, individual and social, simultaneously with their interpenetration or communion; this echoes Watsuji's notion of the human being as *ningen*.

Let us return for a moment to the idea of the mirror mentioned above. The mirror, then, is a totalizing framework—one that seeks sameness and rest. This kind of relation that supports identity as sameness, as I have argued in more detail elsewhere, is what Edouard Glissant would term "totality."[29] Binary frameworks are totalizing; they leave no room for change or relation with the other, whereas fluidity, mucosity, and *ningen* do allow for a communion with the other (what Glissant terms "Relation") that does not mean the appropriation or subsuming of him or her, but rather a relation that includes continual becoming.

In Watsuji, this becoming is expressed through a movement of negation that he sees as a fundamental structure of the human being. He identifies three moments that the negation inherent in being *ningen* encompasses: "fundamental emptiness, then individual existence, and social existence as its negative development. These three are interactive with one another in practical reality and cannot be separated. They are at work constantly in the practical interconnection of acts and can in no way be stabilized fixedly at any place" (WTR 117). Relations between people continually perform this double movement of negation. Watsuji characterizes the fundamentally negative dialectical structure of a human being as such that "the negative structure of a betweenness-oriented being is clarified in terms of the self-returning movement of absolute negativity through its own negation. This is a human being's fundamental structure, which makes its kaleidoscopic appearance in every nook and cranny of a human being" (WTR 117). Central to this is the constant negating of this negation—it is something rich and dynamic that, contrary to nihilism, links us fundamentally to others. What is particularly interesting for us in our comparison is that, as *ningen,* this process of becoming never comes to a standstill—the fundamental structure of *ningen,* then, expresses the articulation of the becoming and remaining self in Irigaray's concept of relational identity. In *The Way of Love,* she speaks of a letting go that I maintain is a part of this articulation: "Releasing all hold would be carried out toward a future of which the equation escapes us, and with regard to an other irreducible to the same for each subject. Letting go then gives access to a truly open space-time where co-belonging is still to be created."[30] This resonates, I believe, with the process of becoming to be found in *ningen,* with Irigaray adding to Watsuji that this would be a space for *both* the male and female subject to truly come together. Irigaray acknowledges the role of negation in such becoming: "In order to meet with the other, I must first let be, even restore, the nothing that separates us. It is a negative path which leads to the approach of the different and the possible relation with him, or with her."[31] If the process of becoming stops for *ningen,* and for Irigaray, the betweenness collapses; if it continues, however, "the movement of the negation of absolute negativity is, at the same time, the continuous creation of human beings" (WTR 117–18). Watsuji maintains that this is the fundamental structure of our existence—in other words, we are constantly, if we are being fully human, becoming. We are always influencing the world and people we come into contact with and the world and people we are in-the-between with are influencing our individual selves. This mutual and constant emptying and filling is at the heart of this way of conceptualizing the self. In *ningen,* the difference between self and other is transcended, *yet this transcendence is not a fixed unity:*

> Each of us is both one and many, both an individual as isolated *and* inextricably interconnected with others in some community or other. As *ningen,* we negate our individuality to the extent that we are communally connected, and we negate our communality to the extent that we express our individuality. We are both, in *mutual* interactive negation, as well as being determined by the group or community, *and* determining and shaping the community. As such, we are living self-contradictions and therefore living identities of self-contradiction, or unities of opposites, in mutual interactive negation.[32]

Despite the centrality of the notion of negation then, Watsuji's study of the human being-in-the-world is anything but nihilistic. In fact, Robert Carter argues that precisely *because* of the double negation inherent in *ningen,* there is a ground for a very deep sense of relatedness to others. This negation, letting go, or forgetting of the self "results in an opening of self to a sense of relatedness—intimate relatedness—with a greater whole, whether it be that of people in love or that of family, group, nation, or even some sense of cosmic consciousness."[33] Such a sense of self, I believe, allows for thinking the kind of sexual difference that Irigaray advocates.[34] Irigaray argues that on the Western philosophical model there is no betweenness, no genuine encounter with the other. We reduce the other to ourselves for we are caught in the identity of sameness, searching for our own reflection in the other, rather than being open to a true encounter with the other. Irigaray and Watsuji each enrich the other here and potentially, in dialogue, provide us with a new framework that allows for and furthers a way of rethinking relational identity and selfhood, as called for by Irigaray.[35]

Conclusions: Between and Beyond Watsuji and Irigaray

One problem readers who are familiar with Watsuji's work will note is that his concept of *ningen* can also be read as undermining difference (precisely what Irigaray rejects and works to overcome in the Western tradition). As John Maraldo explains:

> Watsuji writes "self-other" as a single word (*jita*) that stands on one side of a negative equation whose second side (or negation) is a totality or greater whole. An individual's other half is not really an other individual but the world (*seken*) that makes one a human being. . . . The relevant relationship, for better or worse, is not the relation between self and other.[36]

But what if we re-imagine or re-think this betweenness where self and other are not separate? Maraldo rightly notes that Watsuji puts betweenness above individual and communal, subject and object, self and other—but what if we think this as also just a moment in human existence? What occurs if we reinterpret Watsuji here, infusing his concept with Irigaray, and read the between of the community as a space from which individuals both emerge and return to, transformed in some way by losing self in that between but not necessarily subsuming the other or being subsumed by the other in the process? On this reading, the between becomes a space that allows for creative, generative tension or interplay—a space of true communion with the other in a mutual, nonhierarchical manner—the truly open space-time that Irigaray aspires to above. If we take this reading, mindful of Watsuji's description of the continuous movement of negation, then one cannot get stuck in the between where one gives over one's self—for it is just a moment.

This may be, in fact, the very sort of transcendence of binary poles Irigaray is looking for—and in turn, infusing feminism into Watsuji here might address Maraldo's critique of him. Irigaray writes of a transcendence of the other in a relationship (or betweenness) that does not reduce him or her to me or mine. In our initial encounter with the other, there is wonder:

> Awakening us, by their very alterity, their mystery, by the in-finite that they still represent for us. It is when we do not know the other, or when we accept that the other remains unknowable to us, that the other illuminates us in some way, but with a light that enlightens us without our being able to comprehend it, to analyze it, to make it ours.[37]

Normally, however, we flee from this strangeness through integrating the other into ourselves—stuck at the pole of individuality as a static subject. If, however, we enter into relation in the between—negating for that moment both self and other—might this not be the open space for wonder of the sort that Irigaray seeks? In the between, the other is not reducible to me because there is no other, there is no me; and yet, I maintain, this does not mean that there is an *absolute,* static unity, that there is no space for alterity.

"Not one, not two" is the way Zen Buddhism expresses this notion, and as Maraldo points out in a discussion of the *Ten Oxherding Pictures* of Zen Buddhism, it might be that "the conviction that self and other are 'not one and not two' better promotes the very kind of equality the alterists desire. This is not the '"conceit" of equality between real selves' but rather true impartiality."[38] In this space there is no hierarchy. Irigaray notes that the

> transcendence of the *you* as other is not yet, really, part of our culture. . . . This letting go of the subject, this letting be of the *I* toward what it is, knows, and has made its own, this opening of a world of one's own, experienced as familiar, in order to welcome the stranger, while remaining oneself and letting the stranger be other, do not correspond to our mental habits or our Western logic.[39]

Bringing in Watsuji's structure of *ningen,* whereby one preserves and dissolves oneself in a welcoming of the other, addresses some of Irigaray's concerns. She urges us, in much of her work, not to move directly from a celebration of "one" to a celebration of "multiplicity" and calls us to recognize the two, male and female, as subjects in their own right. She calls us to rethink what being-in-relation is and what its implications are, concluding that this relation has been, in Western systems of logic, unthought—it calls for a different type of thinking.[40] The idea of betweenness and a Zen Buddhist "not one, not two" that is neither a celebration of multiplicity nor a static absolute is, I believe, one different type of thinking that might allow for the kind of selfhood, relationality, and ethics that she seeks.

Irigaray suggests that one thing necessary for this kind of relational identity to occur is a new model of sexual relations—one which, unlike what is found in Sartre, for instance, is not about possessing the other or surrendering to the other. She refers to a "carnal sharing" in love, and suggests that love "takes place in the opening to self that is the place of welcoming the transcendence of the other."[41] This place—this space of betweenness, of transcendence—

> becomes the place not of a repression or of an exploitation of the flesh but of a poetic, even mystical, progression of love, a path of renunciation of absolute love

of oneself with a view to carry out love with the other in the giving up of both self and other, emotionally as well as intellectually . . . It becomes abandonment to the opening of self and other toward wisdom still unknown.[42]

One would come out of such a union, such a communion, altered yet not lost, presumably with a better or transformed sense of self and other yet one which requires a moment of dissolution of self and other—a moment, perhaps, of *jita*. One's individuality, then, can be preserved and yet influenced and mutually informed by an other: it dissolves into community and then reemerges as individual again, only to resume the process, to continue becoming. What then if we extend this metaphor of sexual relations through to being-in-the-world as *ningen*? Then, I suggest, betweenness provides a model for transcendence of the *you* and the *I* that is embodied (but not necessarily sexual), and is extendable not just to relations within and between genders but even between cultures and philosophical traditions.

The problem of course, is *how* to live this. One cannot simply re-imagine selfhood from a purely theoretical standpoint. In fact, one of the most powerful aspects of bringing these two philosophers together is that even though they might have different epistemological foundations, taking both Irigaray's grounding as a feminist philosopher and Watsuji's grounding in Japanese philosophy seriously requires an engagement in some sort of practice or praxis . . . some sort of cultivation of this new way of being-in-the-world. At the very least, I hope that the critical exchange of their ideas in this chapter has not only illuminated aspects of their respective philosophies but that, following the model of *ningen,* ideas about selfhood, ethics, and the body have emerged transformed by this encounter. Perhaps even imagining boundaries between self and other as more porous, recognizing the interdependency and interconnectedness of human being-in-the-world, rethinking what it is to be a self, we just might be more open to our next encounter with the other and truly meet him or her in the between—and that might be one step toward cultivating open understanding in the world.

NOTES

The present essay is drawn from material in Erin McCarthy, *Ethics Embodied* (Lanham, Md.: Lexington Books, 2010), and is reprinted here with permission of the publisher.

1. Elizabeth Spelman, "Woman as Body: Ancient and Contemporary Views," *Feminist Studies* 8, no. 1 (Spring 1982): 111.

2. Drew Leder, "A Tale of Two Bodies: The Cartesian Corpse and the Lived Body," in Donn Welton, ed., *Body and Flesh: A Philosophical Reader* (Oxford: Blackwell, 1998), 117.

3. Leder, "A Tale of Two Bodies," 119.

4. See David Edward Shaner, *The Bodymind Experience in Japanese Buddhism: A Phenomenological Study of Kūkai and Dōgen* (Albany: State University of New York Press, 1985), esp. chap. 2, for an in-depth discussion of this concept.

5. Ibid., 99.

6. Elizabeth Grosz, *Volatile Bodies: Toward a Corporeal Feminism* (Bloomington: Indiana University Press, 1994), 4.

7. Ibid., 5.

8. See Iris Marion Young, *On Female Body Experience: "Throwing Like a Girl" and Other Essays* (Oxford: Oxford University Press, 2005), 5.

9. Shaner, *Bodymind Experience in Japanese Buddhism*, 121; cit. Yoshito Hakeda, *Kūkai: Major Works* (New York: Columbia University Press, 1972), 89.

10. Yuasa Yasuo, "Cultivation of the Body in Japanese Religions," trans. Shigenori Nagatomo (unpublished essay given to the author by Yuasa), 17–18. The key element to note here is the resonance of Yuasa's analysis of the lack of the feminine voice in Western philosophy—this is not to say that there are not problems with depth psychology from a feminist perspective, but the key here is Yuasa's critique of the Western philosophical tradition's emphasis on rationality and the resulting dichotomies that get put into place as given.

11. Grosz, *Volatile Bodies*, 5.

12. Shaner, *Bodymind Experience in Japanese Buddhism*, 148.

13. Yuasa, "Cultivation of the Body in Japanese Religions," 13.

14. Elizabeth Hirsh and Gary A. Olson, "Je—Luce Irigaray: A Meeting with Luce Irigaray," *Hypatia* 10, no. 2 (Spring 1995): 97.

15. Luce Irigaray, *Between East and West: From Singularity to Community,* trans. Stephen Pluháček (New York: Columbia University Press, 2002), ix.

16. Ibid., ix.

17. Irigaray, *Sexes and Genealogies,* 112.

18. See Alison Martin, "Luce Irigaray and the Culture of Difference," *Theory, Culture, Society* 20, no. 1 (2003): 1–12.

19. Tamsin Lorraine, *Irigaray and Deleuze: Experiments in Visceral Philosophy* (Ithaca, N.Y.: Cornell University Press, 1999), 21.

20. Irigaray, *Sexes and Genealogies,* 5. For a more detailed discussion of how bringing together Irigaray and Watsuji can help promote a sustainable peace see Erin McCarthy, "Towards Peaceful Bodies," in *Philosophieren über den Krieg: War in Eastern and Western Philosophies* (Berlin: Parerga, 2008), 147–64.

21. John Maraldo, "Watsuji Tetsurō's Ethics: Totalitarian or Communitarian?" in Rolf Elberfeld and Günter Wohlfart, eds., *Komparative Ethik: Das gute Leben zwischen den Kulturen* (Cologne: Edition Chōra, 2002), 185.

22. Ibid., 185.

23. Irigaray, *Sexes and Genealogies,* 5.

24. Luce Irigaray, *Why Different? Interviews with Luce Irigaray,* trans. Camille Collins, ed. Luce Irigaray and Sylvère Lotringer (New York: semiotext(e), 2000), 159–60.

25. Philippa Berry, "The Burning Glass," in *Engaging with Irigaray*, ed. Carolyn Burke, Naomi Schor, and Margaret Whitford (New York: Columbia University Press, 1994), 232. In *Speculum of the Other Woman,* trans. Gillian C. Gill (Ithaca, N.Y.: Cor-

nell University Press, 1985), Irigaray goes on to invert the mirror or the speculum, using the "burning glass" to point the way toward, as Berry states it, "a radically new nondualistic mode of physical, metaphysical, ethical speculation" (243). In this work, however, I have chosen to work with the theme that emerges more often after *Speculum*—that of mucosity and fluidity, as I find if more useful for challenging the way we think about corporeal boundaries and for thinking about nondualism.

26. Irigaray, *Sexes and Genealogies*, 65.

27. See also Erin McCarthy, "Ethics in the Between," *Philosophy, Culture, and Traditions* 2 (2003): 63–78, for a more in-depth discussion of this. Watsuji uses examples of the mother-baby relationship and the desire of friends to be physically close to one another to articulate betweenness.

28. Lorraine, *Irigaray and Deleuze*, 15.

29. Erin McCarthy, "Comparative Philosophy and the Liberal Arts: Between and Beyond—Educating to Cultivate Geocitizens," *Canadian Review of American Studies* 38 (2008): 293–309.

30. Luce Irigaray, *The Way of Love*, trans. Heidi Bostick and Pluháček (London and New York: Continuum, 2004), 83.

31. Ibid., 168.

32. Robert E. Carter, "Strands of Influence," in WTR 340.

33. Ibid., 334.

34. Though there is more to be said on this topic, there is no space to do so in the present essay. The history of power and privilege of patriarchy and the male subject must be taken into account—for it is too easy to think that it would simply disappear if the male subject ascribes to *ningen*. This is perhaps one point at which Irigaray and Watsuji differ, in that Irigaray's project as a feminist philosopher is inherently political and aspirational, while despite its roots in Japanese philosophy, which often demands a praxis of some sort, Watsuji's project may be more descriptive.

35. Irigaray, *Why Different?* 162.

36. John Maraldo, "Between Individual and Communal, Subject and Object, Self and Other: Mediating Watsuji Tetsurō's Hermeneutics," in Michael F. Marra, ed., *Japanese Hermeneutics: Current Debates on Aesthetics and Interpretation* (Honolulu: University of Hawai'i Press, 2002), 84.

37. Irigaray, *Between East and West*, 123.

38. John Maraldo, "Alterity and Nonduality in the Oxherding Pictures of Chan/Zen," unpublished paper presented at the American Academy of Religions, Buddhism Section, November 2000.

39. Irigaray, *Between East and West*, 125.

40. Irigaray, *The Way of Love*, 90–91.

41. Irigaray, *Between East and West*, 115.

42. Ibid., 116.

13

Overcoming Modernity:
A Critical Response to
the Kyoto School

Bernard Stevens

The fundamental intention of this essay is the wish to clarify what is meant by the philosophical concept of modernity and what it can possibly mean to speak of "postmodernism," or even to attempt the "overcoming" of modernity, as a number of Japanese thinkers sought to do in the early 1940s. Indeed, in this context it is extremely important to revive the memory of the ideological disaster that the project of "overcoming modernity" caused in the Japanese tennōcentric (emperor-centered) regime at the time of the Fifteen Year War. My aim is not to perversely reawaken extinguished passions and old controversies. On the contrary, my concern here is twofold: first, to "save," so to speak, the remarkable philosophical and humanistic message of the Kyoto School by extricating it from its political misadventures; and second, to resist what is happening today in both the West and the East, namely, a progressive erosion of the commitment to democracy and the resurgence—sometimes obvious, sometimes hidden—of what can only be called "neo-fascism." Whether it is in the neo-liberal scheme in the Atlantic style (the heritage of Adam Smith) or in the developmental interventionism of the East Asian style (the combined heritage of Friedrich List and Neo-Confucianism),[1] not to mention the various forms of fundamentalism of which Islamism is only the most spectacular, the global triumph of capitalism (asserted far more today than it was at the beginning of the twentieth century) is once again (just as it did eighty years ago) generating various symptoms of an ideological and pathological syndrome. Any intellectual who has a modicum of civic consciousness has no other choice but to resolutely oppose this—maybe not, principally, through any militancy, but at least by actively seeking to clarify the ideas at stake. Such is the primary objective of the present essay.

Under the general expression "modernity and its overcoming" we actually have an extremely vast subject matter within which I propose to distinguish three great thematic blocks. These blocks are linked by the common project of criticizing modernity, but they are separated by the particular context within which each of these critiques developed, as well as by their respective forms and ideological stakes. These thematic blocks are: (1) the original Japanese project of "overcoming modernity"; (2) the more recent cultural movement of "postmodernism"; and (3) the still present conceptual phenomenon of "postmodernity."

The first theme—"the overcoming of modernity" (*kindai no chōkoku*)—covers the subject of the notorious Tokyo symposium of 1942: the monumental ambition of surmounting modern Western civilization. As has become customary since the publication of a famous article by Takeuchi Yoshimi,[2] I associate the symposium in question with the so-called *Chūōkoron* discussions of the same period, in which some representatives of the Kyoto School who were also present at the symposium participated. These forums debated many of the same problems (more cultural in the case of the symposium, more political in the case of the discussions). The question of "overcoming modernity" primarily concerns ultranationalist Japan in its confrontation with Europe and the United States. But today more than ever, it can also be related to other civilizations in their problematic relations to the West, and finally, in certain respects, it can be linked to the Nietzschean-style genealogical critique of modernity within Europe itself.

One could believe, at first sight, that the criticism of the modern, contained in the Japanese ambition of "overcoming modernity," is basically similar to that of René Guénon, when he (for example in *La crise du monde moderne*)[3] attacks Western modernity on behalf of the Oriental tradition. For Guénon it would simply mean terminating all those technical and juridical novelties which originated in the West but which are destroying the ancient values and ways of living in the East. If, however, there actually is a traditionalistic dimension in the ideology of overcoming modernity, then the latter, in a typically Japanese mode, is not insensitive to the seduction of the new—proper to modernity—and its relation to such a modernity will thus be fundamentally ambiguous. The traditionalism of the upholders of "overcoming modernity" is therefore not exclusively nostalgic and includes, one could say, "the tradition of the new,"[4] which implies a take on the course and meaning of history. This characteristic conjunction of traditionalism and modernism, moreover, is quite comparable to the mindset of the "conservative revolution" in Germany during this time. A comparison between the two movements would certainly prove most fruitful.

The second theme, which is more specifically Western, concerns the opposition between modernism and postmodernism. The academic dimension of the modernist movement developed itself most conspicuously in a specific field: postwar American art criticism (most notably, Clement Greenberg).[5] The discussions around modernism and postmodernism can clarify the ideological implications of the initial theme of overcoming modernity. They demonstrate in particular the reasons behind the ideologically reactionary dimension of all attitudes that go under the label anti-modern or post-modernist criticism, in spite of their claim to radical novelty.

In the eyes of art criticism, the formal aesthetic researches of architectural and pictorial European modernism from the 1920s to the 1960s[6] were accompanied by an emancipatory and progressive ideal. The American postmodernism of the 1980s and 1990s abandoned this not for aggressively reactionary reasons, but rather in favor of an accommodating submission to the demands of the market and the ever more anti-aesthetic and anti-humanistic values of a triumphant and uncontested capitalism. It is within such a context that there reappears some shady nostalgia for the *Einfühlung* aesthetics of which the Fascist styles (Mussolinian, Hitlerian, and Stalinistic) have been the most extreme examples.[7]

All this simply confirms what was obvious during the first appearance of the word "modernism" within the doctrinal debates of the nineteenth-century Catholic Church. It is indeed well known that in those debates the emancipatory modernism of political liberalism appeared as a threat to the theocentric authority of tradition. Not unlike what is happening in the contemporary Islamic world, liberalism created a reaction—at first anti-modernistic, and then bluntly fundamentalist—which led to highly suspect political compromises.[8]

Finally, the third great theme is that of postmodernity such as it has appeared first in France in the 1970s, with Jean-François Lyotard and the poststructuralists, and which, via an American detour, has had a considerable impact in Japan in the 1980s, notably with Karatani Kōjin. This phenomenon has since fostered at-times ambiguous relations with the thematic of postmodernism as well as with that of overcoming modernity. This is due, among other things, to the perpetuation or rediscovery of Nishida philosophy by Ōhashi Ryōsuke and Nakamura Yūjirō.[9] Here again, without showing any obvious longings for any type of neo-fascism, it is the accommodating submission to a capitalistic ideology, wherein the political emancipatory intention is silenced in favor of the exclusively economic dimension of indefinite growth. This growth generates a state of mind that surreptitiously allows for the erosion of democratic commitments and simply abandons the critical and subversive role of the intellectual in favor of the mainstream of consumer society.

It is this complex triangulation that I wish to clarify by means of an investigation developed along two distinct registers: (1) ontological and topological (or theoretic and cognitivistic); and (2) political (or practical and ideological). On the horizon of this entire investigation, after having gone through these multiple problematics, one could attempt to redefine the project of overcoming modernity under the form of a "self-subversion of modernity": some type of "subversive rationalism" that would be reminiscent, but in a self-critical mode, of what Nishitani Keiji had in mind when he called for a "self-overcoming of nihilism."[10]

I therefore propose, if only approximately at first, two clearly distinct definitions of modernity, directly linked to the difference of register that I insist on establishing between the practical-political dimension and the ontological-topological dimension of thought. This will be followed by a few precise observations concerning this distinction in the context of an examination of the ideology inherent to the original project of overcoming modernity. In that original project such a difference is precisely *not* taken into account, and this, I believe, is the very reason, or at least one of the main reasons, for the well-known political missteps of the Kyoto School. It is important to make this point since there is no guarantee that such missteps will not reappear today under one guise or another in the East and/or the West. This appears to be a distinct possibility when one considers, among other things, the regularity with which the claim is repeated, in Far East Asia in particular, that the questions of the 1942 symposium, if not its solutions, still apply to the world today.

Ontological Modernity and Political Modernity

The field within which the problematic of "place" (*basho*) is developed, as well as the major part of the Nishida philosophy that generated from it, is typically ontological-topological and resolutely unpolitical. The philosophy of Nishida, as well as that of the major part of the Kyoto School (with a few notable exceptions, such as Tanabe's "logic of species"), is basically unpolitical and clearly metaphysical, even though it is a metaphysics that endeavors to be non-idealistic and, after the fashion of Husserlian phenomenology, close to "the things themselves," to the concreteness of the "life world" (Gn. *Lebenswelt*), of lived body (Fr. *corps propre*), of existential time, etc. One can say much the same about Watsuji who, in a less speculative and more descriptive manner, develops, as Augustin Berque has written,[11] a true phenomenological geography, a phenomenology of lived space and environment (Jp. *fūdo*).

For Nishida, the problematic of place is a stage, probably the most decisive, in the path along which the Japanese thinker tries to find a Western philosophic expression for an ontological intuition that is fundamental in the East, though it is "rhizomatic" or multiformal: the intuition of emptiness (*kū*), of Indian origin; the more specifically Sino-Japanese intuition of inner nature (*shizen*); and also the intuition of nothingness (*mu*), which is omnipresent in Far Eastern metaphysics. These three notions are distinct and yet all contribute jointly to expressing the fundamental relation of traditional Oriental humanity to being.

If for Nishida the natural or environmental dimension is not foreign to his intention, it is clearly the notion of nothingness that is questioned most insistently along his path, from the investigation of "pure experience" through that of the "historical world," to that of "place." (Nishida's conception of *basho* draws near to the Platonic concept of *khōra*, in a sense that seems to announce Derrida's reinterpretation of the same concept.[12]) This insistence on the concept of nothingness is such that Nishida's thought has occasionally been called a "topology of nothingness," an attempt to define the *topos*, the place or site, of nothingness. This Oriental "nothingness" is explicitly put in an oppositional relation to Western "being." Nishida tries to overcome this opposition by criticizing the Western commitment to an ousiological or substantialistic ground, reaching back to the Scholastic interpretation of Aristotle. He also (and chiefly) attempted to overcome it because of its anthropological or subjectivistic (or transcendental) founding of modern ontology.

Nishida's ontological critique of modernity stands in basic agreement with the related one made by Watsuji, as well as with Heidegger's position. If we reduce these three thinkers to what they have in common on this topic, modernity is understood here as the period of the history of metaphysics during which occur two fundamental interpretations of the being of beings (*das Sein des Seienden*). First, the being of beings is interpreted from the perspective of the abstract categories of cognitive human reason and not from the concrete way of the being of beings themselves. The second interpretation is that beings in general are reduced to objects, not only of observation for a subject that masters them rationally, but also for casual handling by a humanity that has become estranged from its own environment, which it subjugates materially and, in so doing, destroys an essential dimension of its own relation to things and its own being-in-the-world.

Modernity, in the ontological sense, is thus the age in which the being of beings is deprived of its own essence in order to be submitted to a cognitive and objectifying reason, inherent to the transcendental ego, which in this manner becomes the site of the substantialistic foundation of beings. In such a perspective, to overcome modernity would mean, with the help of a new paradigm, to reinvent a relationship to the environment that would be the occasion of the reunion of humanity with its own vital milieu as well as with its own essence. To return today to the project of such an overcoming, considering in particular the renewed environmental concerns of our time, would reveal itself to be of a striking topicality, if not a true urgency.

And this—I wish to stress emphatically—is what should be kept in mind and considered foremost as the positive message of the Kyoto School.

Considering now the practical-political definition of modernity, during both the symposium on "overcoming modernity" and the connected *Chūōkoron* discussions, we notice a jumble of ideas surrounding the ontological-cognitive dimension. This is an explicitly and massively political dimension, in which modernity is identified with Western ideology and Western colonial imperialism, and the overcoming of modernity signifies the military overthrow of Western hegemony in favor of a Japanese hegemony that would re-establish the ancient order of things and would give back to the peoples of Asia their despoiled identity. All this would be relatively justifiable if, effectively, the political notion of modernity met perfectly with the ontological notion. Overcoming modernity, in that case, would mean altogether to overthrow an oppressive Western imperialism and a perverted relation to the world that results from Western imperialism. But the reality is more complex.

In the register of political philosophy, the notion of modernity covers something quite different and it is important to recall its significance. Although such a meaning is obvious for whoever has a shred of political consciousness, it went dramatically unrecognized by the Kyoto philosophers and also by a great many of the European and American philosophical heirs of the genealogical critique of modern rationality in the Nietzschean-Heideggerian style, as well as by a number of those who would like to revive the project of overcoming modernity.

As Maruyama and Habermas have stressed, political modernity, stemming from the French Enlightenment, is an incomplete project—not in terms of subjecting nature to a cognitive-instrumental reason, cut off from its roots, but rather of emancipating humans from a socio-economic and politico-juridical order that is obscurantist and oppressive, linked to the *ancien régime* and to its avatars in the contemporary capitalistic system of profit and exploitation. Such a modernity is not founded on a transcendental, rationalistic, and objectifying subject that would be the ontological and *a priori* foundation of being, but on a plurality of socialized subjects that are the elements of a communicative and praxis-oriented reason that remains in a constant process of becoming.

In short, modernity in the political sense is the still-incomplete effort to emancipate humanity from what oppresses it, including Western imperialism. This kind of modernity allows one to grant meaning to expressions like "progress," "humanism," "democracy," "the rule of law," and "human rights." These are all positive and desirable ideas, and they justify considering modernity as a project that, far from having to be overcome, has yet to be achieved either in the West or in the East.

It is obvious that such a distinction is not made within the ideology of overcoming modernity and that, as a result of this ignorance of the specificity of the political, the confusion of the ontological-cognitive and the juridical-political is carried on to the point of aiming explicitly at overthrowing every aspect of Western modernity, including its sense of progress, humanism, democracy, and the rule of law. Moreover, this overthrow problematically excludes the militaristic and economic means of modern industrial national power.

In their rejection of modernity, this bracketing of the "military industrial complex" is symptomatic of the second great weakness of the ideologists of overcoming modernity: in addition to the confusion of the ontological and the political, there is, linked to the ignorance of the specificity of the political, a total lack of knowledge regarding the socio-economic conditions that help determine the historical and cultural development of nations. It is no coincidence that, among the many authors of the German Idealist and post-Idealist tradition that the Kyoto philosophers so carefully examine, Marx is conspicuously absent. Consequently, we end up with a paradoxical situation in which the only aspect of modernity that they should have seriously disputed—namely, the capitalistic system of profit, growth, and exploitation (which were, in turn, the chief mechanisms of Western imperialism)—is the only one that the Kyoto philosophers pass over in silence in their generalized criticism of modernity. Not only do they pass over it in silence, but they also actively collaborate with a regime that, in a proper fascist fashion, pushes toward the systematic development of the military industrial complex, thereby fostering an expansion of the most harmful aspect of that modernity against which they wanted to oppose themselves. The flaw is all the more serious because, as Maruyama, Arendt, and Habermas have understood it, we are presented with only one possible link between ontological modernity and political modernity.[13]

The "Fascist Predisposition" of Japanese Intellectuals in the Prewar Period

It is important to understand better what, in the intellectual, social, and cultural context of the decades prior to start of War World II, might have predisposed these philosophers to have missed the distinction between registers discussed above, and to have allowed themselves to be so easily seduced by the ideological fiction of tennōcentrism.

This distinction between the ontological and the political—to think at the intersection of similar distinctions, one made by Paul Ricouer, between the rational and the reasonable, and another by Jürgen Habermas, between objectifying transcendentalism and communicative action—is perhaps most clearly formulated by Hannah Arendt. What she says about it can be directly applied to our topic. At the risk of being overly schematic, I will refer to the manner in which Arendt has rethought the ancient Aristotelian distinction between the contemplative life (*biōs theōretikos*) and the active life (*biōs politikos*)[14] as a tension between the literal singularity of philosophical existence (heir of the ideal of *sophia*, wisdom, that was Plato's main concern) and the plurality of life within the city (heir of the specifically Greek experience of *politeia*).

The political ideal corresponds to *praxis*, that is, action within the *polis*, in the common world of plurality. It requires the virtue of *phronēsis* (prudential judgment within a given situation) and the faculty of *logos*, understood literally as the "spoken word" (dialogue, communication, rhetoric, dialectic, persuasion, argumentation, demonstration, etc.). As for the contemplative ideal, it corresponds to *theōria*, the intellectual vision of being and the divine. It also requires a higher and rare intuition, the *noūs*, pure thought, that is in itself *aneu logou* (beyond words) and capable of perceiving the primary ontological principles. However, in order to be expressed in a discursive way, the contemplative ideal uses a *logos* that is extricated from its insertion within the communicative relation: It is the solitary dialogue of the self with itself that is at the foundation of metaphysical speculation.

Whereas the *logos* of political *praxis* is at the source of what will be called later, notably by Kant, "practical reason," and still later "communicative reason," the *logos* of speculative contemplation will be at the source of "theoretical reason" or "cognitive reason." There are thus two clearly distinct usages of *logos* or reason to be applied to two clearly distinct fields of human activity—precisely those I intended to identify under the notions of the political-practical and the topological-ontological.

The political perversion, typically speculative (found among the Kyoto philosophers and Heidegger alike), is to treat questions relative to *praxis*—namely, the active life within the world of plurality which is also the world of common sense—with a terminology and a conceptuality adapted to *theōria* or, in our case, to the "pure experience" of "absolute nothingness" (*zettai mu*) which, according to Nishida and his disciples, is enabled by Zen thought thanks to a superior intuition, beyond language. Plato inaugurated this typical speculative perversion when he favored theoretical knowledge over practical action, endeavoring to submit the latter to the former under the form of a science that only the contemplator of ideas would possess. This perversion even blunts the capacity to distinguish good from evil. Indeed, retiring from the world of action, the thinker atrophies her or his power to judge (since judging implies the capacity to share the point of view of others). Such a thinker therefore tends to lose the power to judge the difference between good and evil. This is enhanced by the fact that the thinker erodes the capacity to perceive the evil or pain that others can feel, and also forfeits the ability to see their own action from the perspective of others. Moreover, since the submission of politics to theory signifies, at the same time, the submission of will to thought, the prospective attitude of the will, turned toward the future of uncontrollable action, is no longer determined by the necessity of following the dictates of one's conscience, distinguishing in each present situation between good and evil. Rather, it is determined by the programmatic calculation of thought, nourished by the retrospective look at the past and turned toward the mastery of the world of action within the timelessness of a knowledge that aspires to be absolute. Such an attitude has the tendency to dictate action by rules that are beyond good and evil—evil being no more than a detail within the greater vision of the progress of history.

The Platonic preference of *theōria* to the detriment, not of "life," as Nietzsche would have it, but of *praxis,* as both Arendt and Habermas observe, has resulted in the *déformation professionnelle* of philosophers throughout the history of Western metaphysics, including its adoption by the so-called Oriental philosophy of the Kyoto School. The fact is, on the occasion of the numerous and generally unfortunate usurpations of practical reason by theoretical reason, the submission of the first to the second was the rule (notably in Hegel and Marx) rather than the exception (as in Aristotle and Kant). In fact, during the greater part of its history, philosophy, which merges with what Heidegger has called metaphysics or onto-theology, has constantly been tempted by a totalizing view of human activity in which justice was not meted to the specificity of action—its factual finitude, its communicative dimension, its uncertain and untotalizing plurality. It knew nothing of the intrinsic conflict of a *praxis*-oriented situation whose ambiguity and unpredictability is forever impossible to master. Faced with the intrinsic imperfection of *praxis,* one finds here the *hubris,* the arrogance and impatience of the human mind that would like to subjugate events to the perfection of a disembodied vision, an arrogance that Greek tragedy always emphatically condemned.

Does one not recognize such *hubris* and impatience not only in Plato and Heidegger, but also among the philosophers of the Kyoto School? This is indeed my conviction. And I agree here with the interpretation by Japanologist Robert H. Sharf who, without developing it, has glimpsed the issue. He writes:

> Impatience with plurality and uncertainty in the intellectual realm can lead all too readily to impatience with plurality and uncertainty in the realm of politics. It may not be mere coincidence that a surprising number of those who saw Zen as a solution to spiritual anxiety were drawn to authoritarian or totalitarian solutions to social and political unrest. In a similar vein, Hannah Arendt has commented on the "exasperation" we sometimes feel when confronted with the fact that Plato and Heidegger were drawn to "tyrants and Führers." Arendt suggests that this may be more than happenstance; it might in fact attest to a *déformation professionnelle.* . . . It may well be that the apostles of "pure Zen," accepting wondering as their abode, fell prey to this *déformation professionnelle:* they yearned to realize in the world of human affairs the "perfection" they found in their Zen.[15]

This *déformation professionnelle* of the speculative philosopher, denounced by Arendt, combines moreover, among the Kyoto philosophers, with a cultural predisposition whose general characteristics Maruyama Masao, Nakamura

Hajime, and Ichikawa Hakugen,[16] among others, have explained. Sparing the details, I would just like to recall here their general ideas.

Maruyama demonstrates how, from the Meiji era on, the ambition of the new Japanese state, constructed to a great extent after the example of the enlightened despotism of Prussia, intended to catch up with and overtake the West in order to protect itself from the imperialistic designs of the latter. This ambition encouraged an economic and political interventionism that put its mark on all aspects of social and cultural life. To limit ourselves to the political question, the decision to submit the private sphere to the public dimension of state authority smothered the development of what Hegel used to call *Moralität,* that is, the moral internalization necessary for the creation of political judgment and for a sense of civic responsibility. Now if Hegel is right in saying that there is no true *Sittlichkeit* (objective morality, internally diversified) without the mediation of a *Moralität* (subjective morality), it was not just the foundations for the true rule of law that were lacking in prewar Japan, but also the foundations for an actual political consciousness.

In addition to this absence of political consciousness, there is, through the imposition of state Shintō, the systematization of a whole series of cultural attitudes that tend to predispose individuals to the ideological fiction of tennōcentrism. Here the analyses of Nakamura Hajime prove to be the most revealing and penetrating. These cultural attitudes, which are more on the register of affect than conscious thought, converge toward a feeling of non-differentiation between the sacred and the secular realms, that is, a feeling of symbiosis with the elements of nature and of social communion with the enlarged group. When the Emperor is construed to embody such a non-differentiation, symbiosis, and communion, one then understands the fact that there is no individually responsible subject, but only a collection of the Emperor's subjects, and that all morality will be a social ethics of conformity with the group and of submission to authority, something to which Confucianism, the other great ethical tradition of Japan, also contributes.

Finally, there is the tradition of Zen to consider, which more directly inspired the Kyoto thinkers. Zen shares with Shintō the feeling of a presence of the absolute within the concrete phenomenality of things rather than in transcendent and universal ideals. It also shares the feeling of a spirituality that is intimately linked to one's own cultural specificity, which would be like the quintessence of all human spirituality—that is, some sort of cultural nationalism. But moreover—and this is what Ichikawa Hakugen has denounced— Zen has accumulated in its history a series of shortcomings that go against the fundamentally non-violent, anti-nationalist, and compassionate message of its origins in ancient Buddhism. Specifically, in abandoning the supranationalist universality of the *Dharma,* Zen (pursuing the examples of Chinese Chan) has often opted without hesitation for temporal power. In the past, it also chose to become an integral part of the military training of the samurais. Furthermore, in creating a distinction between "secular freedom" and "absolute freedom" (purely ontological), and by stressing (in a very Platonic way) the superiority of the latter over the former, it has suppressed all possibility for the Zen practitioner to foster any awareness of a social or political mode. For Zen, the issue is to cultivate ontological freedom in an intuitive dimension of spiritual awakening—that is, not just "beyond words" but also "beyond good or evil," free from the distinctions or discriminations of an "all-too-human" consciousness. This disposition also fosters the acceptance of the political circumstances of the moment—including militarism. Since such affairs are all-too-human, they are not worthy of being taken into account.

It is toward all this that the fundamentally non-political or apolitical thought of Nishida converges. Indeed, according to a paradox that is only apparent, it is his apolitical stand (his lack of political sense and reflection) that is to a great extent responsible for his more than ambiguous political choice when, driven by circumstances, he had to engage himself politically. The same is true for most of the Kyoto School philosophers. The attitude of the speculative thinker is apolitical—concerned with ontology but ignorant of the common affairs linked to human plurality. The attitude of the Japanese prewar intellectual is apolitical, theoretically educated in Western culture, but without sharing the internalization of its ethico-juridical sense. The attitude of the Shintoistic subject, for whom the highest virtue is the devotion to the Emperor, symbol of the vital cosmos and social harmony, is apolitical. The attitude of the Zen practitioner, devoted to mystical contemplation but contemptuous of the socio-economic condition of his fellow men, is also apolitical.

From *An Inquiry into the Good* to the "logic of place," the whole of Nishida's thought is marked by an ontological monism that blurs the distinctions of register and blinds one to the communicational and non-cognitive dimensions of philosophical thought. This goes to the point where the Hegelian influence, determinative for Nishida and for the Kyoto School as a whole, will go massively in the direction of its monistic tendency, ontologically totalizing and politically totalitarian, to which this philosophy is vulnerable when the (necessary) stages and mediations are neglected, progressing then toward a culmination in the chimera of an absolute knowledge that could identity itself with the immediacy of pure experience.

For Nishida as for Zen, it is a matter of becoming one with the absolute that is present in the locus where one dwells, be it the immediacy of "pure experience" or the space-time of the "historical world." In accordance with the paradoxical logic of Zen, it is a matter of finding the "self-identical contradiction" that exists between the individual and the universal, the self and the historical world, the totality of brute facts and the absolute. In each case it is a monism, a systematized non-duality that leads, among other things, to a non-distinction between being and the "ought," between what is and what ought to be. As Ichikawa has stressed, Nishida's philosophy of self is an undifferentiated monism where the autonomy of the modern subject is not yet acquired, where the inner space necessary for a moral consciousness and a civic and critical responsibility is not developed, and where the presupposed ontological harmony blinds one to the conflicts and contradictions intrinsic to reality—notably, the socio-economic reality about which Nishida was silent.

Prospective Remarks

The question at hand is not a determination of the degree or exact nature of the relationship between Nishida, his disciples, and the tennōcentric regime. Rather, it is to understand—on the level of a whole attitude that is simultaneously existential and professional—the reasons and conditions for such obviously disreputable arrangements, not in order to institute once again proceedings against Nishida and the Kyoto School, and even less with the intention of rejecting their teaching. On the contrary, it is in order to resume on a new basis the Kyoto School's prodigiously daring project of a philosophical thought that is built at the meeting point of the cultures of the East and of the West, and that can, on such an enlarged foundation, confront the current global problems with which the whole of humanity is confronted, including, most notably, the environmental crisis. In brief, then, it is to resume the project that the Kyoto School missed on the political level, even though it had sketched it remarkably well on the ontological level—namely, the project of a thought that is concretely universal because it is effectively cosmopolitan. As this would imply a number of things, I will limit myself to three considerations.

First of all, this would imply a vast mediation between all that the thought of the Kyoto School ignored and what some of its postwar critics have tried to rectify: (1) the communicative dimension of modern reason and its emancipatory project; (2) the internal diversification of Hegelian philosophy, notably its philosophy of law, and more specifically its reintroduction of subjective morality; and (3) the taking into account of the socio-economic questions in the philosophy of history, etc.

Second, it would imply continuing the political watchfulness of the immediate postwar critics of which the present fashion of postmodernity might not be capable. My repeated warning does not concern, then, the obvious ideological misadventure of a political choice in favor of any particular rise of neo-nationalism, but rather the inadvertent perpetuation of the *défaut professionnel* denounced by Arendt. Inasmuch as such watchfulness necessitates a clear distinction between the theoretical and practical registers, as well as sub-registers within these, it is extremely important to know at which level we are when we speak of modernity and its connected notions (the subject, place, humanism, etc.). This discernment does not aim to sequester one type of discourse from another type of discourse, but rather to be better equipped this time around if we want to realize their desirable intersections.

I know also that few are interested in Zen today,[17] so no one risks inheriting its ontological monism (partially responsible, let us recall, for many disastrous confusions and the leveling of basic conceptual distinctions). But monism can reappear under other forms in postmodern thought: for example, within the one-dimensionality that was once denounced by Herbert Marcuse but is present more than ever; in the incapacity of a thinking that is entirely dialectical and subversive; and in the acceptance, both unconditionally and playfully, of the *status quo* that is called today, in a most ambiguous way, the "global triumph of democratic liberalism," but which is really a global pervasiveness of late capitalism.

It is indeed under the moniker of the capitalist triumph that the thematic of "postmodernity" develops today. Appearing first in France in the structuralist movement, and then becoming fashionable in American literary circles, the notion of postmodernity has also achieved considerable success in Japan, also within circles linked essentially to academic literary criticism, where people enjoyed considering the Japan of the 1980s as the embodiment *par excellence* of postmodern society. Ideologically very ambiguous, postmodernity presents itself as a fact that is peculiar to advanced industrial societies, independent of political options. A whole series of elements that the anti-capitalism of yesteryear, from right to left, tried to put into question are now being accepted as being part of an undisputed environment. The paradoxical situation today is then that the thematic of postmodernity, originating with thinkers who are generally from a politically correct left, becomes the pretext for an unconditional acceptance of triumphant capitalism, just as in the past the ideologists of overcoming modernity accepted the domination of the military-industrial complex in an uncritical way. This can be seen, for example, in the thinking of Gianni Vattimo, who tries to reconcile the discourse of postmodernity with that of Nietzschean-Heideggerian genealogy, taking advantage of the notions of post-history or the "end of history" while avoiding a deeper socio-economic reflection on the present situation.

In light of such a situation many former anti-capitalistic themes, notably those linked to the Frankfurt School (Adorno, Benjamin, Marcuse), regain their timeliness and judiciousness—yet also a paradoxical proximity to some of the legitimate ambitions among Japanese proponents of the overcoming modernity ideology. It is an ideologically delicate situation, originating in our current crises, that pushes us to re-question the global significance of the criticism of modernity and of modernism. While doing so, we also should maintain our commitment to, as Habermas says, the modern "project" from the perspective of its completion, which should bring us then ultimately to propose a still-hypothetical formulation of the self-subversion of modernity. Briefly stated, what should ideally be included here is another immense essay: what has to be subverted, in the main, is the way in which the triumph of capitalism is savagely destroying the natural environment that is the very condition for human life on earth.

The third consideration aims to detect everything that, in the Japanese cultural tradition and more generally in the Asian tradition, can feed the communicative reason specific to the political modernity that is still to achieved, in order to establish the latter on the "concrete universality" which the Kyoto philosophers discuss with such insistence. To give an example: the reflections of Watsuji and Kimura Bin move in this direction when they concern the notion of the "human being," understood here not in a solipsistic manner (as in transcendental philosophy or even phenomenology), but rather in terms of social relationships. This is evident when they stress that the expression *ningen* (human being) includes the kanji for *aida* (what is "between" humans: their relations).[18] One also finds Maruyama moving in a similar direction when he attempts to bring to the fore, among the thinkers of the Tokugawa era, and notably with Ogyū Soraï, embryonic elements of a modern political consciousness (the freeing of the political from the moral, the distinction between private and public, etc.).[19]

The Tokugawa era, as announcing a not yet accomplished modernity, and not a regressive postmodernity, would be one of the research programs. The eminently modernist predisposition of traditional Japanese aesthetics also serves as a confirmation and guide here. Another guide might well also be this intuition of one of the most surprising thinkers of the twentieth century in France, Alexandre Kojève, who in one of his most enigmatic and provocative remarks writes:

> I was brought to the conclusion that the American way of life was the type of existence specific to a post-historical period—the way the United States were present in the world being a prefiguring of the future "eternal present" of the whole of humanity. And thus, the return of man to animality appeared, not just like a possibility still to come but also like an already present certainty.
>
> It was after a recent trip to Japan (1959) that I radically changed my opinion on this point. I observed there a society that is unique, because it is the only one to have had almost three centuries of existence in a state of the "end of history." . . . This allows me to believe that the recently initiated interaction between Japan and the Western world will finally lead, not to a renewed barbarism of the Japanese, but to a "Japanization" of the Westerners (including the Russians).[20]

NOTES

1. See the writings of Karel Van Wolferen, Chalmers Johnson, James Fallows or, more interestingly, David Williams's *Japan: Beyond the End of History* (New York and London: Routledge, 1994). I personally endeavored to give an overall interpretation of East Asian capitalism in "L'autre capitalisme: le système nippo-asiatique," *Les Temps Modernes*, no. 591 (December 1996–January 1997): 35–91.

2. Takeuchi Yoshimi, "Kindaika to dentō" [Modernization and tradition], in *Kindai Nihon shisōshi kōza*, vol. 7 (Tokyo: Chikuma Shobō, 1959); quoted in James W. Heisig and John C. Maraldo, eds., *Rude Awakenings: Zen, the Kyoto School, and the Question of Nationalism* (Honolulu: University of Hawai'i Press, 1994), 194. The book edited by Heisig and Maraldo is my main source concerning the Tokyo symposium and the *Chūōkoron* discussions. I have also used Alain-Marc Rieu and Araki Tōru, "Le dépassement de la modernité," *Ebisu* 6 (July–September 1994).

3. René Guenon, *La crise du monde moderne* (Paris: Gallimard, 1946/1973).

4. Harold Rosenberg, *The Tradition of the New* (New York: Da Capo Press, 1960; repr. Cambridge, Mass.: Perseus, 1994).

5. See in particular Clement Greenberg, "Modernist Painting," in *Art and Literature* 4 (1965); also *Art and Culture* (Boston: Beacon Press, 1961).

6. There is of course no question here of negating the dogmatic turn that modernism has too often taken, particularly in architecture, nor to negate the numerous catastrophic urbanistic realizations in which the most extreme doctrines of the so-called "international style" were applied. What I would like to reevaluate—but this would need some further developments—is the fundamental intention of modernism which, aesthetically, means a purification of language and means, ideologically, an emancipatory ideal.

7. I use the expression *Einfühlung* in the sense developed by Wilhelm Worringer, *Abstraktion und Einfühlung* (Munich: R. Piper, 1911): figurative representation where the spectator can identify himself emotionally, in an almost cinematographic manner, to the figures represented. Malraux is probably one of the first authors to have shown how hypertrophied *Einfühlung* (what he calls "the art of assuaging") is utilized by totalitarian states, from fascism to sovietism. See André Malraux, *Les voix du silence* (Paris: Gallimard, 1951), 541ff.

8. Emile Poulat, *Histoire, dogme et critique dans la crise moderniste* (Paris: Castermann, 1962); also, *Intégrisme et catholicisme integral* (Paris: Castermann, 1969).

9. On postmodernism and postmodernity in Japan, see Masao Miyoshi and H. D. Harootunian, *Postmodernism and Japan* (Durham, N.C.: Duke University Press, 1989). On the transmission of the Kyoto School philosophy, see the remarkable book by Ōhashi Ryōsuke, *Die Philosophie der Kyōto-Schule: Texte und Einfürungen* (Munich: Karl Alber, 1990).

10. Nishitani Keiji, *Nihirizumu* [*The Self-Overcoming of Nihilism*], 1949. The project was pursued in *Shūkyō to wa nanika* [*Religion and Nothingness*].

11. Augustin Berque, "Milieu et logique du lieu chez Watsuji," in Bernard Stevens, ed., *La réception européenne de l'école de Kyōto*, in *La Revue Philosophique de Louvain* 4 (November 1994): 495–507.

12. I developed this idea in "Basho et khōra: Nishida en son lieu," *Etudes Phénoménologiques* 21 (1995): 81–109.

13. What I am expressing here in a condensed way has been developed in a number of articles, among which are "Arendt et Maruyama: deux approches complémentaires du totalitarisme," *Approches critiques de la pensée japonaise du XXème siècle* (Montreal: Les Presses de l'Université de Montréal, 2001), 227–41; and "Un regard japonais sur la modernité: la pensée politique de Maruyama," *Du bon usage des droits de l'homme*, in *Esprit*, no. 312 (Paris: Février, 2005), 117–33.

14. Each type of life should, again, be subdivided: the contemplative ideal divides into religious and metaphysical contemplation, whereas active life divides into the three great fields of political action, human creative work, and the ever-recurring productivity of labor. But the limited dimensions of the present essay force an impoverishing schematization on us. We can refer here to Hannah Arendt's major work, *The Human Condition* (Chicago: University of Chicago Press, 1958).

15. Robert H. Sharf, "Whose Zen?" in *Rude Awakenings*, 50.

16. A number of studies, among which are Maruyama Masao, *Thought and Behaviour in Modern Japanese Politics* (Oxford: Oxford University Press, 1963); Nakamura Hajime, *Ways of Thinking of Eastern Peoples* (Honolulu: University of Hawai'i Press, 1964); Ichikawa Hakugen, "Zen and Contemporary Thought," cited in *Rude Awakenings*, 16ff.

17. And this fact is most unfortunate since Zen thought remains inescapable in order to understand the ontological reach of Nishida's philosophy. Moreover, beyond all the deviations that a particular institutional Zen has inflicted upon the *Dharma*,

it would be important to see to what extent Zen might remain—as D. T. Suzuki suggested, notably in *Zen and Japanese Culture* (Princeton, N.J.: Princeton University Press, 1970)—the best access road for an opening of Western consciousness to the fundamental message of Buddhism.

18. See, among others, Watsuji Tetsurō's *Rinrigaku,* translated as *Watsuji Tetsurō's Rinrigaku: Ethics in Japan* by Yamamoto Seisaku and Robert E. Carter (Albany: State University of New York Press, 1996); and Kimura Bin, *Zwischen Mensch und Mensch: Strukturen Japanischer Subjectivität* (Darmstadt: Wissenschaftlicher Buchgesellschaft, 1995).

19. Maruyama Masao, *Studies in the Intellectual History of Tokugawa Japan,* trans. Mikiso Hane (Princeton, N.J.: Princeton University Press, 1974).

20. Alexandre Kojève, *Introduction à la lecture de Hegel* (Paris: Gallimard, 1968), 437; my translation.

14

Heidegger and Japanese Fascism: An Unsubstantiated Connection

GRAHAM PARKES

If one moves in academic circles having to do with modern Japanese political philosophy, it soon becomes clear that Japan's most renowned thinkers of the twentieth century, members of the so-called Kyoto School, were primarily responsible for "defining the philosophic contours of Japanese fascism," and that the major impetus for this nefarious project came from the German philosopher Martin Heidegger.[1] This impression is given by a number of books, some of which are written by celebrated scholars and published by prestigious university presses.[2] These texts criticize the most prominent figures in the Kyoto School—Nishida Kitarō, Tanabe Hajime, Kuki Shūzō, Nishitani Keiji, and Miki Kiyoshi—for promulgating fascistic and ultra-nationalistic ideas, usually by trying to establish "guilt by association" with Heidegger. But on closer examination, the scholarship turns out to be sadly short on facts and long on neo-Marxist jargon and deconstructionist rhetoric. Ideological concerns have stifled philosophical inquiry and are now promoting a kind of censorship that suggests, ironically, a fascism of the left. This would be of no great consequence if fascism had been eradicated after World War II; but since fascistic movements are still very much with us, scholarly discussions of the phenomenon have a responsibility to identify it properly.

This essay engages several concerns. It extends the argument of an article of mine from 1997, "The Putative Fascism of the Kyoto School," which shows neo-Marxist criticisms of the Kyoto philosophers to be unfounded, and which appears to have gone largely unnoticed in Europe.[3] And since such criticisms of the Kyoto School continue, now on both sides of the Atlantic, it is worthwhile to keep showing how the critics' ideology distorts the picture they present and ignores any studies that point this out. This exercise also serves to outline further, positive dimensions of the political philosophy of the Kyoto

School thinkers. Finally, the appearance of such neo-Marxist criticisms in the United Kingdom prompted an attempt at exchange and dialogue, the failure of which demonstrates how this kind of ideology extends to the politics of publishing in academic journals.

1

So what did the much-criticized Kyoto School philosophers say and write to deserve the moral censure they've been receiving in the Anglophone West? They certainly opposed British, Dutch, and American colonial expansion in East Asia—but only an unregenerate Western imperialist could find their grounds for that opposition invalid. They also venerated the nobler aspects of traditional Japanese culture, and lamented their dwindling vitality under the onrush of mass enthusiasm in Japan for the modern and the Western. Some of them even wrote kind words about the emperor system, and suggested that Japan could become a world power through leading the so-called Greater East Asian Co-prosperity Sphere. For all of this they have been dismissed as fascistic ideologues—when in fact the fascism is being conjured up by projections on the part of morally superior commentators from the side of the victorious Americans. These dismissals have had the dismal effect of stunting the growth of English-language studies of the Kyoto School thinkers, as many potential students have been persuaded that those philosophers are promoters of fascism.

Neo-Marxists love to hate the Greater East Asian Co-prosperity Sphere, denigrating it as "Japan's colonial empire." But if one looks at Nishida's and Tanabe's ideas about how the project should work, it is clear there is nothing fascistic or even imperialistic about them. And the nationalistic aspect of those ideas—since Japan is the only Asian nation not to have been colonized by the West, it is natural that it should play a leading role in the Co-prosperity Sphere—is balanced by a thoroughgoing internationalism. Christopher Goto-Jones has demonstrated the vacuity of the charges of fascism against Nishida's political philosophy and shown the distinctly internationalist dimensions of his thinking.[4] Tanabe's ideas about individual freedom and the multi-ethnic state, and above all his relentless insistence throughout his career on the primacy of reason, definitively preclude his being a fascist philosopher in any sense of the word. This is made clear in a recent study by David Williams that demonstrates, among many other things, the flimsiness of the grounds for accusing Tanabe of fascist leanings.[5] In essays written during the thirties, Kuki expressed optimism about Japan's ability to play a leading role in the Greater East Asian Co-prosperity Sphere and help her neighbors combat Western imperialism in East Asia, but his nationalism is again tempered by an emphasis on internationalism as the appropriate strategy for Japan to become a greater power in a globalizing world.[6]

Nishitani has been especially harshly criticized for his contribution to a series of symposia held in 1941 and 1942 and sponsored by *Chūōkōron*, a well-known literary journal, the transcripts of which were later published under the title *Japan from a World-Historical Standpoint* (1943). In the course of these discussions he said (among many other things) that Japan's assertiveness in its drive to colonize regions of China and South-East Asia, and in its attack on the American fleet at Pearl Harbor (which had happened shortly before), might not be such a bad thing for East Asia, from a world-historical perspective. One can certainly criticize these remarks for being nationalistic and promoting a kind of imperialism, but the context in which they were made was one in which Japan, as the only major East Asian country that had not been invaded by the imperialist powers of the West, was simply beginning to follow their example by trying to obtain an overseas empire on behalf of its own, longer-standing emperor. In any case, nationalism and imperialism are different from fascism—as is the scepticism toward modernism evinced by the Kyoto School thinkers generally, and their reverence for what is great in the Japanese tradition.

It is important to understand these symposia in context, insofar as their basic premise is that the army's influence on the government was dangerously bellicose, and that some rational discussion of Japan's foreign policy was desperately needed. The main theme of the first session (November 1941) was originally to be "How to avoid war [with the United States]," but under pressure from government propagandists after the attack on Pearl Harbor it had to be changed to "How to bring the war to a favorable end as soon as possible, in a way rationally acceptable to the Army."[7] Even though the publisher prudently expurgated the sharp criticisms of the army and General Tojo that appeared in the original transcripts, the published version was immediately attacked by ultranationalist and fascist elements in the government as being too tame, "seditious and anti-war." The army reacted by ordering the suppression of public activities by the "Kyoto faction" and forbidding any further print runs of the book or mention of their ideas in the press.[8] Such measures would have been unnecessary had the participants in the symposium been the raging fascists they are now accused of being. What is clear is that their postwar accusers, if they have read the relevant texts at all, have completely ignored their complicated context.

But why cannot these conflicting views in the contemporary academy be taken simply as a matter of disagreements among scholars who offer differing interpretations, without introducing the contentious concept of ideology? The reason is that what traditionally distinguishes philosophy from ideology is that the former is primarily a *questioning*—a questioning of the purported facts of the matter, of the motives and prejudices behind interpretations of the facts, and of any dogmatism that declines to engage in dialogue. Ideology by contrast tends to discourage questioning of the facts so as to promote belief or faith in its system of ideas, and is correspondingly reluctant to engage in any dialogue that might put into question the origin of those ideas. The neo-Marxist scholarship on the politics of the Kyoto School thinkers and their relation to Heidegger is a perfect example of this latter syndrome.

2

It was not until 1994 that a dialogue concerning the politics of the Kyoto School thinkers got under way, with a conference on the topic in New Mexico, the revised proceedings of which were published the following year under the title *Rude Awakenings: Zen, the Kyoto School, and the Question of Nationalism.* What is interesting about this collection of essays is that positions on the Kyoto School divide more or less along national lines, with the Western authors generally being more critical and the Japanese more defensive.[9] This divide has to be seen against the background of the received view in the Western academy, which conveniently ignores the broader context of international relations formed by Western imperialism—which is that the Pacific War as pursued by the United States was a just war, and the Japanese attack on Pearl Harbor completely unprovoked. It would be hard to take this "Pacific War Orthodoxy" seriously (in David Williams's apt phrase) if it had not been so clearly manifested in the attitudes that underwrote the United States' disastrous invasion of Iraq some sixty years later.

None of the neo-Marxist scholars referred to earlier appears in *Rude Awakenings,* but they figure prominently in my piece on "The Putative Fascism of the Kyoto School and the Political Correctness of the Modern Academy," which appeared a couple of years after *Rude Awakenings.* This essay, which remains more or less neutral with respect to the political ideas of the Kyoto School thinkers, examines the grounds for the allegations of fascism made by scholars such as Harootunian, Dale, Faure, and Pincus against the major Kyoto School thinkers. One would expect to find such allegations to be based on a working definition of fascism and a reading of primary texts containing ideas that meet the criteria for being fascistic. And when Heidegger is invoked as a pernicious influence, one would hope to be shown just which ideas in his works are fascist in tone or orientation, and which fascist currents of thought they fed into in Japan. Yet none of this is to be found in these neo-Marxist excoriations: the allegations remain brazenly unsubstantiated. They depend on quotations taken out of context, tendentious and inaccurate translations, assertions made without justification or argument, and general insinuation and innuendo.

Although I sent copies of the final draft of that article to the authors whose work I had criticized, in the eleven years since its publication I have seen not a single rebuttal of its claims.[10] While the flood of accusations of Kyoto School fascism has abated somewhat, Harry Harootunian continues to prosecute his case. Even though *The Cambridge History of Japan* has been reprinted, the allegations of fascism by Najita and Harootunian in their chapter "Japanese Revolt against the West" remain unchanged. This piece was reprinted without modification in 1998 and again in 1999 in a collection titled *Modern Japanese Thought*.[11] So here is a situation where Harootunian's allegations of Kyoto School fascism in the most prestigious English-language publication on Japan have been shown to be unsubstantiated—and he simply ignores the criticism and keeps on publishing the accusations. See the evil, speak the evil—but keep the ears stopped firmly shut.

A hint of what is behind this tactic can be found in the transcript of a conversation between Harootunian and Naoki Sakai (whose writings on the Kyoto School philosophers are often very critical but always responsibly argued), published in 1999.[12] Here Harootunian criticizes "the model of the colonial regime for area studies" of Japan in the United States, and the resistance to "theory" manifested by the conservative American scholars of Japan who had dominated the field since the end of World War II.[13]

> Theory teaches us to question the object itself, the object of our inquiry. What's revealed . . . is that the object of knowledge is a fiction. . . . The object [in this case] is held together by the complicit relations between American scholars and Japanese scholars. This is why the introduction of theory is seen as so dangerous and why professional journals like the *Journal of Japanese Studies* will do anything to suppress it. *What counts is who has the power to make their fiction stick.* . . . Enor-

mous resources are involved in this. We're not just talking institutional resources; we're talking about social power, status, jobs, fellowships.[14]

He has a point here, insofar as the neo-Marxists have tried to exert a Foucauldian-style power through their knowledge of materials in Japanese that are inaccessible to scholars who do not read the language. And because some of them occupy powerful positions at top universities, people in Japanese studies have been reluctant to question their criticisms of the Kyoto School.

So, now "theory" appears to have supplanted "facts" in the postmodern academy. But can "the object of knowledge" *always* be a fiction? It seems unhelpful to claim so, since the practical distinction between fiction and fact would then collapse altogether. It is reasonable to say, for example, that we know for a fact that Heidegger resigned from the rectorship of Freiburg University in April 1934, twelve months after his being appointed. We can also more or less agree on what kinds of new evidence would require us to reassess that fact and to say that we "now know" that he resigned at a different time. Of course, what we think we know about history and refer to as "historical fact" always obtains within a certain horizon of interpretation; and as horizons of interpretation vary across cultures and change over time, the realm of historical fact is altered accordingly. Yet the general distinction between fact and fiction, while subject to blurring and modification, remains a helpful one—such that one needs compelling circumstances to abandon it.

The first name Harootunian mentions in his book from the following year, *Overcome by Modernity,* and in its very first sentence, is "Friederich [*sic*] Nietzsche." Perhaps his invoking power in connection with fiction is meant in the spirit of Nietzsche's famous (but unpublished) dictum: "There are not any facts, only interpretations."[15] It could derive from a quasi-Nietzschean understanding of the world as a field of interpretive forces, a play of will to power: if one excels at such play, one can make one's fiction stick by having one's will prevail, one's world interpretations hold sway.

Yet when Harootunian says, "What counts is who has the power to make their fiction stick," one is reminded less of Nietzsche than of the American neoconservatives' contempt for members of what they call "the reality-based community." To adapt that laudably forthright statement by the senior adviser to George W. Bush: "We're an empire now, and when we write, we create our own reality."[16] Just as the Bush administration's strategy of endlessly repeating the mantra *Saddam Hussein/Al Qaeda* had two-thirds of the American people believing for several years that Iraq was implicated in the attacks of 9/11, so

Harootunian's mantra *Kyoto School/Heidegger's fascism* seems to be effective in the academic world. Of course the bulk of the American people had to be made to believe in "our own reality," to accede to that interpretation of the world, but this hardly validates it.

Nietzsche was a philologist as well as a philosopher, and through practicing that science he came to appreciate the salutary power of scientific scholarship in general. And so a practice like Harootunian's, whereby one acknowledges sources and texts in the name of doing history but then simply says what one wants regardless of evidence or justification of any kind, is from a Nietzschean perspective utterly inadmissible. By contrast with ego-assertion through "social power and status," will to power at its noblest wills through the world rather than the ego, and exercises power through clear and responsible interpretation.[17]

3

In the introduction to *Overcome by Modernity*, Harootunian explains that the work "grew out of a collaboration with Tetsuo Najita that produced . . . 'The Revolt against the West.'"[18] The reader who consequently expects more on the putative fascism of the Kyoto School is not disappointed, though now the main target is the philosopher Miki Kiyoshi, who is described as "clearly associated with Kyoto philosophy."[19]

The book begins with an account of a well-known symposium on "Overcoming Modernity" that took place in 1942 and some of Nishitani's contribution to it, followed by a discussion of the symposia on "Japan from the Standpoint of World History." It is a relief to find that the "philosophic-contours-of-Japanese-fascism" refrain is now quite muted, being relegated to a dismissive endnote: "But also see Horio Tsutomu, 'The Chūō Kōron Discussions: Their Background and Meaning' . . . for a thinly disguised whitewash of this symposium, whose major orientation was philosophic fascism."[20] The claim that no group in prewar Japan "came closer" than the philosophers of the Kyoto faction to "defining the philosophic contours of Japanese fascism" was merely asserted by Najita and Harootunian in "The Revolt against the West," with not a shred of evidence given in support of it. By contrast, Horio's analysis of the *Chūōkōron* discussions is based on painstaking research into the original sources and makes nonsense of the idea that the group was in any way promoting or supporting fascism. If Harootunian wants to claim that this is "a thinly disguised whitewash" he had better provide some substantive justification, either by showing that Horio is misquoting and/or misinterpreting the transcripts of the symposia, or else by quoting from them himself in order to show just how they constitute "a major orientation [of] philosophic fascism." David Williams's devastating criticisms of Harootunian's account of the symposia show that Harootunian is no more interested in even getting the basic facts concerning them right than in offering interpretations based on readings of the primary texts.[21] Turning to Miki Kiyoshi, Harootunian first introduces him in a tone of some equivocation:

> Miki often skirted with forms of fascist totalizing, even though he also sought to distance himself and Japan from an identity with it. Nevertheless, there is a good deal of folkic totalism in Miki's thinking, which in lesser hands or more determined thinkers . . . easily slipped into fascism.[22]

For readers acquainted with Miki's writings, who was profoundly influenced by Marx and studied and wrote about Marxism for many years, this insinuation of a penchant for fascism will come as a surprise. Even Harootunian himself has to acknowledge that Miki's "Marxian phase . . . in a certain sense remained with him until the end."[23] One would have thought that having such a prolonged Marxian phase would have kept him from slipping into fascism. But perhaps Harootunian will amaze after all by adducing works that have been overlooked by others, or else by demonstrating through analysis of familiar texts an agenda that runs counter to the received view of Miki as a good Marxist.

The first forty pages of the last chapter of *Overcome by Modernity* discuss Miki's political philosophy, which, according to Harootunian, has two sides. One side is introduced by the "guilt-by-association-with-Heidegger" trick: Miki is said to be "deeply implicated in Heidegger," though just what this unusual condition consists in is left unspecified.[24] In fact, Harootunian himself admits two sentences later that Miki distanced himself from the German thinker whose work he had at first admired:

> Despite the hostility he registered in response to Heidegger's Rector address and his decision to join the Nazi party in 1933, there was simply no way of bridging Miki's two sides: the philosopher analyzing the "current situation" (Marxism) and the thinker promoting the space of Asia (fascism). . . . In this sense he remained true to the Marxian analytic, even though his theory of action promising a solution bordered on fascism.[25]

After "skirting with" fascism, Miki's ideas are now bordering on it, thanks somehow to his "promoting the space of Asia." But since a continuing loyalty to Marxism would tend to render one immune to the lures of fascism, expectations of a truly spectacular revelation from Harootunian become ever greater.

Instead, there ensues an exposition (often obscured by the opacity of Harootunian's jargon-ridden prose) of Miki's writings during his explicitly Marxist period, after which the term "fascism" begins to reappear.[26] Referring to Miki's later treatment of the relationship between politics and culture, Harootunian writes:

> Yet this concern surely constituted a sign of a global historical conjuncture where fascism was increasingly the political strategy employed to save capitalism. . . . But this attempt to realign politics and culture . . . showed clearly the linking of fascism and imperialism that . . . others would see as a natural manifestation of the expansion of the communal body.[27]

Whatever these sentences mean, we are given no reasons for believing that, if indeed Miki was concerned with saving capitalism, the strategy he proposed for doing so was fascistic—or that he advocated anything like a linking of fascism and imperialism.

Harootunian goes on to generate a great deal of heat around Miki's concern with the "people" (*minzoku*), which he makes sound sinister by translating the term consistently, and misleadingly, as "folk." Why render a word that means "people" or "nation" by the bizarre term (in this context, at least) "folk"? An associate of Harootunian's, Leslie Pincus, has given the answer in the context of another Kyoto School thinker: "Kuki drew, no doubt, on the semantic resources of the German *Volk*—'folk' in English—and as a translation, 'folk' would have the advantage of invoking the German fascist politics associated with the term."[28] This misleading translation will serve the purpose, then, of linking Kuki, and now Miki, to fascism in Germany. But Harootunian himself has to admit, in discussing Miki's ideas about the Japanese people: "This kind of folkism, observed in Japan and throughout East Asia, differed from the volkisch ideology of national socialism and was not necessarily incompatible with 'globalism.'"[29] Not at all incompatible—and in fact it is central to the political philosophy of the Kyoto School during the 1930s that nationalism and what they call "Japanism" are completely compatible with internationalism.[30] Harootunian's emphasis on the "folk" in Miki serves to bend his thought in the direction of National Socialism, so as to facilitate the underhanded application of the "fascism" label. Underhanded, because Harootunian presents not a shred of evidence for the claim that Miki espoused any kind of fascism, but simply piles on the solemn asseverations.

In Miki's reasoning, the idea of social order that the present required was one that "had to transcend modern gesellschaft to conform to a new gemeinschaft" (14:263). This new gemeinschaft was to be seen not as a throwback to a primitive or feudal community (here, his fascism was both modern and rational), but rather as one that now was capable of sublating (*shiyō*) modern society within itself.[31]

After more than thirty pages of innuendo, it suffices simply to insert a parenthetical remark about the nature of Miki's putative fascism and the case is made. But granted that Miki advocated a new *Gemeinschaft*, we would need to be told what features of this new community make it fascistic. Instead, Harootunian merely raises the specter of "the organicity implied by Miki's conception of fashioning a community"—a bizarre idea, since something that is growing organically can hardly be fashioned—without citing as evidence any text of Miki's discussing organicity. Perhaps we are supposed to be stunned by this utterly unsupported *non sequitur*: "In Miki, this organicism led to political totalitarianism since techné and physis shared a common origin."[32] Again, we would need to hear which features of Miki's putative organicism made the good Marxist go so totalitarian.

Although the climax of Harootunian's discussion begins hesitantly with yet another admission of Miki's distaste for fascism (almost as if made for television, with fair and balanced presentations), it immediately turns unequivocally assertive:

> He often sought to distance himself from historic fascisms . . . even as his analysis of Japan's modernity and his defence of imperialism led him to imagine an order that was just as fascistic, inasmuch as it sought to salvage capitalism and the folk which had been estranged from it in its original form as an organic community. A "modern gemeinschaft" propelled by technological rationality and an organicist folk cooperativeness was simply another name for fascist political totalism.[33]

As if to set a seal of validity on this preposterous claim, the next phrase reads (as the title of the chapter's last section) "Folkism and the Specter of Fascism"—though there is no further discussion of Miki or his work.

We might call Harootunian's method here "the Don Basilio approach," after the character in Rossini's *Barber of Seville* who sings famously of the insidious power of *la calunnia* (slander).[34] Slander should be initiated as "a tiny breeze, a gentle little zephyr, which insensibly, subtly, gently, sweetly begins to whisper," becoming "crescendo, gathering force little by little" until, growing like "the thunder of the storm rumbling in the depths of the forest," it finally "explodes with a crack and crash, like a cannon or an earthquake,"—*fortissimo: il fascismo!*

Over forty pages of text, Harootunian provides no evidence to support the bizarre conclusion that Miki's philosophy turned fascistic. To the minimal extent that there is an argument here, it consists of a travesty of the deconstructive method: Because Miki distanced himself from Heidegger's association with Nazism, he was deeply implicated in it; even though he seemed to remain true to Marxism and was repelled by European fascism, he actually supported the Japanese fascists; in short, because nothing overtly fascistic is to be found in Miki's political ideas, he was in fact advocating "fascist political totalism."

In the light of such a travesty of scholarly argument what is puzzling—and revelatory about the contemporary state of Japanese studies in the United States—is the admiration that *Overcome by Modernity* appears to have generated on the part of some major figures in the field.[35] Has ideology so permeated historical scholarship that reasoned argument on the basis of textual evidence has become *passé*? When the application of the "fascist" label to thinkers one dislikes has been shown to be unfounded, is it praiseworthy simply to ignore this awkward circumstance and go on doing the same thing at greater length?

Another version of the Don Basilio strategy, shorter and *mezzo piano,* is to be found in Goto-Jones's treatment of Miki in *Political Philosophy in Japan.* Here we learn at first that Miki is among those associates of Nishida who "disfigured themselves" (scare quotes in the original) "by explicitly placing solidarity before criticism, becoming 'professional' or 'bureaucratic' intellectuals."[36] We are told that Miki became "a central ideologue of Prince Konoe's New Order Movement," though we hear nothing about the kind of ideology he promoted there. A few pages later Goto-Jones plays the Heidegger card: "In the late 1930s/early 1940s, Miki executed an about face, a 'turn' toward endorsement of the state paralleled by Heidegger's coincident 'turn' in Germany."[37] If the second "turn" here refers to Heidegger's famous (and perhaps never accomplished) *Kehre,* it is not toward endorsement of the state but toward the thinking of Being; if it refers to his earlier involvement with National Socialism, it disregards the fact that Miki became critical of Heidegger as a result of that turn of events in 1933.[38] But now that the mention of Heidegger has presumably triggered the idea of "fascism" in the minds of the *cognoscenti,* there comes, on the next page, the crescendo:

Miki argued [in an essay titled "Principles of New Japanese Thought"] that Japan's unique ability to unite Asia rested on its history of assimilating foreign (Chinese) culture, giving it the understanding to instigate a *kyōdōtai* (cooperative body) in East Asia. Japan's assimilation of Western technology gave it the power necessary to expel the West from China, which was crucial before a peaceful *kyōdōtai* could be established on the principles of cooperativism (*kyōdōshugi*), which he envisioned as an Asian alternative to socialism and liberalism.[39]

So far, so good. Japan had certainly assimilated foreign cultures more comprehensively than any other nation in East Asia, which might well justify a leadership role. And it was certainly the only nation in the region with sufficient military strength to stand a chance of ousting the Western powers from China: A laudable enough aim—except for die-hard imperialists who think the Western powers had some legitimate business in occupying the Central Kingdom. But then, after adding that "much of Miki's language appeared in Prime Minister Konoe's proclamation of the new world order in East Asia" (though without saying exactly what language or specifying its political tenor), Goto-Jones clinches the argument with a startling *non sequitur:* "With Miki, a strand of the Kyoto School is securely woven into fascist thread." Now that this has been established, he is free to drop a remark, in a later footnote, about "Miki's fascist standpoint."[40] But as with Harootunian, the "fascist" label is applied on the basis of nothing in the way of evidence but simply on the claims that Miki had "disfigured himself" as an intellectual, made a Heidegger-like "turn" toward endorsement of the state, and promoted an Asian alternative to socialism and liberalism. But in Asia, as elsewhere, there are ways for intellectuals to disfigure themselves, and to endorse the state, and to pose alternatives to socialism and liberalism, that have nothing whatever to do with fascism.

It is unlikely that Goto-Jones deliberately set out to condemn Miki as a fascist thinker, insofar as the latter is a peripheral figure in *Political Philosophy in Japan* who stands in "Nishida's shadow" as a Kyoto "Rebel." But the insouciance with which Goto-Jones applies the fascist label to Miki (by contrast with his careful and measured exposition of Nishida's political philosophy) suggests that the Harootunian ideology is taking hold in the European academy too.

4

The glad tidings were apparently brought to the shores of Albion a couple of years earlier, by Stella Sandford's article "Going Back: Heidegger, East Asia and 'the West,'" which was published in *Radical Philosophy* in 2003. The opening paragraph begins by invoking Heidegger's influence on Miki, Nishitani, Tanabe, and Kuki.[41] But when Sandford goes on to claim that Miki was the only one, and the only Marxist, to seriously criticize Heidegger after 1933, she goes astray. The philosopher Tosaka Jun was a more committed Marxist than Miki, and he criticized Heidegger often.[42] More importantly, Miki was not alone in criticizing Heidegger for the infamous Rectoral Address. In September 1933 (shortly before Miki's criticisms were published) Tanabe wrote a commentary on "The Self-Assertion of the German University" in which he criticized Heidegger's "championing of the racial significance of German academia."[43] But then Sandford closes the paragraph with a topic sentence making this breathtaking assertion: "The most influential reception of Heidegger's work fed into the philosophical justification of fascism in Japan, as Tanabe's writings in particular show."[44] And where does one learn about this philosophical justification of fascism in Japan? The endnote cites two sources: for Miki, it is the chapter in Harootunian's *Overcome by Modernity,* just discussed and found less than reliable; and for Tanabe, it is an essay by Naoki Sakai titled "Ethnicity and Species."[45]

The impression that the philosophical justification of fascism is going to be a major theme in Sandford's essay is reinforced in the last paragraph of her introduction, where we read that the comparative literature on Heidegger is misleading insofar as it "facilitates the repression of the history of Heideggerian fascism in modern East-Asian, and particularly Japanese, thought." Her fantasy is farther-reaching than Harootunian's: Heidegger's pernicious influence has now apparently spread to fascists in China and Korea as well. Readers keen to learn the identities of these East-Asian fascists who were influenced by Heidegger will be disappointed, since no sources are cited for this expansionist claim. Then, strangely, what appeared to be a key topic—the way "Heidegger's work fed into the philosophical justification of fascism in Japan"—simply disappears from the essay until one page before the end, where Sandford again deplores a supposed "silence on the fascist reception of Heidegger in Japan."[46] That this framing assertion of a Heideggerian fascism in Japan should enclose nothing in the way of justification, or even discussion, shows just how powerful the invocation of Harootunian is expected to be. But non-believers will want to be pointed to the specific Kyoto School texts that go beyond nationalism, patriotism, and militarism as far as "philosophical justifications of fascism"—and to the respects in which these show the influence of Heidegger.

It is strange that Sandford should cite Sakai's essay on Tanabe as a justification for her claim that Heidegger's work fed into the philosophical justification of fascism in Japan, since nowhere in that essay is there any discussion of fascism *or* Heidegger.[47] But in case Sakai does address these topics but indirectly, between the lines as it were, we should examine the argument of "Ethnicity and Species," since it might turn out to be an indictment of Tanabe's Heideggerian fascism after all. The essay is a critical exposition of such ideas as ethnicity and subjectivity as articulated in a series of essays that Tanabe published during the period from 1932 to 1946, and which were eventually collected under the title *Logic of Species.* Sakai also criticizes an infamous lecture Tanabe delivered at Kyoto Imperial University in 1943, "Death and Life," and for which he later expressed profound regret. He sums up the main thrust of the lecture as follows: "Having anticipatorily put oneself on the side of death, and thereby secured one's loyalty to the country, one could in fact transform or even rebel against the existing state under the guidance of the universal idea."[48] Sakai adds that Tanabe was somewhat naive in failing to see that his argument "could easily be distorted or appropriated to serve unintended political interests." Fair enough—but it is hard to imagine the leaders of a fascist state agreeing that their subjects might be justified in "rebelling against the government at any time."

A similar idea is prominent in the *Logic of Species,* where it is clear that "the nation-state is primarily and essentially something to which the individual *chooses* to belong," and where this belonging must be "mediated" by the individual's *"freedom."*[49] For Tanabe, the individual only truly belongs to the nation-state when it tries, as Sakai puts it, to "negate and change it," when it "distances itself" from it, "actively transforming it, according to the dictates of universal humanity."[50] Or, in Tanabe's own words:

> Membership in the state should not demand that the individual sacrifice all its freedom and autonomy for the sake of the unity of the species [in Tanabe's sense of the nation-state]. On the contrary, the proposition would not make sense unless the state appropriates into itself individual freedom as its essential moment.[51]

Sakai then draws the conclusion: "Therefore the view which equates the nation-state with one ethnic community cannot be accepted at all"—whence Tanabe's promotion of the "multi-ethnic state" of Sakai's subtitle. Again, these are hardly ideas that would have delighted the fascists in Japan, or in Europe for that matter—so it remains a mystery why Sandford should think that

"Tanabe's writings in particular show" that the reception of Heidegger's work "fed into the philosophical justification of fascism in Japan."

While Sandford elsewhere in her article makes a valid criticism or two of some of the "comparative literature" on Heidegger, her complaints that commentators (and especially Parkes) have naively overlooked Heidegger's Eurocentrism, nationalism, and association with Nazism, and so have been silent about "the fascist reception of Heidegger in Japan," are groundless.[52] It is true that I have not denounced the fascist reception of Heidegger in Japan, but this is only because the existence of such a phenomenon has never been demonstrated.[53] On the topics of Heidegger's nationalism and putative influence on Japanese fascism, however, I had already published two articles in places where anyone doing research on the comparative literature on Heidegger would easily have found them.[54] So why does Sandford, whose research seems to have been thorough in other respects, fail to take these into account? Either she ignores them because they undermine her main thesis, or else her infatuation with Harootunian's work has blinded her to the existence of anything that contradicts it. In any case, her essay is evidence that Harootunian's strategy of relentless assertion of his ideological position, combined with complete silence in response to criticism and adamant refusal to engage in dialogue with dissenters, is working quite well on the British side of the Atlantic.

After making sure that *Radical Philosophy* was prepared to accept a response to Sandford's article, I submitted a lengthy refutation which pointed out that, among other things, she had misrepresented and criticized my work on the basis of a reading which omitted key contributions such as the "Putative Fascism" essay. The "Editorial Collective" at *Radical Philosophy* (which does not deign to send submissions out for external review, and of which Sandford is a member) turned it down. I sent in a revised version that responded to the few valid minor criticisms they had made, and that was also turned down, again without any attempt to respond to the main arguments.[55]

What we have here is a continuation of the Harootunian strategy of silencing the opposition by pretending it does not exist, and so far it seems to be catching on in the United Kingdom. The reasons for being concerned about this still hold: Prospective students of the Kyoto School thinkers continue to be put off studying them by reading first that they are fascist ideologues, just as Heidegger's involvement with the Nazis justifies not bothering to read his works. The political philosophies of these thinkers continue to be relevant today, even if they contain features that we find disconcerting or distasteful.

These things need to be discussed—especially since fascism is still with us, in pockets of virulence all over the world. It helps to acknowledge the decisive ideas and conditions motivating fascist activity and to correctly identify their sources. It is a distraction to expose and condemn as fascist ideas that are not fascistic—and it is time, instead, to devote our energies to the central tasks of careful inquiry and responsible critique.

NOTES

An earlier version of this essay was published in the journal *Pli* 20 (2009): 226–48, and I thank the editors for their permission to publish a revised version here. Thanks also to Bradley Park, who offered some helpful comments on the initial draft.

1. Tetsuo Najita and H. D. Harootunian, "Japanese Revolt against the West: Political and Cultural Criticism in the Twentieth Century," in Peter Duus, ed., *The Cambridge History of Japan* (Cambridge: Cambridge University Press, 1993), 6: 741–42; Harry Harootunian, *Overcome by Modernity: History, Culture, and Community in Interwar Japan* (Princeton, N.J., and Oxford: Princeton University Press, 2000), 359ff.

2. Peter N. Dale, *The Myth of Japanese Uniqueness* (London: Croom Helm, 1986); Bernard Faure, *Chan Insights and Oversights: An Epistemological Critique of the Chan Tradition* (Princeton, N.J.: Princeton University Press, 1993); Leslie Pincus, *Authenticating Culture in Imperial Japan: Kuki Shūzō and the Rise of National Aesthetics* (Berkeley: University of California Press, 1996); and a journal article by Stella Sandford, "Going Back: Heidegger, East Asia and 'the West,'" *Radical Philosophy* 120 (July/August 2003): 11–22.

3. Graham Parkes, "The Putative Fascism of the Kyoto School and the Political Correctness of the Modern Academy," *Philosophy East and West* 47, no. 3 (1997): 305–36.

4. See the discussions of Nishida in Christopher S. Goto-Jones, *Political Philosophy in Japan: Nishida, the Kyoto School, and Co-Prosperity* (London: Routledge, 2005); also Graham Parkes, "The Definite Internationalism of the Kyoto School," in Christopher Goto-Jones, ed., *Re-Politicising the Kyoto School as Philosophy* (London and New York: Routledge, 2008), 161–82.

5. David Williams, *Defending Japan's Pacific War: The Kyoto School Philosophers and post-White Power* (London and New York: RoutledgeCurzon, 2004), esp. 92–116. This book also contains a translation by Williams of Tanabe's essay "On the Logic of Co-prosperity Spheres: Toward a Philosophy of Regional Blocs."

6. See Parkes, "The Definite Internationalism of the Kyoto School," 164–70.

7. Horio Tsutomu, "The *Chūōkōron* Discussions, Their Background and Meaning," in James W. Heisig and John C. Maraldo, eds., *Rude Awakenings: Zen, the Kyoto School, and the Question of Nationalism* (Honolulu: University of Hawai'i Press, 1995), 301–302.

8. Horio, "The *Chūōkōron* Discussions," 291, 303.

9. See Williams, *Defending Japan's Pacific War,* 147. John Maraldo criticizes Williams's characterization of *Rude Awakenings* in his review of *Defending Japan's Pacific*

War and Christopher Goto-Jones's *Political Philosophy in Japan*, "The War over the Kyoto School," *Monumenta Nipponica* 61, no. 3 (2006): 375–406.

10. By contrast with this silence, a Japanese translation of the "Putative Fascism" essay, "Kyōto-gakuha to 'fuashizumu' no retteru: gendai Amerika ni okeru kado na 'seijiteki na tadashisa' no mondai," was published in the journal *Zengaku kenkyū* 81 (Kyoto, 2002), and was reprinted in Fujita Masakatsu and Bret W. Davis, eds., *Sekai no naka Nihon no tetsugaku* (Kyoto: Shōwadō, 2005).

Several important studies have appeared that give a clearer picture of the political philosophy of Nishida and other Kyoto School thinkers, and one that confirms the essay's premises: Michiko Yusa, *Zen and Philosophy: An Intellectual Biography of Nishida Kitarō* (Honolulu: University of Hawai'i Press, 2002); David Williams, *Defending Japan's Pacific War* (2004); Christopher Goto-Jones, *Political Philosophy in Japan* (2005); and Hiroshi Nara et al., *The Structure of Detachment: The Aesthetic Vision of Kuki Shūzō* (Honolulu: University of Hawai'i Press, 2005).

11. Bob Tadashi Wakabayashi, ed., *Modern Japanese Thought* (Cambridge: Cambridge University Press, 1998).

12. Harry Harootunian and Naoki Sakai, "Japan Studies and Cultural Studies," *positions: east asia cultures critique* 7, no. 2 (1999): 593–647.

13. Ibid., 606–608.

14. Ibid., 611; my emphasis.

15. Nietzsche, *Werke: Kritische Studienausgabe,* 12: 315; *The Will to Power,* §481.

16. Ron Suskind, "Faith, Certainty and the Presidency of George W. Bush," *The New York Times Magazine,* 17 October 2004.

17. For a more detailed explication of will to power as interpretation, see the translator's introduction to Nietzsche's *Thus Spoke Zarathustra,* trans. Graham Parkes (Oxford and New York: Oxford University Press, 2005), xx–xxii.

18. Harootunian, *Overcome by Modernity,* xxxiii.

19. Ibid., 41.

20. Ibid., 421.

21. Williams, *Defending Japan's Pacific War,* chap. 4.

22. Harootunian, *Overcome by Modernity,* xxxii.

23. Ibid., 365.

24. Ibid., 359.

25. Ibid., 359–60.

26. The text is rife with syntactically challenged sentences and orthographic oddities. The attentive reader will be especially baffled by the discussion of Miki's "theory of action through 'poises'" (a misprint for "poses"?) until much later when the word appears italicized and is associated with the Greek *technē*—which confirms that Miki (if not Harootunian) is talking about *poiēsis* (360, 387). Numerous similar errors mar the text. Harootunian's frequent discussions of Heidegger undermine themselves by conflating Heidegger's fundamental distinctions between Being and beings (*Sein und Seiendes:* what he calls "the ontological difference") and between Being and Dasein.

27. Harootunian, *Overcome by Modernity,* 390–91.

28. Leslie Pincus, *Authenticating Culture in Japan: Kuki Shūzō and the Rise of National Aesthetics* (Berkeley: University of California Press, 1996), 55. See the discussion of this mistranslation and its consequences in my "The Definite Internationalism of the Kyoto School," 164–70, and in the context of Nishida and Tanabe, in Williams, *Defending Japan's Pacific War,* 160.

29. Harootunian, *Overcome by Modernity,* 395.

30. See my discussion in "The Definite Internationalism of the Kyoto School," 172–75.

31. Harootunian, *Overcome by Modernity*, 397.

32. Ibid., 398.

33. Ibid., 398–99.

34. "La calunnia è un venticello" in Rossini's *Il barbiere di Siviglia*, act I, aria 6.

35. See the endorsements and excerpts from reviews on the Princeton University Press website: http://press.princeton.edu/titles/6954.html. On the contrast between the current state of Japanese studies in the United States and in Europe, see Williams, 46–49.

36. Goto-Jones, *Political Philosophy in Japan*, 98.

37. Ibid., 104–105.

38. See Miki's essay of November 1933, "Haideggaa to tetsugaku no unmei" [Heidegger and the fate of philosophy], in *Miki Kiyoshi zenshū*, 10: 310–20.

39. Goto-Jones, *Political Philosophy in Japan*, 106.

40. Ibid., 168 n. 4.

41. Sandford, "Going Back," 11, drawing (with acknowledgment) on some of my work.

42. Sadly little of Tosaka's work has been translated into English, but see the selections in David A. Dilworth and Valdo H. Viglielmo, trans. and eds., with Agustin Jacinto Zavala, *Sourcebook for Modern Japanese Philosophy: Selected Documents* (Westport, Conn., and London: Greenwood Press, 1998), 330–71.

43. Graham Parkes, "Rising Sun over Black Forest," note 13, in Reinhard May, *Heidegger's Hidden Sources: East-Asian Influences on His Work*, trans. with an essay by Graham Parkes (London: Routledge, 1996), 109. In the meantime an English translation of Tanabe's essay has appeared in David Williams, *Defending Japan's Pacific War*, 181–87; see also Williams's account of Tanabe's essay, 114–16.

44. Sandford, "Going Back," 11.

45. Ibid., 11 n. 3, 20, which cites Naoki Sakai, "Ethnicity and Species: On the Philosophy of the Multi-Ethnic State in Japanese Imperialism," *Radical Philosophy* 95 (May/June 1999), and Harootunian, *Overcome by Modernity*, 358–414.

46. Sandford, "Going Back," 19.

47. The exception is that at one point in his exposition Sakai resorts to the Heideggerian terms *Geworfenheit* and *Entwurf*, and in an endnote he mentions Tanabe's criticism of Heidegger for failing "to recognize the spatiality of social practice" ("Ethnicity and Species," 39, and n. 24).

48. Sakai, "Ethnicity and Species," 35.

49. Ibid., 35.

50. Ibid., 39–40.

51. Tanabe, "The Logic of Social Ontology," cit. Sakai, "Ethnicity and Species," 41.

52. Sandford, "Going Back," 17–19.

53. For discussions of the receptions of Heidegger's philosophy in Japan, see Parkes, *Heidegger and Asian Thought*, 9–11, and "Rising Sun over Black Forest," 80–81.

54. Six years before "The Putative Fascism of the Kyoto School" appeared, I published "Between Nationalism and Nomadism: Wondering about the Languages of Philosophy," in Eliot Deutsch, ed., *Culture and Modernity: East-West Philosophic Perspectives* (Honolulu: University of Hawai'i Press, 1991), 455–67, in which I criticize Heidegger's nationalism and unfavorably compare his obsessive attachment to a par-

ticular plot of soil with Nietzsche's nomadic and cosmopolitan commitment to "stay true to the earth."

55. See section 5 of a longer version of this essay in James W. Heisig, ed., *Frontiers in Japanese Philosophy* (Nagoya, Japan: Nanzan Institute for Religion and Culture, 2009), 6: 335–60; online at http://www.nanzan-u.ac.jp/SHUBUNKEN/publications/EJPhilosophy/EssaysInJapanesePhil.htm.

PART FIVE

Grammar, Art, and Imagination

15

The Middle Voice
of Emptiness:
Nishida and Nishitani

Rolf Elberfeld

The following attempt to make fruitful a grammatical distinction in Classical Greek and its interpretation relative to the meaning of modern philosophical approaches in Japan is fraught with certain difficulties. In a preliminary fashion, the grammatical form of the middle voice in Classical Greek must first be introduced. In so doing, it will be necessary to interrogate the common interpretations of the middle voice in relation to their implicit philosophical assumptions. These considerations will serve as preparation for posing the question of the middle voice in Japanese. It will be demonstrated that, indeed, in a certain sense, one can speak of the middle voice in Japanese, although in a manner that in significant aspects differs from the one in Classical Greek. After the middle voice and the problem of its application in Japanese have been discussed, the question concerning the middle voice in the philosophy of Nishida, as well as in that of his student, Nishitani, can be posed. In conclusion, there will be a cursory examination of three Western thinkers—William James, Martin Heidegger, Jacques Derrida—who refer directly to the middle voice. In this manner, affinities in thinking between very distinctive philosophical traditions become clear as they cluster themselves around the question concerning the middle voice and its significance for the language of philosophy. Through the retrieval of a grammatical form and its interpretation, a horizon of understanding should open up for basic philosophical approaches that no longer allow themselves to be pigeonholed in the all too facile opposition of Western and Eastern thinking.

The Middle Voice

In the classical European languages, the middle voice as a complete grammatical form and as a descriptive form is found only in Classical Greek. In translations from the latter, the middle voice is for the most part only rendered if a reflexive form is possible, so that from the perspective of either German or English, it appears as a reflexive form. Accordingly, the standard example is *Ich wasche mich* or "I wash myself" (Gr. *louomai*). In this statement, I am simultaneously the subject and the object of the action. Provisionally stated, the middle voice is thus deployed as the form of an action whenever a process does not occur with a clear separation of subject and object.

> The middle voice designates the enhanced internal and external participation of a subject in a process. Almost all of the apparent forms of the middle voice reduce to the following five fundamental types of application; however, a strict separation between them is not always possible. The *direct middle voice* designates an action, which the subject directs immediately toward her or himself (reflexive middle voice). The *indirect middle voice* designates an action, which the subject exercises for her or himself in his or her interest (dative middle voice). The *reciprocal middle voice* designates an action, which the subject performs with other persons with mutual devotion. The *dynamic middle voice* designates an action, which the subject executes with the mobilization of her or his forces and means or in an immediately practical action. The *causative middle voice* designates an action, which the subject lets happen either for itself or in itself. (Some verbs only appear in the middle voice, but do not have any immediately recognizable medial sense for us, for example, *epomai* (I follow) and *gignomai* (I grow).)[1]

The author begins here with the definition as it originates in the action of the subject. The first sentence acts thereby like a fundamental definition of the middle voice. The explanations then all originate from a single subject, so that all of the example sentences can be cited in the first-person singular. But if one were, as an example of the middle voice, to enlist not *ich freue mich* (I am pleased)[2] (Gr. *terpomai*) but rather *wir freuen uns* (we are pleased) (Gr. *terpometha*), the explanation that in the direct middle voice the subject refers back to her- or himself would not be insightful, for the situation in which *wir freuen uns* (we are pleased) would hardly be able to be described in this way.

In the paragraph quoted above concerning the explanation of the middle voice, examples are cited in which it is not really clear why they could only be found in the middle voice. For the interpretation of these medial forms cannot be brought into congruity with the aforementioned explanations. But if one were to consider the Greek word *gignomai*, for instance, more closely, it indeed makes a lot of sense that this verb can only be used in the middle voice.

The two basic meanings of the word *gignomai* are: 1. To attain existence, to originate; (a) said of humans, being generated or born, (b) said of inanimate things, originate, become, happen, occur. 2. To attain a state, become something. Now both of these basic meanings, "originate" and "become," indicate that whatever is to become something is something first of all only in origination and is consequentially not yet there. With reference to the subject, it can also consequently not be said what it is and what it will be. In the cases of "origination" and "becoming," it is not yet clear at the beginning of the process what will finally come out of the process. It is therefore thoroughly illuminating to conceive this happening only in the middle voice, since there exists neither a clear center of activity, nor a merely passive one. For whenever a tree grows, it is itself the growing; it is simultaneously active and passive.

At this point, a further word can be introduced, which, in its verbal form, can only be found in Classical Greek in the middle voice, and which has a special meaning when considered in a philosophical context. This word is *aisthanomai:* "I perceive with the senses." Why does it make sense to render the process of perception exclusively in the middle voice? In conventional explanations, perception is understood either as something purely passive in the sense of a mere taking-in of data or, in more modern times, as a purely active comportment, in which data is constructed by and as the perspective of the subject. If one pursues perception in its fullness more precisely, it indicates that it is neither a purely passive nor a purely active process. It is on the contrary the *founding of a relationship* between the perceiving and the perceived, in which both sides are as active as they are passive. For the perceived is always reflected in the perceiving and the perceiver takes it up and associates it with its context. A place of perception arises here, out of which both the perceiving as well as the perceived come to the fore in the subtlest interplay in the sense of the middle voice.

The Middle Voice in Japanese

The Japanese language possesses a grammaticalized form for the middle voice, which in modern grammars, presumably under the influence of Latin-centric grammar paradigms, is no longer described as such. It is, however, consistently accepted for the grammar of Classical Japanese:[3]

> The middle voice in Japanese in a formal and semantic sense is very close to the passive, in which it indicates a verbally designated process or state, by which the subject is affected, without, however, being caused by an agent, no matter

whether through their own intuition or not. . . . The medial forms of Japanese are ancient and are detectable since the beginning of the literary tradition.[4]

This description of the middle voice, cited from a German Japanologist, shows that here the explanation of the middle voice from the Classical Greek is in effect. The being-affected of the subject in a process or state is explained as the semantic content of the middle voice. The final part of the sentence, however, brings a turnaround in the description, which is not found in Classical Greek. With the statement that the middle voice in Japanese occurs "without being caused by an agent," that is, without subject and/or actor, it coalesces the explanation of the middle voice in Japanese with the question concerning the subject in the sentence. As is generally known, in Japanese, the subject can be dropped without further ado, for it does not stand in the center of the sentence. On the contrary, the happening and/or situation appears in the foreground, in a happening and/or situation in which the subject is not central, but rather the quality of the happening itself. Is there not consequently a contradiction between the part of the explanation in which an affected subject is spoken of and the part in which the middle voice occurs without being caused by an "agent"? The description suggests that a "subject" is presupposed, even when it does not appear in the sentence.

In order to clarify the implications of this manner of interpreting the middle voice in Japanese by way of starting from Classical Greek, a short comparative translation using an example from Classical Japanese literature will be conducted.

In the *Tsurezuregusa,* we find the following phrase: *fude wo toreba, mono kakare.* Taken separately, the individual words here mean the following: *fude* = a "brush" used for writing; *wo* = an accusative particle; *toreba* = "to grasp" or "take" in the conditional form; *mono* = "the matter at hand" (Gn. *Sache*), a thing; *kakare* = "to write" in the grammatical form of the middle voice. No grammatical subject is named in the sentence.

The Japanologist cited above translates the sentence with explicit reference to the description of the middle voice in Classical Greek: "When I clasp the brush, *I (for myself) jot something down.*"[5] In this translation, the reflexive in relation to the subject of the writing is added parenthetically. Presumably, the translator thought of the direct or indirect middle voice in Classical Greek, in which an activity refers back to an actor and/or is performed in the interest of the actor. The "I" as subject is inserted into the first clause, and it is added as well to the verb "to write."

The following sentence provides another translation: "One grasps the brush, and the desire to write sets itself into action."[6] In the first part, instead of naming an "I" as subject, the indefinite pronoun "one" is moved into the subject position, so that the sentence becomes a more universal statement. In the second clause, the middle voice is interpreted in the sense of the dynamic middle voice because the "desire," which is not named in the Japanese sentence, is supposed to bring to expression a particular stake of the process via the subject. The "matter at hand," which is written, drops out of the sentence in the translation.

Before an alternative translation can be given, the middle voice in Japanese must first be explained from the perspective of the Japanese language itself. The following citation comes from a Japanese grammarian, who does not interpret the middle voice of Classical Japanese within the horizon of Classical Greek. Accordingly, the middle voice in Japanese is said to have four distinctive levels of meaning:

1. Spontaneity, an action which occurs without prior intention. (In this sense *ru, raru* shows that a certain action occurs naturally, or a certain condition naturally arises. The original meaning of *ru, raru* was spontaneity, and the other meanings developed from it.)
2. Passive voice. (This passive shows that a certain action is suffered from another person and as a general rule it is used only for people and animals.)
3. Potential. (In this sense the ending shows that a certain action is possible. In the Heian Period *ru, raru* was used with the negative auxiliary verb *zu*, when it expressed potential; but with the arrival of the Kamakura period it was used independently. It is important to note that the potential meaning also includes the sense that a condition naturally arises (spontaneity).)
4. Respect. (It is used to show respect with regard to the action of the person who is the topic of a sentence. . . . *Ru, raru* did not express respect until the Heian Period when many respectful usages were developed.)[7]

The basic meaning of the middle voice, according to this explanation, is the "spontaneity" of an action that occurs in a natural fashion. In the explanation, no word is lost concerning the subject that is affected by the action or something similar. The description puts the quality of the action itself directly in the center and stresses that it is from this basic meaning that the three other meanings are derived. Consequently, the middle voice in Classical Japanese combines in itself four distinctive levels of meaning, all of which interplay and which still obtain today.[8] The first and oldest meaning of the middle voice is an action that acts from itself and in this sense arises naturally. In Japanese, this level of meaning is designated by *jihatsu*, literally, "to come forward from itself." With this explanation, in the description of the middle voice, above all, the self-referentiality of an action appears in the center, and no explicit reference is made to a subject that is affected in the process.

While in the explanation of the middle voice within the framework of European traditions, the subject and its affectivity stood foremost in the center, in the explanation of the middle voice within the horizon of the Sino-Japanese traditions, self-referentiality in the form of a natural happening clearly stands at the center of attention. This difference arises because the middle voice itself, through linguistic habits, and, most of all, through the use of the subject (both grammatical and logical), receives a different emphasis in the respective languages. It is, above all, the status of the subject that the verbal form of the Japanese middle voice can cast new light on.

Proceeding from this explanation of the middle voice in Japanese, an alternative translation of the phrase from the *Tsurezuregusa* can be attempted: "Clasping the brush the writing of something sets itself into action from itself." The word *kakare* designates an attunement of the writing in which, without clear intention, something writes itself down, and by which the writer her- or himself can be afterwards surprised. If one takes the description of the middle voice in the sense of a spontaneous occurrence seriously, then on the one hand, the naming of a subject should be avoided, and on the other, the "from itself" of the occurrence should be stressed. Since in this translation the writing person does not become the subject, which is rather the writing, at least the occurrence of the writing itself can be moved into the foreground.

It belongs to the ironies of linguistic history that the middle voice up to today remains very lively in Japanese, but under the influence of European grammar studies since the Meiji Period, it is hardly ever still described as the middle voice. It is still in linguistic usage and, above all, it is very vital in one's feeling for the language (Gn. *Sprachgefühl*). Matters are exacerbated by the fact that the grammatical category "middle voice" too comes from Europe. Here linguistic usage, grammatical explanation, and philosophical interpretation seem to be hopelessly entangled. In order still to press ahead with the philosophical explanation of the middle voice in Japanese, it now appears sensible to bring contemporary Japanese philosophy into play.

The Middle Voice in Contemporary Japanese Philosophy: Nishida and Nishitani

The thinking of Nishida and Nishitani can be read in a certain respect as a thoughtful development of the middle voice, even though neither thinker speaks explicitly about this grammatical form. This is the central thesis that will be pursued in what follows.

Already the opening passage in Nishida's *An Inquiry into the Good* can be read as a description of the form of an action that comes very close to the middle voice in the sense of *jihatsu*.[9] Nishida here characterizes the basic form of experience, out of which all further conscious determinations first emerge. It is a matter of a form of experience that does not assume the division of subject and object. As paradigmatic situations for this experience, Nishida mentions the seeing of a color and the hearing of a sound. If one hears a sound without any intentions or interpretations, then only the sounding of the sound enters the foreground. In the sounding, an animated space of reference spreads out in which the hearer and the source of the hearing are encompassed. For Nishida, it is important that in this form of experience the ego has not yet emerged. From the perspective of Europe and a conventional explanation of experience, this is rather extraordinary. Is it not precisely the "I," proceeding from which all experience is made, that must accompany all of my representations? What was only suggested by the explanation of the small example from the *Tsurezuregusa* can be comprehended in many literary testimonies in Japanese—namely, the possibility of grammatically correct *subjectless sentences*. Hence, the Nishida passage just referred to does not concern mystical ecstasy, but rather a form of experience that is suggested by the Japanese language. In the latter, the subject can be dropped without further ado and, moreover, the middle voice can determine the expression at multiple levels. The omission of the subject is actually nothing special, but rather the *normal case* for the perception of a happening. Nishida proceeds from this form of experience and develops a philosophizing that time and again links itself back to this "subjectless" action in the sense of the middle voice.

We find a similar constellation in the thought of Nishitani Keiji. He developed Nishida's thinking further in a certain direction, particularly against the background of Zen Buddhist experience, and describes "pure experience" on the concrete level of sensibility. In the essay "On Awareness" (*kaku ni tsuite*), he writes the following about seeing and hearing:

In the originary place that so-called sensibility brings about, that is, in the place of appearing wherein sensibility in its pure simplicity first originates just as it is, there is no distinction between the sensing "something" and the sensed "something." The activity of seeing is immediately one with the being visible [*mieru to iu koto*] of the thing and the activity of hearing is immediately one with the being audible [*kikoeru to iu koto*] of the sound. As said earlier, subject and object are undivided, or thing and ego forget one another, and this refers to this place. We say, "the sea is visible" or "the bell is audible." In these cases, "visible" [*ga mieru*] is something other than either "to see" [*wo miru*] the sea, or the sea "is seen" [*ga mirareru*]. On the contrary, it expresses both sides as inseparably unified. (NKC 13: 106)

Nishitani can, in order to bring his thoughts to expression, refer directly to the medial forms *mieru* and *kikoeru*, presumably without its thereby being known to him that he is using the middle voice. Similar to the opening passage in the Nishida text, it is a matter of describing a place in which the seeing and the seen would arise in an action without the occurence of a subject-object split.

At this point it could be objected that the form of experience in which the middle voice comes to expression constitutes an important point of departure for Nishida's philosophy and Nishitani's philosophy, and therewith their thinking itself is described, but not yet as philosophy. The question posed is thus whether the middle voice and the form of action therewith coming to expression are of central meaning for both of their philosophies and perhaps for the determination of philosophy itself. In order to pursue this question, some further information concerning the Japanese language will first be pursued.

Today there is a still common Japanese word that is in the middle voice: *omoeru*. Its translation into either German or English does not come easily. In the end, we must rely on the reflexive and an "it" so that it can thus be translated: *es denkt mir* or "it thinks to me."[10] This form is clearly distinguished from the form *omou*, which is translated in a context-dependent fashion as "I think" or "you think," etc. But what can the medial form "it thinks to me" mean? If one proceeds from the determination of the middle voice in Japanese given above, then several levels can be in play in the word *omoeru*. Firstly, a thought can emerge in me entirely "of itself," without it being the case that "I" would have "thought it up" in me. In German there is the phrase *mir kommt ein Gedanke* (to me a thought comes), which is used whenever I have a good idea that rather unexpectedly surfaces. A thinking that emerges from itself can consequently even be a creative thinking. Secondly, if a thought comes in this form, then a possibility in thinking becomes clear that heretofore had not yet been thought.[11] These considerations are certainly not known in quotidian linguistic usage, but they indicate a possible action quality of thinking that is critical to the further interpretation of Nishida's thinking.

In the text *Poiesis and Praxis*, Nishida speaks about the phrase *mono to natte kangae mono to natte okonau*. Here it reads:

> The phrase, "to become the matter at hand and think, to become the matter at hand and act," is taken by many people to be something intuitive and illogical. This happens because the Eastern spirit is explained as something illogical. We think, on the contrary, that "to become the matter at hand" must mean to become a state of affairs of the historical world. . . . To become the matter at hand and think, to become the matter at hand and act, must mean to act simultaneously poietically and practically, historically and naturally. (NKZ 10: 158)

Nishida means that when we "become the matter at hand" we thoughtfully and actively enter into the process of historical formation. But this entering is neither simply passive nor simply active. One could here say, in the sense of the logic of place, that it is a process that, above all, comes to expression in the first meaning of the middle voice. The place of historical formation is a process that comes to the fore from out of itself (Jp. *jihatsuteki*), in which all of the moments of the historical formation mutually drive each other forth into expression. Nowhere is an absolute center to be found, because everything is simultaneously in the reciprocal resonance of becoming determined and determining. The shared interpenetration of every moment is called a medial field; and this is what Nishida dubs the "logic of place" (*basho no ronri*). At this point, the question can be posed concerning the manner in which Nishida's own thinking is ordered. Is Nishida *thinking* in the middle voice?

There is, crucially, a word in a certain form that Nishida, already in *An Inquiry into the Good*, often employs and which he uses with increasing frequency in his later texts: *kagae-rare-ru*.[12] This word appears in various phrases: *kangae-rare-ru no de aru, kangae-rare-nakereba naranai, kangae-rare-ru mono de nakereba naranu*, etc.[13] The grammatical form of the words is usually explained either as potential ("to be able to think") or as passive ("is thought") because both possibilities evince the same grammatical suffix. If one looks back at the provenance of both forms, then, first and foremost, the Classical Japanese form of *jihatsu* lies in the background of both meanings. More than anything else, the following is valid for the potential form: "It is important to note that the potential meaning also includes the sense that a condition naturally arises (spontaneity)." Since the description of the modern Japanese language in, for example, German or English does not invoke the middle voice, all words, in which medial meanings still resonate, are assigned to either the potential or the passive form. In Nishida's texts, one cannot really decide if he always means the potential form or the passive form or always both together. But if one wants to disentangle oneself from this decision, then at least the perspective can be considered that Nishida's deployment of *kangae-rare-ru* also resonates in a medial meaning in the first sense. This explanation can perhaps be supported by the previously introduced example. Should that be the case, then this frees one up to see the action of thinking that characterizes Nishida's thought. *In this sense, Nishida does not think "something," but rather a thinking enables itself in him that comes to the fore of itself from out of the place of thinking.* This would precisely be the meaning of the middle voice with regard to thinking. "Thinking thinks itself in the place of thinking" (*Das Denken denkt sich selbst im Ort des Denkens*). Thinking thinking from itself has the consequence that thinking develops itself unremittingly. For without movement, thinking is not the thinking of thinking.

If one looks at Nishida's texts with this in mind, then the thesis begins to emerge that Nishida does not cover over this movement of thinking in his texts, but rather that he made the process-character of thinking itself the central *form* of his texts. In this sense, his predilection for the verb *kangae-rare-ru* allows itself to be understood from out of the manner of thinking and its literary realization. To put a finer point on it, the thesis can now read: Nishida thinks and writes in the middle voice.

It may indeed appear bold, but the phrase *fude wo toreba mono kakare*, cited above from the *Tsurezuregusa*, could be enlisted in order to interpret Nishida's manner of thinking and the forms of his texts. For Nishida's texts evince a form that scarcely has a parallel in the West. The fact alone that certain theses that are included at the beginning of a text in the thought process transform themselves by the end of the text demonstrates that it did not matter to Nishida to publish smooth and unitary texts in which the process of thinking could no longer be traced. Consequently, in his texts themselves, how the thinking and the thoughts originated can be followed and reproduced. This seems to me to be a central dimension of Nishida's thinking. For in this sense the texts are, as little as possible, objectifications in the form of propositions. They are rather exercises and traces of *thinking in its coming to the fore.* Moreover, the special quality achieved thereby is that at the beginning of a text its end cannot really be anticipated. The process of writing (and of reading) thus remains open, even in the sense that during the course of a text new words are introduced that had not yet belonged to Nishida's vocabulary at the beginning of the text. In this sense, the texts themselves are exercises of *jihatsu* and at the same time of *jikaku* (self-consciousness or becoming self-aware).

If the middle voice plays an important role for Nishida predominantly in relationship to the action of thinking, then for Nishitani the emphasis is shifted. Above all for Nishitani it is the realm of sensibility, in which the middle voice plays an important role. As has already become clear in the above quotation, *mieru* and *kikoeru* are medial forms of the verb *miru* (to see) and *kiku* (to hear). In his essay "On Awareness," Nishitani develops an interpretation of sensibility that simultaneously leads to the "place" (*tokoro*) out of which "I" here and now come to the fore as originary experience.

> In the place [*tokoro*] of the opening [*hirake*] in which the activity of the seeing of something and the self-showing [*miete kuru*] of something [that is, the being visible (*miete iru*)] are one, there is also included a kind of pattern of interconnection [*ri*]. In this place only the uniqueness and the unitary accord of the "here and now" prevails, both in relationship to the activity of the sense organs and in the states of affairs that correspond to them. It is the fully and concretely located [*kyokushoka*] place [*tokoro*]. The position that is always absolutely determined in the "here and now" is the position of the one-and-not-two. Sensory knowing originates in such a fully and concretely located place. For this reason, this knowing is an immediate knowing. It is a knowing that already knows before the origination of a concept or a representation, both of which are dependent on the "intellect." The state of affairs that originates in this position is "experience." This is what is at issue in so-called pure experience [*junsui keiken*] or immediate experience [*chokusetsu keiken*], which are the originary sense of experience. (NKC 13: 104)

Similar to the Classical Greek word *aisthanomai,* sensuous perception comes to expression exclusively in the middle voice, in which Nishitani evinces a vital and concrete place in which seeing and hearing eventuate as originary experience. At this level of experience, the ego and its intellectual capacities do not yet play a role. Rather, the intellectual ego develops from out of this level of experience, which in itself is already a form of knowing. The latter is in the highest sense concrete and always originating in the here and now. Nishitani emphasizes that this level of experience is not simply free of contextual interconnectedness, but rather itself contains a pattern of interconnection (Jp. *ri*). This pattern of interconnection can be described and it is not inferior to objective knowing. On the contrary, this level of experience grounds all of the others, and is, moreover, always and everywhere given.

> We catch sight of a beautiful and fragrant flower, and in the moment in which we forget ourselves and see the flower, we forget "ourselves"—in the flower. At the same time, the flower loses its manner of being as a mere thing or object before our eyes [cf. Heidegger's "objectively present": *vorhanden*] and it appears just as it is. This is the meaning of the saying, "The thing and I forget one another." From a quotidian perspective this experience is a special moment, but only because for us the form "I see a thing" has become the normal form of the perception of a thing. But in the case at hand, it is really sensibility that lies at the ground of perception, having already originated as immediate knowing in the original non-duality of subject and object. Only occasionally are we touched by the "beauty" of visible [*miete iru*] things, in which we leave the usual realm of perception behind us and turn towards the ground. Only there does sensibility emerge into appearance [*arawarete kita*] in its originary manner. In sensibility, the forgetting one another of ego and thing is really entirely natural and nothing special. Whenever we see something, we really always forget our "I" and see. (NKC 13: 107–108)

Nishitani emphasizes that our sensibility actually always occurs in the manner in which I and the thing have forgotten one another. Even though we almost constantly, through our intellect and will, combine other motives with this level of experience and overlay the latter with them, it remains for the most part concealed to us that we are always acting in this place and that we come to the fore from out of it. This place opens a world to us, for sensibility in its original manner is the standing-open of the world.[14] This standing open cannot be explained as either active or passive. On the contrary, the world opens itself beyond such crude lopsidedness. If originary sensuous openness is actually experienced, then it shows that I and thing, in this place of sensuous standing open, are empty. The emptiness that is experienced in the place of sensuously executed action is simultaneously both a concrete "here and now" and the highest insight into my own being as emptiness. The highest concretion here connects itself with the highest insight.

Neither for Nishida nor for Nishitani is the middle voice brought into play in a conscious manner as the linguistic form of philosophizing. Rather, it insinuates itself in their thinking because it has been available as a form of expression for ages in the Japanese language without needing to be explicitly problematized. But if one considers the central content of their thinking, then one can get the impression that it concerns the direct description of the middle voice. Even if, in what has been said above, an attempt has been made to highlight the middle voice as the central form of expression in the thinking of Nishida and Nishitani, the task still remains to expand this consideration to include other authors from older times as well as contemporary times. Furthermore, it is necessary to discuss the middle voice in Japanese in greater depth, developing both a grammatical and a philosophical perspective. The last section of this essay will show that these discussions could be meaningful for more than just the Japanese language and Japanese philosophy.

The Middle Voice in Contemporary Western Philosophy

In the following it will be shown, on the basis of three examples from philosophy in the English, German, and French languages respectively, how, in European and North American philosophy since the end of the nineteenth century, the middle voice has been increasingly rediscovered as a form of speech. William James, Martin Heidegger, and Jacques Derrida each happen upon, through specific ways of thinking, linguistic forms that, according to Heidegger and Derrida, are explicitly linked to the form of the middle voice.

The first example comes from James. At the end of the nineteenth century, in a time when psychology had still not decisively separated from philosophy to become a self-standing discipline, James wrote in the opening passage of his first main work, *Principles of Psychology* (1890), the following words, which are quite critical for the development of his own thinking:

> We now begin our study of the mind from within. . . . *The first fact for us, then, as psychologists, is that thinking of some sort goes on.* . . . If we say in English "it thinks," as we say "it rains" or "it blows," we should be stating the fact most simply and with the minimum of assumption. As we cannot, we must simply say the *thought goes on.*[15]

James struggles here to bring to expression in as simple terms as possible the simple fact that in us humans thoughts emerge and again disappear. He does so in order to make this the point of departure for the observation of and research into the human spirit. He uses the possibility "it thinks" to bring to language, in the simplest form of expression thinkable, the process which occurs more or less uninterrupted in us. James indeed names this possibility, but he rejects it with the argument that one could not say that in the English language. In the short quote just given, it becomes clear how certain thoughts and observations, should they be brought into language, demand again and again new grammatical rules and linguistic forms of expression. James wants to bring a level to expression that he dubs "pure experience,"[16] a state in which thoughts simply flow, without specifically being controlled by a subject. Hence, it is important to him in his formulation to avoid the subject in the statement, for the subject is not yet constituted, in the actual sense of the word, in the level he is naming here. James still did not have a special grammatical form for his thoughts, yet he sensed a lack and implied that he considered an "it phrase" to be fitting.[17]

In his epochal work *Being and Time*, Heidegger, in the wake of Classical Greek philosophy, attempts to move phenomenology, founded by Husserl at the beginning of the twentieth century, into a new perspective. For our present concerns, the derivation of the meaning of phenomenology from the Classical Greek language is above all significant. Concerning this, Heidegger writes:

> The Greek expression *phainomenon,* from which the term "phenomenon" derives, comes from the verb *phainesthai,* meaning "to show itself." Thus *phainomenon* means what shows itself, the self-showing, the manifest [*das Offenbare*]. *Phainesthai* itself is a "middle voice" construction of *phainō,* to bring into daylight, to place in brightness (§7, 28). . . . Hence phenomenology means: *apophainesthai ta phainomena*—to let what shows itself be seen from itself, just as it shows itself from itself. (§7, 34)[18]

Heidegger traces the word *phenomenon* back to its Classical Greek origin, where the *genus verbi* of the middle voice can still be found in its complete function. With the middle voice *phainesthai,* there is the middle voice that underlies Heidegger's explanation of the *whole of phenomenology.* "To show itself" and the "self showing" are structures that pertain to the level in which the subject as the one who knows an object has not yet been constituted. In the coming to the fore of the "self showing," there first originates a context out of which the various differences arise. Heidegger thereby begins not with the presupposition of subjects and objects, but rather attempts to show that this separation proceeds from "self showing" understood in the middle voice. It is from here that subjects and objects can receive their meaning. With Heidegger, the grammatical form of the middle voice becomes explicit as the basic form of his phenomenological thinking. But it cannot be decided at this point if the much-asserted proximity of Heideggerian thinking to East Asian traditions of thinking has any serious grounds.[19]

With Jacques Derrida one also finds a direct relationship to the middle voice in a central position. In his famous lecture "La différance," he connects the theme of the whole lecture, and thereby a very deep current in Derrida's philosophy, with the middle voice:

> In a conceptuality adhering to classical strictures "*différance*" would be said to designate a constitutive, productive, and originary causality, the process of scission and division which would produce or constitute different things or differences. But, because it brings us close to the infinitive and active kernel of *différer*, *différance* (with an *a*) neutralizes what the infinitive denotes as simply active, just as *mouvance* in our language does not simply mean the fact of moving, of moving oneself or of being moved. No more is resonance [*résonance*] the act of resonating [*résonner*]. We must consider that in the usage of our language the ending -*ance* remains undecided *between* the active and the passive. And we will see why that which lets itself be designated *différance* is neither simply active nor simply passive, announcing or rather recalling something like the middle voice [*voix moyenne*], saying an operation that is not an operation, an operation that cannot be conceived either as passion or as the action of a subject on an object, or on the basis of the categories of agent or patient, neither on the basis of nor moving toward any of these *terms*. For the middle voice [*voix moyenne*], a certain nontransitivity, may be what philosophy, at its outset, distributed into an active and a passive voice, thereby constituting itself by means of this repression.[20]

Derrida seeks an alternative to the simple active and passive modes of expression. He thereby has a happening in mind that cannot be grasped with these categories. What is at issue is nothing less than breaking through the traditional European conceptual language, which is based on the active-passive distinction. Even if at this point Derrida does not pursue the grammatical form of the middle voice any further, he nonetheless clearly refers to it as another possible perspective in which to get around the unwelcome dichotomy of active and passive.

Because the German language, like all other contemporary European languages, does not recognize the grammatical form of the middle voice, event forms that are neither subject-centered nor object-centered are difficult to bring to expression. They are not suggested in the German language as the central forms of experience. If the matter at hand requires it, they are sometimes brought to language only through a disregard of grammar. So by means of the reclamation of a semantic space of language, through which the grammatical form of the middle voice is developed, certain thoughts—for example, those that attempt to describe sensuously and corporeally executed acts—could probably be more essentially and precisely grasped. Furthermore, mystifications, which all too quickly refer to an all-encompassing unity, could be avoided through the medial linguistic form.

The middle voice is a linguistic form that is still found in many living languages, and so middle voice usages can be researched within an intercultural perspective. This can even contribute to the dialogue between European and Asian philosophical approaches. Preoccupation with the grammatical form of the middle voice allows us, above all, to be consequently more attentive to the particular qualities of actions. Through the shifting of attentiveness, something else emerges in the analysis of processes. Above all, the too-facile distinction between the simply "subjective" or "objective" is thwarted and a new processual level becomes accessible for explication.[21]

Translated from the German by Jason M. Wirth

NOTES

1. E. Happ, F. Maier, and A. Zeller, *Organon: Griechische Grammatik* (Bamberg: Bayerischer Schulbuch-Verlag, 1995), 147.

2. [The English translation of *sich freuen* (to be pleased, happy, or glad) is not reflexive, so I have also preserved the German to keep the thread of the author's example.—Trans.]

3. At this point I cannot go into the various forms of grammar and grammar theory. The present essay can in this respect only go so far as to thematize comparatively a grammatical form in its explanation between two very different languages and make it fruitful for a specific philosophical question.

4. Bruno Lewin, *Abriß der japanischen Grammatik* (Wiesbaden: Harrassowitz Verlag, 1996), 152–53.

5. Ibid., 152. [The German reads: "Wenn ich den Pinsel ergreife, *schreibe ich (so für mich) etwas hin.*"—Trans.]

6. Yoshida Kenkō, *Betrachtungen aus der Stille,* trans. Oscar Benl (Frankfurt am Main: Insel, 1991), 100. [This is a translation of the *Tsurezuregusa;* the German here reads: "*Greift man zum Pinsel, stellt sich die Lust zum Schreiben ein.*"—Trans.]

7. Ikeda Tadashi, *Classical Japanese Grammar Illustrated with Texts* (Tokyo: The Toho Gakkai, 1975), 112.

8. The *genus verbi* is designated in Japanese through the verbal suffix. The active form is not formally designated. The middle voice is designated and it diffuses itself in various meanings. The factitive is also designated, and it expresses a "bringing to" and/or "letting be." In Classical Japanese, the verbal suffixes for the middle voice since the Heian Period (here the variations cannot be gone into) are *ru* and *raru*. In modern Japanese one finds, above all, the suffixes *reru* and *rareru*.

9. "To experience means to know facts just as they are, to know in accordance with facts by completely relinquishing one's own fabrications. What we usually refer to as experience is adulterated with some sort of thought. So by *pure* I am referring to the state of experience just as it is without the least addition of deliberative discrimination. The moment of seeing a color or hearing a sound, for example, is prior not only to the thought that the color or sound is the activity of an external object or the one sensing it, but also to the judgment of what the color or sound might be. In this regard, pure experience is identical with direct experience. When one directly experiences one's own state of consciousness, there is not yet a subject or an object, and knowing and its object are completely unified. This is the most refined type of experience." (IG 3–4)

10. In a South German dialect, the phrase "*es denkt mir, dass* . . ." is today still common.

11. The passive form and the respect form play no particular role at this point, so I do not go into them.

12. In Nishida's *Mujunteki jiko dōitsu* this word appears over a hundred times.

13. In Nishida's writing additional words appear frequently like *serareru, mirareru, iwareru*, etc.

14. See my essay on the interpretations of sensibility in an intercultural perspective, "Sensory Dimensions in Intercultural Perspective and the Problem of Modern Media and Technology," in Peter Hershock, Marietta Stepaniants, and Roger Ames, eds., *Technology and Cultural Values: On the Edge of the Third Millennium* (Honolulu: University of Hawai'i Press, 2003), 478–92.

15. William James, *The Essential Writings,* ed. Bruce Wilshire (Albany: State University of New York Press, 1984), 44.

16. As is well known, Nishida adopts this term from James as a key concept in his work, *An Inquiry into the Good.*

17. It would be its own task to describe the various "it phrases" as substitute forms for the middle voice in the German and the English languages, respectively. When Lichtenberg and Nietzsche say that one should prefer to say, "it thinks" rather than "I think," a clear need for the middle voice as a philosophical linguistic form shows itself.

18. Martin Heidegger, *Being and Time* [1927], trans. Joan Stambaugh (Albany: State University of New York Press, 1996), 25 ("The Concept of Phenomenon") and 30 ("The Preliminary Concept of Phenomenology"), respectively.

19. Cf. Rolf Elberfeld, "Heidegger und ostasiatisches Denken: Annäherungen zwischen fremden Welten," *Heidegger-Handbuch* (Stuttgart: Metzler, 2003), 469–74.

20. Jacques Derrida, "Différance," *Margins of Philosophy,* trans. Alan Bass (Chicago: University of Chicago Press, 1982), 8–9.

21. I have tried to make this bear fruit in terms of a phenomenology of time. See my *Phänomenologie der Zeit im Buddhismus: Methoden interkulturellen Philosophierens* (Stuttgart-Bad Cannstatt: Frommann-Holzboog, 2004).

16

Truly Nothing:
The Kyoto School and Art

Jason M. Wirth

Genjitsu no	Who says
Kaori no yue ni	That the philosophy
Chokkan no	Of intuition
Tetsugaku o yoshi to	Is good
Iu wa tagako zo	Because of the fragrance of reality?

—Kuki Shūzō

This is an essay about the Kyoto School and art. That is to say, it is about the living fruits, the vital traces, of absolutely nothing, of what remains absolutely other to schools, theories, and approaches.

Aesthetics is conventionally considered to be an elective problem within philosophy. This essay will contest that claim, as well as the assumptions underlying it, and will do so by providing some preliminary considerations of Kyoto School aesthetics. The latter is not an application of alleged Kyoto School principles to the question of art, nor is it an issue that speaks within the narrow philosophical parameters of a "school." Rather, it will be argued that this issue is fundamental not only to the manner of philosophizing particular to the Kyoto School, but also that it is an important clue to the coming-to-the-fore of the site of philosophizing itself.

Despite the diversity of philosophical concerns that are somehow collected under the rubric of the Kyoto School, this essay will endeavor to make some general observations regarding the site in which artistic activity both arises and brings into relief the nature of philosophical activity. Although I often tire of the endless proclamations that one's work is only a gesture or hint or preliminary approach to the matter at hand—an endless deluge of unfulfilled promissory notes—I must admit that I believe that the present essay cannot fully escape the deficient relationship between its ambitions and its accomplishments. I, like the Kyoto School in general, am sufficiently Kantian—or perhaps, more to the point, Buddhist—in holding that to appreciate the forces that aesthetic expression holds together demands a more general appreciation of the whole. Aesthetics in such accounts, including the present one, is not a specialty item amid a larger enterprise, a niche problem for those so inclined to address it. It only comes into view within the transformative intensity of the whole. In enlightenment, everyone and everything is at stake; and art expresses enlightenment. "*Kenshō* means to penetrate to the bottomlessly contradictory existence of one's own self. Zen's principle of the absurd must be grasped as this paradox" (LW 108). Art expresses *satori,* in its coming-to-the-fore of itself, before the division of subject and object, artist and artwork. Cultures in which art is viewed as a mere supplement or adornment, an entertainment or investment, an exercise in civic or national pride, or an interesting experience are dangerously unhinged from the site of philosophical activity that is suggested by fundamental aesthetic experience.

After some preliminary orienting remarks, I will turn to the progenitor of the Kyoto School, Nishida Kitarō, and will include brief allusions to Nishida's students, Hisamatsu Shinichi and Nishitani Keiji.[1] Throughout what follows I will remain in dialogue with the Continental tradition, a dialogue at which the Kyoto School for its own part excelled.

Otherwise than *Japonisme*

When speaking of art for the Kyoto School, obviously one must address Japanese aesthetic traditions. How does one begin to approach the *Japanese* in Japanese art?

After the Meiji Restoration, as Japan overhauled or "modernized" major characteristics of its culture to be in some sense more "Western," parts of European culture, especially but not exclusively France, became infatuated with Japanese artifacts. Iconic commodities of Edo-era culture such as intensely colorful woodblock prints (*ukiyo-e*), fans and kimonos and some other wares that they depicted, became profitable and widely available. These colorful and exotic motifs also drew the attention of many European painters, and this Japanese influence is evident in selected works by Van Gogh, Whistler, Monet, Degas, Toulouse-Lautrec, and Gauguin, among others. The French journalist and art-critic Philippe Burty, in an 1876 article, called this enthusiastic trend *japonisme.*[2]

While such curiosity for the culturally exotic does have certain impressive features (its influence on French painting was largely salutary and at-times liberating), it tends to emphasize outward motifs, the external gestures of Japanese art, without much sense for their context and with apparently no sense of their larger cultural trajectory. Despite some striking works like Gauguin's *Nirvana* (1889–1890)[3] and Redon's striking studies of the Buddha,[4] it is hard to argue that *japonisme* displayed a strong awareness of the Buddhist, and especially Zen, roots of the Japanese aesthetic tradition. The celebrated austerity and severity, the *wabi-sabi* resonance, of Japanese Zen art is little evident in the color bombs of *ukiyo-e,* the latter whose name, the "floating world," even if ironically applied, is technically a Buddhist term of disapprobation. The *ukiyo* is the *sahā* world, with its dust and the distress of its many sensuous obsessions.

Moreover, as Roger-Pol Droit has demonstrated, nineteenth-century Europe was at best bewildered, but mostly horrified, by what little they had heard of the Buddhist tradition. They were at least right to recognize that the latter was not a new fad in the bourgeois demand for ever new techniques of relaxation and self-indulgence. The European intelligentsia was generally convinced that the Buddhists were willfully nihilistic, and that their religious salvation, which was supposed by the Christian tradition to preserve one's spiritual being, thereby nullifying death, is for the Buddhists the exact opposite, namely, self-annihilation. The preservation of the self and the nullification of death became the nullification of the self and the preservation of death. Victor Cousin, for example, argued that Christianity and Buddhism are "in absolute opposition" for if "there is anything in the world contrary to Christian doctrine, it is this deplorable idea of annihilation that forms the basis of Buddhism."[5] The Christian adoration of being was threatened by what Cousin called "the worship of nothingness."[6]

Even Nietzsche, whose own philosophy resonates with something like the spirit of Zen, had already in 1871, the time of *The Birth of Tragedy,* claimed that "tragedy should save us from Buddhism."[7] Nietzsche was poorly informed about the Buddha-dharma, understanding it, as did much of nineteenth-century Europe, as a life-enervating doctrine of nothingness, a kind of ontological depression, and hence an anticipation of "European Buddhism" in the wake of the death of God, in which one would rather worship nothingness than not worship at all; or, as Nietzsche predicts the fate of the ascetic ideal in the culminating essay of his *Genealogy of Morals:* "the will would rather will nothing than not will at all."[8] Deprived of God and a divinely meaningful world, one wallows in the subsequent decay of values rather than rethinking and activating the ground of values. European nihilism was the ruinous worship of the empty set of God, who no longer explains human life as something meaningful and thereby valuable.

In this general context, one could say that "Buddhism," either in its decadent metaphysical exhaustion or its current New Age practices of relaxation and the auto-obfuscation of reason, speaks as perceptively of the Buddhadharma as *japonisme* speaks of the roots and soil of Japanese art.

Nietzsche nonetheless remains an important portal to our present reflection because he was among the few to insist on the importance of nihilism, both in its reactive form (the dawning European nihilism, including its permutation as "European Buddhism," as the triumph of *ressentiment* amid the decaying corpse of divine value) and its active form (the self-overcoming of nihilism from within nihilism itself, that is to say, *incipit Zarathustra*). As Nishida's student Nishitani Keiji argued in his early study of nihilism: "Even though there may be in Nietzsche a radical misunderstanding of the spirit of Buddhism, the fact that he considered it in relation to nihilism shows how well attuned he was to the real issue" (SN xxxiii). And: "Ironically, it was not in his nihilistic view of Buddhism but in such ideas as *amor fati* and the Dionysian as the overcoming of nihilism that Nietzsche came closest to Buddhism, especially to Mahāyāna" (SN 180).

Nishitani argued that if one wants merely to know *about* nihilism, as if this were a possible object of knowledge for a discerning and inquisitive subject, then the question was being asked from a standpoint in which nihilism itself ceased to be a question (SN 1). Nihilism yields no information and is not an account of the nature of things, and hence it could not confirm Nietzsche's diagnosis that Europe is afflicted with a "European Buddhism" (reactionary, metaphysical nihilism) as it undergoes the putrefaction of the positive infinity of God into the bad infinity of absolute vacuity—a night in which all sacred cows are black. Nihilism only comes into question when the singular self, no longer able to relegate nihilism into a distant and thereby unobtrusive abstraction, encounters it as a question. This does not occur when an individual asks *about* nihilism, but only when one first finds oneself as having become a question to oneself: "By being thrown into nihility, the self is revealed to itself. Only in such encounters does nihilism (like death) become a real question" (SN 2).

Later, in his meditation on poetic language, "Emptiness and Sameness," Nishitani speaks of the ground of language that exceeds discernment. The Dharma, of course, had long been held to exceed the reach of discursivity, but Nishitani finds this ground even in a certain experience of Christianity:

But if the death of a God who is supposed to be immortal is absurd, the "language" of a God who is supposed to remain eternally a God and is born taking a human body is also absurd. When God emanated words that were within himself, these words became "embodied." The act of "speaking" for a God comes into being by actualizing itself. In the case of Christ, God spoke about God himself. But when he spoke of the "thing," "let the light be," for example, the thing known as the "light" came from nowhere. All existences in this world are creations from nothing.[9]

Poetry is for Nishitani indicative of the *logos* itself: Creation is the activity of absolutely nothing, wholly otherwise than what it brings into being, expressing itself while simultaneously negating itself. It expresses, to use Nishida's famous description, the *basho,* the site in which the ground self-negates in order to self-predicate, the contradictory identity of absolute nothingness and its predicates. The *zettai mujunteki jikodōitsu,* "absolute contradictory self-identity,"[10] is a dharmic iteration of the kind of formulations that one might find amid the tangles of Schelling's *Ages of the World,* despite Nishida's reservation that Schelling in the end considered it unevenly "in the direction of the *noema*" (FP 24):[11] "All life must pass through the fire of contradiction," and the "contradiction that we have here conceived is the fountain of eternal life."[12]

Nishitani locates the ground of poetry in experience, but by the latter he does not mean something set before me, something that *I experience.* I am neither the origin nor the reference point nor the goal of experience. Rather, experience is sensibility (Gn. *Sinnlichkeit*) in its most radical sense. It is not, as Kant argued, either accompanied by a formal point of reference, that is, by the unity of apperception that allows me to say "I think" beside every experience, or as in the third *Critique,* the theater in which the natural and the supernatural, sensible nature and noumenal freedom, intersect *in me,* in my reflective judgment.[13] "In the originary place that so-called sensibility brings about, that is, in the place of appearing wherein sensibility in its pure simplicity first originates just as it is, there is no distinction between the sensing 'something' and the sensed 'something.' . . . It expresses both sides as inseparably unified" (NKC 13: 106). As Rolf Elberfeld argues in this volume, experience occurs of itself, without explicit subject or object (nothingness is not the subject of experience and neither are we its recipients).

Although these initial observations require further elaboration, which is forthcoming, I would like first to hint at the standpoint of a Kyoto School aesthetics by briefly considering the Zen rock garden. In François Berthier's essay *Reading Zen in the Rocks*,[14] he discusses several of Kyoto's striking, obtrusively taciturn stone gardens, with their carefully arranged, somewhat jagged stones, often with outcroppings of moss, in beds of raked pebbles. Turning to Ryōanji, founded in 1450—perhaps Kyoto's, and thus the world's, most admired rock garden—he reflects:

> Rather than interrogating in vain the fifteen rocks of Ryōanji, it is better after a long contemplation, to lend an ear in order to catch their voices, which have been stifled by so many days and nights, and so much talk and noise. What are they saying, exactly? What silent words does this garden contain?[15]

At this point Berthier lets the silence of the rocks speak:

> I am nothing but blocks of stone on pieces of gravel. I am nothing but weight and silence, inertia and density. Nothing will ever learn my secret, or even whether I contain one. The only thing that can penetrate me is the silent cry of the cicada that pierces the heart of summer. Be content to taste the raw beauty of my opaque flesh; look at me without saying a word and ask me nothing; be silent and try, through my hermetic body, to find yourself.[16]

Berthier's reference to cicadas is an allusion to a famous haiku by the incomparable Bashō (1644–1694):

> Prevailing silence—
> And penetrating the rock
> The cicada's cry.[17]

In their silence, inaudible to the atomistic self, the rocks cry out, and their song is the song of all beings. This is not to say, however, that the rocks (the subject) actively sing to us, who become the recipients of the activity of singing. This singing rather happens of itself and this singing in sensibility *is* the rocks. Nishida's student Hisamatsu Shinichi preferred not to call Ryōanji a *seki-tei* or "stone garden," as is customary, but rather a *kū-tei* or "empty garden," an arrangement of and from emptiness (*śūnyatā*), referring to the "depth of the garden, the depth of the Fundamental Subject that is Nothing, of the Formless Self." The sublime austerity of the garden becomes possible because of its sparseness, for "too many stones, or too much variation, would absorb all of our attention and render it difficult for us to sense Nothingness or Emptiness" (ZFA 88).

The stones and moss and pebbles mark the site, the *basho,* of the absolutely contradictory identity of the nothingness of death and the quotidian world. The stones are silence expressing itself from itself. Nishida's term for "expression" is *hyōgen*. *Hyō* literally means "to rise to the surface," and *gen* means something like "to arise or (ontologically) appear." Expression is the self-predication, the coming to the surface, of a subject that is absolutely nothing, that in itself cannot appear and therefore that which self-negates in order to appear. (In this sense, one might speak of a non-subject in the subject position—an *Ungrund*, as Heidegger called it, following Böhme and Schelling—or use the middle voice, which expresses activity without positing either a subject or an object, an actor or an acted-upon.) Art is a site (*basho*) for *hyōgen*: "In art, expression itself is truth" (AM 99). This is not to say that artistic activity, expressive communication, is the same thing as *hyōgen*, but rather artistic creativity originates in *hyōgen*. Nishida was quite clear about this in *Fundamental Problems of Philosophy*: "Therefore, it is not that expressive activity should be derived from artistic creativity, but rather that artistic creativity should arise from the fact that actions are essentially expressive. Art must be the revelation of life. But the artistic should be thought to exist at the point where individual and universal become one in the determination of place [*basho*]" (FP 160).

However, this is not to seek the site of Zen art in grand architectural gestures. In a late essay, the 1941 "Artistic Creation as an Act of Historical Formation," Nishida argued that the "spirituality of Eastern Art" was not found in monumental works or other kinds of objects that demonstrate aggressive mastery of their space. To do so, one might surmise, would be as fruitful as finding this spirituality in *japonisme*. In the case of the latter, one emphasizes the form of the work (the *ism* in *japonisme*), not the formlessness of its origin. For Nishida, this formlessness—this absolute nothing, wholly otherwise than one's self, happening of itself from itself—is found in the "ordinary heart" which "includes heaven and earth in a tea bowl," and hence such works express "the natural process of things as they are."[18]

Heaven and earth are Daoist terms that inform part of the lexicon of East Asian Mahāyāna Buddha-dharma. Nothingness expresses itself as the earth of the tea bowl and, as such, the tea bowl speaks not only to the suchness of itself but of all "things." *Tian*, customarily but also potentially misleadingly translated as "heaven" or "the sky," does not indicate a transcendent actor-creator, but rather the emptiness of the *Ungrund*, the birthing movement of *Dao* (a non-subject in the subject position). *Di*, suggesting "earth" but also "area" or "field," does not literally indicate our planet, nor its surface (soils and other materials). It is akin to the Daoist "ten thousand," that is, to all possible things.

The pair, *tian-di,* operate analogously to "form is emptiness and emptiness is form" in the *Heart Sutra.* In the tea bowl one finds inscribed the expressivity of absolute nothingness itself, and hence, by extension, the expressivity of all of the "earth." Entering into relationship with *tian-di,* "heaven-earth," is akin, to use Nishitani's phrase, "to the heart standing on the wharf or on the beach of the vast sea—an expanse where sky and water merge into each other. If we use the metaphor of the two rivers and the white road," that is, the celebrated seventh-century Chinese Pure Land practitioner Shan-dao's (Jp. Zendō's) image of the road of human suffering that crosses between the river of fire and the river of water on the way to the Pure Land, "I would say that it is like seeing the white road from the midst of the world of suffering while listening to the Buddha's summons."[19]

In what follows I will attempt, beyond the formal qualities of art and otherwise than *japonisme,* to formulate the general aesthetic *standpoint* of the Kyoto School thusly: Aesthetic sensibility is the expression of the Good in the site (*basho*) of the true. The Good is absolutely nothing, but its expression is the beauty of the ongoing life of truth, an expressivity that marks an absolutely contradictory self-identity. To reiterate: this is not to suggest that the Good is a subject. Rather, in the middle voice, the Good self-negates as it self-predicates as the true. The Good, of itself, expresses itself from itself self-contradictorily as the true. The latter expresses the absolute nothingness of the Good. "True life exists by recognizing that which, being 'absolute nothingness,' is self-determining." The Good, like the Word of God, "'lives through dying,' i.e., something which is a contradiction in itself" (FP 106). Reverence for such truth, its wholesale affirmation, is religion, which requires the abdication of the pseudo-dominance of the ego, and hence all good art is true, and the love of art is the love of all things, just as they are.[20]

By *standpoint* I mean to invoke the ancient Buddhist platform, the place or vantage point, from which the Dharma manifests. It is to see as the Buddha saw (but it is not therefore merely to see *what* the Buddha saw). It is to develop what Dōgen (1200–1253), following a long tradition, called the *shō-bō-gen,* the "true Dharma eye." From such a standpoint, Dōgen tells us that the "sound that issues from the striking of emptiness is an endless and wondrous voice that resounds before and after the fall of the hammer."[21]

It is to recover the standpoint of the lotus flower, which preserves its purity while happily living in the mud of the *sahā* world. Or as Nishida formulates it: "We cannot see the fact of seeing in the standpoint of cognition, but by 'seeing seeing' we possess the infinite, objective world of art. We cannot hear the fact of hearing, but by 'hearing hearing' we possess the infinite world of music" (AM 89). It is a pre- and extra-discursive standpoint and hence discursivity can be informed by it, but it cannot provide or demonstrate it. Or as Nishida cites Kumārajīva's disciple, Sengzhao: "heaven and earth are of the same root as the self, and the myriad things are of the same substance as the self." Nishida continues: "We must not seek enlightenment (*bodhi*) above, nor depart from the world of birth and death (*samsāra*) below" (AM 78).

Nishida and the Problem of Expressivity

I would like to begin my discussion of the problem of expressivity in Nishida by way of a brief discussion of the aesthetics of Zen calligraphy. Nishida cultivated his own calligraphic practice, his own Dao of writing (*shodo*), and thus he wrote: "In art, expression itself is truth" (AM 99).

Zen calligraphy is a free expression of *mushin,* or what Hisamatsu called the Formless Self, as it expresses *zenki,* that is, Zen activity or Zen force.[22] It is the active or vital expression of the Zen mind, although this is not to say that this activity is the energy (*ki*) of a self-possessed agent. Zen activity does not express ego-originating agency, nor does it express being overcome and otherwise rendered passive by another agency. Inspiration is not a state or process of being overcome by something.[23] *Mushin,* rather, is the active self-predication of absolutely *nothing,* which therefore does not chiefly express a conscious, goal-oriented striving on the part of the calligrapher-agent, but rather the coming-to-expression of one's "original face." The Formless Self is empty—that is to say, it does not posses being of its own—although it expresses itself with greater energy than any "thing" could. It is the "utterance before voice" and "prior to the separation of heaven and earth" (ZFA 12–13).

Zen calligraphy, therefore, is not merely calligraphy by Zen practitioners, nor is it simply calligraphy with Zen content (phrases from the Zen record, perhaps accompanied by paintings of the first patriarch, Bodhidharma, etc.). The ink is alive, rife with the energy, seeking expression as, in Nishida's words, "the artist thinks through his technique": "The artist does not think idly without taking up his brush. Only when he takes up his brush and faces the canvas does it become clear how he should paint, and an infinite direction opens up before him" (AM 103, 104). As Elberfeld demonstrates in chapter 15 of the present volume, with his rendering of the phrase *fude wo toreba, mono kakare* as "Clasping the brush the writing of something sets itself into action from itself," the brush becomes the manner in and through which thinking and painting occur of themselves. This is much in the vein of Paul Klee, who once spoke of his work as "musing with a line." The artist imaginatively extends the realm of the true as her work expresses an absolutely contradictory identity with the Good, for "there is nothing that is both false and beautiful" (AM 98). Of course, the artist is not the originator, the creative agent determining reality. The artist is the site of the expressive life of the self-negation of the Good as the self-predication of the true. The latter dynamically expresses the absolute nothingness of the Good. Thus Nishida:

> In the actual will subject and object are one, and the self functions in the horizon of behavior. This is precisely the horizon of absolute will. To enter into true reality that is the object of this kind of actual will is aesthetic activity. To enter into this reality, the whole body must become one living power, one activity. (AM 104)

The artwork is the trace of the absolutely contradictory identity of the creation. In this sense all good art—that is to say, the creative discovery or "creative intuition" of the true—is always religious; but this is not in the sense in which religion sides with a superstitious and dogmatic refusal of the true. Creative intuition evades the ego's willful resistance to the true, while "all falsehood destroys the beautiful and defiles the sacred." True religious feeling is the humility and love of an absolute reverence for reality, a "profound adoration of truth" (AM 101); and hence if "we deepen this idea, we can think that each of our movements is also the dance of God" (AM 85).

Here Nishida resonates with Hermann Broch. For the latter, kitsch is the enemy of art—kitsch is a willful resistance to the irrationality of the ground of what matters. It is the flight from the Good, whose force Broch likens to the opacity of death. "One must distinguish between annulling death and fleeing death, between shedding light on the irrational and fleeing from the irrational. Kitsch is found in flight, it is constantly fleeing into the rational."[24] Kitsch, the flight from the dark night of the Good, is not therefore an aesthetic failing. It is an ethical debacle, the obfuscation of the Good with clichés and falsehoods. "The maker of kitsch does not create inferior art, he is not an incompetent or a bungler, he cannot be evaluated by esthetic standards; rather, he is ethically depraved, a criminal willing radical evil."[25]

At the end of Broch's magisterial first novel, *The Sleepwalkers* (1931), which explores the floundering of the various value-producing systems that sleepwalk through the death of God (the decay of values), the narrator, speaking of and from "the profoundest darkness of the world," hears the absolute alterity of the Good, silently and non-discursively operating at the ground of the true: "not to be disowned, the brotherhood of humbled human creatures, from out of whose profoundest Angst the divine grace of the Angst that cannot be disowned or lost shines, the unity of humans that shines through all things, from beyond space and time, the unity from which all light flows as well as the healing of all living things."[26]

For Broch, the novelist-philosopher, and for the Kyoto School philosophers, imbued with Buddha-dharma, philosophy comes into contact with its non-discursive ground.[27] The Zen tradition holds that "there is nothing strange in the Dharma," but an appreciation of this demands more than reflective activity. It demands the standpoint from which creative intuition is possible and hence: "Just as art demands philosophy, so, too, does philosophy demand art" (AM 97). The sacred bond of art and philosophy—indeed, the religious love of truth itself as the ongoing creative life of the Good—demands that the heart become attuned to this site. "When we see things with a pure heart, there is nothing that is not beautiful and good" (AM 165).

Does this not, however, takes us back to the crisis of origins, for does this not indicate the loss of a secure and universally available standpoint? Are not Nishida and Broch turning toward the opacity of origins that degenerated into the disoriented sleepwalking of reactive value systems? Or, in other words, are we not here simply being dishonest? In seeking to explain the artwork, are we not just shrouding it in mystery? And is this shrouding not the obscurantism in which all values are rendered opaque?

This points us to the key issue of the role of the intellectual intuition of the pre-discursive standpoint. This standpoint only emerges for Broch in the humility of thinking amid the decline of values, and for the Kyoto School in overcoming the duality of the discerning subject and the objective world (discernible or otherwise) that makes discursivity as such possible. This standpoint, however, is obviously not available to all rational creatures within the terms set by rationality itself. There is no rational first principle from which to deduce the members of a value system of art. In the Continental tradition, Schelling was among the first to turn to art and aesthetic intuition to ground philosophy itself in his early call for the "return of science to poesy."[28]

If the aesthetic intuition [*ästhetische Anschauung*] is only the transcendental become objective, then it is self-evident that Art is at the same time the single true and eternal *Organon* and document, which always and continuously verifies anew what philosophy cannot present externally, namely the Unconscious in acting and producing and its originary identity with consciousness. Art for this reason is the highest to the philosopher because it opens to him the most holy in which what is sundered in nature and history, and what in life and action, just as in thinking, must fly apart, burns as an eternal and originary unity in a flame.[29]

Hence the sciences, the dynamic works of philosophical reflection and creativity, must also "flow back" like "individual streams into the general ocean of *poesy.*"[30]

It was Hegel who criticized such intuitions as the private and non-demonstrable prerogative of "Sunday's children"—they are not the result of reason's universally accessible orientation to its own activity. The philosophy that relies on the grace and happy accident of intellectual intuition, Hegel argued in *Lectures on the History of Philosophy,* "gave the philosophy of Schelling the appearance of indicating that the presence of this intuition in individuals demanded a special talent, genius, or condition of mind of their own, or as though it were speaking of an accidental faculty which pertained to the specially favored few."[31]

Indeed, Ueda Shizuteru spoke of a "fracture" in Nishida's philosophy between Zen and philosophy,[32] despite Nishida's emphatic efforts to make his thinking an enterprise that operated on a purely philosophical plane. The very notion of Zen philosophy flirts with the oxymoronic. For the Kyoto School, art, to use Adorno's felicitous phrase, bears a wound: "It is self-evident that nothing concerning art is self-evident anymore."[33]

Nishida did not diminish the fruits of Zen practice into Western categories. If anything, what is at stake in Nishida—even from his first, startling treatise, *An Inquiry into the Good* (1911)—is the deployment of Western categories in order to give speech to what is unthought in the West. And this unthought, for Nishida, is also what is most difficult and important to think in any tradition, namely, *the idea of the Good* in all its abyssal darkness—a darkness before which no life can be indifferent. "We can say that the highest truth is the highest good. There is profound meaning in Plato's thought that the Idea of the Good was above all other ideas in dignity and power" (AM 91). Nishida made this quite clear in his 1927 work, *From the Actor to the Seer:*

> It goes without saying that there are many things to be esteemed and learned from in the brilliant development of Western culture, which regards form [*eidos*] as being and formation as the good. However, at the basis of Asian culture, which has fostered our ancestors for over several thousand years, lies something that

can be called seeing the form of the formless and hearing the sound of the sound-less. Our minds are compelled to seek for this. I would like to give a philosophical foundation to this demand.[34]

Elsewhere, Nishida insisted that the starting point of Greek thinking was Being, while Japanese thinking proceeds from nothingness (*mu*) (FP 237). Hence,

> Japanese aesthetics differed essentially from Greek aesthetics in that it was not an aesthetics of *eidos*. Of course, no aesthetics can exist apart from form. But Greek aesthetics saw the formless within form; while not only the distinctive quality of Japanese aesthetics, but also that of all Eastern aesthetics grounded in the idea of Nothingness, lies in employing form to express the formless. Moreover, they were not symbolic, but the revelation of the formless. (FP 249)

Nishida, thinking in the fracture between the Good and the True, attempted to take the resources of the *eidos,* the force of the idea, and to use them to express what transcends the idea, nay, even contests the idea. In a way, Nishida is proposing to use ideas to somehow articulate the idea of that whose *ideatum* always transcends its idea, that whose idea relates to a pre-discursive unified field that cannot be restricted by any idea. It is to see the form of the formless. It is to hear the sound of that which, properly speaking, makes no sound. It is to intuit stillness amid all commotion. Or if one takes seriously Nishida's claim here that the West has traditionally taken *eidos* itself to be the Good—that is, referring to our discussion above, that the idea of the Good is equivalent to the form of all forms, the measure that guarantees the measure of all other measures, that which institutes the domination of form over the formless—then Nishida is proposing to deploy the language and domain of the *eidos* to articulate a Goodness that transcends all its forms and thereby exceeds the discourse that formulates it. Nishida's first work, then, was already an attempt to think the Good beyond being, the Good beyond all goods, a goodness that cannot be approached by the needy ego (the detached, discerning subject) and which demands love, not discursivity. Love is *satori.*

Pure experience is not an experience *of something*. It is not intentional in structure. Rather, it is the undivided continuum, the plenitude of the Good. From the beginning, Nishida links pure experience to Schelling's intellectu-al intuition: "there is no distinction between subject and object in any state of direct experience—one encounters reality face to face" (IG 31). As such, direct experience precedes a denotative account of experience in which an experiencing subject experiences certain objects of experience. Pure experience is an intuition that all that is partitioned, discontinuous, and discrete has been isolated from a pure state of awareness that always remains in excess of all judgments. Meaning emerges only in the betrayal of pure experience. "A truly pure experience has no meaning whatsoever; it is simply a present consciousness of facts just as they are" (IG 4). Meaning is the ineluctable diminution of pure experience. "Meanings or judgments are an abstracted part of the original experience, and compared with the original experience they are meager in content" (IG 9). Pure experience, the abyssal source of all judgments, gives rise to judgments while transcending those very judgments. In a certain sense, pure experience, or I might say here, the Good *kath' auto,* is the meaningless origin of all meaning, the sublime ground of all that matters and of any way in which it might matter.

To invoke pure experience is not, however—as a popular and obscurantist New Age Buddhism would have it—to take refuge in some wish-fulfilling continuum that absolves all the rigors of the idea of the Good into some *satori*-night in which all Buddhas are black. Beyond the subject-object dichotomy, beyond actors performing deeds, the Good individualizes itself, differentiates itself from itself into ceaselessly flowing heterogeneities. Pure experience is the Dao, embraced in a "doing of non-dong" (*wei-wuwei*); pure experience is an "activity without agency" in which the Good is welcomed and affirmed in the unabated flow of its singularities. "From this perspective, what the ancients spoke of as acting from morning to night without acting we might call a stillness in motion, a doing of non-doing. In this way we transcend both knowledge and the will, and in the intuition at their base we can discover their oneness" (IG 33–34).

At this point Nishida's Zen Buddhist commitments should be obvious. In almost all expressions of Buddhism the very block to enlightenment, the impediment to all *satori,* the means by which the ego is always complicit in its own suffering, is the ego itself. The ego is the subject that partitions experience into objects. The ego is the impoverishment of need that hungers for objects that it will never be able successfully to appropriate. *Satori* is the death of the ego in the desire, or what Nishida calls *love* (in the sense of *agapē*), for the Good. "The more we discard the self and become purely objective or selfless, the greater and deeper our love becomes. We advance from the love between parent and child or husband and wife to the love between friends, and from there to the love of humankind. The Buddha's love extended even to birds, beasts, grasses, and trees" (IG 174).

The ego relates to things by wanting things, by wanting *these* things, which appear to the famished ego as good things, and not wanting things whose nature opposes the nature of the things that it wants. The ego wants good things and wants to avoid evil things. The ego wants to do good things and avoid evil. The ego wants to go to heaven, wants to live in the Pure Land, and avoid the sullied, abject, stinking world of evil. The *satori* of pure experience terminates the ego and its grasping for a discrete, logical world. The self is born of this *Great Death*, the dawning of a *Great Doubt* that gives rise to a love that needs nothing and loves everything. "Love is the deepest knowledge of things. Analytical, inferential knowledge is a superficial knowledge, and it cannot grasp reality. We can reach reality only through love. Love is the culmination of knowledge" (IG 175). Such love, such an intuition of the abyss of Goodness at the heart of all judgments, is not possible through the primacy of judgment. "The sword of logic cannot penetrate it and desire cannot move it" (IG 34). Nishida is using the egoism of logic against itself, or to use a more contemporary phrase, to deconstruct itself and thereby unblock the middle voice of the Good as it circulates through self-negation as the true.

Pure experience, the birth of the Buddha's indefatigable generosity, is love in the dawning of a non-constitutable self, a self that exceeds all of its manifest predicates, a self whose energies do not turn inwardly in the direction of self-maintenance and self-enhancement, an abyssal self in the wake of the death of *conatus*. It is a self non-differentiated from the Good and therefore *inseparable* from all things, inseparable from ceaseless flows of heterogeneity. As with Levinas, there is no ring of Gyges, no possibility of separation from participation:

> To acquire this power is to kill our false self and, after dying once to worldly desire, to gain new life. (As Muhammad said, heaven lies in the shadow of the sword.) Only in this way can we reach the union of subject and object, which is the ultimate meaning of religion, morality, and art. Christianity calls this event rebirth, and Buddhism calls it *kenshō*. According to one story, when Pope Benedict XI asked Giotto to show him a work that demonstrated his ability as a painter, Giotto simply drew a circle. In morality, we must attain to Giotto's circle. (IG 145)

Love, for Nishida, is therefore not *my* love for the Other since the Other, the Good in all of its expressions, always precedes any self. "Subjectivity is self-power and objectivity is other-power. To know and love a thing is to discard self-power and embody the faithful heart that believes in other-power" (IG 175). Love opens the ego to the self, to the abyssal Good of the Other. It was this "infinition," to use Levinas's term, of the Good that deprives the ego of its primacy that struck the twelfth-century Zen practitioner and poet Saigyō (1118–1190): "Saigyō exclaimed, 'Though I know not what is enshrined, my tears flow in the face of its awesomeness.' The majesty of morality dwells in an unfathomable realm" (IG 110).

The plenitude of the Good is thought only discretely, even when such judgments are used to say their opposite. And hence the paradox: it is somehow a good thing to say that the Good is not just what is good for us. "Again, reality develops through contradictions and conflicts" (IG 171). Difference, the idea of the Good itself (the absolute nothingness of the Good that haunts the subject position, but which in no way is a subject), substitutes itself from itself as forms, as the countenances of the Good. In fact, Nishida goes much further on this point than Levinas. For many Buddhists, the Good is in "the face" of grass or of stone, in water, in animals, in rain, in trees, even in death. When asked what things had Dao, Zuangzi answered that even shit had Dao. Kitsch flees shit. Aesthetic sensibility knows that *la part maudite* is also a worthy subject.

DEDICATION

For my good friend Ron Carlisle (1942–2007),
a man of the Way, *in memoriam.*

NOTES

The epigraph is from Kuki Shūzō, *Kuki Shūzō: A Philosopher's Poetry and Poetics,* trans. and ed. Michael F. Marra (Honolulu: University of Hawai'i Press, 2004), 92.

1. Sadly, length limitations prevent me from raising the question of art in relationship to the Kyoto School more broadly construed. On the one hand, as Ōhashi Ryōsuke argues in the present volume, Nishida did not found a school *per se,* "but his personality and philosophical thinking attracted many students, who then developed the thinking of their teacher in various directions, albeit departing from the same thinking." On the other hand, a much greater and more diverse set of voices are included in the Kyoto School. I regret especially not having the space to engage Tanabe Hajime, whose turn to Shinran (the True Pure Land sect of Buddhism) adds important dimensions to our discussion. I also regret excluding Kuki Shūzō, who studied with Sartre and Heidegger and was hired by Nishida at Kyoto University, and whose poetry

as well as his groundbreaking analysis of *iki* are seminal contributions. The latter is now available in two English translations.

2. See for example G. P. Weisberg, "Philippe Burty and Early *Japonisme,*" in Yamada Chisaburo, ed., *Japonisme in Art: An International Symposium* (Tokyo: Kodansha, 1980).

3. See Eric M. Zafran, ed., *Gauguin's Nirvana: Painters at Le Pouldu 1889–90* (New Haven, Conn., and London: Yale University Press, 2001).

4. For a strong and fascinating study of the Buddhist influence on Western art, including its influence on Van Gogh, Monet, Gauguin, and Redon, see Jacquelynn Bass, *Smile of the Buddha: Eastern Philosophy and Western Art from Monet to Today* (Berkeley: University of California Press, 2005). More general studies include S. Bing, *Japonisme: Japanese Influence on French Art: 1854–1910* (Kent, Ohio: Kent State University Press, 1975); and Siegfried Wichmann, *Japonisme: The Japanese Influence on Western Art since 1858* (London: Thames & Hudson, 1999).

5. Quoted in Roger-Pol Droit, *The Cult of Nothingness: The Philosophers and the Buddha,* trans. David Streight and Pamela Vohnson (Chapel Hill and London: University of North Carolina Press, 2003), 88.

6. Ibid., 89.

7. Ibid., 144. Nietzsche is certainly ambivalent about Buddhism. On the one hand, his remarks about the historical Buddha in *The Anti-Christ,* while neither altogether flattering nor accurate, place the Buddha on par with the historical Jesus: sensitive types who were too tender for the demands of life. In the same way that Nietzsche separates Christianity from Jesus, he separates Buddhism from the Buddha. What Nietzsche understood of the nineteenth-century German embrace of Buddhism, however, did not win his approval. Schopenhauer's embrace of "Buddhism" as a tonic to the agony of the will is in large part a figment of his own projection. This "Buddhism" emphasized the asceticism of the cessation or diminishing of the will, the latter being the source of suffering. For Nietzsche, however, this was symptomatic of the deflation of the value of life itself. Graham Parkes has also linked Nietzsche's distaste for and poor knowledge of Buddhism to Wagner's embrace of it. (See Parkes's "The Orientation of the Nietzschean Text," in *Nietzsche and Asian Thought,* ed. Graham Parkes [Chicago: University of Chicago Press, 1991], 14.) Hence, the term "European Buddhism," a term that one can find in the *Nachlass* of the 1880s, speaks not to the Buddha but to the life-enervating "Buddhism" of thinkers like Schopenhauer and Wagner. (And hence: any use of the phrase in this essay refers to Nietzsche's disparaging account of this kind of "Buddhism.") We see this clearly in *The Case of Wagner,* where Nietzsche laments that the reworking of *Siegfried*'s conclusion "translated the *Ring* into Schopenhauerian . . . *nothingness,* the Indian Circe, beckons" (cit. Parkes, *Nietzsche and Asian Thought,* 14). Parkes also rightly argues that Nietzsche had no inkling of Zen, which he would have found "much to his own taste" (ibid., 15).

8. Friedrich Nietzsche, *Zur Genealogie der Moral* [1887], *Kritische Studienausgabe,* ed. Giorgio Colli and Mazzino Montinari (Munich and Berlin: Deutscher Taschenbuch Verlag / Walter de Gruyter, 1980), 5: 412.

9. Nishitani Keiji, "Emptiness and Sameness," *Modern Japanese Aesthetics: A Reader,* ed. and trans. Michele Marra (Honolulu: University of Hawai'i Press, 1999), 207.

10. Cf. Nishida Kitarō, "The Unity of Opposites," *Intelligibility and the Philosophy of Nothingness,* trans. Robert Schinzinger (Honolulu: East-West Center Press, 1966).

11. "True self-identity is a universal, and determines the individual as the ultimate determination of the universal" (FP 24); "Self-identity is the unity of absolute

contradictories, and therefore it opposes the self-identity of Schelling" (FP 30); "True self-identity must be considered to be precisely the predicate in the sense of 'absolute nothingness' existing as subject. It must be the self-identity of absolute contradictories as the subject-qua-predicate and predicate-qua-subject" (FP 96). Nishida's standpoint hence differs from Schelling's early negative philosophy (Gn. *Identitätsphilosophie*), but Schelling's *Weltalter* period moves more conspicuously into proximity with Nishida's standpoint. The determination of a place (Jp. *basho*) is the "unity of absolute contradictories" (FP 6–7).

12. In the standard pagination, which follows the original edition established after Schelling's death by his son, and which is preserved in Manfred Schröter's critical reorganization of this material (*Schellings Werke: Nach der Originalausgabe in neuer Anordnung*, ed. Manfred Schröter [Munich: C. H. Beck, 1927]), this is found in *Schellings Sämtliche Werke* (Stuttgart-Augsburg: J. G. Cotta, 1856–1861), 8: 321. This is the third or 1815 draft of *Die Weltalter;* the English translation is *The Ages of the World,* trans. Jason M. Wirth (Albany: State University of New York Press, 2000), in which the standard pagination appears throughout.

13. Alison Ross has recently made a strong case that, for Kant, the "Critique of Teleological Judgment" serves to undermine some of the implications suggested by his account of sensibility. The radicality of the experience of freedom that occurs in sensibility is difficult to reconcile with teleological judgments—and hence Kant's ambivalence toward the incomprehensible prodigality of aesthetic experience and the need to "find in material forms a register of ultimate meaning which is not there" (Alison Ross, *The Aesthetic Paths of Philosophy: Presentation in Kant, Heidegger, Lacoue-Labarthe, and Nancy* [Stanford, Calif.: Stanford University Press, 2007], 16). Kant endeavors to show that the freedom of nature is in some sense *our* freedom: "Nature in its beautiful products displays itself as if it were art, as if it were beautiful *intentionally*" (31). Ross further argues that sensibility becomes increasingly important in the wake of Kant, and especially in the thinking of Heidegger, Lacoue-Labarthe, and Nancy.

14. François Berthier, *Reading Zen in the Rocks: The Japanese Dry Landscape Garden,* trans. Graham Parkes (Chicago: University of Chicago Press, 2000).

15. Ibid., 41.

16. Ibid.

17. Ibid., 148.

18. Quoted in Iwaki Ken'ichi, "Nishida Kitarō and Art," *A History of Modern Japanese Aesthetics,* ed. and trans. Michael F. Marra (Honolulu: University of Hawai'i Press, 2001), 279. Nishida's essay has not yet been translated into English.

19. Nishitani, "Emptiness and Sameness," 209–10.

20. This does not, however, conflate religion with art: "There cannot be anything like an aesthetic religion. Persons may confuse the two through the word intuition, but aesthetic and religious intuition point in opposite directions" (LW 93). Religion points from form to the formless while aesthetic intuition moves from formlessness to form. In this sense, they can be neither separated nor confused.

21. Dōgen, "Bendōwa," *The Heart of Dōgen's Shōbōgenzō,* trans. Norman Waddell and Masao Abe (Albany: State University of New York Press, 2002), 14.

22. According to Hisamatsu, *Zenki* also connotes "wellspring, movement, dynamism, impulse, thrust, spontaneity, immediacy" (ZFA 11).

23. See my *"Blitzkunst:* Towards a Field-Being Conception of Creativity," *International Journal for Field-Being* 3, no. 1 (2006): 35–42.

24. Hermann Broch, "Evil in the Value-System of Art," *Geist and Zeitgeist: The Spiritual in an Unspiritual Age,* ed. and trans. John Hargraves (New York: Counterpoint, 2002), 35.

25. Ibid., 37.

26. Hermann Broch, *Die Schlafwandler* (Zurich: Rhein Verlag, 1952), 761; my translation.

27. Coming into contact with this non-discursive ground, the humus of the earth (which, in our loss of the earth, we ceaselessly perjure), is the theme of Broch's stunning novel *The Death of Virgil* (1945), which enacts at the very moment of death the return—beyond all metaphors and linguistic strategies of containment, beyond any possible empire on earth—to the ground of creation, in excess of the subject-object duality.

28. F. W. J. Schelling, *System of Transcendental Idealism (1800),* trans. Peter Heath (Charlottesville: University of Virginia Press, 1978), 232.

29. Ibid., 231–32.

30. Ibid., 232.

31. See Dale Snow, *Schelling and the End of Idealism* (Albany: State University of New York Press, 1996), 62–66.

32. Iwaki, 261.

33. Theodor W. Adorno, *Aesthetic Theory,* trans. Robert Hullot-Kentor (Minneapolis: University of Minnesota Press, 1997), 1.

34. Quoted in Abe Masao's introduction (IG x).

Logos and *Pathos:* Miki Kiyoshi's Logic of the Imagination

Fujita Masakatsu

Miki Kiyoshi's philosophy is remarkably multifaceted. He exerted a significant influence on the Japanese intellectual world during the period of his thought when he inclined toward Marxism; and yet his first book was *A Study of Human Being in Pascal* (1926), and his posthumously published work, left behind when he died in prison a little over a month after the end of the war, was titled *Shinran* (1945). In the interim, he published a large number of works, including *The Materialistic View of History and the Consciousness of the Present Age, The Philosophy of History, Aristotle, Notes on a Theory of Life,* and *The Philosophy of Technology.* But in the end, were we to single out one of Miki's works as being his magnum opus, it would in all likelihood be *Logic of the Imagination.*

One reason why *Logic of the Imagination* should be accorded this status is that he worked on this text over a number of years during the latter part of his life. To be precise, in May 1937, when he was forty years old, the first part of the first chapter on "Myth" was published in the journal *Shisō,* and in July 1940, two years before his death, the last part of the fourth chapter on "Experience" was published. Moreover, the fact that in this work he addressed problems that had remained unresolved, and reconsidered issues that not been fully dealt with in his earlier works, would seem to give us sufficient reason to refer to it as his magnum opus.

On the other hand, however, it should be pointed out that even though in 1939 the first three chapters appeared together as *Logic of the Imagination Part One,* the various chapters of *Logic of the Imagination* were originally published intermittently as journal articles, and not composed in a unified form. Moreover, although at the end of chapter 4 Miki announces a plan to discuss the problem of language, this plan was never realized. Hence, inasmuch as he had the intention of adding such a discussion, in its present form the text must be considered incomplete.

In his preface to *Logic of the Imagination Part One,* Miki himself stated that the papers contained in the book were originally "written in the form of research notes," and that their present articulation remained excessively "complicated." In short, he wrote these articles without having first determined the composition of the entire work, and without having a clear conception of the organic connection between the parts. In this preface he also wrote that "a complete systematic articulation must begin from the point that this study has reached at the end. The present discourse will first of all take the form of phenomenological description, and then later it will be given a purely logical form" (MKZ 8: 3). This statement clearly implies that Miki regarded the chapters actually published as a "phenomenological" description, and thought that it remained necessary to supplement this basis with more "logical" reflections (though we might consider chapter 4 as the beginning of such reflections). In this sense, also, *Logic of the Imagination* remained an unfinished work.

Nevertheless, this book plays a special role in the development of Miki's thought. To begin with, it was written with the intention of providing a solution to a certain problem that, although extremely important to his thought, remained unresolved in his earlier works. This problem is, in a word, the "unification of *logos* and *pathos*." In his preface to *Logic of the Imagination Part One,* he expresses this issue as follows:

> After the publication of *The Philosophy of History,* the problem which had continuously occupied my mind was that of how the objective and the subjective, the rational and the irrational, and the intellectual and the emotional could be united. During that period I formulated this problem as that of the unification of *logos* and *pathos,* and worked mainly on analyzing the two elements of *logos* and *pathos,* which can be found in each and every historical phenomenon, and on articulating the dialectical unification of these elements. (MKZ 8: 4)

While Miki depicted the aim of his thought since *The Philosophy of History* (1932) in this manner, he also remarked that his considerations had previously remained "too abstractly formal," in other words, that he had not been able to sufficiently clarify precisely "where one should find" the unification of *logos* and *pathos.* He then adds: "In the course of pursuing this problem, and by recalling that Kant assigned to the imagination the function of uniting understanding and sensibility, I was led to conceive of the logic of the imagination" (MKZ 8: 5). We can infer, then, that *Logic of the Imagination* was conceived with the intention of carrying out the task left unachieved in the development of Miki's thought after *The Philosophy of History*.

I would also like to point out the fact that various aspects of Miki's thought prior to *Logic of the Imagination* flow organically into his theory of the imagination. In particular, this theory was made possible on the bases of his previous theories with regard to human being, *logos/pathos,* technology, *poiesis,* body, history, literature, and so forth. Conversely, one could say that his theory of the imagination takes up, develops, and even synthetically unites the content of these previous theories.

Finally, I would like to point out that even while this work remains unfinished, the various novel conceptions that appear in its pages are replete with possibilities for further development. For example, Miki's consistent stance throughout this text is to understand human being, not simply as a being endowed with intellect, but also as an embodied existence. The issues of *praxis, poiesis,* technology, and so forth are each discussed from the point of view of human being as an embodied existence, that is, as a being of *pathos.* What is particularly noteworthy is the manner in which Miki attends to the important role that the formation of images plays in *praxis* and *poiesis.* Moreover, these images—which he also called "forms"—are things produced, fictions rather than facts of life. Yet Miki argues that reality is to be found precisely within such fictions, and this is indeed the main emphasis of his *Logic of the Imagination.* Here too we find a point in Miki's thought which, even from a contemporary perspective, appears novel and stimulating.

It will not be possible, needless to say, for me to discuss every aspect of this work. I shall limit myself here to the task of bringing to light the impetus behind Miki's conception of a "logic of the imagination," and to clarifying what he aimed to problematize and accomplish through this idea. A consideration of the profound implications—and latent possibilities—of his logic of the imagination, on the other hand, will for the most part have to be deferred to another occasion.

The Body in Subjectivity

In the beginning of the chapter on "Myth" in *Logic of the Imagination*—in the context of referring to Alexander Baumgarten's "logic of the imagination" (Gn. *Logik der Einbildungskraft*) or "logic of fantasy" (*Logik der Phantasie*), Pascal's "logic of the heart" (Fr. *logique du coeur*), and psychologist Théodule Ribot's "logic of the sentiments" (*logique des sentiments*)—Miki raises the question of whether there exists "a logic distinguished from that of abstractive thought" or "a logic differing from that of reason." Indeed he states that this is precisely the question with which he is concerned. Hence, we may first of all understand his "logic of the imagination" as a "logic distinguished from that of abstractive thought."

Why is it necessary to raise the question of a logic that differs from that of abstract thought and formal logic? With regard to this question, Miki writes:

> It is through the body that we strike up against things themselves in their physicality. We, as things ourselves, strike up against things. Now, if we refer to the body in its subjectivity as *pathos*, a logic of things will have to be more than simply a logic of *logos*; for it will need also to relate to matters of *pathos*. (MKZ 8: 15)

Judging from this, we can surmise that what Miki was seeking was not just a "logic" in the sense of laws of thought, but a logic or a philosophy that brings to light the essence of human being as an embodied existence that acts through the medium of its body, and also the reality that is encountered within the field of this activity. In this sense, his "logic of the imagination" is not simply a "logic of knowledge" but rather a "logic of praxis" (MKZ 8: 15).

As can be seen in these passages, Miki's "logic of the imagination" is closely connected to his understanding of human being, that is, to his unique anthropology. Although we find his anthropology expressed in *Logic of the Imagination*, he had in fact previously written a work called *Philosophical Anthropology*. This previous work, however, was never presented to the public. It was rewritten several times between 1933 and 1937, and yet, even though the manuscript proofs had been prepared, the work never reached publication. Judging from the fact that in May 1937 the first part of chapter 1 on "Myth" was published (as previously mentioned) in the journal *Shisō*, we can infer that at this time he abandoned the publication of *Philosophical Anthropology*, and in its place began writing *Logic of the Imagination*.

In chapter 1 of *Philosophical Anthropology*, "The Concept of Anthropology," Miki distinguishes anthropology from other sciences as follows. Anthropology, he says, is characterized by the fact that it treats the human being in its entirety, while the other sciences—for example, physiology or psychology—take only one part of the human being as their object of study. Anthropology entails, above all, "not abstracting human being from the body." This implies not reducing human being simply to consciousness or mind. The body is not to be abstracted from human being as a mere object of objective analysis, but rather taken as an "'animated or ensouled [*kokoro ni ikasareta*]' (*beseelt*) body" (MKZ 18: 149). Expressed in the terms of a passage quoted earlier, it is "the body in subjectivity." It could be said that the dual task of the anthropology envisioned by Miki involves, on the one hand, thinking the body *as the human being's* body, and, on the other hand, understanding human being *as an embodied existence.*

It is from such a standpoint that Miki refers, in the chapter "The Concept of Anthropology," to the anthropology of Maine de Biran. As opposed to Descartes, who dealt with self-awareness from a merely intellectual standpoint, de Biran argued that desire or volition (*vouloir*) itself is "the primitive fact" (*le fait primitif*). Miki appreciates de Biran's development of this idea, as well as his discussion of the connection between this primitive fact of volition and the outer world. Miki quotes the following lines from de Biran's *Nouveaux essais d'anthropologie ou de la science de l'homme intérieur* (New essays in anthropology or the science of the interior human): "The will (*vouloir*) is a simple, pure and instantaneous act of the soul (*l'âme*), in which or through which this intellectual and active force manifests itself both externally, and to itself internally" (MKZ 18: 140–41).[1] Miki highly regards the fact that here the self that desires and strives is considered, not just in its self-relation, but in its relation with things which resist the self.

It is worth noting here that Miki's appreciation of Maine de Biran is shared by Nishida Kitarō. Nishida's interest in de Biran was likely stimulated by the various debates on philosophical anthropology that took place following the publication of, among other works, Max Scheler's *Human Being's Position in the Cosmos* (1928) and Helmuth Plessner's *The Stages of the Organic and Human Being* (1928). Nishida published an article titled "Anthropology" in *Collected Philosophical Papers in Honor of Dr. Tomonaga's Sixtieth Birthday* in 1930, and also referred to de Biran's *Nouveaux essais* in "The Operation of Consciousness as the Self-Determination of Place" (included in *The Self-Aware Determination of Nothingness*), which was written during the same period as the above-mentioned article. We find Nishida's fundamental conception of anthropology expressed in the following sentences: "Philosophy, it can be said, includes one type of, or rather the true meaning of anthropology. But this must be an anthropology of the self-aware human being. It must be not a science of the exterior human being (*homo exterior*), but rather that of the interior human being (*homo interior*)" (NKZ 6: 112). Just before this, Nishida writes that "philosophy originates on the basis of the fact of self-awareness itself, which, through becoming nothingness, determines itself." This understanding of philosophy underlies Nishida's claim that philosophy is "the true anthropology" or "the anthropology of the self-aware human being." It also explains his sympathy with de Biran's "science of the interior human."

While strongly sympathizing with de Biran's anthropology, Nishida was nevertheless conscious of its one-sidedness. In the article "Anthropology," he writes:

> Although it is true that human being is human being only due to its interiority, and in this sense we have many things to learn from Maine de Biran who takes as his point of departure *homo interior,* on the other hand, human being exists not only in himself, but also in the flesh. Moreover, human being exists not only in the flesh, but also in society, and not only in society, but also in history. We human beings cannot be understood merely from the interior. Anthropology must, therefore, be approached from both directions. As opposed to an anthropology that starts from the interior, we must establish one that starts from the exterior. (NKZ 12: 25)

While Nishida uses the expression "flesh" (Jp. *nikutai*) here, he obviously intends that human being be grasped as "an embodied existence" (*shintaiteki sonzai*)—and, moreover, as a "social" and "historical existence."

It can be said that Miki's interest in de Biran is based upon Nishida's understanding of anthropology, and so is Miki's criticism of de Biran. In his *Philosophical Anthropology,* Miki writes:

> I think that [de Biran's] anthropology has not yet reached the standpoint of actual praxis. His study remains at the standpoint of interior sensation or inner experience, and is limited to analyses of the interior human that appears in such sensation or experience. . . . Actual praxis transcends consciousness and gets out of the inner world. It is by way of the body that praxis exits the inner world, and it is impossible to consider praxis without the principle of embodiment. (MKZ 18: 141)

Miki's criticism of de Biran here is in accord with that made by Nishida. Miki writes, "it is a concrete fact that, rather than becoming reflectively aware of myself on my own, I return to myself through the resistance of the objective world" (MKZ 18: 143), and he emphasizes the point that we encounter "the resistance of the objective world" through acting as an embodied existence. Although de Biran had given consideration to the fact that self-awareness occurs through the medium of some resistance to the self, Miki points out that it is through the medium of "the body" that we truly encounter resistance, and that self-awareness genuinely comes into being. On the basis of Nishida's criticism of de Biran, Miki was thus able to further clarify the significance of the body in self-awareness. Miki expresses this in the following words: "Our standpoint of anthropology is that of active self-awareness. Without abstracting human being from the body, this approach is able to grasp human being subjectively and socially" (MKZ 18: 147).

Pathos and the Body

As the preceding quotation makes clear, Miki understands *pathos* in its relation to "the body in subjectivity." Let us now examine this relation. In "The Concept of Anthropology," the first chapter of *Philosophical Anthropology,* Miki points out that there are two aspects or "directions" of *pathos*. On the one hand, with reference to the etymological derivation in Greek of *pathos* from *paschein,* meaning "to suffer from" or "to receive the action" of another, Miki understands *pathos* to imply a passivity, wherein we receive something that places or "situates" us within a certain disposition or affect. The "body" is nothing other than the place in which *pathos* as disposition or situatedness arises, that is, takes place. In this sense, the body is said to be the "place of passivity" (MKZ 18: 152). It follows that *pathos* is a certain passivity that arises, takes place, in this "place of passivity."

But Miki discovers at the same time a "fundamental activity" within *pathos*. Transformations of the situation, which take place in the "place of passivity," are not limited to being mere transformations; they also manifest a power of self-expression which is aimed outward. In other words, *pathos* has an "impulsive" character; it urges us to action through our bodies. It is because of this active side of *pathos* that the body is not simply a material object, but is rather a "body in subjectivity." Miki writes in this regard: "Pathos is regarded as connected with the body. It is first by means of pathos that the body is, so to speak, 'endowed with heart and mind' as the human body, and that the heart and mind are embodied and concretized as human heart and mind. At the basis of human praxis lies pathos" (MKZ 18: 399). It is due to pathos that the body is not a mere material object but an "ensouled" body, that is, a "body animated by the heart and mind" (*kokoro ni ikasareta shintai*), and, at the same time, that our mind is not a mere consciousness but an "embodied/incarnated" (*shintaika shita*) mind, an "embodied/concretized" (*gutaika shita*) mind.

Having now disclosed these two aspects of *pathos,* how are we to think their connection with one another? In other words, where is the point of contact between them? With regard to this question, it is worth looking at how, prior to *Philosophical Anthropology,* Miki had introduced the concept of "inner body" in "On Pathos" (January 1933) and "Literature and the Contemporary Problem of Ethics" (April 1933).

After the publication of *The Philosophy of History,* between 1932 and 1936 Miki published many articles on art and especially on literature. Among these, the article "On Pathos" addresses the question of creativity or innovation in literature. In this context, Miki discusses what he calls "double transcendence." Specifically he writes:

> There is a double transcendence of consciousness. On the one hand, the relation in which consciousness is determined by external beings, which transcend consciousness in an outward direction, may be termed "reflection" or "imitation." On the other hand, the relation in which consciousness is determined by the inner body, which transcends consciousness in an inward direction, may be referred to as "expression" or "exhibition." (MKZ 19: 582)

Miki holds that consciousness is related, on the one hand, to external beings—that is, to beings that transcend and determine it from the outside. On the other hand, consciousness is related to something that transcends it internally. Because the inner body determines consciousness—that is to say, because the inner body "seeps up into consciousness"—"expression" is possible. Hence, the "inner body" is regarded here as that which underlies and enables artistic creation.

It is presumably because Miki considers the inner body to have a kind of substantiality (physicality) or materiality that he refers to this inner transcendent being as the "inner body"; at times he also calls it "inner substance." We might say that unformed material is there "imaged," prior to being given concrete form in "expression." In the article "Ideology and the Logic of Pathos" (1933), written immediately following "On Pathos," Miki argues that materiality is more original than form: "Contrary to the Greek way of thinking," he writes, "that which is material or physically substantial is more primary than that which has form or is ideal. Animal spirits are more substantial than bodies with form" (MKZ 21: 210).

"Animal spirits" (Fr. *esprits animaux*) is, as we know, the name of the substance posited by Descartes in support of the "activity of body" in his explanation of "passion (the passivity of soul)." Miki is presumably using this notion of "animal spirits" as one model for his discussion of the "inner body." Miki does not, of course, directly accept the Cartesian idea of "animal spirits." For Descartes, "animal spirits" constitute one part of physical substances; but Miki clearly rejects this idea. For Miki, animal spirits do not belong to the external body, but rather lie deep down "inside" as "the formless something" that underlies the activity of artistic expression. In relation to this "inner body," Miki defines *pathos* as follows: "Pathos, passion, emotion and enthusiasm refer to the state of consciousness determined by the subject that transcends consciousness inwardly" (MKZ 19: 582).

Now, the question of "double transcendence" or "transcendence toward the subject" is also discussed in *Philosophical Anthropology,* but the term "inner body" is carefully avoided there. In its place, Miki speaks in this text of "nothingness." For instance, in "The Expressiveness of Human Existence," chapter 4 of *Philosophical Anthropology,* he writes:

> Originally praxis must be thought, on the one hand, to fully imply that the human being actively makes, and yet, at the same time, it must also be thought to fully imply that the human being is made. In other words, human praxis entails an aspect of being determined by "something other." Now, if this "something other" were an objective existence or "being," praxis would lose its subjective meaning, and then it could not be called praxis. . . . On the other hand, if this "something other" were taken in the sense of a [Platonic] Idea, praxis would lose its creative meaning, and then we would be unable to conceive of such matters as artistic creation. Consequently, this "something other" is nothing other than "nothingness." (MKZ 18: 348–49)

Miki argues here that not just artistic creation, but praxis in general has both a voluntary or subjective aspect as well as an involuntary or nonsubjective aspect. It could be said that he has in mind the impulsive aspect of being urged to praxis by "something." What is referred to as "something other," in this context, is precisely what is called "inner body" in the articles "On Pathos" and "Ideology and the Logic of Pathos." Although Miki does not explicitly relate the reason for its reconceptualization as "nothingness," one occasion for this change may have been his encounter with Helmuth Plessner's anthropology.

As is evident from Miki's citations, one of the books that he referred to in writing *Philosophical Anthropology* was Plessner's *The Stages of the Organic and Human Being.* In this book, Plessner analyzes the different positional character or "positionality" (Gn. *Positionalität*) that plants, animals, and humans each have in their respective worlds, and attempts to explain human nature in terms of this structural difference. He argues that plants do not have the "center" (or central organ) which unifies an organism, nor do they have the "subjectivity" which delimits the self from its surrounding world. In this sense, plants have a free or open relation to the external world. By contrast, animals have a central organ. By means of this, an animal delimits itself from, and maintains an isolated relation to, the external world. But an animal is not *aware* of this manner of its existence; Plessner claims that the "here and now" are absolute for an animal. To live submerged in the "here and now" is the only possible form of existence for an animal.

By contrast, through reflection human beings liberate themselves from an absolute immersion in the "here and now," as well as from the manner of existing merely as a "center." In other words, the human being does not simply exist as a center, but at the same time transcends this center and stands behind it. This "behind" cannot be temporally or spatially determined as a particular "when and where." It is rather, so to speak, temporally a "no-when" and spatially a "no-where." Plessner states that it is, indeed, "nothingness." Human beings transcend themselves toward "nothingness," and gaze at themselves from "nothingness." Plessner finds this to be the peculiar positional character of human being, and defines it as "excentricity" (*Exzentrizität*).[2]

On the basis of Plessner's ideas, Miki writes the following in *Philosophical Anthropology*: "It can be said that the world is opened up and revealed to us in the consciousness of nothingness. The human being is subject insofar as he is the being that transcends toward nothingness" (MKZ 18: 267). For the animal, which is always a "center," the objective world is merely that which surrounds its own center; it is no more than an "environment" (Gn. *Umwelt*). By contrast, world (*Welt*) is revealed as world only for humans who can go beyond their center and stand behind it; that is to say, world is revealed only for the subject that transcends toward "nothingness."

We can infer that the influence of Plessner's anthropology lay in the background of the fact that Miki came to describe the "something other" which lies at the base of *pathos* and urges us to praxis, as "nothingness." Yet Miki's conception of "nothingness" did not necessarily remain within the framework of Plessner's notion of "nothingness." For in fact, Miki's conception of "nothingness" implies more than simply the positional character in the relation of subject to object.

In chapter 3 of *Philosophical Anthropology*, Miki refers to Karl Jaspers's concept of "limit situation" (*Grenzsituation*) when examining the "situatedness" of human being. Miki claims, however, that the "nothingness" we face in the anxiety of a "limit situation"—for example, in the face of death—is nothing more than "nothingness" experienced as a limit from the perspective of being; it is a mere "nihility," and not yet the "genuine nothingness" that is nothing less than human being's "ground of existence." Clearly, then, Miki understands "nothingness" not as the mere positional character of human being, but as its very "ground of existence."

Miki elaborates on this point as follows: "It [what is arrived at by stepping over the limit] is the ground of human existence that transcends human existence. Such a ground is 'nothingness.' Moreover, it is not the relative nothingness that is thought to be the utmost limit of being, but rather the nothingness that envelops even objective being" (MKZ 18: 293). "Nothingness" in this sense, presumably, could no longer be modified by the adjective "inner." It is rather "what transcends the inner and the outer of human being in its entirety" (MKZ 18: 292).

Miki then redefines "pathos" in relation to this idea of "nothingness." "Nothingness is what transcends the subjective and the objective and envelops them. To be determined by this nothingness is what we call *pathos,* and such *pathos* lies at the base of expressive activity. All creation has the meaning of 'creation from nothingness,' and creation from nothingness is always determined by *pathos*" (MKZ 18: 340). "Pathos" thus implies being determined by the "nothingness" that lies at the base of our existence. All creative activity is supported and carried forth—not, for example, by mere *mimesis*—but rather by this "pathos" and, moreover, by the "nothingness" that lies at its ground.

The Logic of Image Formation

Now, having examined how human existence is embodied, and how *pathos* lies at the base of human activity, why is it necessary to go on to raise the question of "imagination"? What prompted Miki to develop a "logic of the imagination" in addition to his original anthropology?

Miki provides the answer to this question in chapter 1 of *Logic of the Imagination,* in the form of a criticism of the French social theorist Georges Sorel. There Miki quotes the following lines from Sorel's *Reflections on Violence:* "What creates action is not the imagination. It is hope or fear, love or hatred, desire, passion and the impulse of egoism or the ego."[3] On the contrary, Miki argues:

It is impossible to think imagination in abstraction from embodiment. Imagination is precisely connected to hope or fear, love or hatred, desire, passion, impulse and so forth, and it is for this reason that Descartes and Pascal regarded the imagination as the origin of error. Imagination is connected to, and creates its images from, emotion. Through the imagination, emotion can be transformed into something objective, strengthened as such, and made permanent. (MKZ 8: 49)

Here we may clearly infer that Miki understands human action or praxis not as a simple exhibition of emotion, passion, or impulse, but rather as an activity of constructing images out of these, in other words, as an activity of giving form to the formless. What "transforms" *pathos* into something objective or formed is the power of the imagination. We may surmise, then, that for Miki human praxis is distinguished *as* human praxis by the fact that it does not merely "exhibit" *pathos,* but rather confers on it a different systematic order.

As a concrete instance of the formation of images, at the beginning of *Logic of the Imagination* Miki discusses the example of "myth." Myth is not, as is commonly thought, a direct expression of emotion or passion. Myth is the activity of portraying, or quite literally "drawing out" (Jp. *egakidasu*), a new world (reality) on top of the natural world, and this cannot be achieved without the intellect. In this chapter, Miki objects to eighteenth-century Enlightenment philosophy and nineteenth-century positivism, insofar as they consider myth to be nothing more than an unscientific ancestor of and obstacle to science. He approves, rather, of Bronislaw Malinowski's view,[4] according to which "myth, in fact, is not an idle rhapsody, not an aimless outpouring of vain imaginings, but a hardworking, extremely important cultural force . . . a pragmatic charter of primitive faith and moral wisdom" (MKZ 8: 20). Here it can clearly be seen that myth is not simply an outflow of *pathos,* but is rather a religious or moral "wisdom," that is to say, an endeavor that involves *logos.*

It is because *pathos* does not in and of itself take a distinct form that Miki posited the power of imagination as a special faculty, a faculty that enables human activity by transforming *pathos* into images—that is, into things with form. In order to transform *pathos* into something formed, a place must be opened up wherein affectivity and intellect can intermingle. One could say that it is precisely the faculty of imagination that opens up such a place, and that gives birth to images from out of this intermingling.

This is what Miki means when he writes that "the imagination is not merely emotion, but is at the same time the power to produce intellectual images" (MKZ 8: 49). It must therefore be said that "the logic of the imagination" is not simply a logic of emotion or a logic of *pathos,* but more precisely a "logic of formed images [*keizō*]" (MKZ 8: 46). However, this formation of images does not originate solely from the intellect, inasmuch as the formed image that is produced by the imagination is "not a pure Idea, but, so to speak, an Idea that has a body, an embodied Idea" (MKZ 8: 62). We might, in other words, call it a desire or impulse that has obtained form.

Just as Kant took imagination to be what connects sensibility to understanding, what Miki calls the imagination has the function of lying between, and binding together, what is emotional and what is intellectual.

As mentioned in the beginning of this article, in the preface to *Logic of the Imagination Part One*, Miki tells us that what had been at the center of his thought since the publication of *The Philosophy of History* was "the problem of how the objective and the subjective, the rational and the irrational, and the intellectual and the emotional could be united"—in other words, the problem of a "dialectical union" between *pathos* and *logos*. This problematic finds expression in "Ideology and the Logic of *Pathos*," where Miki sets his study of *pathos* over against ideology, and also in "Literature and the Problem of Neo-Humanism" (1933), where he proposes a "new humanism" that would connect humanity with sociality.

In the same preface, Miki expressed regret over the fact that his attempt to unify *logos* and *pathos* had remained "too abstractly formal," that is, that he had not been able to concretely demonstrate just *where* this unification takes place. We can surmise that his "logic of the imagination" was developed precisely in order to compensate for this shortcoming. We may furthermore conclude that the development of Miki's unique philosophy was made possible on the basis of the fact that he discovered, in the imagination, a power capable of giving logical (i.e., *logos*-informed) expression to the impulses of *pathos*, which we inevitably harbor insofar as we exist as embodied human beings.

Translated from the Japanese by Bret W. Davis,
with Moritsu Ryū and Takehana Yōsuke

NOTES

This essay is a slightly revised version of Masakatsu Fujita, "Logos and Pathos: Miki Kiyoshi's Logic of the Imagination," *Synthesis Philosophica* 19, no. 1 (2004): 117–28, and is reprinted here with permission of the publisher.

1. "Le vouloir est un act simple, pur et instantané de l'âme, en qui ou par qui cette force intelligente et active se manifeste au dehors et à elle-même intérieurement" (Maine de Biran, *Oeuvres*, ed. François Azouvi [Paris: J. Vrin, 1989], 10: 179).

2. Helmuth Plessner, *Die Stufen des Organischen und der Mensch*, 3rd edition (Berlin: Walter de Gruyter, 1975), 292.

3. Georges Sorel, *Réflexions sur la violence*, 6th edition (Paris: Éditions de Seuil, 1925), 45; *Reflections on Violence*, trans. with intro. T. E. Hulme (London: Allen & Unwin, 1916). As Miki mentioned, however, this part is adopted from John Henry Newman's *An Essay in Aid of a Grammar of Assent*.

4. Bronislaw K. Malinowski, *Myth in Primitive Psychology* (London: Kegan Paul, 1926), 14–15, 23.

Contributors

Thomas J. J. Altizer is Professor Emeritus of Religious Studies at Stony Brook University. A pioneer in the Buddhist-Christian dialogue, he is the author of fifteen books, beginning with *Oriental Mysticism and Biblical Eschatology* and including *Genesis and Apocalypse: A Theological Voyage Toward Authentic Christianity; The Genesis of God: A Theological Genealogy; Godhead and the Nothing;* and most recently, *Living the Death of God: A Theological Memoir.*

Bret W. Davis is Associate Professor of Philosophy at Loyola University Maryland. He is author of *Heidegger and the Will: On the Way to* Gelassenheit; translator of Martin Heidegger, *Country Path Conversations* (Indiana University Press, 2010); editor of *Martin Heidegger: Key Concepts;* and editor, with Fujita Masakatsu, of *Sekai no naka no Nihon no tetsugaku* (Japanese philosophy in the world). In addition to earning a PhD in Western philosophy from Vanderbilt University, he spent more than a decade researching and teaching in Japan, during which time he completed the coursework for a second PhD in Japanese philosophy at Kyoto University. His research focuses on Continental, Buddhist, and Japanese philosophies, areas in which he has published numerous articles in English and Japanese, including the article on the Kyoto School for the online *Stanford Encyclopedia of Philosophy.*

Steffen Döll is a research assistant at Ludwig-Maximilians-University in Munich, Germany, where he earned his Dr. phil. with a dissertation on *Yishan Yining und die frühen Jahre des Diskurses in den Fünf Bergen* (Yishan Yining and the early years of Five Mountains Discourse). He spent three years in the Department for the History of Japanese Philosophy at Kyoto University and is author of *Wozu also Suchen? Zur Einführung in das Denken von Ueda Shizuteru* (Why bother searching? An introduction to the thought of Ueda Shizuteru). He has also translated from the Japanese Kubota Nobuhiro's *Das Klima des japanischen Polytheismus* (The climate of Japanese polytheism) and Imamichi Tomonobu's *Eco-Ethica: Eine Einführung in die Umweltethik* (Eco-ethica: An introduction to environmental ethics). His current research project focuses on the history of the literati in China and Japan.

Rolf Elberfeld is Professor of Philosophy of Culture at Hildesheim University, Germany. He is author of *Kitarō Nishida (1870–1945): Moderne japanische Philosophie und die Frage nach der Interkulturalität* and *Phänomenologie der Zeit im Buddhismus: Methoden interkulturellen Philosophierens*. He has also edited *Komparative Ästhetik: Künste und ästhetische Erfahrungen in Asien und Europa; Komparative Ethik: Das Gute Leben zwischen den Kulturen; Was ist Philosophie? Programmatische Texte von Platon bis Derrida;* and with Ōhashi Ryōsuke, *Dōgen, Shōbōgenzō: Ausgewählte Texte: Anders Philosophieren aus dem Zen.*

Fujita Masakatsu is Professor and Department Head of Japanese Philosophy at Kyoto University. He is author of *Philosophie und Religion beim jungen Hegel; Gendai shisō toshite no Nishida Kitarō* (Nishida Kitarō as a modern thinker); and *Nishida Kitarō.* His many edited books include *Kyōto gakuha no tetsugaku* (The philosophy of the Kyoto School); *Higashiajia to tetsugaku* (East Asia and philosophy); and with Bret W. Davis, *Sekai no naka no Nihon no tetsugaku* (Japanese philosophy in the world).

David Jones is Professor of Philosophy at Kennesaw State University, editor of the journals *Comparative and Continental Philosophy* and *East-West Connections,* director of the Atlanta Center for Asian Studies, and has been visiting professor of Confucian Classics at Emory University. His books include *The Fractal Self and the Evolution of God,* with John L. Culliney; and *Zhu Xi Now: Contemporary Encounters with the Great Ultimate,* edited with He Jinli. He is also co-editor of *Asian Texts—Asian Contexts: Encountering the Philosophies and Religions of Asia* and *The Gift of Logos: Essays in Continental Philosophy;* and editor of *Confucius Now: Contemporary Encounters with the Analects* and *Buddha Nature and Animality.* He is President of the Comparative and Continental Philosophy Circle and was the East-West Center's Distinguished Alumnus in 2004–2005.

Gereon Kopf is Associate Professor of Asian and Comparative Religions at Luther College. In addition to numerous articles on the religious philosophies of Dōgen and Nishida, he is author of *Beyond Personal Identity: Dōgen, Nishida, and a Phenomenology of No-Self* and editor, with Jin Park, of *Merleau-Ponty and Buddhism.* He is the recipient of fellowships from the Japan Foundation and the Japan Society for the Promotion of Research, which supported his research at the Obirin University in Machida (1993–1994) and at the Nanzan Institute for Religion and Culture in Nagoya (2002–2004). He is currently developing a systematic philosophy of non-dualism and a philosophy of diversity based on the works of the Kyoto School philosophers.

John C. Maraldo is Professor Emeritus of Philosophy at the University of North Florida and held the Roche Chair in Interreligious Research at Nanzan University in 2008–2009. He is the author or editor of seven books, including *Der hermeneutische Zirkel. Untersuchungen zu Schleiermacher, Dilthey und Heidegger* and with James W. Heisig, *Rude Awakenings: Zen, the Kyoto School and the Question of Nationalism.* He has published numerous articles in Japanese, German, and English on Japanese and Continental thought, including "Contemporary Japanese Philosophy" in the *Companion Encyclopedia of Asian Philosophy,* and the entries on Nishida in the *Routledge Encyclopedia of Philosophy* and the online *Stanford Encyclopedia of Philosophy.* He is currently co-editing *Japanese Philosophy: A Sourcebook* and writing a book on *Alternatives: The Promise of Japanese Philosophy.*

Erin McCarthy is Associate Professor of Philosophy at St. Lawrence University, where she also teaches in the Asian Studies and Gender Studies programs. She completed her doctorate at the University of Ottawa. She is author of *Ethics Embodied* and has published on comparative philosophy in the journals *Philosophy, Culture and Traditions* and *Canadian Review of American Studies,* and in several anthologies in French and English. She has served as Chair of the Board of Directors of ASIANetwork.

Ōhashi Ryōsuke is Professor at Ryukoku University and a central figure in the tradition of the Kyoto School. After graduating from Kyoto University, he went on to receive his doctorate and later *Habilitation* at universities in Germany. He is the author of numerous books on philosophy and aesthetics in Japanese and German, including *Zeitlichkeitsanalyse der Hegelschen Logik: Zur Idee einer Phänomenologie des Ortes; Nihon-tekina mono, Yōroppa-tekina* *mono* (Things Japanese and things European); *Nishida-tetsugaku no sekai* (The world of Nishida philosophy); and *Japan im interkulturellen Dialog;* and is editor of such works as *Kyōtogakuha no shisō* (The thought of the Kyoto School) and *Die Philosophie der Kyōto-Schule.*

Graham Parkes is Professor of Philosophy and Head of the School of Philosophy and Sociology at University College Cork, in Ireland, and a former senior fellow at the Harvard University Center for the Study of World Religions. Among his numerous publications, he is author of *Composing the Soul: Reaches of Nietzsche's Psychology;* editor of *Heidegger and Asian Thought* and *Nietzsche and Asian Thought;* and translator of Nishitani Keiji's *The Self-Overcoming of Nihilism* and François Berthier's *Reading Zen in the Rocks: The Japanese Dry Landscape Garden.*

Brian Schroeder is Professor and Department Chair of Philosophy and Director of Religious Studies at Rochester Institute of Technology. He is author of *Altared Ground: Levinas, History and Violence* and principal co-author of *Pensare ambientalista: Tra filosofia e ecologia* (Environmental thinking: Between philosophy and ecology). His edited and co-edited books include *Thinking through the Death of God: A Critical Companion to Thomas J. J. Altizer; Contemporary Italian Philosophy: Crossing the Borders of Ethics, Politics, and Religion; Levinas and the Ancients* (Indiana University Press, 2008); and *Between Nihilism and Politics: The Hermeneutics of Gianni Vattimo.* He is currently completing a book titled *Atonement of the Last God: Absolute Nothingness and the Problem of a Postmetaphysical Ground.*

Bernard Stevens is a researcher at the Catholic University of Louvain, in Belgium, and a frequent visiting professor at the Collège International de Philosophie in Paris. A philosopher specializing in hermeneutical phenomenology and, more recently, in contemporary Japanese philosophy, he has introduced the philosophy of the Kyoto School to the French-speaking academy. His essays have appeared in numerous journals, including *Les Temps Modernes, Esprit, Philosophie, Etudes phénoménologiques,* and the *Revue philosophique de Louvain.* His most important books are *L'apprentissage des signes: lecture de Paul Ricœur; Topologie du néant: une approche de l'école de Kyôto; Le néant évidé: ontologie et politique chez Keiji Nishitani; Invitation à la philosophie japonaise: Autour de Nishida;* and *Le nouveau capitalisme asiatique: le modèle japonais.*

Sugimoto Kōichi earned his PhD in the Department of Japanese Philosophy at Kyoto University with a dissertation on Nishida's philosophy of history, and now lectures on Japanese philosophy and intellectual history at Osaka Education University. His major research interest is in the Kyoto School's relation to Zen. He has published a number of articles on the Kyoto School, including "Nishida Kitarō no 'kōiteki-chokkann' to rekishisei" ("Acting intuition" and the problem of historicity in Nishida Kitaro), in *Shūkyōtetsugaku kenkyū* 21 (2004): 49–61; and "Shōwa shoki Kyōtogakuha ni okeru 'rekishi' no mondai no hōga" (The emergence of the problem of history in the Kyoto School in the early Showa period), in *Nihonshisōshigaku* (Journal of Japanese intellectual history) 36 (2004): 197–215.

Ueda Shizuteru is Professor Emeritus of Philosophy of Religion at Kyoto University and member of the Japan Academy. He is the successor of Nishitani Keiji and the current leading figure in the tradition of the Kyoto School. His numerous works on Zen, mysticism, and Nishida's philosophy, as well as his own developments of a religious phenomenology of self and world, have been collected and published in an eleven-volume edition, *Ueda Shizuteru shū*. His works available in Western languages include *Die Gottesgeburt in der Seele und der Durchbruch zu Gott. Die mystische Anthropologie Meister Eckharts und ihre Konfrontation mit der Mystik des Zen Buddhismus; Zen y filosofía*, trans. R. B. García and I. G. Comín; "'Nothingness' in Meister Eckhart and Zen Buddhism: With Particular Reference to the Borderlands of Philosophy and Theology," trans. J. W. Heisig, in F. Frank, ed., *The Buddha Eye: An Anthology of the Kyoto School*; and "Language in a Twofold World," trans. B. W. Davis, in J. W. Heisig, T. P. Kasulis, and J. C. Maraldo, eds., *Japanese Philosophy: A Sourcebook*.

Jason M. Wirth is Associate Professor of Philosophy at Seattle University. He works in the areas of aesthetics, Continental philosophy, comparative philosophy, and Africana philosophy. He is author of *The Conspiracy of Life: Meditations on Schelling and His Time*; editor of *Schelling Now: Contemporary Readings* (Indiana University Press, 2004) and *Zen No Sho: The Calligraphy of Fukushima Keidō Rōshi*; and translator of the third draft of Schelling's *The Ages of the World*. He is currently finishing work on a book on Milan Kundera as well as a monograph on Schelling's middle period, called *Schelling's Practice of the Wild*.

Index

Lightning Source UK Ltd.
Milton Keynes UK
UKOW03f1915090417
298728UK00001B/27/P